WHAT SILENT LOVE HATH WRIT
A Psychoanalytic Exploration of Shakespeare's Sonnets

Martin S. Bergmann & Michael Bergmann

version .91

©2008 by Gotschna Ventures, Inc.   400 East 77th Street   New York, NY 10075

TABLE OF CONTENTS

INTRODUCTION: BACKGROUND AND CONTROVERSY

This book offers readers who wish to get to know Shakespeare's sonnets the chance to read them with a commentary and in a sequence which provides a guide to the major themes of the poems and illuminates the thought processes of the character we call the Poet of the Sonnets, the "I" who is the speaker in each of the poems. A universally quoted line such as "Shall I compare thee to a summer's day" does not make one feel the need to know much about the person who is speaking but "Sin of self-love possesseth all mine eye" makes us more curious. The sonnets can be read together as if they are all spoken by one person and afford us a chance to get to know him by understanding what he writes and what he means in his various moods. Shakespeare's sonnets, anxious in their homosexuality and angry in their heterosexuality comprise a most unusual body of love poems. Awesomely skillful and limitlessly beautiful, they are a pleasure to get to know while also being deeply disturbing.

The technique of combining insight drawn from various sources into one gestalt is a standard psychoanalytic way of thinking, but in clinical psychoanalysis we have a living analysand either to confirm or to disprove a hypothetical construction. This check on our imaginative construction is not open to us here; but on the other hand we can do no harm as no interpretation of a great work of art precludes other interpretations. "From fairest things we desire increase," is how Sonnet 1 begins (it's the 20th sonnet we discuss). Our readers will have to judge for themselves if our approach increased their ease in getting to know these poems and deepened their pleasure in reading them. Readers who wish to test out this experience should themselves, before reading further in this book, read the discussion of four sonnets in Chapter 1, with which we introduce both the character of the Poet of the Sonnets and the major themes of the poems. You will soon see if our analysis makes you want to read more.

The analysis of the four sonnets that is the subject matter of Chapter 1 leads to understanding why the Poet of the Sonnets was more afraid of death than ordinary mortals are. This is the subject of Chapter 2, the longest in this book. The insights gained from Chapter 2 illuminated for us the strange preoccupation of the Poet with the wish that the Young Man he loved should procreate. This is the content of Chapter 3 (in which we finally discuss Sonnet 1). Chapters 4 and 5 are put together to highlight the Poet's contribution to the understanding of love. Chapters 6 and 7 deal with the heterosexual component, and why the homosexual and heterosexual components could not coexist without an inner war between them. The second part of the book compares Shakespeare the playwright with Shakespeare the Poet of the Sonnets. The last chapter deals with what Freud learned from Shakespeare and how Freud's insights made Shakespeare understandable to us in a new way.

We have taken the liberty of regrouping the sonnets according to what seemed to us development of major themes. We were encouraged to take this liberty because Shakespearean scholarship established that there is no reliable way for us to know in what sequence the sonnets were composed and in what sequence Shakespeare himself would have wanted them to be printed. We have retained the traditional numbering of the sonnets, however.

THE CURRENT POPULARITY OF THE SONNETS

Shakespeare's sonnets enjoy an astonishing popularity in our generation; only the literature on *Hamlet* exceeds the literature on the sonnets. According to Katherine Duncan Jones (1947), this popularity is a new phenomenon, as the sonnets remained largely unappreciated throughout the seventeenth, eighteenth and nineteenth centuries. When the first quarto was published in 1609, it was greeted by silence. The sonnets were not published again until 1640 in an edition that made the poems written to a man appear as if they were written to a woman. Only in 1709 did a responsibly edited version appear, and another half-century followed before other editions were printed. William Hazlitt, a sensitive critic writing in 1817, had this to say about Shakespeare's sonnets:

> Our idolatry of Shakespeare (not to say our admiration) ceases with his plays. In his other productions, he was a mere author, though not a common author. It was only by representing others, that he became himself. He could go out of himself, and express the soul of Cleopatra; but in his own person, he appeared to be always waiting for the prompter's cue. In expressing the thoughts of others, he seemed inspired: in expressing his own, he was a mechanic. The licence of an assumed character was necessary to restore his genius to the privileges of nature, and to give him courage to break through the tyranny of fashion, the trammels of custom. In his plays, he was 'as broad and casing as the general air:' in his poems, on the contrary, he appears to be 'cooped, and cabined in' by all the technicalities of art, by all the petty intricacies of thought and language, which poetry had learned from the controversial jargon of the schools, where words had been made a substitute for things (p. 346-7).

This is a powerful indictment of Shakespeare as a poet, though even Hazlitt concluded that many of the sonnets were beautiful, and singled out for praise Sonnets 29, 73, 102 and 105. (Of these four sonnets, 29 and 73 have retained their popularity, but 102 and 105 are no longer so appreciated; see table on pages 21-23). Hazlitt reserved the brunt of his criticism for poems other than the sonnets. Shakespeare is accused of being able to create a Cleopatra, but not to speak meaningfully about himself. Today, after Flaubert's famous confession—"Madame Bovary *c'est moi*"—we are inclined to believe that Shakespeare represented himself in different and complex ways in all the characters he created, including the women. On the other hand, we recognize that Shakespeare and the "I" in whose voice the sonnets are written—the character we call "the Poet of the Sonnets"— need not be the same person.

A similar disdain for the sonnets is found in J. Middleton Murray's essay "Shakespeare and Love" (1922).

> We shall hold that the sonnets represent an episode in Shakespeare's experience that caused a momentary but a complete overclouding of the reflection in the mirror of the plays. The episode passes and the reflection becomes calm and serene once more. The sonnets gave us, as it were, a year in Shakespeare's attitude to love; the plays give us a lifetime (p. 12)

After Freud such terms as "momentary overclouding of the reflection in the mirror" do not appear adequate, particularly when this supposed overclouding resulted in so magnificent a poetic vocabulary. Modern temper calls for a rereading and a different appreciation of the sonnets.

If we go from Hazlitt to a contemporary view of the sonnets, for example to the late Anthony Hecht (1996), we learn that the sonnets outsell everything that Shakespeare wrote and that is in spite of the fact that the popular plays like *Romeo and Juliet* and *Hamlet* are taught in schools and the sonnets are not.

> In England in the 1590s there was a vogue of sonnet-writing in which poets admonished themselves, in the words of Philip Sidney, to look in their hearts and write. Such introspection and honesty are not easy in any age, and it is the general consensus that, of all the sonneteers, Shakespeare was beyond question the most penetrating. He was also the one who seemed most perfectly to adapt the form itself to his analytic or diagnostic and deeply dramatic purposes (p. 5).

Such a radical change in public opinion over 200 years suggests that our generation is more interested, more puzzled, and more ready to explore the mysteries of love than were our ancestors. Unlike the Victorians, we have accepted more readily the clash between different forms of love—self-love, homosexual love, and heterosexual love—and recognize that they can be at war with each other within one person. We are less frightened by the possibility that Shakespeare's sonnets contain a homosexual component. We have become more tolerant and therefore interested in the complexity of loving. We are a little less afraid of inner conflicts evoked by love and, hence, better capable of appreciating Shakespeare's sonnets as a document recording an inner struggle as described by the greatest genius that the English language has produced.

We cannot however dismiss Hazlitt's appraisal for it contains a kernel of truth. Hamlet, Falstaff, King Lear or women like Rosalind and Cleopatra vibrate with life. They are palpable human beings whom we learn to know even though we never encounter a person like them in our lives. The same cannot be said about the Young Man the Poet of the Sonnets loves or his dark mistress. We gain no picture of them as human beings, and should we meet them there would be no way for us to recognize them. The men, be it man or men, to whom most sonnets are addressed is, or are, idealized figures, lacking any discernible personal character. The same can be said about the Dark Lady, even though she is mostly negatively described. However, when it comes to the Poet of the Sonnets, whether he was the actual Shakespeare or merely created by him, we can get to know him, but have to work harder at it. To compare the sonnets with the dramatic works, as we do in Chapter 9, is to realize how hard the dramatist works at making his dramatic personae understandable to us. In classical Hellenic art, the face is usually serene and often blank. To find inner individual life in a painting, we had to wait for Caravaggio or Rembrandt. The sonnets can be compared to Rembrandt's self-portraits. They show the Poet in a great variety of moods as if he were wearing a variety of costumes comparable to a series of self-portraits by Rembrandt.

The twentieth century nearly destroyed civilization during the two world wars, but it had one advantage over the nineteenth: it was less afraid of sexuality. As a species, we are unique in the animal kingdom in spending so much energy deciding who our mate should be. It may be that the professional commitment to psychoanalysis has made us particularly sensitive to this problem. The number of men and women who seek help because they cannot find a permanent mate is great. Add to this the number of people who have entered into a marriage or a permanent relationship over a long period of time, but are most unhappy with the partner they have selected without being able to free themselves from that relationship. To these two groups, a third one should be added that includes men and women who do not find it possible to be happy with one person and need two or more as long-term companions. Some of these people are bisexual, requiring simultaneously, or in sequence, relationships with both men and women. The Poet of the Sonnets, if not Shakespeare himself, belongs to that group. It was Freud who began a journey that still engages us in understanding why the unhappiness in loving is so prevalent and the selection of a mate so difficult. One of us traced this history in a previous book [*The Anatomy of Loving*, 1987]. However, a deepening acquaintance with the sonnets led to the conviction that Shakespeare, although universally praised for the beauty of his language when dealing with love, was never given a serious place in the history of love as it unfolded in Western thinking. One of our aims in this book is to give these sonnets a place in the history of love in Western literature. This recognition is responsible for a special chapter, "Meditations on the Nature of Love."

Mores were different in Elizabethan England. Finding the right person to love was not as central a concern as it is today. We are therefore all the more amazed at how much Shakespeare discovered when he set out to explore the complexity of loving in these poems.

SHAKESPEARE'S SONNETS IN THEIR CULTURE AND HISTORICAL CONTEXT

Shakespeare was born in 1564, the year that Michelangelo died. These two giants of the Renaissance have much in common. The Christian past that dominated the Middle Ages is still palpable in their work, but no longer compelling, and the classical past has come back to life. There is also a notable difference: Michelangelo lived in Florence and in Rome at the very center of where the "Renaissance miracle" took place; Shakespeare lived in England, a province by comparison with Italy. Michelangelo became increasingly religious as he became older; to our knowledge no similar development took place in Shakespeare. Shakespeare occasionally uses metaphors, images and vocabulary that the Christian religion provided, but from his Christian heritage he seems to have inherited only a profound sense of guilt. When the Poet of the Sonnets faces death (and death plays a prominent role in the sonnets) he is engaged in a personal struggle against death's power. There is no merciful God awaiting him in a world to come. Michelangelo's teacher was the famous statue of the *Torso* in the Vatican, a magnificent Hellenistic sculpture. Shakespeare's teachers, the sonnets reveal, were Plato and Ovid. The Poet's affirmation of homosexual love, if not of homosexuality, is expressed in Sonnet 20; it is matched by Michelangelo's David and the Ignudi, the naked and restless figures of the young men painted on the Sistine Chapel that both separate and energize the Biblical stories. Michelangelo was regarded as "divine" already in his lifetime, almost the equal of popes and kings. Shakespeare's contemporaries held him in high esteem but it would take another century and a half for Shakespeare to be recognized as a genius outstripping all contemporaries. Michelangelo also wrote sonnets, but they are not popular today.

Unlike the sonnets of Shakespeare's predecessors and even unlike the sonnets that appear in Shakespeare's plays, the majority of the sonnets are not traditional hymns to love, but expressions of an inner conflict. Three types of love compete with each other: homosexual love for a young man, heterosexual attraction for a dark lady and self-love.

As to the relationship of the three types of love to each other, Freud believed, and our own clinical experience has amply confirmed, that the three types can flow back and forth into each other. A disappointment in heterosexual love can strengthen the homosexual love or self-love. Conversely, a new and richer heterosexual love, when subjected to psychoanalytic scrutiny, may show that the sense of wonder it evoked was based on components of self-love and homosexual love that have become newly available to the heterosexual relationship.

The three types of love could presumably coexist side by side were it not for aggression; in an intrapsychic conflict each one of these loves wants to eliminate the other two. The writer of the sonnets is richly endowed with aggression, which becomes particularly noticeable in the heterosexual domain. The amount of hostility that the Poet of the Sonnets expresses toward the woman he presumably loves is, to our knowledge, unique in the poetry of love. The hostility to the male lover seems less pronounced, or at least better covered-over by the Poet's idealization. In the homosexual sonnets, aggression is mostly directed at the Poet's own aging self or at "Devouring Time." Love expressed in the sonnets is mainly triadic, linking three people, rather than dyadic (confined to two). Most of the poetry of love, including the literature among Shakespeare's contemporaries, (as available, for example, in a new Oxford book of Sixteenth Century verse) is dyadic.

Whether the three types of love can live in harmony with each other or engage in an intrapsychic war depends in part on the attitude of the culture toward homosexuality as well as the amount of aggression with which an individual has been endowed. Classical Greek culture is usually cited as an example of a culture tolerant toward a particular form of homosexuality as well as more tolerant toward self-love. K.J. Dover, an authority on the subject, found that the Greeks differed from us in their readiness to recognize the alternations between homosexual and heterosexual preferences in the same individual and the implicit denial that such alternation created problems either for the individual or his society (p. 1).

> Plato takes homosexual desire and homosexual love as the starting point from which to develop his metaphysical theory; and it is of particular importance that he regards philosophy not as an activity to be pursued in solitary meditation and solitary communication in ex-cathedra pronouncements by a master to his disciples, but as a dialectical progress which may well begin with the response to an older male to the stimulus afforded by a younger male who combines bodily beauty with beauty of the soul (Dover, p. 12).

Shakespeare's love and praise for the beauty of the Young Man would have sounded familiar to Plato.

Unlike the dramatist, the lyric poet does not gradually unfold the story he wishes to tell; he does not protect us from a sense of shock. The poet is less concerned with the mental equilibrium of the readers. In his ability to give a voice to inner conflict, Shakespeare was not only ahead of his time but has not, to our knowledge, been surpassed, even by Proust.

WHY THIS BOOK IS CONTROVERSIAL

Helen Vendler in her recent book has suggested that:

> The true "actors" in lyrics are words, not "dramatic persons;" and the drama of any lyric is constituted by the successive entrances of new sets of words, or new stylistic arrangements (grammatical, syntactical, phonetic) which are visibly in conflict with previous arrangements used with reference to the "same" situation. Thus, the introduction of a new linguistic strategy is, in a sonnet, as interruptive and interesting as the entrance of a new character in a play (p. 3).

With this statement we are in full agreement. Expanding on this theme, Vendler explains further:

> Precisely because he was a dramatist by temperament and by training, Shakespeare could, in the 1609 Quarto, turn the external dramatic enactment we see here into the interior meditative drama of lyric. Because the drama of the 1609 poems has less to do with their themes than with the way those themes are stylistically dramatized through grammar, syntax, and word choice, any treatment of the sonnets that focuses chiefly on their themes loses almost all of their aesthetic richness (p. 7).

On this point we are of a different opinion. There is a closer connection between theme and aesthetic richness than Vendler recognizes. Furthermore the theme is not always self-evident and easy to decipher. Different themes may be struggling against each other in a given sonnet.

Somewhat mitigating what she had said earlier, Vendler cites Wallace Stevens, that a poem must exhibit double beauty, "the poetry of the idea and the poetry of words" (p. 4). Vendler goes on to emphasize that the poetry of the sonnet is inward, meditative and lyrical, while the poems in Shakespeare's dramas tend to be outward, expository and narrative (p. 13).

She reaches the conclusion that "lyric poetry, especially highly convention-alized lyric of the sort represented by the sonnets, has almost no significant freight of 'meaning' at all in our ordinary sense of the word (p. 13)." Mock-ingly she adds "I have insomnia because I am far away from you" is the gist of one sonnet; "even though nature wishes to prolong your life, time will eventually demand that she render you to death" is the "meaning" of another.

While we have no wish to deny the extraordinary role of carefully ar-ranged words in the sonnets, we cannot agree with Vendler's belief that the sonnets have no "freight of meaning." We would rather say that nowhere else has Shakespeare the dramatist so fully freed himself from the con-straints of narrative. A narrative has occurred; some series of events has be-fallen the Poet of the Sonnets and these events are different from the events in any of the plays, but we glimpse them only partially because in the son-nets Shakespeare has not left us a story, but rather a record of the feelings that story evoked in its central character. We will insist that in the beautiful choice and skillful arrangement of the words we hear wishes and fears often at war with each other and themes and meanings emerge. Vendler's book adds much to the pleasure of reading the sonnets by drawing attention to the skill with which they are crafted. We offer the reader a different kind of reading of the sonnets, one that emphasizes conscious, but even more unconscious, meaning. It is our hope that this meaning, once accessible, enhances the pleasure of reading the poems.

Every sonnet, in our view, represents a new balance of intrapsychic forces that are alive within the Poet, and seeks expression in ever-fresh ways of looking, experiencing, and verbalizing his inner conflict. We are deeply impressed by the number of ideas that Shakespeare managed to include in a mere 14 lines and hold them together in one poem.

There is yet another and even more important disagreement between Vendler and ourselves that is of interest. Vendler writes:

> As to what Shakespeare may conceal from the reader, or even from himself, such a supremely conscious writer conceals, it seems to me, very little (p. 11).

Vendler assumes that being a "supremely conscious writer"
there is little that was unconscious in the Poet when he wrote the s͏   ͏s.
We assume the very opposite: that in every sonnet a great deal is hidden
from us as well as from the Poet himself. The wish to reveal and conceal at
the same time often gives rise to magnificent metaphors.

It may be useful at this juncture to draw attention to a line of demarca-
tion between the writer of prose and the poet. Writers of prose write with a
certain audience in mind and have a message they wish to convey to their
audience; the prose writer aims to explain and persuade, or to narrate.
Poets are burdened by something within them that demands expression,
and may resort to strict forms in their search for a container for emotions
that threaten to overwhelm them. Their desire to resolve may be greater
than their desire to communicate. What it is that they wish to express may
only partially be conscious. If Freud was right, poets also wish to conceal
another part of their message and safeguard it from the intrusive eyes of
others. The poem is a success if these two contradictory wishes reach a
satisfactory equilibrium.

Poetry written 400 years ago within a culture very different than the
one familiar to the reader may require an intermediary who knows more
than the reader about the way poems were written in Elizabethan culture.
Scholars have spent years on their hidden structure; years mastering Shake-
speare's work and the world he lived in to make the poems more accessible
to our understanding. We can claim no expertise in any of these fields, and
often have recourse to quoting some of the better scholars; what we regard
as our special area of competence is a willingness to consider the text and
accept what is written until we can decipher trends that remained uncon-
scious but nevertheless transmit derivatives of these repressed unconscious
thoughts to the attentive reader. Once more, if Freud was right, the poet
even more than the prose writer—because he or she wishes both to reveal
and conceal, often in metaphor—says more than he or she intended to
say consciously, and given a certain skill, what has been hinted at can be
reconstructed enriching our experience of the poem. This terrain between
conscious and derivatives of the unconscious is the area to which we are
now drawing the attention of the reader.

Our disagreement with academia is broader and richer in meaning. We can easily put Susan Langer in the place of Vendler, who wrote:

> A poem is not like a dream, a proxy for libidinal ideas, intended to hide wishes and feelings from oneself and others; it is meant to be always emotionally transparent. Like all deliberate expressions, it needs a public standard of excellence.

Langer goes on to say that one does not say that a sleeper dreams clumsily, nor that neurotic symptoms are carelessly strung together. But a poet may be charged with inaptitude or carelessness (Langer 1953, p. 244-5). We agree that a poem must meet a public standard of excellence. However, Langer was wrong on clinical as well as literary grounds. Clumsy dreams do in fact exist; they lack what Freud called "secondary revision" and are thus lacking in coherence. Because they lack coherence they often turn into anxiety dreams that awaken the sleeper. There is a group of mentally ill patients that suffers greatly because their symptoms are "carelessly strung together."

Fortunately, this disagreement does not prevent us from enjoying Langer's chapter titled "Poesis" (1953). We agree that language can be used in two ways: to convey information and to stimulate feelings in the reader. We also agree that Blake's Tyger in "Tyger, tyger burning bright in the forests of the night" is not the beast for British sportsmen to hunt and that a common tiger is not likely to burn in the forest of the night. We do believe, however, that this tiger may have been a dream before it became a poem and was a metaphor for something unconscious in the poet.

THE SIGNIFICANCE OF METAPHOR

Philosophers like Susanne Langer and her mentor Cassierer have acquainted us with the idea that metaphors have made possible the intellectual development of mankind. The beginning of the psychoanalytic understanding of the role of metaphor took place in a 1940 essay by the British psychoanalyst Ella Freeman Sharpe. She found metaphors particularly useful when there is simultaneously a wish to reveal and a wish to conceal.

She also found that in the course of analysis, metaphors are used to reveal forgotten experiences. In Shakespeare's case we are usually dealing with original metaphors coined by the Poet. For example, in the opening scene of *King Lear,* the king proclaims

> Know that we have divided
> In three our kingdom; and 't is our fast intent
> To shake all cares and business from our age,
> Conferring them on younger strengths, while we
> Unburden'd crawl toward death (I.i.38-42).

The metaphor "crawl toward death" gains its power from condensing infancy and old age, because it not only conveys the slow passage of time in old age but also, more deeply hidden in the unconscious, the wish to return to childhood, when crawling was the form of locomotion.

The ability to coin original metaphors enabled Shakespeare to fuse nature and sexuality in a way that is still astonishing. For example, from *Antony and Cleopatra,* "old Cesar plowed her and she cropped" or, from *A Midsummer Night's Dream,* Titania speaks the truly wondrous metaphor:

> When we have laugh'd to see the sails conceive
> And grow big bellied with the wanton wind (II.i.128-129)

Most of us have often watched with pleasure the wind propelling a sailboat, but how many have been in contact with their unconscious so that they can experience the wind as impregnating the sail? And to experience the wind as wanton because it will impregnate every sail in its path! If psychoanalysis is right, we all had some of this capacity (though not the ability to choose and arrange the words so concisely and so musically) before sexual repression banished such thoughts to the realm of the unconscious.

In the same play Titania says:

> And never, since the middle summer spring,
> Met we in hill, in dale, forest, or mead,
> By paved fountain, or by rushy brook,
> Or in the beached margent of the sea,
> to dance our ringlets to the whistling wind (II.i.82-86)

and all nature responds to their quarrel:

> Therefore the winds, piping to us in vain.
> As if in revenge have suck'd up from the sea
> Contagious fogs; which falling in the land
> Have every pelting river made so proud
> That they have overborne their continents (II.i.88-92)

Winds are alive and capable of revenging themselves and rivers can be so proud they overflow. Nature is neither inanimate nor impersonal.

In Sonnet 1 the Poet is urging a young man too much in love with himself to reproduce. Self-love is described in that sonnet metaphorically as "thou contracted to thine own bright eyes." Is the metaphor only a synonym of self-love or does it go further to imply that the eyes play a significant role in self-love? If the metaphor has an autonomous meaning of its own the line will be remembered apart from the sonnet.

To us, "contracted to thine own eyes" emphasizes the role of the eyes as a sexual organ. One of the great limitations of self-love is our inability to see our own eyes except in the mirror. We are unable to delight in their brightness. Even Narcissus could only accomplish the feat he is famous for by seeing himself mirrored. Does "contracted to thine bright eyes" mean that the Young Man is looking at himself in the mirror? Furthermore, the word contracted is of interest. Literally it means "committed to by contract" in other words engaged to be married. But love also restricts and limits choice. The Poet wishes to tell the Young Man not only that he is not free but also that his self-love is making his world small.

In Sonnet 137 the Poet feels betrayed by his own eyes.

> If eyes corrupt by over-partial looks
> Be anchored in the bay where all men ride (lines 5-6)

In a state of love the otherwise roving eyes have become anchored, a beautiful metaphor for constancy, but this "anchoring" has "corrupted" the eyes, implying that they are useless in evaluating the loved one. In this case they became anchored in a bay where all men ride, another original metaphor for the woman's promiscuity. Psychoanalysis has shown that loving a promiscuous woman is a compromise between homo- and heterosexual feelings. What remained unconscious to the Poet is that the very promiscuity he deplores is the very reason for his being "anchored" in her. Complex ideas, largely unconscious, lend themselves (in talented hands) to being condensed into metaphors.

Poets of the greatness of Homer or Shakespeare are wordsmiths of a very special kind. They deal with realms that have not yet been articulated, realms that conceptual language has not yet conquered. To do so, they rely primarily on an unusual capacity to create metaphors and similes that only, at a much later date, will be translated into conceptual language. Metaphor is particularly useful in the quest for insight, as our inner life is usually accessible only through metaphors. The metaphor fuses sense experience with thought. Metaphors can be understood without their full meaning becoming conscious to the listener or reader. The metaphor is a communication between the preconscious of one person and the preconscious of another, without the pain or embarrassment that might be created when the message is stated starkly. Much of the communication between poet and reader takes place on this level.

A poet is a musician who combines words in melodic ways. This emphasis on melody is no longer fashionable among critics of poetry who prefer to compare poetry to sculpture, but in 1951 Dylan Thomas wrote:

> I wanted to write poetry in the beginning because I had fallen in love with words. The first poems I knew were nursery rhymes, and before I could read them for myself I had come to love just the words of them, the words alone... And these words were, to me, as the notes of bells, the sounds of musical instruments, the noises of wind, sea, and rain, the rattle of milk carts, the clopping of hooves on cobbles, the fingering of branches on a windowpane might be to someone, deaf from birth, who has miraculously found his hearing... I cared for the shape of sound...I cared for the colors the words cast on my eyes (Gibbons p. 184)

Shakespeare's sonnets are among the most musical, as, for example: "When to the sessions of sweet silent thought" (Sonnet 30), "as sweet seasoned showers to the ground" (Sonnet 75), "Like as the waves make towards the pebbled shore,/So do our minutes hasten to their end" (Sonnet 60).

It is this joy in the melody of words that the Poet transmits to us his readers. We can go on to quote from Dylan Thomas:

> …words were their springlike selves, fresh with Eden's dew, as they flew out of the air. They made their own original association as they sprang and shone… until I knew that I must live *with* them and *in* them, always… I knew I had to know them most intimately in all their forms and moods, their ups and downs… What I like to do is to treat words as a craftsman does his wood or stone (p. 185).

Words are alive and animated to the poet. He has a relationship to them and they in turn relate to each other. Because the words are alive for the poet he can reanimate the world of our childhood that maturation and trauma have made nearly lifeless as we come to render words subservient to realistic aims. The great poet also uses words to speak about what we dare not verbalize. He does this by coining original metaphors in which words become alive again. But contributing to the magic spell cast by the poet, there is also the unconscious reality of the poet. This unconscious is unknown to the poet but the poet's unconscious, like everybody else's unconscious, has an energy of its own and it seeks ways to burst out of its obscurity.

The concept of metaphor was just coming into use during Shakespeare's lifetime. The concordance to his writings shows that Shakespeare himself used the term "metaphor" four times in his writings; three times in Act V, Scene II in *All's Well That Ends Well*. There, Parolles, whose name means "words," introduces the term metaphor by exposing it to ridicule.

> *Parolles:* Nay, you need not stop your nose, sir. I spake but of a metaphor.
>
> *Clown:* If your metaphor stinks, I will stop my nose;
> or against any man's metaphors (V.ii.11-13).

In Act I, Scene III of *Twelfth Night* Sir Andrew asks Maria, "What is your metaphor?" And Maria answers, "It's dry," (lines 72-73) consciously a reference to Sir Andrew's drinking and less obviously a sexual rebuff to Sir Andrew. Although Shakespeare made light of the term metaphor, he used metaphors as they had never been used before.

POETRY AND BIOGRAPHY

In the absence of biographical data, the question as to whether the Poet of the Sonnets is Shakespeare himself has evoked an extensive study and controversy. There are those who believe that the greater the genius the more complete will be the severance of the poetry from the personality, or, stated differently, "the poetical is rarely identical with the personal ego." The opposing opinion states that however objective poets tries to be, they cannot help but betray their own secrets. The confessional spirit of our own age takes it for granted that the writer of fiction is writing thinly veiled autobiography and lyric poets today often introduce their poems when they read them to an audience by describing the personal circumstance that led to their creation.

A recent case where data are available may throw light on the complex relationship between the fictive author and the person. The narrator of Proust's *A La Recherche du Temps Perdu* was gentile and heterosexual; the author was half Jewish and mostly homosexual. Does this fact invalidate the observations the author made concerning jealousy when he presented it in a heterosexual context? Painter, Proust's biographer, maintained on one hand that the novel cannot be fully understood without the knowledge of Proust's life. On the other hand, however, he stated that Proust altered "material reality" to make it conform to "symbolic reality." Painter calls the novel "the symbolic story of his life" and therefore, "a creative autobiography." Harold Bloom in his *Western Cannon* saw Proust as rivaling Shakespeare in his portrayal of sexual jealousy. In Bloom's view "jealousy is hell in human life but purgatorial splendor in *Materia Poetica* (396)."

In the popular novel *Possession* by A.S. Byatt a professor warns a graduate student not to choose a certain author for a doctoral dissertation because "it was uncertain ground, a kind of morass like Shakespeare's sonnets (p. 127)." The "morass" to which the professor alludes is the question that absorbed the interest of so many writers, the identity of the Dark Lady and whether the Poet and his lover did or did not have a sexual relationship.

We wish to share another thought with our readers. Let us assume that some diligent researcher of Elizabethan archives came up with a document that discloses who Mr. W. H., "the only begetter of the sonnets," was—whether he was of a higher social rank, how long his love relationship lasted, and what the age difference between the two was. And let us also assume that similar information were known about who the Dark Lady was—how many times and with whom she was "foresworn." How much difference would such a discovery make to the analysis in this book? It is likely that some interpretations would come to seem irrelevant, or conversely, we might be congratulated for our capacity to deduce relevant biographical material from the sonnets. But ultimately, we must take Ben Johnson's advice when he urged readers, in his caption to the portrait of Shakespeare at the beginning of the First Folio to "look not on his picture but his book." The mystery would still remain, for it is not the Poet's biographical reality that matters but the alchemy that makes it possible to transform psychic pain or great joy into memorable poetry. Let us now assume another hypothesis: a manuscript was found, written in Shakespeare's hand, and in that manuscript, the date of every sonnet had been recorded. In this case, we would learn much more that is valuable because we would be able to connect the sonnets with each other and with Shakespeare's plays in a more meaningful way, incorporating the sonnets into the chronology of his works. This discovery would be significant because both the sonnets and the plays open windows into Shakespeare's way of feeling and thinking. However, since we have the answer neither to the first nor the second question, our imagination is left free to roam.

THE ANTHOLOGIES

When we found sonnets such as Sonnet 20 or 129 particularly important as a source of psychological information, we became curious to see how they ranked in importance as a poem. But how does one judge the importance of one sonnet by comparison with another? A crude but interesting way of doing this, we thought, was to consult anthologies and see what sonnets were selected as being significant. In the table that follows we tabulated the Shakespeare sonnets that six anthologies included.

We turned to six well-known anthologies: W. H. Auden, Louis Untermeyer, Emrys Jones, Lionel Trilling, Robert M. Bender and Charles L.

Squier, and Harold Bloom. Untermeyer and Auden were themselves poets and Jones is an authority on 16th century poetry; Trilling was a highly respected critic and teacher of English while Bender and Squier are teachers of English. Harold Bloom is an eminent literary critic. Auden included 24 sonnets, Untermeyer 22, Jones 40 (in an anthology that covers only the 16th century), Bender and Squier 48, and Bloom 14. Among the six, they anthologized 72 sonnets. Four sonnets were selected by all six anthologies: 30, 55, 73 and 129, while five sonnets—18, 19, 29, 87 and 116—were chosen by five of them. One poem, Sonnet 66, was included by four anthologies. These 10 sonnets can therefore be considered Shakespeare's most popular or influential.

An additional 10 sonnets—15, 33, 71, 86, 97, 106, 107, 130, 138 and 146—are found in three anthologies. Altogether 20 sonnets out of the complete cycle of 154 were selected in three or more of the six. For the convenience of the reader, we have added a further column listing the chapter in this book in which these sonnets are discussed. Of the 154 sonnets, 63 were selected by at least one anthology, and in our work we have covered 109 sonnets. That makes this book an anthology of a sort. We have included those sonnets about which we thought we had something interesting to say.

Auden	Trilling	Untermeyer	Jones	Bloom	Bender & Squier	Discussed in Chapter
		1				5
			2		2	5
					6	5
					9	5
					11	5
			12		12	3
					14	5
		15	15		15	2
					17	5
18	18	18	18		18	2
19		19	19	19	19	2

Auden	Trilling	Untermeyer	Jones	Bloom	Bender & Squier	Discussed in Chapter
			20			1
					22	2
					23	3
					25	2
29	29	29	29		29	3
30	30	30	30	30	30	3
31						3
		33	33		33	4
			35			4
					38	
					44	6
					49	4
			53	53		3
55	55	55	55	55	55	2
57			57			6
			60		60	2
61						
62						1
			64		64	2
			65		65	2
66		66	66		66	2
		71	71		71	2
73	73	73	73	73	73	2
					74	2
75						4
			76			
					79	
					85	
			86	86	86	4
87		87	87	87	87	4
90			90			4
94		94	94	94	94	4

Auden	Trilling	Untermeyer	Jones	Bloom	Bender & Squier	Discussed in Chapter
		95				4
		97	97		97	6
			98			
				99		3
					101	
			104			1
		106	106		106	2
	107		107	107		2
			110			4
			112			3
116		116	116		116	2
121			121	121	121	3
		123			123	2
			124			2
			125			
					126	2
					127	7
129	129	129	129	129	129	1
			130	130	130	7
138		138	138			7
			140			7
141		141				7
				144	144	8
					145	
146		146			146	2
147						7
151			151			7
					152	7
					153	
					154	

When we completed the writing of this book, we were startled to discover that six of 10 selected sonnets—18, 19, 55, 66, 73 and 116—were in the chapter "When Love is at War with Time and Death," two poems—29 and 30—in the chapter "Meditations on the Nature of Love," one sonnet—129—in the chapter on the pivotal sonnets and one other sonnet—87—in the chapter "As Love Declines." Conversely the sonnets in the chapters on the heterosexual relationships, on the procreation sonnets and on separation between lovers did not evoke in the anthologizers the same depth of feeling or admiration.

There is no way for us to know why a given anthologizer selects one sonnet rather than another, but we felt safe in our assumption that all anthologizers select those sonnets they personally feel are the best.

ACKNOWLEDGEMENTS

In writing this book, we wish to express our gratitude to many commentators on Shakespeare whose books have been helpful to us in understanding the sonnets. We have regularly consulted John Dover Wilson's *The Sonnets* (Cambridge University Press, 1966), Steven Booth's *Shakespeare's Sonnets* (Yale University Press, 1977), *The Sonnets*, edited by G. Blackmore Evans (Cambridge University Press, 1996), *The Arden Shakespeare's Sonnets*, edited by Katherine Duncan-Jones (1997), Helen Vendler's *The Art of Shakespeare's Sonnets* (1997), *The Oxford Shakespeare Complete Sonnets and Poems*, edited by Colin Burrow (2002), and *The Penguin Books: William Shakespeare, The Sonnets and a Lover's Complaint*, edited by John Kerrigan (1999). We have learned a great deal from all of them. We have also been greatly helped by the *Harvard Concordance to Shakespeare* by Martin Spivak and Harold Bloom's *Shakespeare: the Invention of the Human* was always a stimulation, even when we disagreed with him, as we often did.

Without the commentator's glossaries, many of the sonnets would have remained opaque and refractory to our understanding. For us, the sonnets' mystery begins after the commentator's elucidation has helped us overcome the obscurity of the language. Only then did we feel free to hear the Poet speaking to us and to wrestle with the mystery of the sonnets.

We owe a debt of gratitude to Charles Rosen's book, to his emphasis that each part of a poem, closely read, has a specific and individual phonetic character of its own (p. 194). In Rosen's view, the Poet should be almost pathologically sensitive to the suggestiveness of purely phonetic aspects of words (p. 195). As Rosen puts it, the "radiating word," alliteration, assonance, rhyme, rhythmic pattern—any form of poetic repetition—is part of the essence of poetry. The richness of meaning in the sonnet depends on the release of language from its normal function of conveying information (p. 207). When the poetic "message" is freed from too intimate a tie with a specific sender or receiver, the latent meanings in the text are released and come alive, and the sonnet is open to the reader to interpret as irresponsibly as he pleases. A love poem, unlike a proposal of marriage, does not derive its meaning by being fixed in time and space. The poem has its action in an indeterminate space, and its time is whenever it is read (p. 221).

Rosen quotes with approval the German Romantic author Schlegel: "A poem is written for everyone and no one. If the poet writes for someone in particular, he deserves to go unread." Everyone knows that Elizabeth Barrett Browning wrote her sonnets to Robert Browning, but the alchemy of poetry has so transformed them so that they are not only private love letters; there is a wider audience beyond the recipient for these love poems. The Poet of the Sonnets flagrantly preferred his male lover to his mistress. We should not ignore or even repress this fact, but this preference should not be allowed, in our opinion, to blind us to the wealth they contain for readers of any sexual orientation.

We wish to express our gratitude to Maria V. Bergmann for reading and commenting on every draft, to Karen Duda for typing the manuscript, to Meredith Bergmann for the cover drawing and a final careful read, to Sarah Starbuck for proofreading, and to Kathy Kovacic and Blackthorn Studio for designing the book.

CHAPTER 1:
FOUR PIVOTAL SONNETS:
SONNETS 20, 62, 104, 129

In this chapter we have selected four sonnets for special consideration, as taken together they illuminate the Poet's most prevalent concerns, including his horror of aging and his bisexuality. We will be referring to these sonnets again and again throughout this book.

If we allow ourselves to assume that the "I" of the sonnets is a single character (whether that is Will Shakespeare himself or a character of his creation doesn't matter) we can connect seemingly disparate material into a revealing, coherent picture. By so doing we are well aware that we have ventured beyond the relatively safe harbor of the psychoanalytic hour where a living patient can confirm the analyst's insights and we recognize that what seems evidence to us may not be convincing to some readers. But the approach has one certain benefit: by following it we will gain access to the major themes of the sonnets and get to know this astonishing body of poems very well.

The Poet of the Sonnets, being a man of the Renaissance, made full use of classical mythology but was also capable of coining new myths of his own making and creating an imagery so beautiful that, once compre-

...ed, it remains with us even if we do not share the Poet's interior psychic conflicts.

SONNET 20

A woman's face with nature's own hand painted,
Hast thou the master mistress of my passion,
A woman's gentle heart but not acquainted
With shifting change as is false women's fashion,
An eye more bright than theirs, less false in rolling:
Gilding the object whereupon it gazeth,
A man in hue all hues in his controlling,
Which steals men's eyes and women's souls amazeth.
And for a woman wert thou first created,
Till nature as she wrought thee fell a-doting,
And by addition me of thee defeated,
By adding one thing to my purpose nothing.
    But since she pricked thee out for women's pleasure,
    Mine be thy love and thy love's use their treasure.

In the first five lines the feminine aspects of the Young Man are stressed, as is his superiority over women. The next three lines will emphasize his masculine aspects. In line 6, this androgynous man-woman is compared to the sun: "Gilding the object whereupon it gazeth." The act of gilding, as distinguished from gilded, appears only twice in Shakespeare's work, in this sonnet and in Sonnet 33:

> Kissing with golden face the meadows green,
> Gilding pale streams with heavenly alchemy (Sonnet 33, lines 3-4)

In mythology the sun is usually a masculine symbol, whereas the "pale" moon is experienced as feminine; the use of the term gilding emphasized the masculine aspect of this bisexual youth.

A gender change is introduced in line 7, when the Young Man is addressed as "A man in hue, all hues in his controlling." The word "hue" had in Shakespeare's time many connotations, such as appearance, bearing, and grace. In these lines, the Poet seems eager to counteract the feminine impression he conveyed in the first six lines. "Masculine" means being in control of all his hues so that nothing that emanates from him is beyond his control. In Sonnet 94 a similar praise appears: "They are the lords and owners of their faces," meaning that those whose face does not betray what they feel are masculine. Commentators have also noted that "controlling" in line 7 contains a pun on "cunt." In that case the faint echo of "his cunt" in "his controlling" increases the sense of the Young Man as hermaphroditic.

Line 8 affirms the Young Man's appeal to both men and women: "Which steals men's eyes and women's souls amazeth." We note that the appeal is not equal on both genders. The Young Man evokes admiration from men, "stealing their eyes," implying taking men's eyes away from women. The Young Man has an even deeper effect on women, whose "souls he amazes." Blackmore Evans believes that the asymmetry is intended to convey that men responding with their eyes are more intellectual, while women, responding with their souls are more richly endowed with emotions. However, we will see that the eye is often the principal sexual organ in Shakespeare's sonnets—perhaps because it is the organ used to read them—so to "steal men's eyes" has sexual undertones.

The third quatrain introduces a legend that Shakespeare created for this occasion. Nature was engaged in creating a woman when she "fell a-doting"—that is, in love with the woman she was creating. Being heterosexual, Nature decided to add a penis for her own sexual pleasure. The Poet suggests that he was ready to love the woman nature was creating, but nature defeated him by the addition of the penis, making a sexual relationship between the Poet and the Young Man impossible. Hence, "me of thee defeated." Nature can have him but the Poet cannot. The verb "painted," found in the first line, appears in Shakespeare's work 58 times and is mostly used as a metaphor, often to connote the opposite of genuine as in "your painted counterfeit" in Sonnet 16. In this sonnet, when nature paints a woman, the woman comes to life, and when she adds a penis the woman becomes a bisexual person.

The term "a-doting" appears only in this sonnet. In the quarto edition, the line reads: "fell a doting." In Sonnet 131 the Poet speaks of "my dear doting heart." In Sonnet 141 the Poet tells us that his heart is "pleased to dote." And in Sonnet 148 the Poet speaks of "my false eyes dote." In these sonnets, as well as in other works of Shakespeare, doting means loving to excess, or loving foolishly. However, to be the recipient of such a love may not be undesirable. Thus, in *Much Ado About Nothing* we are told that Beatrice loves Benedick with an "enraged affection." Don Pedro muses "I would she had bestowed this dotage on me" (Act II, Scene III). An extreme form of dotage takes place in *A Midsummer Night's Dream* when Titania tells Bottom, transformed into an ass, "Oh, how I love thee; how I dote on thee." Oberon comments, "Her dotage now I begin to pity." Dotage can be a painful emotion.

Who is this nature so charmingly anthropomorphized? If we turn to other sonnets to discover who nature is, we will find, in Sonnet 4, that "Nature's bequest gives nothing, but doth lend," meaning that the loveliness of the Young Man was not given to him as a permanent right, but only lent to him by "nature," obliging him to pass on his beauty to the next generation. In Sonnet 18 we are told that "nature" is far from constant: "nature's changing course untrimmed." In Sonnet 60 "nature" can be in conflict with time, when time "Feeds on the rarities of nature's truth." In Sonnet 67 "nature" can be experienced as bankrupt, and when that happens there is no reason to live on. Depressing is also that "nature" uses the Young Man as a kind of souvenir of times now past. In Sonnet 126 "nature" is described as "sovereign mistress over wrack." At times "nature" is equated with life itself, a ruler over destruction, as for example in Sonnet 122: "so long as brain and heart/Have faculty by nature to subsist." Nature can be playful and goddesslike; she sometimes helps and at other times hinders our effort. Basically, in this sonnet, nature is portrayed by the Poet as narcissistic and irresponsible, pursuing her own ends indifferent to human wishes. In other sonnets discussed in Chapter 2 she is a sort of stand-in for the Poet himself, keeping the Young Man youthful as a souvenir of the beauty she had long ago. This idea seems strange but we will come to know it well, beginning with the discussion of Sonnet 62 later in the chapter.

There is a bawdy play on words in line 12: "adding one thing" is a reference to the penis; "to my purpose nothing" is the opposite of "one thing" and a reference to the vagina. It is likely that line 14 in Sonnet 8—"Thou single wilt prove none"—is also a reference to the female genital. There is a famous scene in *Hamlet* that can also be cited as confirmation of the Elizabethan equation between vagina and nothing:

Hamlet: Lady, shall I lie in your lap?
    Lying down at Ophelia's feet.
Ophelia: No, my lord.
Hamlet: I mean, my head upon your lap?
Ophelia: Ay, my lord.
Hamlet: Do you think I meant country matters?
Ophelia: I think nothing, my lord.
Hamlet: That's a fair thought to lie between maids' legs.
Ophelia: What is, my lord?
Hamlet: Nothing [Act III, Scene II, 119-28.].

In the third quatrain of Sonnet 136, (a sonnet we do not otherwise include in this book) we read:

Among a number one is reckoned none.
Then in the number let me pass untold,
Though in thy store's account I one must be.
For nothing hold me, so it please thee hold
That nothing, me, a something sweet to thee (lines 8-12).

The Poet asserts that one is no number, and that one is to be reckoned as none. That one is none is a proverb in many languages. For example, the German "Einmal (once) ist Keinmal (never)." A favorite strategy used by seducers is to persuade that one intercourse is no intercourse. "Store's account" contains an allusion to cunt. "Nothing" in line 11 can be read as "no thing" and therefore again as a reference to the vagina. The psychoanalyst Bertrand Lewin (1948), without reference to Shakespeare stated, "When a patient in analysis says he is thinking of nothing, he or she will soon be talking about the female genital."

The Poet has fallen in love with a very attractive and effeminate young man, but the Poet knows that homosexual relationships are forbidden under Elizabethan law. He may also share the abhorrence for homosexual activities, or may only be careful not to express them. In any case, he hopes homosexual love that does not lead to homosexual activity can be made acceptable to the reader. No wonder, then, that in subsequent years this poem evoked controversy, some using it to prove Shakespeare's homosexuality while others employed it as a proof that he was not. It is hardly surprising: an overt homosexual would never have written this sonnet, but neither would it have occurred to a heterosexual man.

The Young Man in this poem represents a solution to a particular problem that the Poet experiences. The Young Man is as beautiful as a woman but, being a man, is free from the character defects that the Poet attributes to women. The Poet of the Sonnets leads us to believe, at least in his case, that love and sexuality run along different tracks: the Poet's feelings of love are easily and unselfconsciously directed towards a man, but his feelings of sexual attraction remain directed towards women. Both feelings are presented as natural, so as to require no explanation to the reader.

In Sonnet 20, the beauty of women is regarded as self-evident, as the poem begins by attributing to the man "a woman's face." Written in an exuberant mood with a great deal of humor, many original ideas, and unexpected puns, this sonnet is a charming fable. One would have expected that it would rank among Shakespeare's more popular sonnets, but only one anthology included it. We suspect that it did not fare well because in spite of the Poet's denial so charmingly stated, the implicit homosexuality was too disturbing to many readers. To our knowledge, Sonnet 20 is unique in celebrating love based on the bisexual appeal of the person chosen.

In real life there are heterosexual women who love their female friends, and enjoy their company and have much more in common with them than they do with their heterosexual mates. The reverse is equally common: men who spend most of their time and pleasure in the company of other men and yet seek sexual gratification from a woman or from more than one woman. In psychoanalytic terms such solutions are called compromise formations between homo- and heterosexual wishes. Many masculine women and feminine men exert a special fascination on their partners, appearing bisexual; as both man and woman, they represent a possible solution to a conflict between homo- and heterosexual wishes. As a rule, however, the perceived bisexuality of the partner remains unconscious. However in Sonnet 20, this knowledge has not only become conscious but was transformed into a highly original poem. Sonnet 20 is an attempt at compromise formation based on love for a man who seems to the Poet to possess the attributes of both genders; the Poet admits openly that it is the bisexuality of the Young Man that is attractive, but denies that the Young Man is sexually attractive. Bisexuals attract for the same reason that narcissists are attractive: they are or at least appear self-sufficient. Psychoanalysts often discover that both envy and jealousy often interfere with the capacity to love, but love for a bisexual person who is believed to have within her or his orbit all that is the best in both genders must evoke also a great deal of envy. Falling in love with a hermaphrodite, as the Young Man is experienced in Sonnet 20, contains an obstacle. Anyone experienced in fantasy as hermaphroditic fantasy is bound to seem self-sufficient and therefore incapable as well as unwilling to love the other.

On the surface, this sonnet is in praise of a young man the Poet adores, or to use Shakespeare's term, "dotes upon." There are many sonnets in praise of this or another young man, but the nature of the praise bestowed in this sonnet is unique. The Young Man is exalted because he has androgynous qualities; because he combines masculine and feminine tendencies, being both master and mistress is proclaimed to be unique. This dual nature is captured in the second line: "the master mistress of my passion." In Shakespeare's time, the term "mistress" had not yet acquired the connotation it has for us—that of a "kept woman," or a woman who belongs to a man, usually married, who is financially supporting her. The term "master" here refers to a person endowed with the right to command. A note of submission to this hermaphroditic creature is introduced.

Shakespeare's commentators have interpreted that "but not acquainted" puns as not having a cunt. Whether this interpretation is accepted or not, it is clear that a strong anti-femine attitude is present when the Young Man's eyes are seen as "less false in rolling," namely, more loyal than woman's eyes. This belief in the lover's constancy will not be sustained in the subsequent sonnets. Patrick Mahony (1979) noted that the syntactical structure of Sonnet 20 contains many inversions (changes in the words' order), ellipses (omission of words necessary to complete the sentence), paralaxis (change in direction), and hypotaxis (subordinate clauses). The sonnet is unique in having fourteen hypermetric lines (exceeding the established meter of the sonnets). The bisexuality is also reflected in the binarity of the lines, two different ideas being pressed into the same line. He noted that to be accepted with the reverse side, or back side, is a reference to anal eroticism, so prominent in homosexuality. What Mahony discovered is a connection between the style of the poem and what the Poet tried to repress. What is repressed in the content, the anal homosexual wish, resurfaces in the style.

In psychoanalytic practice, one occasionally encounters men and women who have fallen in love with someone of their own gender, but this love or even sexual attraction notwithstanding, they insist that they are not homosexuals. As the Poet declares in Sonnet 20, they only happen to have fallen in love with this particular person. With humor and irony some people wear a button that says, "I'm not gay, my lover is."

One of the important contributions of psychoanalysis to the understanding of homosexuality was the insight that in addition to overt homosexuality, two other types have to be added: latent homosexuality, where homosexual wishes, insufficiently held back by repression, require fear and hatred of homosexuals to contain the homosexual wishes in a state of repression. Latent homosexuals rely heavily on projection (attributing their feelings to others, not themselves) and reaction formation (feeling repelled by what unconsciously attracts them) to keep their homosexuality repressed. Another diagnostic group comprises desexualized homosexuality; such men and woman have passionate love relationships with members of their own gender, including jealousy when the loved one prefers someone else, but the relationship does not include direct sexual wishes. In Sonnet 20 desexualized homosexuality is the Poet's ideal. It is possible to read all the love sonnets to the Young Man as examples of desexualized homosexuality, but the heterosexual sonnets discussed later in this book (Chapter 7), including the painful triangle, cast doubt on the fact that the desexualization idealized in this sonnet was actually achieved.

In the Poet's unconscious there was a choice: he could desire the Young Man's penis as a woman would and find that he is a homosexual. Or he could ask for friendship based on admiration but devoid of sexual interest, thus sublimating homosexual wishes into a "mere" friendship. Unwilling to accept the implication of homosexuality, the Poet created Sonnet 20. Resigned to the fact that nature "pricked" the man he loves, that is, endowed him with a penis for woman's pleasure, he asks only for the Young Man's love and suggests the Young Man's sexuality, here called "love's use," should go to women. What the Poet advocated was a radical separation between love and sexuality; as we will see in other poems, sexless love also implies loveless sexuality.

SONNET 20 AND THE CLASSICAL PAST

Shakespeare very likely wrote under the influence of the Roman poet Ovid, who in his famous book *Metamorphoses* told the story of the sculptor Pygmalion, who fell in love with and caressed the statues of a young woman he had created. Venus granted is prayer that the statue come to life and become his wife. In psychoanalytic terms both Shakespeare's Nature and Ovid's Pygmalion are not capable of loving a real person and fall in love with what they themselves have created.

Whether Shakespeare read Ovid in the original in his student years or whether he read it in the Golding translation that had just appeared in 1565 is not clear, but the bisexuality was described by Golding thus:

> Her countenance and her grace
> was such as in a boy might well be called a wench's face,
> and in a wench be called a boy's (Golding 10:429-36)

Ovid's story of Salmachis and Hermaphroditus is also relevant to Sonnet 20. The water nymph Salmachis did not enjoy the hunt, preferring to look at herself in the water mirror and comb her lovely hair (we will meet her masculine equivalent as Narcissus). Hermaphroditus, the son of Hermes and Aphrodite, was a beautiful lad fifteen years old. He came to a pool translucent to the very bottom and it was the pool that Salmachis was using as mirror to her self-love. She sees Hermaphroditus, admires his beauty, desires him and pleads for kisses. Hermaphroditus is reluctant. Salmachis lures him into the water and once there, serpentlike, she coils herself around him. She prays to the gods, "May no day ever come to separate us." Her prayer was answered. Their bodies merged, becoming one person, both man and woman. "Two beings and no longer man and woman but neither and yet both" (Ovid *Metamorphoses*, 4:285-388, Humphries translation).

"Master mistress of my passion" goes even further back to the fable told in Plato's *Symposium*. The best-known part of the *Symposium*, the one that has influenced Western culture most profoundly, is the legend told by Aristophanes to explain the nature of love: originally mankind was composed of double creatures, having two heads, four arms, four legs, and two genitalia. Some were double-males, others double-females, and still others were composed male and female. These creatures threatened the gods because being self-sufficient they felt no need to sacrifice to the gods and the gods were in turn desperately dependent on human sacrifices. So the gods decided to cut each creature in half and since then the two halves are yearning to be reunited.

The legend told in the *Symposium* explained also why some people are heterosexual and others homosexual: sexual orientation depends on the gender of the person with whom we were originally united. We should note the wisdom of this legend. The hermaphrodite is self-sufficient and does not need the help of the gods, and therefore will feel no need to sacrifice to the gods. Being self-sufficient themselves, these gods nevertheless "need" the sacrifices offered by mortals for their own gratification; therefore they have a narcissistic relationship with mortals. These gods are interested in mortals only as sacrificers.

Our analysis of Sonnet 20 leads us to believe that this sonnet has been underestimated by the commentators and anthologizers. There is first the original use of the classical heritage and its transformation beyond what had been transmitted by the tradition. But there is more; whenever in the course of psychoanalysis sexual or love wishes for someone of one's own gender emerge, anxiety of becoming homosexual or bisexual surfaces. Shakespeare was capable of taking this anxiety-laden subject and treating it lightly and with humor; a taboo subject was given permission to become articulated. A weight of guilt and shame was lifted, if only for the time it takes to read this sonnet.

In Sonnet 20 we encounter the Poet who can bring to life the classical past, but is capable of creating a personal myth modeled on the classical past. Shakespeare's humor goes beyond Ovid; his nature is not a goddess-like Aphrodite who grants the sculptor's wish. She herself falls a-doting and for her own sexual satisfaction adds the penis the Poet claims not to need. We can look upon this sonnet as a compromise between homo- and heterosexual wishes. If the Poet had succeeded to live up to this division we would not have had the conflicts that animate the other sonnets. Because the sonnet is an erudite and funny compromise it remains inherently unstable. An unstable compromise is a wonderfully promising dramatic premise and since the rest of the sonnets show that the compromise of Sonnet 20 did not lead to a permanent resolution, we selected this poem as the gateway to one of the Poet's major inner struggles.

SONNET 62

Credit for the discovery of self-love as a third form of love after hetero-sexual and homosexual love goes to Ovid. This love still carries the name of his legendary character Narcissus and is called narcissism. Ovid, being a poet and not a systematic thinker, created a legendary character, not a psychological concept.

According to Ovid, Narcissus was a youth of wondrous beauty. Perceptively, Ovid made him not the child of a loving couple but of the nymph Leiriope, who was ravished by the river god Cephisus, who encircled her with his winding streams. Leiriope consulted the prophet Tiresias as to whether Narcissus would reach old age; the prophet replied, "Only if he never knows himself." It has been pointed out that the seer's answer was Ovid's ironical reversal of the Greek ideal "know thyself," inscribed on Apollo's temple in Delphi. Beautiful youths, men, women and nymphs fell in love with Narcissus but he rejected them all. In response to a rejected lover, Nemesis, the goddess of vengeance, inflicted upon Narcissus the pain he caused others, to love without being loved. Exhausted from the hunt, Narcissus reaches a fountain whose waters are unruffled. In the silvery waters he is smitten by love for the image that stares at him from the water. Narcissus cannot tear himself away and dies gazing at his image.

Among those who fell in love with Narcissus was the nymph Echo, who was punished by Juno to be unable to have independent speech and was capable only of repeating what she was told.

> Out of the woods she came with arms all ready to fling around his neck, but he retreated. "Keep your hands off," he cried, "and don't touch me. I would die before I would give you a chance at me." "I'd give you a chance at me," was all that poor Echo could reply (Ovid *Metamorphoses* 3, Humphries' translation).

This story, in our opinion, shows how profound a psychologist Ovid was. Milder narcissists may not be able to love an independent person but at least they can find a partner who mirrors them, who, echo-like, reflects back what they are. That Narcissus could not even love Echo doomed him to utter loneliness.

With these preliminaries behind us, we turn to Sonnet 62.

> Sin of self-love possesseth all mine eye,
> And all my soul, and all my every part;
> And for this sin there is no remedy,
> It is so grounded inward in my heart.
> Methinks no face so gracious is as mine,
> No shape so true, no truth of such account,
> And for my self mine own worth do define,
> As I all other in all worths surmount.
> But when my glass shows me my self indeed
> Beated and chopped with tanned antiquity,
> Mine own self-love quite contrary I read:
> Self, so self-loving were iniquity.
>> 'Tis thee (my self) that for my self I praise,
>> Painting my age with beauty of thy days.

The very first words of the sonnet are a surprise. Why is self-love a sin? There is hardly a passage in the Bible where self-love is denounced with such vehemence. What has usually been condemned is the sexual expression of self-love, masturbation. True, during the Middle Ages vanity had the status of a sin. But there is little evidence that the author of the sonnets was a believing Christian.

"Self-love possesseth all mine eye" tells us that the eye is the crucial organ in self-love. This self-love permeates the Poet's soul and every part of him. The expression "possesseth" implies that self-love, like other forms of love, can overwhelm the person in love, who has the feeling of being taken captive by the love. To feel possessed implies that love is experienced passively as something that overwhelms us, not actively as something we choose to do. This self-love first conquered the eye, then the soul and then "every part." This self-love is so grounded in the Poet's heart that there is no remedy for it. The first quatrain is stated as an overwhelming fact; the second quatrain opens with "Methinks." It is not as absolute as the first quatrain, for "Methinks"—the equivalent of "it seems to me"—mitigates the absoluteness of the first quatrain. It was this all-conquering self-love that made the Poet think that "no face so gracious is as mine/ No shape so true, no truth of such account." The last statement is of special interest because even if something is believed to be truth it can be held weakly or uncertainly, or, as it happened to the Poet, so strongly that no other truth compares to it and is of similar account. The second quatrain ends with the declaration that the Poet feels he surmounts, or surpasses, everybody else.

In the first two quatrains the Poet, like Narcissus, is in love with himself. Regarding self-love as a sin, he knows no cure for it. In the third quatrain, however, the remedy for self-love is discovered. The same mirror that trapped Narcissus has a sobering effect on the Poet.

Shakespeare transformed Ovid's tale. The very glass that trapped Narcissus awakens the Poet out of his narcissistic slumber. His age, in this sonnet called "tanned antiquity," causes him to fall in love with someone who reminds him of his own now-lost self-love while he was young. This is expressed metaphorically in the last line, "Painting my age with beauty of thy days."

It is only when he happens to look in the mirror ("but when my glass shows me myself indeed" sounds like something that happens, not like something that happened once) he is suddenly reminded that he is praising the Young Man. The Poet moves beyond his self-love when he can no longer maintain it because of aging. This moment allows him to write uniquely because he gained some distance from his self-love.

Thus for all its debt to Ovid, Sonnet 62 tells the story of a "Narcissus" who became a lover of someone else. The young man who looks at his reflection and falls in love has become an old man who loves himself until he sees his reflection and then finds a young man to love instead (this idea is the inspiration for the drawing on the cover of this book). Where a more ordinary mind would have had the Poet roused from his narcissism by the beauty of another (one, perhaps, who reminded him of himself), Shakespeare gives us a story of self-love that is thwarted by the Poet's horror of old age. This is of great importance, for the relationship because the man the Poet loves will himself age, which, in other poems, will raise the question of whether the Poet will be able to love him as he gets older.

The term "self love" appears in Sonnet 62 three times: in lines 1 and 11, and in line 12 as "self loving." In all of Shakespeare's writing, "self love" appears eight times and "self loving" three times. In Sonnet 3 "Who is so fond will be the tomb/Of his self love to stop posterity." Sonnet 62 alone would have assured for Shakespeare a prominent role in the Western understanding of the nature of narcissistic love. Love is a dominant theme in all poetry, but self-love has rarely been seen as a worthy topic for poetry. Poetry communicates one's love to the other; as a communication to the self it seems cumbersome.

The couplet

> 'Tis thee (my self) that for my self I praise,
> Painting my age with beauty of thy days.

Can be read in two different ways depending on how we interpret "thee." Most commentators think that "thee" refers to the Young Man. In this interpretation the Poet used the Young Man as a kind of deceptive mirror to persuade himself that he was young. But the parentheses around the word myself suggests another and deeper possibility: that it refers to the self-love of the Poet as a Young Man. The cunning poet may have wished to convey the two interpretations simultaneously, obliterating the difference in the state of love between himself and the Young Man.

Vendler believes that the Poet created this delusory self-image in order to be able to believe in the Young Man's affections for him. We, by contrast, believe that the Poet fell in love with the Young Man in order to prolong or recapture the illusion of his own youth and beauty. The love of the Young Man was in the service of the Poet's restoration of his own narcissism.

It was in 1914 that Freud recognized that self-love, or as he preferred to call it "narcissism," can give rise to a special kind of love, which he called "narcissistic love." In that love, we love someone else who reminds us of ourselves either as we are or as we had once been or as we wished to have been. It is a love that is based on converted envy. When we read Sonnet 62, we can see that Shakespeare had this insight three hundred years before Freud. But, because the Poet condemned his own self-love, he also condemned his narcissistic love for the Young Man. Only Auden included this sonnet in his anthology. From a psychoanalytic perspective, the transformation of narcissism into a narcissistic love as depicted by the Poet is a milestone in the understanding of self-love.

SONNET 104 (crucial)

Sonnets 62 and 104 have in common the fear of aging. In Sonnet 62 aging forced the Poet to change his self-love for the love of the Young Man. In Sonnet 104 the Poet is amazed that his love for the Young Man lasted for three years without his lover showing signs of aging.

> To me fair friend you never can be old,
> For as you were when first your eye I eyed,
> Such seems your beauty still: three winters cold,
> Have from the forests shook three summers' pride,
> Three beauteous springs to yellow autumn turned,
> In process of the seasons have I seen,
> Three April perfumes in three hot Junes burned,
> Since first I saw you fresh which yet are green.
> Ah yet doth beauty like a dial hand,
> Steal from his figure, and no pace perceived,
> So your sweet hue, which methinks still doth stand
> Hath motion, and mine eye may be deceived.
> > For fear of which, hear this thou age unbred,
> > Ere you were born was beauty's summer dead.

The poem has a unique structure. The first two lines are addressed to the Young Man, assuring him that he can never be old. The next six lines are a description of three years and their respective seasons, implying the Poet's amazement that the youth did not appear to have aged in the last three years. In the third quatrain this peculiar certainty has gone; the Poet has become suspicious: time is compared to a "dial hand" that moves so slowly that beauty can be stolen from the Young Man's figure without the pace being "perceived," that is, without us noticing that the shadow on the sun dial has moved at all. In line 11 what was a certainty in the first lines has been reduced to a mere "methinks;" the Poet suggests that the Young Man has aged in these three years but the Poet's eyes have been deceived.

The couplet is addressed to future generations, here called "age un-bred," and the Poet tells them that even before they were born "beauty's summer," a reference to the Young Man, beauty had died. The couplet thus takes back what the poem tried to affirm.

The traditional division of the sonnet into three quatrains in contrast as well as in communication with each other has not been observed. In-stead, the theme of the second quatrain extends over six lives, giving the changes of the season extra power.

The second line brings in the role the eye plays in the Poet's falling in love. Love took place literally at the first sight, when "your eye I eyed." Once more we can confirm that the main sexual organ for the Poet is the eye and this displacement from the penis to eye helped the Poet separate love from sexuality. When the eye takes over the function of the genital, psychoanalysis uses the term "displacement." Already in Sonnet 20 the lover was praised as having "an eye more bright than theirs/Less false in rolling;" and in Sonnet 62, "sin of self love possessed my eye." There are a number of other sonnets in which the eye plays a prominent role in the love feelings of the Poet. For example in Sonnet 1: "But thou contracted to thine own bright eyes;" Sonnet 14: "But from thine eyes my knowl-edge I derive;" Sonnet 47: "Mine eye is famished for a look;" Sonnet 49: "Scarcely greet me with that sun, thine eye;" Sonnet 61: "It is my love that keeps mine eye awake;" Sonnet 93: "There can live no hatred in thine eye;" Sonnet 139: "Wound me not with thine eye, but with thy tongue."

Nature, we note, is experienced as both active and hostile as well as passive and enduring. Active forces playing havoc alternate with passing events that could not be prevented, "three winters cold" is experienced as the aggressor, who "shook three summers' pride." In the fifth line, "beaute-ous spring to yellow autumn turned" without anyone actively bringing this change about. The next metaphor is a powerful one, "three April perfumes in three hot Junes burned," implying that April perfumes linger until they are burned up by the hot June. The Poet repeats that these changes have taken place three times since the two have met. In the third quatrain, the Young Man himself is introduced into the cycles of nature. Three years ago, he was green, but unlike nature human life is not cyclical and subject to the power of time.

In line 9, a major shift takes place. What impresses the Poet now is not nature, but the clock.

The word dial appears in Shakespeare's work nine times, the word dial's four times, and dials twice. The full term sundial was not used by Shakespeare. Two references to dial appear in Sonnet 77:

> Thy glass will show thee how thy beauties wear,
> Thy dial how thy precious minutes waste.

And again,

> Thou by thy dial's shady stealth mayst know
> Time's thievish progress to eternity;

The phrase "dial's shady stealth" refers to the fact that in the shade the dial cannot register the changing hours, and this is how time can steal. In psychoanalytic terms, the dial is a symbolic representation of the superego; it admonishes the Poet to note how precious moments are wasted, but it is also an instrument used by time as in "thievish progress to eternity," where time allegedly steals from us our hours. The reference to eternity is one of the few places where the Poet speaks in religious language.

The metaphor used by the Poet in line 10: "Steal from his figure, and no pace perceived;" is of special interest because it illustrates how a creative poet can use the paranoid idea of stealing and transform it into poetry. Beauty is compared to a "dial hand" (sundial) that moves so slowly that no movement is noticed, expressed as "no pace perceived." Beauty itself, in line 10, is accused of stealing from the figure of the Young Man. Beauty also fades imperceptibly like the dial hand. What the Poet means is that because aging takes place, the beauty of the Young Man is stolen from him, a striking example of how a paranoid idea can become transformed into an original metaphor. Because the idea is paranoid, lines 9 and 10 are difficult to decipher logically. To make sense of them, we have to divide the thoughts that have become condensed. Beauty is accused of stealing (sneaking away) from the Young Man's figure and treated like a possession that can be stolen. Another metaphor is then added: beauty behaves like a dial hand that moves so slowly that we did not ever perceive the motion. The Poet frequently used the metaphor of stealing to connote lack of legitimacy; for example, in Sonnet 63 time is described as "Stealing away the treasure of his spring."

As we reach line 11, the certainty of the first line has vanished. The bold statement "you never can be old" has become the hesitant "methinks still doth stand." The metaphor of the dial hand in line 9 is still animating line 12. The dial can deceive the eye by moving in such a way that the motion itself is not noticed. The Young Man can age without the Poet noticing it. The fear of not noticing the effect of time grips the Poet. The Young Man was never supposed to age, and by loving him the Poet would also stay young. This was beyond the power of Eros to achieve. The Young Man may still be "green," but the Poet knows that he will not stay young forever. The Poet cannot accept that beauty is transient. "Sweet hue" in line 11 refers to the Young Man's complexion. "Hue," as we saw in Sonnet 20, is a word the Poet usually uses to describe masculinity. The Poet is no longer sure that a Young Man's "sweet hue…still doth stand." He begins to feel that his eyes, which have not noticed aging, may have deceived him. What the Poet feared becomes a certainty in the couplet. With "thou age unbred" the Poet addresses future generations and tells them (us) that with the aging of his lover, "beauty's summer" died. Thus the personal tragedy of the Poet, seeing the Young Man he loves aging, becomes a universal tragedy because his beauty will never be replicated. The coming generation will no longer know the beauty that died with the summer. Future generations should know that when the Poet's Young Man aged, summer's beauty died.

What is striking, particularly to older readers, is that three years seems such a long time to the Poet. In Sonnet 116, Shakespeare expressed the opposite feeling that love is "not time's fool, though rosy lips and cheeks within his bending sickle's compass come." In Sonnet 104, the mere anticipation of aging frightens the Poet. He does not explain this sonnet and we cannot be sure that we grasped it fully, but a hypothesis does come to mind. There are three years that make a very big difference: these three years may have been so crucial if they embrace the years during which the Young Man will have reached puberty. This hypothesis cannot be entirely dismissed because we encounter in real life people who can love either boys or girls as long as they are pre-pubescent (Charles Dodgson's desexualized love for Alice Liddell gave us *Alice in Wonderland*). If this was to any degree true of the Poet of the Sonnets, we gain a new understanding of the procreation sonnets which begin the sonnets in the traditional published sequence and which we describe in Chapter 5. They are addressed to the Young Man the Poet loved who is now reaching sexual maturity. If this was the case we can also understand better the enmity between the Poet and time. It is normal to have difficulty in accepting aging, but if love is confined to the few years before pubescence sets in, there will be a deeper reason to be at war with the destructive power of time. Sonnet 104 leads to the hypothesis that the Young Man the Poet loved was not only young, but not yet a man.

We have included Sonnet 104 in this chapter because in this sonnet the Poet allowed insight into his sexual and love life that he has not granted elsewhere. We are aware of the fact that no other interpreter of the sonnets has interpreted it the way we have, and we may be mistaken in our surmise. But if we are right, then one more puzzle about the Poet's love life will have yielded its secret. What has alerted us to the uniqueness of the sonnet is that the Poet himself seems amazed that his love had lasted for three years. If the Poet had used thirty years we would not have been surprised. But does anyone consider a relationship that lasts for three years particularly remarkable?

Since we assigned a pivotal role to Sonnet 104, we were naturally curious how the other commentators dealt with this problem. Vendler ignored it. Blackmore Evans, on the authority of Rollins, suggested that "'three' may be not a specific historical allusion but a poetically conventional number for commemorating such meetings (p. 212)." He draws attention to the fact that Sonnet 104 as well as Sonnet 107 is so often discussed in terms of the controversy of who the youth was, Southampton or Pembroke. Burrow noted that Sonnet 104 "does not break decisively from the poems that precede it" and that it contains "a significantly higher proportion of late rare words and lower proportion of early rare words than those which preceded them (p. 109)." We seem to be alone in the significance that we assigned to this sonnet. The sonnet contains some beautiful nature metaphors but if we were right in our surmise of its perverse implication it is hardly surprising that it was included in only one anthology.

SONNET 129

The three sonnets we have looked at so far cover a wide range of variations on falling in love, and what we think of as normal or at least typical falling in love ("boy meets girl" in American popular culture) is noticeably absent. Absent, too, is the theme of sexual desire or the fulfillment of love through the sexual act.

Sonnet 129, by contrast, concerns itself directly with desire and lust and ranks among Shakespeare's best-known sonnets and was chosen by five anthologies. The sonnet has its own unique structure but it is also one of the most savage ones. The word "lust" did not at first have the sinister connotation it has in this sonnet; though a deadly sin in the Christianity of the Middle Ages it was synonymous with pleasure and delight. However, by the time the sonnet was written the word lust acquired the meaning of strong, excessive or inordinate desire followed, once gratified, by loathing.

When a minister in one of his sermons fulminates against lust, we are not surprised. It is, so to speak, his métier. But Shakespeare? There is nothing in the other sonnets to prepare us for the vehemence with which lust is denounced in this sonnet, except the similar denunciation of self-love in Sonnet 62.

SONNET 129

Th' expense of spirit in a waste of shame
Is lust in action, and till action, lust
Is perjured, murd'rous, bloody full of blame,
Savage, extreme, rude, cruel, not to trust;
Enjoyed no sooner but despised straight,
Past reason hunted, and no sooner had,
Past reason hated as a swallowed bait,
On purpose laid to make the taker mad:
Mad in pursuit and in possession so,
Had, having, and in quest, to have, extreme;
A bliss in proof and proved, a very woe,
Before a joy proposed behind a dream.
   All this the world well knows yet none knows well,
   To shun the heaven that leads men to this hell.

"Th' expense of spirit," the opening words in this sonnet, are as striking as they are puzzling. The word expense was used by Shakespeare 19 times and only this once in the sonnets. It is the only place in his work where the word is used metaphorically rather than concretely. Commentators interpreted "Th' expense of spirit" as waste of vital energy, which results in a "waste of shame." By putting the two words "waste" and "shame" under the same yoke the Poet created a term that never existed before.

Something more can be learned from Shakespeare's use of the word waste, which appears in his works 51 times. Words can be wasted, breath can be wasted, and also memory, and above all the treasure of time can be wasted by idle hours. Man can waste time but time can also waste the man. One can also make "waste in brief mortality (*Henry V,* I.ii.28)." Because the Poet was, as we shall demonstrate in the next chapter, at war with time, he was highly sensitive to any waste. In the sonnets the word waste appears seven times, as for example in Sonnet 30, "And with old woes new wail my dear time's waste," or Sonnet 77, "Thy dial how thy precious minutes waste."

"Waste of shame" evokes the image of desolate territory—a desert inhabited by shame, possibly a non-flattering reference to the vagina. Lust is an action; it lasts only as long as the action lasts. The third and the fourth lines are lines of invectives; altogether nine invectives are hurled against lust. These invectives tell us what happens after lust has passed. The second quatrain repeats explicitly what was implicit in the second line. It emphasizes the brevity of the enjoyment and the guilt feelings that follow after consummation, expressed as "despised straight." In lines 6 through 8, the use of "past reason hunted" and "past reason hated" portray the double nature of lust. One feels first hunted by it and then overcome by hatred of it. Reason cannot explain either the haunting quality of lust nor why it is so powerfully hated after consummation. "Past reason" is repeated in lines 6 and 7; it is the Poet's term for what we call the "irrational." The Poet then goes on to compare the person seized by a lust to a fish that swallowed bait—a highly compressed metaphor, the word fish being eliminated. A person overtaken by lust is struggling like a fish that just swallowed bait, struggling in vain to free itself from the bait.

In line 8 a paranoid idea emerges. Lust has the character of conspiracy imposed upon us by some mysterious evil designer "to make the taker mad." The couplet emphasizes human helplessness in avoiding lust, even though we know full well its destructive power.

The Poetic impact of the sonnet is due in part to its structure: four nouns in line 1; the repetitive reversal of the words "lust" and "action" in line 2; three adjectives in line 3, followed by four adjectives in line 4. Together, they give the first quatrain a strong declarative and impersonal quality.

The second quatrain is constructed differently. It contains one sentence per line, but each sentence contains two ideas. The third quatrain is structurally similar to the second; all lines until the couplet consisting of six to nine words, while the couplet is longer, consisting of ten words. However, it is the content, the savage denunciation of lust that is most striking.

We are fortunate to have the analysis of Sonnet 129 by the distinguished linguist Roman Jakobson (in collaboration with Lawrence Jones, quoted by Rosen). In his analysis of that sonnet, Jakobson relied on the principle of binary opposition, which played so fundamental a role in his systematization of the study of sound structure in language. This binary opposition highlights the collision of pairs that provides a linguistic representation of the collision of two bodies in the act of fulfilling lust. And since, to Shakespeare, lust was the opposite of love, the structure of the sonnet captures and repeats the enmity between these two emotions.

Inserting vertical lines into the sonnet emphasizes the binary opposition.

I   Th' expense of Spirit / in a waste of shame
       Is lust in action, / and till action, lust
       Is perjured, murd'rous, / blouddy full of blame,
       Savage, extreame, rude, / cruel, not to trust,
II   Injoyd no sooner / but dispised straight,
       Past reason hunted, / and no sooner had
       Past reason hated / as a swallowed bayt,
8   On purpose layd / to make / the taker mad.
III Mad[e] in pursuit / and in possession so,
       Had, having, and in quest, / to have extreame,
       A blisse in proofe / and provd, / a[nd] very wo,
       Before a joy proposd / behind a dreame.
IV All this the world / well knows / yet none knowes well,
       To shun the heaven / that leads / men to this hell.
       (Rosen, p. 199)

As the vertical lines show, the binary opposition is maintained until line 8. In the first seven lines the grammatical parallelism has been maintained, while line 8 is built on five dissimilar grammatical forms. Equally striking for Jakobson is the fact that this sonnet alone among the 154 contains no personal or possessive pronouns, giving the sonnet an abstract structure, making it possible for Jakobson to speak of the "poetry of grammar." The impersonal structure of Sonnet 129 is in sharp contrast to the most personal theme of fornication and its bitter aftermath. Even the fornicator is never referred to directly, except in dependent clauses. Charles Rosen, who quoted Jakobson's work in a chapter entitled "Concealed Structures," noted that "the ability of the grammatical structure of language to assume a poetic life of its own is fundamental to music, which imitates this aspect of language."

After quoting Jakobson, Rosen also suggested an alternate analysis. He noted that the four consonants of s.p.r.t. dominate the first 12 lines.

1   Expence, Spirit, waste (sp sp st)
2   lust, lust (st st)
3   Is perjurd (s p r r)
4   Savage, extreame, trust (s str tr st)
5   despised straight (sp s str t)
6   Past reason hunted (p st r s t)
7   Past reason hated (p st r s t)

Rosen differentiates between what he calls the canonical interpretation, which deals with the interrelationship between the three quatrains and the couplet, and the "microscopic analysis," to which Sonnet 129 was subjected by Jakobson. If Shakespeare had attempted to achieve both kinds of symmetries, it would require an enormous amount of work and concentration. It is therefore likely that Shakespeare was so sensitive to language that such hidden structures occurred to him effortlessly and even unintentionally. Words occur to the Poet the way melodies occur to the composer.

A biblical passage is probably the oldest text to describe the pernicious effect of lust. Amnon, one of King David's sons, was so vexed by his desire for his half sister, Tamar, that he fell sick: "For she was a virgin; and Amnon thought it hard for him, to do anything to her." Following the advice of a lecherous friend, he pretended to be sick, and when King David visited him, he asked as a special favor that Tamar come and cook for him so that he can recover. King David complied, and Tamar came and cooked for him. Amnon then sent away all servants and when the two of them were left alone, the following happened.

(11)   And when she had brought them unto him to eat, he took hold of her, and said unto her, Come lie with me, my sister.

(12)   And she answered him, "Nay, my brother, do not force me; for no such thing ought to be done in Israel: do not thou this folly.

(13)   And whither shall I cause my shame to go? And as for thee, thou shalt be as one of the fools in Israel. Now therefore, I pray thee speak unto the King: for he will not withhold me from thee.

(14)   Howbeit he would not hearken unto her voice: but, being stronger than she, forced her and lay with her.

(15)   Then, Amnon hated her exceedingly; so that the hatred wherewith he hated her was greater than the love wherewith he had loved her. And Amnon said unto her, Arise, be gone.

(16)   And she said unto him, there is no cause: this evil in sending me away is greater than the other that thou didst unto me, but he would not hearken unto her.

(17)   Then he called his servant that ministered unto him, and said, Put now this woman out from me, and bolt the door after her (Samuel II, Chapter 13).

In the biblical passage, the essence of lust is an overwhelming desire before consummation, followed by an even more powerful disgust after the sexual act has been completed. The Bible offers no explanation for the radical shift in mood.

One of the influences of Freud's ideas on our way of feeling is that we no longer feel as inimical to lust as earlier generations were. We know today that the main enemies of love are more likely to be hatred or jealousy rather than lust. The term lust connotes a powerful sexual attraction driven by hostility that takes hold of a person after the sexual act has been completed. Lust can take place between two consenting partners but is more commonly experienced in isolation. It is usually a powerful sexual attraction to a person considered a forbidden partner, as when incest is involved, or as in happened in *The Winter's Tale*, where the coveted woman was the wife of the childhood friend. (However, there is no evidence that Polixenes actually lusted after Hermione, wife of his childhood friend Leontes. Rather, the sexual attraction between the two appears to be a product of Leontes' paranoid imagination.) Within the Freudian sphere of influence, lust takes place within the sexual sphere of narcissism, where the partner's needs are ignored; if the welfare of the partner is taken into account, lust will not be the word chosen. Lust is the sexuality of those who cannot love.

Wilson (1966) noted that unlike most sonnets, this sonnet was not written in quatrains, conveying to us the impression of being written in one breath, the form imitating the content. Wilson also put forth the idea that Sonnet 129 comprises all the different stages of lust: the after-lust period (had), the actual experience of lust (having) and the anticipation of lust (in quest) and that the extremes of lust are felt—all these stages (to have extreme). He credits Laura Riding and Robert Graves for this observation. In the biblical account that we presented, this chronological order was followed, but it ended in disgust, avoiding repentance. In psychoanalytic terms, if the capacity for repentance is present, the person who succumbed to lust is functioning on a higher psychological level of development than the one who stops at the level of disgust.

The psychoanalyst André Green (1975) differentiated between the object of need and the object of desire. In a relationship in which need predominates the gratification of the need leads to a loss of interest in the object. In a relationship of this kind once the sexual need has been gratified the other is of no further interest. If, however, the partner is the object of desire, gratification does not lead to satiety, and no one knew this difference better than Shakespeare.

Cleopatra is clearly the object of desire and not an object of need in *Antony and Cleopatra*. As Enobarbus puts it:

> Age cannot wither her, nor custom stale
> Her infinite variety; other women cloy
> The appetites they feed, but she makes hungry
> Where most she satisfies; for vilest things
> Become themselves in her, that the holy priests
> Bless her when she is riggish (II.iii.240-246).

To our knowledge no one equaled Shakespeare in describing the object of desire. What is astonishing is that the same man who wrote Sonnet 129 knew also of the bliss of which Enobarbus speaks.

The place of Sonnet 129 among Shakespeare's sonnets is a puzzle. Why should a cycle of love poems be interrupted to make room for a vehement denunciation of lust? If religious scruples, ideas of hell and punishment after death, were in the Poet's mind, surely this was the sonnet in which to express them. But there is no hint of religious feelings in this sonnet.

It therefore seems to us that Sonnet 129 was the result of the Poet's inability to maintain the split between love and "love's use" that the Poet tried to maintain in Sonnet 20. In our view the Poet would not have written Sonnet 129 had he been able to keep his sexual wishes out of the relationship with the Young Man. The sonnet suggests that the Poet could neither abstain nor accept his homosexual wishes.

Sonnet 129 has been placed within the series of the heterosexual sonnets devoted to the Dark Lady. The general tendency of the Poet to direct his feelings of love to the Young Man and his sexual feelings to the Dark Lady support a heterosexual reading of the poem as does phrase "waste of shame" in the first line suggesting an unflattering reference to the vagina. But if Sonnet 129 documents a moment when the Poet's deep love of the Young Man finally overcame his inhibition against desiring his beloved, then the failure of the avowal of sexual disinterest in Sonnet 20 could well account for the bitterness, rage and linguistic violence that permeate the poem. The sonnet itself gives us scant evidence as to whether lust was experienced in a homo- or heterosexual relationship, but makes it clear that sex and desire were not, for the Poet of the Sonnets, happy components of life.

We have selected these four sonnets for special consideration because they seem to us, individually and taken together, to yield an introduction to the major themes of the sonnets. We will see the Poet's war with time played out with astonishing richness. No man, one would think, can win the battle against time, but time was a worthy adversary for a pen as great as Shakespeare's and it will be left to the reader to judge who is winning. The Young Man's self-love will haunt many other poems, as will the Poet's attempt to love people other than himself. Nature, too, will return again and again, not as the goddess of Sonnet 20 but as the object of the Poet's immense affection as he describes trees, flowers and sunlight with great tenderness. In fact, we will see that it is the Poet's indisputable love of nature that makes us believe him when he says he loves the Young Man and the Dark Lady.

CHAPTER 2: WHEN LOVE IS AT WAR WITH TIME AND DEATH

SONNETS 116, 18, 19, 55, 107, 123, 124, 106, 15, 22, 115, 60, 63, 64, 65, 67, 68, 66, 74, 71, 73, 126, 146

I n the previous chapter we discussed four sonnets that we felt, taken together, opened a window into the ways in which the Poet of the Sonnets loves and the conflicts with which he struggles. What we gleaned in the previous chapter, particularly his hatred of his own aging as expressed in Sonnet 62 and his dread of his lover aging as expressed in Sonnet 104, makes it understandable that the Poet would have a particularly powerful fear of aging and death.

Because of some unusual mutations, our species is the only one to know that death is inevitable, but this knowledge is difficult to bear and we go to great lengths to undo this knowledge. While the fear of death is nearly universal, the role of that fear in individual life varies a great deal. In the work of the Poet of the Sonnets the fear of death is central and that is the reason why this chapter is the longest in the book. We will show in Chapter 9 that Shakespeare the playwright had a much richer and more nuanced attitude towards death than the Poet of the Sonnets did, another reason to regard the Poet of the Sonnets as a character created by Shakespeare rather than as Shakespeare himself.

Great poems at the crossroads between love and death have been written by many. We need only think of Andrew Marvel's poem to his coy mistress. But we know of no sustained body of love poetry in which death plays as central a role as it does in Shakespeare's sonnets. The two lovers are never alone: subtly, the fear of death transforms the dyad into a triad.

Nothing represents the harshness of this reality more than time. We have no power over it and cannot prevent its passage. We are all slaves to time; time injures our sense of sovereignty and our self-love. The Poet's indignation over the passage of time may be more pronounced than our own, but we need no empathy to appreciate these poems; our own narcissism makes us sympathetic to the Poet's war on time.

LOVE TRIUMPHANT OVER TIME AND DEATH

SONNET 116

Let me not to the marriage of true minds
Admit impediments, love is not love
Which alters when it alteration finds,
Or bends with the remover to remove.
O no, it is an ever-fixèd mark
That looks on tempests and is never shaken;
It is the star to every wand'ring bark,
Whose worth's unknown, although his height be taken.
Love's not Time's fool, though rosy lips and cheeks
Within his bending sickle's compass come,
Love alters not with his brief hours and weeks,
But bears it out even to the edge of doom:
   If this be error and upon me proved,
   I never writ, nor no man ever loved.

To our knowledge, no sonnet has undergone so powerful a re-evaluation as Sonnet 116. Wordsworth called it "Shakespeare's best." It is Shakespeare's best-known sonnet, frequently cited during marriage ceremonies and anniversaries; one cannot imagine any anthology not including it. In 1966, Dover Wilson could still write of its perfection:

> Seventy-five percent of the words are monosyllables; only
> three contain more syllables than two; none belong in any
> degree to the vocabulary of "poetic" diction. There is nothing
> recondite, exotic, or metaphysical in the thought… The Poet
> has employed one hundred and ten of the simplest words in
> the language and the two simplest rhyme-schemes to produce
> a poem which has about it no strangeness whatever except the
> strangeness of perfection.

Steven Booth, writing in 1977, has a very different evaluation:

> Sonnet 116 is one of the most universally admired of Shake-
> speare's sonnets. Its virtues, however, are more than usually
> susceptible to dehydration in critical comment. The more
> one thinks about this grand, noble, absolute, convincing, and
> moving gesture, the less there seems to be to it. One could
> demonstrate that it is just so much bombast, but, having
> done so, one would have only to reread the poem to be again
> moved by it and convinced of its greatness.
>
> A major problem about literary art is that abstract general as-
> sertions do not feel any truer than their readers already believe
> them to be; they carry no evidence of their truth and very
> little of the life (p. 387).

Helen Vendler, writing in 1997, is equally harsh:

> The Young Man even though concealing his motives behind
> his euphemizing vagueness, has been exposed (by his unpack-
> ing-by-reiteration of his very words *alter* and *bends*) as a man
> in thrall to the sensual bloom of youth; when he sees the sickly
> bend, he must, he has said, bend with it, remove himself when
> he sees beauty removed, and find another as-yet-unreaped
> beauty (p. 490) .

We regard Sonnet 116 as a kind of secular prayer, an expression of
what the Poet would like to attain, but cannot. There are many men and
women who have not succeeded in loving beyond a short duration, but
who nevertheless harbor the wishes expressed in this sonnet.

The first line, "let me not" invokes the language of prayer. An example
can be found in Psalm 31:17-18: "Let me not be confounded oh Lord."
The word impediments also invokes the marriage ceremony—"if either of
you know any impediment why you may not be lawfully joined in mat-
rimony then ye confess it." The term "marriage of true minds" makes ex-
plicit the reference to the marriage ceremony, "for better or for worse until
death do us part." The marriage of true minds is a far nobler undertaking

than carnal marriage, and we read this nobility in Sonnet 116 a little differ-ently after our study of Sonnet 20 in the previous chapter.

The fourth line, "Or bends with the remover to remove" is not easy to interpret. To bend must imply some changing, some lowering in the Poet's fixed love (in erotic terms the losing of an erection), but who is the remov-er? The object of the Poet's love, in which case he is declaring that he will go on loving unrequited if his lover loses interest? Is "the remover" Death, in which case the Poet is promising love even beyond the grave? Vendler interprets "remove himself when he sees beauty removed," so the Poet is promising to go on loving the Young Man after Time has taken his beauty away. Time is the culprit in any case, whether because with the passage of time love will wane or the beloved's beauty will fade, and Time appears explicitly in the third quatrain of this poem. Continuing the metaphor of the navigating ship, the Poet avers that true love looks on tempests, but is never shaken. In the next line, the true lover is compared to the "ever-fixèd mark," a reference to the north star, a metaphor for everlasting constancy, a star that never changes course. If the "wandring bark" is a lover whose interest may be straying, then true love is the star by which he can find his way again. Line 8 also deals with the same celestial body; "whose worth's unknown," should be interpreted as worthy beyond any measure, while "Although his height be taken," refers to the process of determining a ship's position by the height of the star from the horizon.

The third quatrain highlights the paradoxical relationship between love and time. Love, we are told, is "not Time's fool," meaning it is not subject to time's power, even though time can affect "rosy lips and cheeks" and lovers come "within his bending sickle." The bending sickle is a met-onym for death which makes the lovers into a crop that must be harvested. Line 10 affirms the power of Time to bring death but line 11 asserts the opposite; it is a ringing declaration that "love alters not with his brief hours and weeks." Line 12—"bears it out even to the edge of doom"—is an enigmatic and powerful line. Interpreters have tended to translate "doom" as a reference to the Last Judgment and "bears" as synonymous with en-dures. For us "bears" introduces the theme of bearing witness, so central to the end of the poem. The phrase "the edge of doom" is very powerful, whether it refers to the Last Judgment, as it does more clearly in Sonnet 55, or to some other major unspecified catastrophe that inevitably lies ahead.

Thus line 12 gives the whole poem an ominous character. We believe that at least preconsciously this line affects the reader in a direction opposite from the conscious reading and that it has contributed significantly to the special appeal of this sonnet. The couplet brings in the Poet's surest weapon against time, the immortality of his writing, but the declaration, though it should be ringing and confident, somehow conveys doubt even though no doubt is in the words. Perhaps the seed of doubt is sewn by "if this be error" for even the admission of the possibility of error is in stark contrast to the assertive tone the Poet strives for. We recall that Shakespeare is the author of the line (and the first conceptualizer of the idea) that we still use to indicate our suspicion of too-forceful an assertion: Gertrude in *Hamlet* saying "the lady doth protest too much methinks." Even if the sonnet is read as affirmation, the enumeration of what it is not sounds suspicious in an age influenced by Freud's thinking on the power of denial.

Sonnet 116, read carefully, must be felt in two ways, as a grand affirmation *and* as a confession of what the Poet wished but doubted he could reach. The Poet knows but wishes to deny that love alters, that love bends, that it is shaken by tempest, that love is "time's fool" and succumbs to the "bending sickle" of death as it alters with "brief hours and weeks" and he is willing to stake all of mankind's love and all of his writing on his denial.

SONNET 18

Shall I compare thee to a summer's day?
Thou art more lovely and more temperate:
Rough winds do shake the darling buds of May,
And summer's lease hath all too short a date:
Sometime too hot the eye of heaven shines,
And often is his gold complexion dimmed,
And every fair from fair sometime declines,
By chance, or nature's changing course, untrimmed:
But thy eternal summer shall not fade,
Nor lose possession of that fair thou ow'st,
Nor shall death brag thou wand'rest in his shade
When in eternal lines to time thou grow'st,
    So long as men can breathe or eyes can see,
    So long lives this, and this gives life to thee.

The Poet compares his lover to a summer's day, and finds more constancy in the lover than the summer day can offer. Nothing in nature is permanent, nor can nature boast being the lover's equal. Calling the buds of May "darling" animates nature, a beautiful example of a phenomenon we shall see over and over again in these poems: however complicated the Poet's love for his lovers may be, his love for nature is simple, pure and complete.

The business of real estate is not usually called up to supply the metaphors for love poetry, but a lease as a metaphor for life's or love's duration was a favorite term of the Poet; Sonnet 146 contains the line "why so large cost, having so short a lease." And Juliet, impatiently awaiting her tryst with Romeo cries out "O I have bought the mansion of a love but not possessed it."

In the second quatrain of Sonnet 18 the sun, called "the eye of heaven," can be too hot and conversely is often in "his gold complexion dimmed" a reference to clouds that cover the sun. We know that the eye had a special meaning to the Poet of the Sonnets. When nature is anthropomorphized the sun becomes heaven's eye. Line 7 summarizes the Poet's complaint about transience; nothing is permanent and "every fair from fair sometime declines."

The decay can set in by chance, through accidents, or by the inevitable change that seasons bring, referred to in line 8 as "nature's changing course." "Untrimmed" refers to sails that are not trimmed in proper navigation, reminding us of the metaphor of the "wandring bark" from Sonnet 116. By the addition of "untrimmed," nature's changing course seems suddenly more navigable, more influenced by what man can do and therefore nature's changing course becomes not just a metaphor for the progression of the seasons but a metaphor for the fading of love in response to the passage of time. This shadow passes over the poem to be pushed away in line 9 when the Poet exclaims triumphantly, "thy eternal summer shall not fade:" the loved young man's "summer," meaning youthful beauty, will never be supplanted by age. The concept of fading had a special appeal to the Poet, for in Sonnet 19 we find "fading sweets" and in Sonnet 146 the Poet's body is described as a "fading mansion." In line 10, the Poet assures us that the beauty of the young man will never fade, expressed as "Nor lose possession of that fair." The beauty "thou ow'st," condenses a complicated idea in a couple of syllables. The Young Man owns his beauty but owes it as a debt to nature that nature will inevitably collect, harvesting that beauty, meaning that the Young Man must age and lose his beauty. Since what is harvested is usually to be devoured there is a distant but unmistakable attribution of oral aggression to nature when she will come to harvesting the Young Man's beauty. The Poet's intervention will enable the Young Man to keep the beauty he owes. In the eleventh line the Poet challenges death directly: "nor shall death brag thou wand'rest in his shade." The Poet is confident death will be cheated by the immortality of his lines. Line 12 is even bolder; the Poet feels confident that not only will death be unable to brag that the young man wandered in death's shade, the Young Man will even continue to grow in the Poet's "eternal lines." Time therefore will be unable to destroy the Poet's lover; on the contrary, time's effect will be to make him grow in beauty and fame. There is probably no other moment in the sonnets to rival this one for the Poet's confidence that he will not only defeat time but force time to do his bidding.

When death is introduced, a triangle is established. The Poet selects death as his rival. The Poet feels victorious over death and, in the last three lines, celebrate his triumph. In the couplet the Poet is confident that "so long as man can breathe or eyes can see," the lines of the Poet will bestow immortality on the Young Man. So far the Poet's boast has proven true, though whether the immortality is conferred upon the Young Man or the Poet himself is more of a question. We can glean nothing about the Young Man from the sonnets. Was he tall? Was his eye blue? Did he limp? What sort of voice did he have? Nothing so particular is important enough to make its way into the sonnets. Shakespeare must have known, as we all do, that it will be the Poet, not the object of his love, who gains immortality. Had Dante not met Beatrice and Petrarch not met Laura, other women would have fulfilled the same function.

Upon first reading, the poem is in praise of love as more permanent than the summer. But as we look more deeply, the power of death grows in our awareness. Death is not directly mentioned in the first quatrain, but its presence can be felt. Death is the power behind the "rough winds [that] do shake the darling buds of May," and death is also implied in "summer's lease hath all too short a date." As the sonnet progresses, the Poet's struggle with time and death, and his challenge to death, move into a central position. Until the couplet, the melancholy atmosphere where everything succumbs to transience prevails.

The poem contains an interesting compromise with the young man's self love. The poem is about his beauty, but what is the young man really asked to love but the fact that the Poet has immortalized him. The Poet's efforts, therefore, are directed towards the young lover's own narcissism. The Poet does not ask to be loved by the young man but merely appeals to the lover's self-love. Even if the Poet were to succeed and the lover were persuaded that he will gain immortality through the Poet's sonnets, how much love would the Poet reap? Strictly speaking, this is not a love poem but a poem in which the Poet tries to make his lover experience the Poet's self-love. Incapable of loving, the Poet gives or at least loans his own self-love to the young man. The strength of self-love that we stressed in the previous chapter is palpable in this sonnet.

In the so-called "procreation sonnets" (discussed in Chapter 3) the Poet makes it clear that the main reason for the Young Man to have a sexual relationship with a woman is to defeat the destructive power of time by begetting a child who will carry his beauty forward as he ages. Thus when the Poet speaks of immortalizing the Young Man's beauty in his verse he is setting his ability as a poet in competition with the ability of women to bear the Young Man's children.

Sonnet 18 is one of the best known of Shakespeare's sonnets and five of the six anthologies included it. We conclude that the assertion that love is more permanent than nature's seasons, and the triumph over death as a rival. evoked a powerful positive response in readers that makes this sonnet among the best-known poems by Shakespeare. If the printed sequence of the sonnets is to be trusted, Sonnet 18, coming right after the procreation sonnets, may be interpreted as the Poet overcoming his jealousy of women, which unconsciously haunted many of the 17 procreation sonnets. The Poet now feels that his poetry is equal or perhaps even superior to the capacity of women to grant men immortality by reproduction. Having overcome the envy of women, the Poet feels that his poetry offers a more permanent immortality than progeny.

SONNET 19

Devouring time, blunt thou the lion's paws,
And make the earth devour her own sweet brood;
Pluck the keen teeth from the fierce tiger's jaws,
And burn the long-lived Phoenix in her blood;
Make glad and sorry seasons as thou fleet'st,
And do whate'er thou wilt, swift-footed time,
To the wide world and all her fading sweets:
But I forbid thee one most heinous crime,
O carve not with thy hours my love's fair brow,
Nor draw no lines there with thine antique pen;
Him in thy course untainted do allow
For beauty's pattern to succeeding men.
    Yet do thy worst, old Time, despite thy wrong,
    My love shall in my verse ever live young.

Edith Sitwell, in her *Poet's Notebook* (1943), praises this sonnet as, "in all probability, the greatest sonnet in the English language with its tremendous first lines." She singled out for praise the majestic double vowels in "devouring" and "lions" in the first line. She speaks of the "gigantic system of stretching double vowels, long single vowels, muffled by the word 'earth' in the second line." In line 4, the alliterative "B" in "burn" and "blood" is noteworthy. In a similar vein, Vendler speaks of the "murderous vitality" of the first quatrain. Challenging death to a kind of duel over who will own the young man, the sentiment that animated Sonnet 18, gives way to awe before the destructive power of time. The term "devouring time" was taken from Ovid, who called time the devourer of things. Death is not only animated but becomes alive with oral aggression; insatiable hunger is attributed to time. Time transforms the earth into a cannibal, into a mother eating "her own sweet brood." Because people are buried in the earth after they die, the Poet sees earth as a cannibalistic mother devouring her children. Behind the cannibalistic mother is a more destructive father figure called "devouring time." Time can even pluck the teeth from the "fierce tiger's jaws." Tiger's teeth are themselves a symbol of oral aggression, but devouring time is endowed with so much hostility that it can pluck out the very symbol of oral aggression. The implicit double orality may not become conscious to the reader, but it impresses itself on our preconscious. That a father can eat his children is horrible enough,—we think of Goya's painting of Saturn in the Prado Museum—but a mother "devouring her sweet brood" is even more difficult to contemplate. From a psychoanalytic perspective the first two quatrains express in magnificent imagery an early state of oral anxiety when both parents are experienced as ready and willing to devour the child.

In the second quatrain, fleeting time creates the glad seasons (spring and summer) and the sorry seasons (autumn and winter). Time is not only fleeting but also swift-footed, having dominion over "the wide world and all her fading sweets." "Fading" emphasizes the declining aspect of the cycle of nature. "Sweets" refers back to line 2: "sweet brood."

What impressed commentators in Sonnet 19, is the contrast between the sweeping all-conquering majesty of the first two quatrains assigned to the destructive power of "swift-footed time" which nothing can withstand and the third, a quatrain of defiance wherein the Poet forbids time a "most heinous crime."

The Poet steps in with his prohibition in line 8, the last line of the second quatrain. Thus he does not allow the power of Time two full quatrains, but steps in, more boldly than if his assertions had begin in the third quatrain. By so doing the Poet obtains mastery over time, that had been so powerful and frightening in the first eight lines.

And what is this heinous crime? Carving the beloved young man's brow with time's hours, an everyday occurrence that happens to every man and every woman. If we keep Sonnets 62 and 104 in mind, the reason why the "crime" of aging is experienced as heinous becomes understandable and "old" in line 13 is a horrible insult. In line 10, time is described as using his "antique pen" to draw lines on the Young Man's brow, a striking metaphor. The term pen was used in the sonnets 10 times, and the term "antique pen" appears in this sonnet and in Sonnet 106, where "I see their antique pen would have expressed" appears in line 7. Since any pen must be the Poet's, giving Time a pen implies a certain identification with Time, and calling the pen "antique" perhaps evokes the Poet's former loves which were more subject to the passage of time. This is the love, after all, which the Poet thinks will be different. This is the love which will endure. Thus the Young Man's beauty should remain inviolate to represent ideal beauty for later generations of ideal beauty, expressed as "for beauty's pattern to succeeding men." In the couplet, the Poet changes course. He will allow time his destructive work because the Poet's verse is beyond time's power to destroy.

That aging should be so heinous a crime to the Poet lends support to our interpretation in the previous chapter that the Poet was compelled to stop loving when the first signs of aging or perhaps even the first signs of maturity appeared in the boy he loved. The Poet's love, which animates his skill in writing, triumphs over the destructive powers of time in the couplet, but not until he gives up fighting to preserve the youthful beauty in the actual physical body of his beloved. This is a great truth about love: it must endure beyond the initial physical attraction if it is to last a long time. In Sonnet 19 the Poet gives up the physical preservation of the Young Man's beauty the way he gave up any sexual desire for him in the couplet of Sonnet 20. He moves on to the purer, or at least less physical love represented by a timeless love poem. To our ear the defiance in the third quatrain and the "happy ending" in the couplet do little to dispel horror evoked by the first two quatrains. If psychoanalytic experience is any guide, the happy ending of a fairy tale is usually forgotten, while the horror remains alive.

The fact that both sonnets 18 and 19 were selected by five of the six anthologies suggests to us that the relationship between time and love evokes a strong interest, regardless of whether the supremacy is granted to time or to the Poet's work.

SONNET 55

Not marble, nor the gilded monuments
Of princes shall outlive this powerful rhyme,
But you shall shine more bright in these contents
Than unswept stone, besmeared with sluttish time.
When wasteful war shall statues overturn,
And broils root out the work of masonry,
Nor Mars his sword, nor war's quick fire shall burn:
The living record of your memory.
'Gainst death, and all-oblivious enmity,
Shall you pace forth, your praise shall still find room,
Even in the eyes of all posterity
That wear this world out to the ending doom.
    So till the judgment that your self arise,
    You live in this, and dwell in lovers' eyes.

The sonnet opens on a note of triumph; the Poet's powerful rhyme is stronger than "marble and gilded monuments" that rulers erect in their quest for immortality. His lover will outshine all of them in the "contents" of the lines of the Poet. In line 4, "unswept stone" refers to dust on gravestones, neglected because all the people who loved the person who was buried there have died, so the memorial inscription has become illegible by the work of "sluttish time," which has "besmeared" it. Time is promiscuous because it destroys everything equally. Combining "sluttish" with "besmeared" lends a strong anti-sexual feeling to the line. Wasteful war can overturn statues, but poems do not perish. "Broils" in line 6 refers to internal disturbances within the country, as distinguished from external wars. Civil wars, like external wars, root out the works of masonry, but are powerless to destroy poetry. "Oblivious enmity" in line 9 refers to hostilities that create oblivion by destroying monuments. But the young man will "pace forth," or march on, and his praise will "find room" in immortal poetry. In this sonnet, as in many others, what endures is the Poet's praise of the man he loves. Once more we note the narcissistic nature of this love relationship. The Poet does not believe he will be loved because he has won the young man's love, but because he has made him immortal. On the other hand his joy in the power of his poems is palpable.

The sonnet ends with a reference to the Day of Judgment and the expected resurrection. The ending, however, is ambiguous. Line 11 is still secular: The lover will live in "the eyes of all posterity." Line 12, "That wear this world out to the ending doom," is similar to line 12 in Sonnet 116, "But bears it out even to the edge of doom." It is again a surprising concept because the Last Judgment does not typically belong to love poetry. The line has a strange and powerful beauty to it. In the couplet, both the Day of Judgment and the Young Man's resurrection are affirmed. But until that day, the last line tells us the lover lives in the Poet's lines and in all "lovers' eyes." Resurrection is the ultimate immortality, but until that time, a secular immortality will be the Young Man's lot, in the eyes which lovers use to read the poem, perhaps to each other.

Given the ubiquity of sly Elizabethan puns, we note the undertone of a secular reading of the couplet in which the "judgment" is whatever the Young Man would have to think to "arise" that is to get an erection. In this meaning, the poem serves as the asexual love-alternative to the Young Man's sexual relationship until he develops one. This use of "rise" is explicit in other sonnets as we shall see, particularly in the heterosexual Chapter 7.

Vendler has drawn attention to the strategic placement of the word "live." The sonnet as a whole is a defiance of death. Hence, the emphasis on "live." There is "outlive" in line 2, "living" in line 8, and "oblivion" in line 9. Finally the word "live" appears in the very last line.

Dover Wilson pointed out that Sonnet 55 is rooted in Ovid's famous epilogue to his *Metamorphoses*. We cite from Humphries's translation:

> Now I have done my work. It will endure,
> I trust, beyond Jove's anger, fire, and sword,
> Beyond Times' hunger. The day will come, I know,
> So let it come, that day which has no power
> Save over my body, to end my span of life
> Whatever it may be. Still, part of me,
> The better part, immortal, will be borne
> Above the stars; my name will be remembered
> Wherever Roman power rules conquered lands,
> I shall be read, and through all centuries,
> If prophecies of bards are ever truthful,
> I shall be living, always.

Ovid has not been mistaken about his immortality. We would like to compare the Ovid translation familiar to us with the Golding translation that Shakespeare drew upon:

> Now have I brought a work to end which neither Joves feerce wrath,
> Nor sword, nor fyre, nor freating age with all the force it hath
> Are able to abolish quyght. Let comme that fatall howre
> Which (saving of this britle flesh) hath over mee no power,
> And at his pleasure make an end of myne uncerteyne tyme.
> Yit shall the better part of mee assured bee to clyme
> Aloft above the starry skye. And all the world shall never
> Be able for to quench my name. For looke how farre so ever
> The Romane Empyre by the right of conquest shall extend,
> So farre shall all folke reade this work. And tyme without all end
> (If Poets as by prophesie about the truth may ame)
> My lyfe shall everlastingly bee lengthened still by fame.

This concern with personal immortality is foreign to classical Greek culture, as it would also be to the authors of the Bible. It seems to have appeared for the first time in Horace who said of his poems *aedificavi monumentum aere perennius*, "I have built a monument more lasting than bronze." Ovid developed this theme more fully and it passed on from him to the Poet of the Sonnets.

Ovid clearly states that his poetry will assure his own immortality. Shakespeare transformed the idea to celebrate the immortality of the man he loved, a significant borrowing across centuries, but also a creative transformation. Ovid brags that his creation is beyond the reach of Jupiter's anger, his fire and sword. He experiences time as hungry and Shakespeare took the metaphor of "hungry time," so basic to the sonnets, from Ovid. But Ovid makes a peaceful division between himself and time. Time will get his body at the end of his span of life, but the better part of him will gain immortality. Unlike Shakespeare he is not at war with time or death. A similar transformation occurs in Shakespeare's poem *Venus and Adonis*. In Ovid's version of the tale, Cupid was playing with his mother, Venus, quiver on his shoulder, when a barb grazed her breast, and that is why she fell in love with the mortal Adonis. She warned Adonis not to hunt for dangerous animals but he paid no attention and was gored by a boar. Adonis as a reluctant lover was Shakespeare's invention. He gave the legend a distinct homosexual connotation of a beautiful youth struggling against a seductive older woman.

In the previous chapter we discussed the enmity between the three types of love: heterosexual, homosexual and narcissistic. Judged from this point of view, Sonnet 55 is predominantly a narcissistic sonnet. The Young Man is praised but there is little doubt that the Poet is most impressed with the power of his pen to give the man he loves the immortality the Poet believes his lover so ardently desires. Sonnet 55 is one of Shakespeare's most popular sonnets, having been selected by all six anthologies.

SONNET 107

Not mine own fears, nor the prophetic soul
Of the wide world dreaming on things to come,
Can yet the lease of my true love control,
Suppos'd as forfeit to a confin'd doom.
The mortal moon hath her eclipse endur'd,
And the sad augurs mock their own presage;
Incertainties now crown themselves assur'd,
And peace proclaims olives of endless age.
Now with the drops of this most balmy time
My love looks fresh, and Death to me subscribes,
Since, spite of him, I'll live in this poor rime,
While he insults o'er dull and speechless tribes:
　　And thou in this shalt find thy monument,
　　When tyrants' crests and tombs of brass are spent.

We mentioned, in connection with the previous sonnet that the Poet claimed he was conferring immortality upon his lover but likely knew that he was conferring it upon himself instead. But reading Sonnet 107 makes us accept as sincere the intention of Sonnet 55, for in this sonnet the Poet grants himself the immortality of his verse and the poem has far less energy and enduring power than we find in the ones which seek to keep the Young Man young and alive. In fact if Shakespeare's immortality had rested solely on this sonnet it might not have been assured. However narcissistic the Poet's love may have been, his love for the Young Man and his need to keep him young provided the Poet with a powerful muse whom we miss in this poem.

Duncan-Jones connects this sonnet's first two lines and the emphasis on balmy days as alluding to the year 1603, which saw the peaceful accession of James I, upon which Shakespeare's patron, the Earl of Southampton, was freed from imprisonment in the Tower and the fortunes of William Herbert, third Earl of Pembroke, also improved.

Vendler has emphasized the various "puns" and similarities among the words "prophetic" and "proclaim," "supposed" and "subscribed," "control" and "confined," "confined" and "final," "endured" and "endless," "olives" and "I'll live," "incertainties" and "assur'd."

The first line is very strange in that the Poet thinks that the world as a whole is watching the outcome of his love. The eclipse of "the mortal moon" has been interpreted as a reference to the defeat of the Spanish Armada in a battle the prospect of which frightened the British very much. The pessimists, here called "sad augurs," "mock their own presage," implying that a widely held prediction did not come true. The Poet celebrates the new age of certainty's victory over a previous age of anxiety, which has brought "balmy time." The word balmy means healing and was used by Shakespeare only three times, here and twice in Othello: "To have their balmy slumbers wak'd with strife" (II.iii.258) and "O balmy breath, that dost almost persuade" (V.ii.16), but the combination of balmy and time is unique to this sonnet.

Lines 9 and 10, "My love looks fresh, and Death to me subscribes,/ Since, spite of him, I'll live in this poor rime," imply that the Poet himself has won a victory over death. Death can only insult by his victory "o'er dull and speechless tribes," that is, those who, unlike the Poet, cannot speak. The couplet is the by now familiar assertion that in his poems a monument was built by the Poet for the lover more durable than brass, though there is something melancholy in the Poet's comparison of his poem to a tomb.

Sonnet 107 celebrates the Poet's victory over death; two anthologizers have included this poem.

SONNET 123

No! Time, thou shalt not boast that I do change,
Thy pyramids built up with newer might
To me are nothing novel, nothing strange,
They are but dressings of a former sight:
Our dates are brief, and therefore we admire,
What thou dost foist upon us that is old,
And rather make them born to our desire,
Than think that we before have heard them told:
Thy registers and thee I both defy,
Not wond'ring at the present, nor the past,
For thy records, and what we see doth lie,
Made more or less by thy continual haste:
    This I do vow and this shall ever be,
    I will be true despite thy scythe and thee.

In this sonnet it is the Poet himself, not his beloved, who is threatened by Time's destructive power. This sonnet, like many before, declares war against time, and like many of its predecessors it is a poem of defiance. The sonnet opens with a powerful "No!" Time is personified and boasts that the Poet has changed,—we might first think aged—and therefore under time's dominion. The Poet refuses to be impressed by time's power, and even the pyramids that to many seem to successfully defy time do not impress the Poet, nor is he impressd with what one might call time's body of work, "his registers and records." The line "They are but dressings of a former sight" is difficult to decipher, since the Poet doesn't specify what he means by "a former sight" but we may speculate that behind the manifest meaning, leftovers of something that was once worth looking at, he is referring to a love felt for someone in the past.

The second quatrain opens with the insight that because "our dates are brief" we admire structures that defy time. The Poet feels that time has foisted these architectural miracles upon us. In Line 8 the Poet introduces his own medium, writing, when he says "Than think that we before have heard them told." The Poet refuses to admire anything in the present or in the past because time is not telling the truth, expressed in line 11 as,

"For thy records, and what we see doth lie." The Poet feels that the end of his ability to love is fast approaching and he projects this feeling onto time experienced as "thy continual haste." In the couplet the Poet reveals what the change is that time is attempting to induce in him: the fading of his love, expressed as his promise to "remain true." The Poet's truth is thus contrasted to the lies of time in line 11.

Time, for the Poet, induces infidelity. Thus, two wars are joined: the war against time and the inner conflict over infidelity. The Poet promises to remain true in spite of time and death, represented as a metonym by the scythe. In Shakespeare's preconscious, time, the universal destroyer, became equated with infidelity. In general we expect that, when a lover falls out of love and is unfaithful with someone else, that a new relationship is forming. But if we read this sonnet together with Sonnet 32 (in Chapter 3) we can surmise that the threat comes from the Poet's reawakened love of former lovers. The pyramids then stand in for the souvenirs of the Poet's previous love relationships which he is striving to keep—like the Pharoahs—entombed.

Two anthologies included this sonnet.

SONNET 124

If my dear love were but the child of state
It might, for fortune's bastard, be unfathered,
As subject to time's love or to time's hate,
Weeds among weeds, or flowers with flowers gathered.
No, it was builded far from accident;
It suffers not in smiling pomp, nor falls
Under the blow of thralled discontent,
Whereto th'inviting time our fashion calls:
It fears not policy, that heretic,
Which works on leases of short-numbered hours,
But all alone stands hugely politic,
That it nor grows with heat, nor drowns with showers.
    To this I witness call the fools of time,
    Which die for goodness, who have lived for crime.

The imagery is taken from the political world of Shakespeare's time. The sonnet opens with a declaration that if the Poet's love had been the "child of state," it would have been in danger of being born unfathered, lacking the constancy a father is supposed to give to the child and therefore subject to changes brought about by fortune, or, in the language of this chapter, time's love and time's hate.

For us, living in a relatively safe bureaucracy, to be a "child of state" may have a positive connotation of permanence and social security. But for a poet living in the Elizabethan era, living as a child of state meant to rise and fall at the whim of a monarch or nobleman, to be inherently unstable, to remain insecure and fatherless, the very opposite of true love.

Such love would be no more than "weeds among weeds," (plants that grow unwanted) or "flowers with flowers gathered," ("gathered" means that these desirable flowers that are cut and killed because they are desirable) another metaphor for lack of permanence. The echo of the other meaning of "state," the condition that something is in at any given moment, furthers the theme of whether or not the Poet's love is changeable.

The second and third quatrains proclaim the constancy of the Poet's love. Since it is not a "child of state" it need not suffer from the two conditions that are so destructive to a monarch, "smiling pomp" and "thrilled discontent." These two monarchial plagues also have their analogue in issues that concern the Poet very deeply when he considers his love. The Poet of the Sonnets is much concerned with the ability of flattery to deceive a lover and "thralled discontent," a magnificently condensed phrase that means the unhappiness of those who are enslaved is a serious matter for a lover who is unhappy in his love but unable or unwilling to be free of it, a condition that appears often in the sonnets.

"Policy" in line 9 is the expedience that causes public actions (but also love) to remain constant for only such short periods of time. The word "leases," a favorite in the sonnets ("summer's lease hath all too short a date"), is an image of a legal commitment, though one of short duration. "Heretic" in line 9 is used because the Poet wants his love to be understood as a matter of unassailable belief that will not alter or admit any dangerously contrary ideas.

The sonnet is not easy to decipher, but the phrase "was builded far from accident" may imply that "accident" refers to the sexual event which causes the begetting of an unwanted child. There is certainly a punning reference to the penis in "neither grows with heat nor drowns with showers." The Poet may be suggesting that his love is the more constant because it is asexual.

As in Sonnet 116, the Poet tries to impress upon us the constancy of love, even though the bulk of the sonnets deal with betrayal and infidelity. The Poet implies that his love is steady and free from wide fluctuations. The extensive use of political vocabulary in this sonnet suggests a reference to the effects (explicit in other sonnets) that differences in rank played in the Poet's love for the more noble Young Man. Booth has suggested that the key to the poem's power may be in the word "it," which, like all pronouns, is specific, hard, concrete, and yet imprecise and general—able to include anything or nothing. In this sonnet the word "it" appears close to the beginning of line 2, line 5, line 6, line 9 and line 12, contributing to the power of the poem. The word always refers to love.

In the last line the "fools of time," those who fear time and obey the power of time "die for goodness" while they "lived for crime." The line is enigmatic. Burrow believes it has a political meaning, referring to virtuous martyrs who died "for goodness" but earlier "lived for crime." Blackmore Evans believes the line refers to those who made deathbed repentance for crimes done in their "days of nature" (*Hamlet* I.v.12). It is not out of the question that Shakespeare would refer to repentant sinners as "fools of time," but in this case the last line would be out of place in the poem because it would no longer refer to love.

We do not know whether those sonnets that affirm the permanence of love against the destructive power of time correspond to a period of stability in the Poet's life, or whether they testify to his fluctuating moods. Only one anthology included this puzzling sonnet.

Sonnet 116 and Sonnet 124 have the same aim—to affirm the permanent quality of the Poet's love—but the difference is great. With all the reservations of Sonnet 116, it has a profound emotional appeal, while Sonnet 124 is confined by specific references that we can no longer decipher.

SONNET 106

When in the chronicle of wasted time
I see descriptions of the fairest wights,
And beauty making beautiful old rhyme,
In praise of ladies dead, and lovely knights;
Then in the blazon of sweet beauties best,
Of hand, of foot, of lip, of eye, of brow,
I see their antique pen would have expressed
Even such a beauty as you master now:
So all their praises are but prophecies
Of this our time, all you prefiguring;
And for they looked but with divining eyes
They had not skill enough your worth to sing;
    For we which now behold these present days
    Have eyes to wonder, but lack tongues to praise.

Prefiguration became an integral part of Christian theology when the Church decided to keep as holy scripture both the Old and the New Testaments. Thus, the unconsummated sacrifice of Isaac was seen as prefiguring the sacrifice of Christ, and the prophets of the Old Testament were seen as prefiguring the coming of Christ. In Sonnet 106, the Poet took the Christian idea of prefiguration and secularized it by claiming that all former beauties of antiquity only prefigured the man he loves. This transformation into the secular could have had a blasphemous connotation, but because the metaphor appears only in lines 9 and 10 the impact is softened.

"Wasted time" means time which has passed and is therefore no longer of any value: it has become waste. It does not quite have as its principal meaning the sense in which we now use it: as time misspent or spent unprofitably, but that meaning is clearly present as an echo. It is possible that the now-common phrase "wasted time" appears for the first time in this sonnet (the *Oxford English Dictionary* has no earlier citation for he phrase and cites the first use of it in the contemporary sense as having occurred in 1741). Here the Poet uses the word "waste" as meaning ruin, and because time is such a destroyer the past is equated with having been ruined by time.

Historians are in the habit of writing the chronicle of significant events, so the very idea that there exists a "chronicle of wasted time" comes as a surprise. Being a mock historian, the Poet finds in the "chronicle of wasted time" descriptions of fair enough to enable earlier poets to make beautiful old rhymes. In the fourth line, the Poet differentiates between "ladies dead" and "lovely knights," where usually one would refer to ladies as lovely, and knights as brave, showing a preference for men over women.

The second quatrain makes heavier demands on the reader because the "fairest wights" from the first quatrain are broken up into anatomical parts: hands, foot, lip, eye and brow. What the Poet hints at is that time ruins the beauties of the past by dismemberment. The various parts of these long dead beauties—their hands, feet, lips, eyes, and brows—are now used to create a kind of coat of arms ("blazon") to serve as a monument to beauty gone. In Line 7 the Poet sees that the antique pen, meaning older poets, would have expressed "beauty as you master now," though cataloguing the specific beauties of the Young Man is one poetic convention to which the Poet steadfastly refuses to participate in. In the sonnets to the Dark Lady the Poet mockingly describes parts of her which he finds unattractive, but a praising description of the Young Man's beautiful parts will not be found in the sonnets. The Poet offers us his explanation: the Poets of old couldn't do it because they had no such beauty to inspire them and we who are alive today, though we can see the beauty lack the "tongue" to praise. Whether that means the skill or whether that means that the Poet is struck dumb by the beauty is left to the reader to decide.

We are asked to believe that in his young man beauty reached its highest level in all history. This will strike many as an example of what Shakespeare elsewhere called "the Poet's rage." Nevertheless the sonnet was included by three of the six anthologies, bestowing upon this sonnet greater praise than we would have considered its due.

SONNETS OF INNER CONFLICT

One of the discoveries of psychoanalysis is the significance of ambivalence in psychic life. In this section we assembled sonnets in which ambivalence towards a lover found expression.

SONNET 15

When I consider every thing that grows
Holds in perfection but a little moment,
That this huge stage presenteth nought but shows
Whereon the stars in secret influence comment;
When I perceive that men as plants increase,
Cheered and checked even by the self-same sky,
Vaunt in their youthful sap, at height decrease,
And wear their brave state out of memory;
Then the conceit of this inconstant stay
Sets you most rich in youth before my sight,
Where wasteful time debateth with decay
To change your day of youth to sullied night,
    And all in war with time for love of you,
    As he takes from you, I engraft you new.

This very beautiful sonnet can profitably be read together with Freud's short essay on transience (1915). In that essay, Freud described a summer walk through the countryside with a young and already famous poet (Rilke). The poet could experience no joy on this walk because "All this beauty is fated to extinction." Freud interpreted this state of the poet to mean that transience gave him a foretaste of mourning over his own death. This foretaste of transience, as Freud called it, was painful and it inhibited enjoyment of the beautiful day. It would have been interesting to know how Freud would have reacted to Sonnet 15, where another great poet experienced the same sense of transience. The Poet of the sonnets here differs from Freud's companion because he is led to associate that life is like a play, obliterating the difference between life and theater.

In the first two lines the Poet remembers that everything that grows can hold perfection only for a moment. From there he is led to the idea that the world is a huge stage. The idea that life itself is nothing but a show recalls *As You Like It.*

> All the world's a stage
> And all the men and women merely players:
> They have their exits and their entrances;
> And one man in his time plays many parts (Act II, Scene VII)

And *Macbeth:*

> Life's but a walking shadow a poor player
> that struts and frets his hour upon the stage,
> and then is heard no more (Act ,V Scene 5).

Shakespeare was an actor and a playwright who meditated deeply on the nature of life. To obliterate the difference between real life and "shows" and look upon one's own life as a stage requires a degree of de-realization of one's own life that may enhance one's creativity but is costly in terms of experiencing one's own life as real.

The fourth line brings in astrology. It has caused Shakespeare's commentators some difficulty. If we believe in astrology, the word "comment" is too weak. But if Shakespeare neither fully believed in astrology nor totally disbelieved it, then the word "comment" would mirror his ambivalence: the effect of the stars is not known to men, and therefore remains secret. The Poet of the sonnets is not obliged to have a scientific position on astrology; he is writing to record his feelings. To include the word "secret" in "in secret influence comment," gives a conspiratorial hue or a paranoid connotation to astrology. The possible power of the stars increases the Poet's helplessness.

In the second quatrain, a radical change in the basic metaphor takes place: the Poet perceives man as a plant. The sky is experienced as cheering and encouraging the plant to grow up to a certain point until time turns adversary and is checking this growth. "Cheered and checked" is a wonderful way to express ambivalence when that term was not yet coined. The comparison between men and trees makes it possible for the Poet to speak, in line 7, of "youthful sap." The inclusion of the word "vaunt," meaning to exult or rejoice, suggests that the young men feel victorious as long as they feel the youthful sap running in their veins. The quatrain is pessimistic; "wear their brave state out of memory" suggests that the youthful feeling of being "cheered" by the sky will not always be a sustaining memory.

The third quatrain changes the metaphor once more to bring us back to the idea that life is a show. The word "conceit" in line 9 means that which is conceived in the mind and therefore the thought of life as an "inconstant stay." The Poet's lover is "most rich in youth," but even as the lover still seems youthful he is already subject to a dispute between "wasteful time" and decay as to which one of the two will destroy him, with each one demanding the right "to change your day of youth to sullied night." The Poet of the sonnets often used hideous night as the enemy of the brave day, but now night is sullied, that is, the darkness is dirty.

"Nought but shows" is a complex idea, because if we denigrate what happens in the theater because it isn't real or significant, that judgment comes when we compare what happens on the stage to real life. If real life is no more important than a play then we are left without anything at all that *is* important. A theologically inclined man of the Middle Ages might take this position to argue that only what happens in heaven is solid and important, but in Shakespeare there is no hint of anything more important than life and beauty. Today we conceptualize the state that the Poet evokes as "depressed." Shakespeare didn't have the verbalized concept but he created magnificent descriptions of depression in *Hamlet* and elsewhere in the sonnets as we shall see. In sonnet 15 the Poet celebrates his active war against Time on behalf of the Young Man as an antidote to depression. The poem is a strong one and three of the six anthologies included this sonnet.

SONNET 22

My glass shall not persuade me I am old
So long as youth and thou are of one date;
But when in thee time's furrows I behold,
Then look I death my days should expiate:
For all that beauty that doth cover thee
Is but the seemly raiment of my heart,
Which in thy breast doth live, as thine in me;
How can I then be elder than thou art?
O therefore love be of thyself so wary
As I not for myself, but for thee will,
Bearing thy heart, which I will keep so chary
As tender nurse her babe from faring ill:
    Presume not on thy heart when mine is slain;
    Thou gav'st me thine not to give back again.

The mirror cannot persuade the Poet that he is aging as long as his lover is young expressed as "youth and thou are of one date;" but when he detects "time's furrows" on the young man's brow he will want to die. This sonnet sheds some light on why drawing furrows on the Young Man's brow was seen as such a heinous crime in Sonnet 19.

In the second quatrain, the Poet tells us that the lover's beauty is only a "seemly raiment," meaning a handsome cloth or dress to cover the Poet's heart, an unusual way to express the fact that he Young Man's youth is a precondition for the Poet' love. The poem goes on to make use of the familiar Renaissance metaphor that lovers exchange hearts. The idea is used to support the claim that if they exchange hearts, they thereby become one. Then the Poet goes on to explain how each must take care of the other's heart. The Young Man must take care of the Poet's heart by remaining young. If he doesn't, the Poet will die and the Young Man will die too, because it is the Young Man who has—and is living on—the Poet's heart. In the couplet the Poet says that the Young man should not look to get his own heart back again if the Poet's heart dies because the Young Man ages. Stripped of its metaphorical language, the Poet is telling the Young Man not to expect to recover when he loses the Poet's love by ageing.

The Poet in his turn promises to take care of the Young Man's heart as if it were a baby he is nursing. A feminine identification is thus introduced. The Poet alludes to the regression to the helplessness of infancy that is part of the emotional essence of falling in love.

Two kinds of battle against time are in play here: the regression to infancy that is part of normal falling in love and the Poet's own unique need for his lover to stay young. The Poet has used the convention of the lovers' exchange of hearts to describe the unique situation in the Sonnets in metaphoric language that is difficult to decipher because the ideas themselves are difficult, and only one anthologizer selected this sonnet. But while the fate of such a love is necessarily tragic we cannot help but stand in awe of what the Poet has revealed to us about the nature of his love.

SONNET 115

Those lines that I before have writ do lie,
Even those that said I could not love you dearer;
Yet then my judgement knew no reason why
My most full flame should afterwards burn clearer.
But reckoning Time, whose millioned accidents
Creep in 'twixt vows, and change decrees of kings,
Tan sacred beauty, blunt the sharp'st intents,
Divert strong minds to th'course of alt'ring things—
Alas, why, fearing of Time's tyranny,
Might I not then say "Now I love you best,"
When I was certain o'er incertainty,
Crowning the present, doubting of the rest?
    Love is a babe: then might I not say so,
    To give full growth to that which still doth grow.

Sonnet 115 is full of the Poet's happy surprise that his love, which he had previously thought to be as great as possible, has nevertheless grown.

We know the Poet well enough now to be surprised by the second quatrain and what follows. In the second quatrain the Poet once again pays homage to the power of "reckoning time" and tells us that he did not take time into consideration when declaring his love. He also tells us in lines

10-12 that he declared his love to be at its zenith because he feared the destructive power of time. Nevertheless, in this poem the surprise that Time dealt the Poet was an increase in his love, not the expected decay.

Line 12 is of particular interest because the overcoming of ambivalence is called "crowning the present." The moment in which love has overcome all misgivings—"certain o'er incertainty" is the moment that love should be crowned. However, the Poet is aware of the fact that both past and future are clouded by ambivalence, expressed as "doubting of the rest." The last line is an optimistic one. The Poet expresses the wish "to give full growth" to that which is still growing within him. The conflict over the perfection of love and love as a continuously developing process is resolved in favor of development.

A number of commentators have noticed that this sonnet is indebted to a poem by John Donne:

> I Scarce believe my love to be so pure
> As I had thought it was,
> Because it doth endure
> Vicissitude, and season, as the grasse;
> Me thinkes I lyed all winter, when I swore,
> My love was infinite, if spring make it more.

In the couplet, love is called a babe. This has generally been interpreted as Amor, the god of love, being portrayed as an infant. The Greek and Roman view of Amor as a babe also contains a piece of psychic truth, a dim presentiment that love has something to do with infancy. If we compare Sonnet 115 to Sonnet 22 we find the Poet calling his own love, rather than his beloved's, "a babe." In the language we have been developing here we would say that the Poet understood that love based on the lover's unconscious regression into infancy can grow, whereas love based only upon the narcissistic need to remain young can only decline with time.

SONNET 60

Like as the waves make towards the pebbled shore,
So do our minutes hasten to their end,
Each changing place with that which goes before,
In sequent toil all forwards do contend.
Nativity once in the main of light,
Crawls to maturity, wherewith being crowned,
Crooked eclipses 'gainst his glory fight,
And Time that gave, doth now his gift confound.
Time doth transfix the flourish set on youth,
And delves the parallels in beauty's brow,
Feeds on the rarities of nature's truth,
And nothing stands but for his scythe to mow.
    And yet to times in hope, my verse shall stand
    Praising thy worth, despite his cruel hand.

The first two lines in this sonnet are lines of rare beauty. The striking image in Sonnet 60, where minutes like waves exhaust themselves against a pebbled beach in lines 1-4, was conveyed to Shakespeare by Ovid. The comparison is made between breaking waves and minutes that presumably "hasten" to their end. We know that minutes move at a steady pace—unlike people, they can neither hasten nor tarry—but to the Poet, deeply concerned about the aging of his young lover, they seem to hasten. It is as if the wave carried within it its own suicidal intent.

We have an opportunity to observe the borrowing of one great poet from another. Shakespeare took the analogy between time and tide and even the simile of one wave driving the other forward from Ovid, but unlike Ovid, Shakespeare endowed the waves with a suicidal tendency, in the phrase "hasten to their end."

In *Metamorphoses,* Book 15, Ovid is summarizes the teachings of the Greek philosopher Pythagoras. The relevant passage reads:

> Things eb and flow: and every shape is made to passe away.
> The tyme itself continually is fleeting like a brooke.
> For neyther brooke nor lyghtsomme tyme can tarrye still. But looke
> As every wave drives other foorth, and that that commes behind
> Bothe thrusteth and is thrust itself: even so the tymes by kind
> Doo fly and follow bothe at once, and evermore renew.
> For that that was before is left, and streyght there dooth ensew
> Anoother that was never erst. Eche twinkling of an eye
> Dooth chaunge (Ovid, Golding translation, Book 15, lines 198-206).
>
> From that tyme growing strong and swift, he passeth foorth the space
> of youth: and also wearing out his middle age apace,
> Through drooping ages steepye path he ronneth out his race.
> This age dooth undermine the strength of former yeares, and throwes
> It downe (Golding translation, lines 247-250).

The second quatrain turns from nature to human destiny. Once born into the light from the womb Nature leads man to "crawl to maturity." Once maturity is reached he is crowned, and begins to decline. The crowning in Sonnet 115 which marks the moment the Poet overcame his ambivalence is used here to mark the moment when, as in Sonnet 15 man is "checked" and begins to "decrease." Reading the poems together suggests that the Poet experienced love as something that would rise and fall much as a man reaches maturity and then declines into old age and death. This is particularly true when the Poet loves the Young Man but fears he won't be able to go on loving him once the Young Man matures.

Crawling is the opposite of what the minutes do when they hasten to their end. After this decisive entrance into life, time moves more slowly. Whether childhood rushes or crawls to maturity depends on how happy childhood is. That it seemed to the Poet to crawl is an intuitive understanding of childhood unhappiness, which for him repeats itself in love.

Shakespeare often used crawling to designate the passage of time in reverse when men refuse to go on being mature men, often under the pressure of advancing age. Examples include the famous line by King Lear after he divided his kingdom is "while we/Unburden'd crawl toward death" (I.i.40-41) and Hamlet's savage self-accusation in Act III, scene I (beginning on line 121), where Hamlet advises Ophelia, "Get thee to a nunnery:

why would'st thou be a breeder of sinners?" ends by saying, "What should such fellows as I do crawling between earth and heaven?"

"Crooked eclipses" in line 7 is a reference to the malignant influence of the stars. The eclipse as darkening the power of the sun must have greatly impressed Shakespeare, for it is a favorite image to describe the loss of happiness and good fortune. In the third quatrain, time which from nativity to manhood was on the side of the struggling man now confounds, or overcomes the man. What it gave him during his youth it now takes back again. The Poet experiences time as changing sides. As so often in the sonnets, time is experienced in oral terms as a devourer. In this sonnet time "Feeds on the rarities of nature's truth." Time is felt as particularly desirous of eating that which is rare, in this case an especially beautiful young man. Time's mowing scythe is all-powerful. And yet the couplet affirms the Poet's hope that his verse and praise of his lover will stand in spite of time's "cruel hand."

SONNET 63

Against my love shall be as I am now
With Time's injurious hand crushed and o'erworn,
When hours have drained his blood and filled his brow
With lines and wrinkles, when his youthful morn
Hath traveled on to age's steepy night,
And all those beauties whereof now he's king
Are vanishing, or vanished out of sight,
Stealing away the treasure of his spring:
For such a time do I now fortify
Against confounding age's cruel knife,
That he shall never cut from memory
My sweet love's beauty, though my lover's life.
 His beauty shall in these black lines be seen,
 And they shall live, and he in them still green.

In Sonnet 63 the Poet visualizes the day the Young Man will reach the age the Poet is now (and hates). The ideas in it are familiar to us by now, but this beautiful sonnet is remarkable for the detail in which the Poet imagines the horror that is to come. In this poem he seems confident in the power of his verses to preserve the Young Man's beauty, and the poem gains much of its power from the tension between the image of the Poet busily writing away to preserve his memories of his lover's beauty and the actual content of the poem which is taken up with imagining and describing the horrors of his lover's ageing.

The structure of the poem conveys the rhythm of the Poet's thought. The first word "Against…" needs the couplet to complete the thought which is, in its entirety:

> Against my love shall be as I am now
>> His beauty shall in these black lines be seen,
>> And they shall live, and he in them still green.

The Poet cannot, however, say this without getting distracted by the horrors he is working against, which occupy the next 7 lines. In line 9 the Poet tries again with:

> For such a time do I now fortify

But he becomes distracted again, this time sending the Young Man not merely into old age but into death itself. "Steepy night" in line 5 is a metaphor for death but it does not yet quite mean the Young Man will die; that thought becomes explicit in line 12. The couplet envisions the Poet reading the poems to preserve his memory of someone who has died. The death of love which the Poet fears will be brought on by the Young Man's ageing has become conflated with death itself. There is a sort of "medical theory" in lines 3-4 that wrinkles occur because the blood is drained out which makes actual death begin to hover over the poem. The term "steepy" appears in Golding's translation of Ovid: "Throogh drooping ages steepye path he ronneth out his race (book 15, line 249)."

In the third quatrain the Poet makes another connection: the wrinkles are cut with a cruel knife (not with an antique pen as they were in Sonnet 19) and that knife murders the Young Man from whom Time has stolen his youth, expressed as "Stealing away the treasure of his spring." The thought process that the Poet has condensed here implies that the Young Man's youth is a treasure and because it is a treasure it can be stolen.

Therefore time is seen as a thief, not just as a destroyer. "Treasure," as we have noted, can, in Shakespeare, be a pun on the male orgasm, as when Emilia in *Othello* speaks of unfaithful husbands as "pouring our treasure into foreign laps."

The Poet writes as if he is trying to paint us a picture of himself busily at work creating protective verses which will stand up to the ravages of time the way farmers prepare their homes and lands for the ravages of winter. Instead, the Poet writes not about what he says he's writing about, which would be a loving description of his lover's beauty but about the horrors to come. The reason for this is given in the first line: the Poet has given us a picture of himself trying to write about the Young Man but writing, instead, about himself.

We find this sonnet a beautiful poem and a moving evocation of the Poet struggling, although it evoked no similar response in the anthologizers, who did not include it.

SONNET 64

When I have seen by Time's fell hand defaced
The rich-proud cost of outworn buried age,
When sometime lofty towers I see down-rased,
And brass eternal slave to mortal rage.
When I have seen the hungry ocean gain
Advantage on the kingdom of the shore,
And the firm soil win of the watery main,
Increasing store with loss, and loss with store.
When I have seen such interchange of state,
Of state it self confounded, to decay,
Ruin hath taught me thus to ruminate
That Time will come and take my love away.
    This thought is as a death which cannot choose
    But weep to have that which it fears to lose.

Like Sonnet 60, this sonnet was inspired by Ovid. Each quatrain opens with "when I have seen," once again stressing sight and the role of the eyes.

The corresponding lines in Ovid read:

> For I have seene it sea which was substantial ground a late
> againe where sea was, I have seene the same become dry land
> (book 15, line 288-289)

Even the metaphor of time as a cannibal is found in Ovid: "Thou tyme the eater up of things" (line 258).

Helen Vendler has commented on this sonnet:

> The ruin of the three quatrains pertains to the inanimate
> world; the couplet departs from this to the true concern of the
> speaker: the death of his living beloved. In retrospect, we can
> see the first twelve lines as a long defense—by thinking about
> the end of inanimate things—against thinking about the
> death of a living person (p. 301).

In Vendler's view, the sonnet represents a state of mourning before the fact, a kind of anticipatory mourning. We see the animation of the inanimate world as a special characteristic of Shakespeare's sonnets. We are deeply impressed by the Poet's capacity to see the ocean as hungry and to experience the same ocean as gaining advantage on the kingdom of the shore as if the two were armies in mortal combat. Also magnificent is the Poet's capacity to see brass as "eternal slave to mortal rage." The very idea that slavery can be eternal while the rage that destroys it is mortal is a staggering combination. To bring life to inanimate nature reduces the Poet's loneliness allowing him to feel in tune with nature's cycles. Two anthologies have included this sonnet.

Sonnet 65 is similar in mood and imagery to Sonnet 64.

SONNET 65

Since brass, nor stone, nor earth, nor boundless sea,
But sad mortality o'ersways their power,
How with this rage shall beauty hold a plea,
Whose action is no stronger than a flower?
O how shall summer's honey breath hold out,
Against the wrackful siege of batt'ring days,
When rocks impregnable are not so stout,
Nor gates of steel so strong but time decays?
O fearful meditation, where alack,
Shall Time's best jewel from Time's chest lie hid?
Or what strong hand can hold his swift foot back,
Or who his spoil of beauty can forbid?
    O none, unless this miracle have might
    That in black ink my love may still shine bright.

Sonnet 64 ended with the victory of time, with the Poet weeping over what he fears to lose; in Sonnet 65 he takes up the battle against time once more. This time he is less despairing and all of time's destructive powers are listed as questions. Though the Poet regards it as a miracle if the his verses have enough power to protect against time, he nevertheless considers the possibility. In this poem the Poet cedes ownership of the Young Man's beauty to time by calling it "time's best jewel." Time attacks life like an army besieging a fortified town. Hence, the "wrackful siege of batt'ring days." The days are experienced as the destructive machines employed by time against walls of the fortress of life.

SONNET 67

Ah wherefore with infection should he live,
And with his presence grace impiety,
That sin by him advantage should achieve,
And lace itself with his society?
Why should false painting imitate his cheek,
And steal dead seeming of his living hue?
Why should poor beauty indirectly seek,
Roses of shadow, since his rose is true?
Why should he live, now nature bankrupt is,
Beggared of blood to blush through lively veins,
For she hath no exchequer now but his,
And proud of many, lives upon his gains?
    O him she stores, to show what wealth she had,
    In days long since, before these last so bad.

This beautiful but enigmatic sonnet can begin to be understood if we assume that the state of affairs described in Sonnet 63 has worsened. If we take the word "infection" to be the Poet's disgusted reference to himself, the first quatrain declares in the most brutal terms that the Young Man should not spend time with the Poet. The "false painting" in line 5, which is Shakespeare normally refers to the application of makeup by women, in this case refers to the Poet's "covering himself" with the Young Man's beauty so he won't have to experience his own horrid old age. He refers to his own love as "Roses of shadow" and sees no reason why the Young Man would want it. This original and wonderful phrase makes use of Plato's metaphor of the cave.

Having begun to talk in terms of nature, the Poet continues and assigns to the lover a central place in the world, in which Nature uses the young man in order to deny how bad things are. Because the Poet's love for the Young Man is fading, the world is experienced as dying; lacking inner life of its own to keep alive. Except for the young man the Poet loves, nothing is alive in the world. The memory of his love is now only an obstacle to an all-enveloping melancholia.

The idea of theft in line 6 shifts the atmosphere from a predominantly depressed one to something close to paranoia. We see with some amazement that the Poet hovers between a melancholic and a paranoid outlook. That infection is rampant and that the presence of the loved man graces impiety are depressive thoughts. That sin obtains an advantage through him, stealing his living hue, represents paranoid trends of thought. The idea that someone (Nature, the Poet) close to death wishes to steal the living hue of the Poet's lover is an example of paranoia transformed into poetry. (Paranoid ideas are among the most resistant to transformation into art.) "Roses of shadow," evokes roses of the world of the dead, and they envy his living rose.

In the third quatrain the Poet tells us that nature is bankrupt, so why should his lover continue to live? Anemia has set in; nature is experienced as "beggared of blood" and therefore not strong enough to create blushes, and nature envies the blood running in the young man's veins. We remember that when time was to carve furrows in the Young Man's brow in Sonnet 63 it was because all the blood had drained from his face. Line 11 continues the metaphor of bankruptcy. Nature's treasure, here called "exchequer," is empty, except for her possession of the Young Man. She keeps him only as a relic to show how wealthy she was at some previous time, which we surmise was the time when the Poet really loved the Young Man. Nature, once privileged ("proud of many") now can exist only by feeding on the young man's life. In the couplet nature keeps the Young Man from ageing to remind herself of the wealth she once possessed in days long ago. The Poet is projecting onto nature exactly what he has told us he does in Sonnet 62.

What happened that so darkened the outlook of the Poet is left unexplained, but a psychic catastrophe must have taken place. For reasons not revealed, the Poet's hostility towards his young lover greatly increased. The hostility gave rise to death wishes against the young man. These death wishes were intolerable to the Poet and were projected by the Poet onto nature. Because the Poet withdrew his interest from the outside world, the world was experienced as empty and dying. (In psychoanalytic language this is called withdrawal of libido from the outside world.) As long as the Poet was able to experience his lover's youth and beauty as his own he was protected from feelings of envy. Now his envy of the Young Man breaks through and is projected onto nature, which is experienced as jealous as well as envious.

We surmise that the Poet felt that he was trying to live by draining the life of the Young Man. To experience his love as draining life out of the man he loved combines paranoia and melancholia. One can imagine that the idea that the Poet's inner life had come to an end and that he then tried to live off the young man's vitality was most painful to the Poet. The resulting melancholia was then projected onto nature.

The combination of high praise and death wishes creates an atmosphere of oppressive beauty. As the Poet loves the Young Man less, nature herself is experienced as a shadow of what she once was. We are accustomed to the opposite, that a state of being in love enhances and strengthens the sense of reality. This feeling is frequently reported by lovers when they say that the sunset in the presence of the beloved is infinitely more beautiful than when viewed alone. What we find remarkable in this sonnet is the Poet's capacity to project his dying love for the Young Man onto nature, conveying to his readers the horror of nature's bankruptcy. Shakespeare's love for the young man was receding, but his capacity to find bold and creative metaphors for this state of feeling was, if anything, heightened.

The savage, cannibalistic depression that we find to be at the core of this sonnet has not been noted by academic commentators. Vendler comments: "The beloved has outlived the Golden age, his era; he is a museum piece, a living relic, maintained alive by nature as her exhibit of what beauty and truth were (p. 313)."

True, but the depression that produced these lines has gone unnoticed. Other commentators sought refuge in the social realm, emphasizing the corruption in society. Burrow finds the sonnet overwritten, with abstract concerns (p. 514).

We notice also that the same theme of stealing beauty is the subject matter of Sonnet 99, but there it is treated with humor and kindness. That such disturbing emotions could be transformed into a poem is admirable. The anthologizers must have experienced difficulty in responding to this very depressed sonnet, for none of them included it. The mood of this sonnet recalls Hamlet's description of his illness to Rosencrantz and Guildenstern.

I have of late, but wherefore I know not, lost all my mirth, forgone all custom of exercises; and indeed it goes so heavily with my disposition that this goodly frame, the earth, seems to me a sterile promontory; this most excellent canopy, the air, look you, this brave o'erhanging firmament, this majestical roof fretted with golden fire, why, it appears no other thing to me than a foul and pestilent congregation of vapours. What a piece of work is a man! how noble in reason! how infinite in faculty! in form and moving how express and admirable! in action how like an angel! in apprehension how like a god! the beauty of the world! the paragon of animals! And yet, to me, what is this quintessence of dust (II.ii.307-321)?

That the energy behind all these destructive emotions could be channeled into a poem of great beauty inspires awe before the Poet's genius.

SONNET 68

Thus is his cheek the map of days outworn,
When beauty lived and died as flowers do now,
Before these bastard signs of fair were born,
Or durst inhabit on a living brow;
Before the golden tresses of the dead,
The right of sepulchres, were shorn away,
To live a second life on second head,
Ere beauty's dead fleece made another gay:
In him those holy antique hours are seen,
Without all ornament, it self and true,
Making no summer of another's green,
Robbing no old to dress his beauty new,
    And him as for a map doth Nature store,
    To show false art what beauty was of yore.

The melancholia of Sonnet 63 and Sonnet 67 continues in this astonishing sonnet in which the Poet has expertly fused the celebration of the Young Man's beauty with his lament for his own old age. The explicitness of Sonnet 62 is a great help in understanding this poem. The Young Man's cheek is a reminder of the Poet's youthful cheek, expressed as a "map of days outworn," to look at his cheek is to see how beautiful the Poet used to be. Therefore the Young Man is still young, still beautiful. The phrase "bastard signs of fair" is not easy to interpret but it seems to suggest that the Young Man's beauty is an illegitimate offspring of the Poet's own. And yet the Poet goes on to assert his lover's legitimacy at the expense of his own, when he says that the Young Man is "making no Summer of another's Green," a poetic way of chiding himself for what he is doing with his love of the Young Man.

Lines 3-4 suggest that erstwhile beauty had already died when beauty first touched the Young Man. These lines contain the insight that the Poet had to overcome his self love before he could respond to the Young Man's beauty, and also strengthen the sense that we got from Sonnet 104 that the Young Man may be very young indeed.

The Poet has an even more melancholy comparison in store in the next quatrain in which he offers a new and powerful metaphor. Its power is derived from the dread most people feel when corpses are violated. In Shakespeare's time it was customary to use the hair of the dead for wigs. The inherent horror of this custom is alive for the Poet, because he calls it a violation of "the right of sepulchers." A greater horror took place during the Holocaust, when the used body parts of their victims for commercial purposes. Because of the melancholic tone of the poem and some ideas that the Poet makes explicit elsewhere, particularly in Sonnet 31, it is possible to read additional relevance into the tresses metaphor if we have the courage to accept the idea that the Poet is already thinking of a transfer of his love from the young man to some future lover. The idea, however, is abhorrent to another part of the Poet's unconscious, and that is the reason why he is horrified by the violation of the "right of sepulchers."

> To live a second life on second head,
> Ere beauty's dead fleece made another gay

Line 8 continues the metaphor, but the hair has been replaced by "fleece," the wool of sheep. It will now falsely decorate another head and make another man happy ("gay"). It is not easy for us, the Poet's readers, to accept what the Poet has dared to tell us, for he has compared signs of aging with death itself, and then added that just as the tresses of the dead can be used to decorate another head, so the Poet will take some part from the young man and transfer it to some future lover.

In the couplet Nature, and not the Poet's verses, is keeping the Young Man young, as a souvenir of what beauty she used to have at her disposal. In Sonnet 62 the Poet told us that he is using the Young Man's youth as a way to keep himself young. The couplet of this poem is a beautiful, metaphorical way to express this idea. In other poems the Poet will add the warning that but for Nature's desire to keep the Young Man beautiful as an aide-memoire the Young Man would age and die, meaning that when the Poet ceases to love the Young Man he will hurtle toward the fate that awaits us all. This poem makes use of the same ideas as several others but the tone is deeply melancholic. We may construct a narrative: that first the Poet was happily in love and now his love is waning, but that would be to impose our construction on the poems. What is certain is that the Poet has left us a dramatic range of different moods as he works the same material over and over again, like the waves upon the pebbled shore.

The sonnet is emotionally difficult to accept and no anthology selected it. From a psychoanalytic perspective there is much to admire in this sonnet, for the Poet dared view and put into words thoughts that are frequently repressed.

SONNET 66

Tired with all these for restful death I cry,
As to behold desert a beggar born,
And needy nothing trimmed in jollity,
And purest faith unhappily forsworn,
And gilded honour shamefully misplaced,
And maiden virtue rudely strumpeted,
And right perfection wrongfully disgraced,
And strength by limping sway disabled,
And art made tongue-tied by authority,
And folly (doctor-like) controlling skill,
And simple truth miscalled simplicity,
And captive good attending captain ill.
    Tired with all these, from these would I be gone,
    Save that to die, I leave my love alone.

"Tired with all these," the Poet tells us in the first line, he cries for "restful death." The long battle against death that animated so many earlier sonnets has here been given up. When the Poet's mood was determined by aggressive orality, death was experienced cannibalistically, being eaten by hungry time, but Death is now welcome as restful. The usual vitality of the sonnets, based on a lively relationship between three quatrains and a couplet, is here submerged behind ten identically constructed lines, each beginning with the word "and;" they convey the impression that we are walking in a slow funeral procession. This sonnet was anthologized by four of the six anthologies, to us an unexpectedly high evaluation, suggesting that its unique poetic structure and the bitter depressive content, contributed to making this sonnet memorable.

SONNET 74

But be contented when that fell arrest
Without all bail shall carry me away;
My life hath in this line some interest,
Which for memorial still with thee shall stay.
When thou reviewest this, thou dost review
The very part was consecrate to thee;
The earth can have but earth, which is his due,
My spirit is thine, the better part of me;
So then thou hast but lost the dregs of life,
The prey of worms, my body being dead,
The coward conquest of a wretch's knife,
Too base of thee to be remembered:
   The worth of that, is that which it contains,
   And that is this, and this with thee remains.

In this sonnet the Poet has moved from resisting his death to imagining himself dead. We find him musing over his lover reading the sonnets after his death. A variation on the repeated "and" in Sonnet 66, the rhythm of this one is carried by the repetitive "th": "that" in the first line, "without" in the second, "this" in the third, "thee" in the fourth, "thou" twice and "this" in the fifth, "the" and "thee" in the sixth, "the" and "earth" twice in line 7, and "thine" and "the" in the eighth line, "then," "thou" and "the" in the ninth. The final line has "that," "thee" and "this" twice.

The poem opens with the words "But be contented," a strange opening, as if we have entered into an ongoing conversation between Poet and lover, with the Poet asking the lover to be contented, after the Poet's death, with the poems left behind. "Fell arrest" is a metaphor for death. Literally the term is used to describe an arrest without a chance of posting bail, equivalent to "the country from which no traveler returns." Shakespeare has used the same metaphor in *Hamlet:* "As this fell sergeant death/is strict in his arrest" (V.ii.347-48). The fell arrest will carry the Poet away, but because of "this line," meaning the current sonnet, the life of the Poet retains "some interest." It will stay with the lover as a memorial for the Poet; when the lover will read the sonnet he will realize the "very part," meaning the very sonnet, is "consecrate to thee," a linguistic statement that recalls the marriage commitment.

In the seventh line the Poet reiterates an idea that meant a great deal to Shakespeare: "The earth can have but earth, which is his due." In Genesis, when God created Adam he created him out of earth and therefore the body must return to earth, or be "due" to earth, while the spirit of the Poet, embodied in the poem, will remain with his lover. This spirit is "the better part" of the Poet. In the language of Sonnet 20, the compromise of asexual love has been realized permanently. A "part," in Elizabethan English, can have a connotation of referring to a penis and so the Poet calls his verses his spirit, "the better part" of himself. In traditional religious terms the spirit returns to God, but in the Poet's mind the "better part" will survive him and will remain with the lover. The passage brings to mind the famous exchange between Prince Hal and Falstaff.

> *Hal*: Why thou owest God a death.

> *Falstaff*: Tis not due yet: I would be loath to pay him before
> his day. What need I be so forward with him that calls not on
> me. (*Henry IV, Part I*, V.i.126-129).

In the *Book of Common Prayer* this idea is expressed as "I commend thy soul to God the father almighty and the body to the ground, earth to earth, ashes to ashes, dust to dust." In the poem the lover has replaced God. The religious distinction between body and spirit is retained but subverted into the continuation of the love relationship after the Poet's death, rather than "life everlasting" in heaven.

The last quatrain is Medieval in tone. The body is referred to as "the dregs of life" and "prey of worms." The body is "too base" to be worth remembering. In line 11 death is maligned as "The coward conquest of a wretch's knife;" wretch here literally means a worthless person, such as might kill someone in a robbery, but we also know that knife from the other poems as belonging to Time. The mood in which this sonnet was written is in opposition to what the Poet expresses in Sonnet 71, to which we turn next. Of the two, the anthologies preferred 71. Sonnet 74 is a powerful but depressing poem. Only one anthology included this poem.

SONNET 71

No longer mourn for me when I am dead,
Than you shall hear the surly sullen bell
Give warning to the world that I am fled
From this vile world with vilest worms to dwell:
Nay if you read this line, remember not,
The hand that writ it, for I love you so,
That I in your sweet thoughts would be forgot,
If thinking on me then should make you woe.
O if (I say) you look upon this verse,
When I (perhaps) compounded am with clay,
Do not so much as my poor name rehearse;
But let your love even with my life decay.
    Lest the wise world should look into your moan,
    And mock you with me after I am gone.

The Poetic structure of this sonnet is built around the sounds we associate with the letters W and V, alternating with the sound of the letter S. We have "when" in the first line, "warning" and "world" in the third, and "vile," "world," "vilest," "worms" and "dwell" in the fourth. In the sixth line we find "love," and "sweet" and "would" in line 7. Line 8 contains "woe," line 9 "verse," and line 10 "when" and "with." Finally, the Poet uses "love" and "with" in line 12, "wise" and "world" in line 13, and "with" in line 14.

As to the S sound, there are "surly" and "sullen" in line 2, "this," "vilest" and "worms" in the fourth line, "this" in line 5, "so" in line 6, "sweet" and "thoughts" in line 8, "say" "this" and "verse" in line 9, and "perhaps" in line 10. The last S sounds in the sonnet are "so" and "rehearse" in line 11, and "lest" and "wise" in line 13.

Ostensibly what the Poet tries to do is to persuade his lover not to mourn for him after his death. By itself this is a strange request because the "work of mourning," as Freud called it, is necessary in order to obtain liberation from the lost lover. Since the publication in 1917 of Freud's essay "Mourning and Melancholia," psychoanalysts tend to believe, contrary to the Poet's view in this sonnet, that those who cannot mourn the loss of an old love will have greater difficulty finding a new love than those who have mourned and finished the work of mourning. Depression, conscious or unconscious, will befall anyone who cannot mourn the loss of a loved one. It is strange that so profound a psychologist as Shakespeare should so preposterously err in this sonnet. To sympathize with the Poet in this sonnet we must assume that the Poet feared mourning.

The official reason given for this prohibition of mourning emerges in the couplet. We are asked to believe that the world will mock the young man if he shows signs of mourning. The reason for the Poet's fear that he will be mocked is not stated. It has been assumed that this was an allusion to the difference in social rank between them, but it could also reflect the Poet's depression and his conviction that he does not deserve to be mourned.

Depression is the significant theme in this sonnet, as indicated by the main metaphors chosen. The Poet did not die; he "fled/From this vile world," not into a better world in the hereafter, but in order to dwell "with the vilest worms."

The first quatrain is written as a kind of will or testament. For a fee, the heirs of a dead person could get the church bell to toll once for every year the deceased had lived. The Poet of the sonnet asks that this custom not be used at his funeral. The Poet forbids mourning for him once the bell announcing his death has tolled. Mourning should not last longer than the sound of the bell. The bell is experienced as "surly" and "sullen." The word "surly" implies stern, haughty, arrogant, or imperious behavior, while "sullen" suggests gloom or melancholia. Associating the two words with the sound of the bell sends a double message, a prohibition on mourning, combined with a sense of gloom. Death is experienced in hostile, oral terms, as being eaten by the "vilest worms."

There is something hostile in this insistence that the Poet not be mourned, hiding behind the innocuous wish to cause no woe to the lover. In line 9, the idea is repeated; even if the lover will look upon "this verse" at a time when the author is already "compounded with clay" he should refrain from rehearsing the Poet's name.

The Poet twice instructs his lover not to remember him, both times when he is reading this very poem, thus advocating the suppression of mourning. The fact that three of the six anthologizers included this sonnet suggests that many readers respond strongly to the Poet's wishes to spare his lover the need to mourn him. The post-Freudian notion that mourning is both necessary and a psychically healing response, and conversely, that the inability to mourn is conducive to mental illness, was not within the orbit of Shakespeare's thinking or the thinking of all those who celebrate this sonnet.

In our view, since no one can love and not mourn the loss of the person loved, the injunction against mourning amounts to a prohibition on loving.

SONNET 73

That time of year thou mayst in me behold,
When yellow leaves, or none, or few do hang
Upon those boughs which shake against the cold,
Bare ruined choirs, where late the sweet birds sang.
In me thou seest the twilight of such day,
As after sunset fadeth in the west,
Which by and by black night doth take away,
Death's second self that seals up all in rest.
In me thou seest the glowing of such fire,
That on the ashes of his youth doth lie,
As the death-bed, whereon it must expire,
Consumed with that which it was nourished by.
  This thou perceiv'st, which makes thy love more strong,
  To love that well, which thou must leave ere long.

In sonnet 73 the Poet's age has become the very reason for his lover's love. And because the Poet perceives himself as loved *because* of his old age he can write about himself with the love and tenderness he reserves for descriptions of nature. In sharp contrast to Sonnet 71, here the Poet expresses his full capacity for self-mourning.

Sonnet 73 is among Shakespeare's best-known sonnets, selected by all anthologies.

In the first line the Poet boldly states that the Young Man (or an unknown onlooker, and by implication, we his readers), sees him in old age expressed as at that season of the year "when yellow leaves, or none, or few do hang." The logical sequence of the seasons has deliberately been changed when a "none" precedes "a few." The seasons of nature are highly regular, but the moods of the Poet are not. In his inner life, winter can come before autumn. The scene that in the first two lines was static becomes full of movement in the third line, when the wind, not directly referred to, makes the boughs shake against the cold. For the Poet nature has become animated; the trees shake as human beings do, especially older people, when exposed to inclement weather. The new metaphor introduced in the fourth line is darker. Preconsciously we know that barren boughs will become green again in the next season, but the addition of "ruined" to "bare ruined choirs" eliminates the hope of renewal. Blackmore Evans has suggested that several levels of meaning are implied. Picturesquely we see the ruined remains of a church choir. The arches, like branches, are open to the elements. Historically this may be a reference to the destruction of the monasteries carried out under Henry VIII. Some commentators even suspect that Shakespeare was referring to choirboys. What seems significant to us is that, as in other sonnets, the Poet excels in creating images that describe the desolation of old age while simultaneously evoking the time past of youthful beauty, here the time when sweet birds sang there. The next line, "in me thou seest the twilight of such a day," is so powerful because the Poet himself has merged with the twilight: he and nature have become one. He is also the day that "after sunset fadeth in the west." Black night appears in line 7; it is animated and endowed with a capacity to take away the previous day. The Poet's invocation of sleep, described as "death's second self that seals up all in rest," rather than death itself, adds an element of healing that mitigates the bleak picture and lends sweetness to the poem.

Perhaps the mitigation of sleep has had an encouraging effect on the Poet, because, not being dead yet, he compares himself to embers in the third quatrain, comparing his love to the hottest kind of fire. Alas the fire burns upon "the ashes of his youth." Burning on top of ashes, the fire must soon expire. In the twelfth line the Poet points out that and fire consumes the very matter that it is nourished by, adding a cannibalistic note to this very bleak picture. We recall the cannibalistic metaphor in Sonnet 19, "make the earth devour her own sweet brood."

WHEN LOVE IS AT WAR WITH TIME AND DEATH

This sonnet contains one of the most pessimistic appraisals of love found in Shakespeare, more pessimistic than the one we found in *Venus and Adonis*. Love is a fire that burns more strongly when one is young. The early love turns into ashes, and these ashes threatened to suffocate the love of maturity. We may go so far as to suspect that deeply in his unconscious the Poet attributes to love the same suicidal quality he attributed to fire. This is reminiscent of the line in *Hamlet:* "There lies within the very flame of love a kind of wick or snuff that will abate it" (IV.vii.114-115).

It seems likely that Sonnet 73 was in Edna St. Vincent Millay's mind when she wrote one of her famous sonnets. The same tree that (in Millay's words) does not know what "birds have vanished one by one" and "yet knows that its boughs are more silent than before" appears in both Millay's sonnet and Sonnet 73.

What lips my lips have kissed, and where, and why,
I have forgotten, and what arms have lain
Under my head till morning; but the rain
Is full of ghosts tonight, that tap and sigh
Upon the glass and listen for reply,
And in my heart there stirs a quiet pain
For unremembered lads that not again
Will turn to me at midnight with a cry.
Thus in the winter stands the lonely tree,
Nor knows what birds have vanished one by one,
Yet knows its boughs more silent than before:
I cannot say what loves have come and gone,
I only know that summer sang in me
A little while, that in me sings no more.

SONNET 126

The sonnet contains a well-known anomaly; it has only twelve lines instead of the customary fourteen. We have no way of knowing whether it was purposely shortened by the author or whether discretion made the publisher omit two lines. In the printed sequence it is the last of the sonnets addressed to the Young Man. One senses that the relationship—or at least this particular way of viewing and thinking of the Young Man—has come to an end and in this poem the Poet comes to terms, in a sad but also humorous acceptance, with the end. We re-encounter in this sonnet the myth created by Shakespeare and familiar to us from Sonnet 20, that nature herself fell a-doting on the Poet's lover, as well as the idea that she is keeping him young for her own purposes in her war against time.

> Oh thou my lovely boy who in thy power,
> Dost hold Time's fickle glass his sickle hour:
> Who hast by waning grown, and therein show'st,
> Thy lovers withering, as thy sweet self grow'st.
> If Nature (sovereign mistress over wrack)
> As thou goest onwards still will pluck thee back,
> She keeps thee to this purpose, that her skill
> May time disgrace, and wretched minutes kill.
> Yet fear her O thou minion of her pleasure,
> She may detain, but not still keep her treasure!
>> Her audit (though delayed) answered must be,
>> And her quietus is to render thee.

"Oh thou my lovely boy" as a form of address is found only in this sonnet, according to Burrow. It is a more directly homosexual address than we have yet seen. If the sequence of the sonnets is to be trusted, then in the last sonnet to the Young Man Shakespeare expressed homosexual wishes more overtly, perhaps because he was saying farewell. This sonnet combines the theme of the Young Man keeping the Poet young with his youth with the theme of time coming to destroy the Young Man. In the opening two lines the young man is given extraordinary power to "hold," or stop, "Time's fickle glass," a reference to the hourglass in which the sand, signifying the passage of time, is running. The "sickle hour" refers to the hour of (the Poet's) death which the Young Man can also prevent. In the first two lines, the lovely boy is victorious over aging as well as death: fickle glass and sickle hour form a striking poetic pair. In the third line death has become night as the moon is invoked by "waning" which here is used to mean here symbolizes growing older; unlike the Poet, the Young Man has become more beautiful as time passed on, while the Poet (and the lovely boy's other lovers) have only withered as they've grown older.

The second quatrain introduces the legend with which we are already familiar. The Young Man is seen as the battleground between nature and time. He has not aged because nature "plucked him back" from aging, being herself mistress over destruction or "wrack." Her aim is to confound time, to win victory over time, and to kill the "wretched minutes" that do time's bidding. The whole idea that nature and time are at war with each other over who has dominion over the young man suggests nature as a feminine and maternal figure at war with the masculine and paternal figure of time. A similar battle over an Arabian boy gives rise to a disagreement between Oberon and Titania in *A Midsummer Night's Dream*. It was a theme that seemed of particular interest to the Poet. In psychoanalysis such a battle over a child represents a consolation over the loneliness of the child excluded from the sexual experience of the parents, for in this consolation the parents do not desire each other but fight over the boy. The Poet did not claim this coveted position for himself but assigned it to the young man he loves. The Poet thus created an imaginary triangle in which time and nature fight over who will possess the young man. This triangle anticipates the triangle of the dark lady sonnets. Victory, the Poet predicts, will go to time.

However, nature in Sonnet 126, unlike nature in Sonnet 20, has not herself fallen in love with the young man; the young man is only a "minion of her pleasure." Minion here means favorite or darling and the original phrase "minion of her pleasure" is a highly original way of describing narcissistic love. Nature is using the young man to show her skill and her ability to compete with time. The Poet projects onto nature exactly what he said he was doing himself in Sonnet 62. In the last quatrain, the young man is urged not to trust nature, for she merely exploits him as her minion, serving to give her pleasure. Since nature is a woman, there is no love between nature and the lovely boy, his being only her toy to play with. Ultimately, nature will prove powerless against time. She can detain the boy, that is, keep him from aging, but in the end all she can do is delay his aging. In the last line, the verdict is issued: the lovely boy will become her "quietus," a technical term indicating the settling of a debt. The word "quietus" according to the O.E.D. originally meant "a receipt given on payment," like audit; "quietus" is another metaphor for death, made explicit in the line from Hamlet's most famous soliloquy where Hamlet refers to suicide as "when he could his quietus make with a bare bodikin." Nature can no more keep him from (ageing and) dying than Venus could have prevented the death of Adonis.

Only one anthology included this sonnet, but for us it summarizes the conflict of the Poet of the sonnets in an original way. The elevation of the Young Man to a cosmic significance as the battleground between two narcissistic divinities, each fighting to possess him but neither loving him but merely exploiting him. It should, in our opinion, be understood as a mythological extension of Sonnet 104, described in the previous chapter.

SONNET 146

Poor soul, the center of my sinful earth,
Feeding these rebel powers that thee array,
Why dost thou pine within and suffer dearth,
Painting thy outward walls so costly gay?
Why so large cost, having so short a lease,
Dost thou upon thy fading mansion spend?
Shall worms, inheritors of this excess,
Eat up thy charge? Is this thy body's end?
Then, soul, live thou upon thy servant's loss,
And let that pine to aggravate thy store;
Buy terms divine in selling hours of dross;
Within be fed, without be rich no more:
    So shalt thou feed on Death, that feeds on men,
    And Death once dead there's no more dying then.

Commentators have apparently found this a difficult sonnet to decipher. Booth needed 16 pages to explain it, while the adjacent sonnets required only one or two pages. Vendler needed six pages while adjacent sonnets required only two.

Sonnet 146 is surprising because we have become accustomed to seeing Shakespeare as representing the man of the Renaissance and in this sonnet he speaks to us in the language of the Middle Ages, in which, traditionally, a debate between soul and body takes place. This sonnet reminds us of some of the religious poetry written by John Donne. It has been called Shakespeare's Christian sonnet and is the one sonnet to which the word "religious" applies; it could almost be called a sermon. Barrow compared this sonnet to those that explored a dialogue between body and soul. But this is hardly the case, for neither body nor soul speak; we hear a voice criticizing and admonishing, but we do not find out who "the speaker" is. Instead, the speaker is an inner voice of the Poet that has become detached from the feelings of the Poet and addresses the soul of the Poet as if it were a foreign voice. It is a voice we recognize, which often speaks to Hamlet, and a voice Freud would describe as the voice of the superego.

To us the poem reveals the Poet's feelings absent his relationship with the Young Man, either before he fell in love as described in Sonnet 62 or after he freed himself from this love. He is left alone with his disparaged ageing body, exhorting himself to nourish his spirit upon his body's decay rather than to nourish his heart by rejoicing in his love for his younger self. It's a beautiful poem but rather traditional and familiar in content: an ageing man urges himself to turn away from investing his libido (that is, his loving energy) in his vanity and turn to the nourishment of the spirit instead. Reading this poem is such a jolting return to territory familiar from the writings of other authors that we can't help missing the (admittedly frequently disturbing) relationship with the Young Man for the richness of invention that love inspired in the Poet.

Many critics have looked upon this sonnet as revealing Shakespeare's personal attitude toward death. Caroline Spurgeon, in *Shakespeare's Imagery*, expresses this point of view.

> Only once does Shakespeare in his own person seem to tell us
> directly what he himself thinks about death, and that is in the
> grave 146th sonnet, addressed to the soul of man. Here we see
> the medieval picture reversed, and the greedy feaster on the
> flesh of men subdued and annihilated in his turn by the spirit
> of man grown strong, and here Shakespeare points out to us
> the way of life, and so of the defeat of death (p. 185).

Since we have taken the position that the Poet of the Sonnets is only
one of the characters created by Shakespeare, we see no reason to believe
this sonnet is more personal to Shakespeare than Hamlet's famous solilo-
quy and Claudio's terror of death in *Measure for Measure*.

This sonnet echoes some Pauline passages from the New Testament:
"For I delight in the law of God after the inward man. But I see another
law in my members warring against the law of my mind and bringing me
into captivity to the law of sin that is in my members" (Romans 7:23-24).
In line 11 we are told that by starving the body it will "Buy terms divine
in selling hours of dross." Dross refers to what is left over from metals in
smelting, with the further implication of impurity in general. The term
dross appears in Shakespeare's work five times, always metaphorically: "my
love admits no qualifying dross (*Troilus and Cressida* IV.iv.9)" or "A golden
mind stoops not to shows of dross (*The Merchant of Venice* II.vii.20)."

However, in this sonnet there are no references to any specific Christian
themes, such as the resurrection and salvation. A Pagan stoic philosopher
could almost have written the sonnet. There is no reference in this sonnet
to love or to any human relationship. In significant ways this sonnet is sim-
ilar to Sonnet 129, where lust was denounced with similar vehemence.

The couplet:

> So shalt thou feed on Death, that feeds on men,
> And Death once dead there's no more dying then.

Is like this couplet in Donne's "Death be not proud:"

> One short sleep past, we wake eternally
> And death shall be no more: death thou shall die.

Or from Donne's "Divine meditation:"

> I run from death and death meets me fast
> And all my pleasures are like yesterday

As different as this sonnet is from the rest, we recognize many familiar images and themes. The mansion is here again, though this time it is the ageing body and not a metaphor for love. The lease is here again with its short date but this time, without the Young Man for inspiration, it isn't "summer's lease." The Poet's "poor soul" is the center of "his sinful earth," evoking the Poet's opposition to the feminine and the sexual. In the other sonnets considered in this chapter, the Poet regards it as natural that he should react so badly to his ageing body. Only here does he admonish himself to turn away from "painting" and other vanity, and seek to overcome death by feeding upon his own decay. It is not clear exactly what he means by this but the cannibalism that has appeared before has become explicit. Worms, in the second quatrain, will get to eat the body in any case. What a contrast to Rosalind in *As You Like It*, who declares "men have died from time to time and worms have eaten them but not for love." A worm can also symbolize a penis, as in *The Rape of Lucrece*, "why should the worm intrude the maiden's bed" (848). Oral hunger runs through the whole poem. The word "feeding" opens the second line, and in lines 7 and 8 again the hungry worms are central. The word "fed" appears in line 12 and appears twice in line 13. Death, to the Poet is always hungry, but in this poem it is implied, although not directly stated, that the purified soul has devoured death itself.

This chapter illustrates that the Poet of the sonnets, unlike a philosopher like Socrates, does not have a permanent, stable attitude toward death. His feelings fluctuate; triumph contends with defeat, hope with despair, but in all moods he carries us with him by the magic of his words and metaphors. The seven sonnets that describe the defeat of love by time are in the minority, seven out of 24. The preponderance of the Poet's feelings in this chapter implies that love is no match against aging and death; its strength is only the strength of a flower. Collecting these poems in one chapter transmits a sense of depression.

The sonnets we have discussed in this chapter are very beautiful, and yet this chapter was not easy for us to write and it may not have been easy for many readers, for we all wage the same battle against time and death. The ferocity with which the Poet of the Sonnets described this battle and the feelings he admits to himself and shares with us are sometimes almost too difficult to bear, yet the beauty of these sonnets brings undoubted joy. And as we promised in the Introduction, we are beginning to get the sense that we know him.

CHAPTER 3: MEDITATIONS ON THE NATURE OF LOVE

SONNETS 29, 30, 31, 114, 23, 36, 96, 53, 99, 112, 121

I n this chapter, more modest in scope than the previous one, we have assembled 11 sonnets that, taken together, represent the Poet's reflection on the nature of love and the changes love can bring about. We start with the more optimistic ones, which celebrate love's capacity to win over envy and jealousy (Sonnet 29) and love's capacity to awaken the pain of earlier loves (Sonnet 30). We do not expect our readers to find difficulty with these two sonnets. Sonnet 31, on the other hand, is likely to evoke stronger opposition, since the Poet claims to have transferred parts of the earlier lovers to the current lover in a rather concrete way. Continuing in the order in which we present them: Sonnet 114 deals ambivalently with love's capacity to bring about the "alchemy" of idealization. Sonnet 23 is about the inability to speak in a love relationship, and Sonnet 36 deals with the Poet's difficulty in feeling merged with his lover. Sonnet 96 focuses on the complex relationship between love and self-love. In Sonnets 53 and 99 the Poet plays with Platonic ideas in an original way, and last, Sonnet 112 and Sonnet 121 deal with the impact of scandal and gossip on the love relationship.

SONNET 29

When in disgrace with Fortune and men's eyes,
I all alone beweep my outcast state,
And trouble deaf heaven with my bootless cries,
And look upon my self and curse my fate,
Wishing me like to one more rich in hope,
Featured like him, like him with friends possessed,
Desiring this man's art, and that man's scope,
With what I most enjoy contented least,
Yet in these thoughts my self almost despising,
Haply I think on thee, and then my state,
(Like to that lark at break of day arising
From sullen earth) sings hymns at heaven's gate,
 For thy sweet love remembered such wealth brings,
 That then I scorn to change my state with kings.

Sonnet 29 celebrates love as a cure for envy. It is a sonnet that lovers can read to each other with great hope and pleasure because envy is such a prevalent and painful emotion. A sudden freedom from envious feelings, brought about by love, can be experienced as the lifting of a burden. There is much to be said in favor of love if it can free us from such painful feelings. It is therefore not surprising that this sonnet has been selected by five of the six anthologies.

In psychoanalytic work we often hear a woman in love exclaim: "No one has anything better than I have," or "I must be the happiest woman in New York," or a man saying "I used to look at nude pictures of women and be jealous of the men who can have them—this feeling is entirely gone since I have known you." Sonnet 29 says all of that and more in incomparable language.

Depressed people are particularly susceptible to the painful feeling of wishing to be someone else. Normally we are protected from such painful feelings by healthy narcissism. We envy one person's attainment or another person's popularity, but we are not willing to become this other person. In depression, however, the self-rejection can go so far that we would like to be someone else. In love, and particularly in homosexual love, the envy described in this sonnet can become the very reason for selecting someone who has all the qualities we lack, making her or him the person with whom we fall in love.

In the first two lines, fortune, like the muse in other sonnets, is personified. The Poet of the Sonnets frequently uses religious imagery, but does not express religious feelings, and "Deaf heaven" is his synecdoche for Fortune as an unresponsive God.

The word "bootless," meaning useless, appears in Shakespeare's work 23 times: for example, "bootless inquisition" in *The Tempest* (I.ii.5), "bootless rhymes" in *Love's Labor's Lost* (V.ii.64) and "bootless prayers" in *The Merchant of Venice* (III.iii.20). The Poet, despairing like the biblical Job, curses his fate. In the fifth line, his envy breaks through when he wishes to be like another person, "rich in hope." In the next line—"Featured like him, like him with friends possessed"—the Poet expresses the wish to look like another man, and wishes to be as popular as him. He desires this man's skill as well as another man's range, likely meaning his influence or knowledge. The phrase "rich in hope" is apt, for we feel richer when we experience hope. Envy has become intense, and although the Poet does not envy material riches or status, he uses these as metaphors for optimism, hope, understanding and companionship.

The eighth line, ending the second quatrain, brings to completion the long list of painful feelings the Poet suffered. With the phrase "With what I most enjoy contented least," the Poet introduces an unexpected insight. In the contrast between "most enjoy" and "contented least" the Poet realizes that what he most enjoys also deprives him of contentment. When a person says, "I enjoy…" and specifies what he or she likes, that person is describing an active, participatory emotion. When another person tells us that he or she is content, what is being described is a passive state of contentment with one's life as it is. If, however, what is enjoyed most brings least contentment, we are dealing with an inner conflict and contradictory feelings, because enjoyment and contentment should complement rather than be in opposition to each other. To become aware of such a complex state of feelings requires insight and self-knowledge. These thoughts, the Poet tells us, cause him to "almost" despise himself.

As so often in Shakespeare's sonnets, the third quatrain represents a sharp departure from the previous two. After the hint of relief in Line 9 afforded by the mitigating adjective "almost," in line 10 the very thought of the lover changes everything. The Poet now compares himself to the "lark at break of day." The lark was proverbial because it was thought of as flying straight up from "sullen" earth to heaven, a heaven that seemed "bootless" in line 3 but which now opens its gate to the rising lark. While formerly the Poet envied other men, he now declares "I scorn to change my state with kings." The third quatrain and couplet form a hymn celebrating the power of love to bring about a radical change in feelings and a dramatic improvement in self-esteem.

Sonnet 29 ranks among Shakespeare's best-known sonnets. Vendler, in her interpretation, stressed that the sonnet moves from the hierarchical social world, dominated by the wheel of fortune and with the speaker outcast and in disgrace, to the hierarchy of the natural world, consisting of heaven and the earth from which the lark rises. We would add at this point that the social world is the oppressive one, and nature, by contrast, liberates the Poet. The lark symbolizes, among other ideas, social mobility; it arises out of the sullen earth which is equivalent to the Poet's "outcast state" and is transformed into a member of a celestial choir singing hymns of praise." The word "arising," associated with the dawn, is also associated with the joys of erection.

The psychoanalyst Ella Sharpe analyzed this sonnet from a different perspective (Sharpe 1946). She stressed the theme of banishment, so prominent in *King Lear* and *The Tempest*. She interpreted "my outcast state" as another example of Shakespeare's interest in banishment and related it to "deeply unconscious sources" experienced in childhood situations that were relived in this sonnet and in the two plays.

If a poem is supposed to be what the ancient Greeks called *mimeses*, that is an imitation of life, a critical reader of this sonnet may deduce that the Poet's love is not a deep one, because the Poet experiences all the bitter emotions of envy in the first eight lines and only in the third quatrain remembers his lover. But if the poem is a metaphor for the dramatic change in feelings from a state in which one is not in love because one is completely self-involved, to a state in which love is re-discovered, the sharp line of demarcation in this sonnet evokes the transformative magic of love.

SONNET 30

When to the sessions of sweet silent thought,
I summon up remembrance of things past,
I sigh the lack of many a thing I sought,
And with old woes new wail my dear time's waste:
Then can I drown an eye (unused to flow)
For precious friends hid in death's dateless night,
And weep afresh love's long since cancelled woe,
And moan th' expense of many a vanished sight.
Then can I grieve at grievances foregone,
And heavily from woe to woe tell o'er
The sad account of fore-bemoanéd moan,
Which I new pay as if not paid before.
    But if the while I think on thee (dear friend)
    All losses are restored, and sorrows end.

This sonnet shows sensitivity to an issue usually overlooked in the literature on love, namely the reactivation of previous loves when falling in love again. In current vocabulary, we would say that painful memories of past loves ordinarily undergo repression. But in the Poet's view, when new love comes, the repression of previous loves gives way and the pain of their loss becomes activated. In Sonnet 30, the Poet uses the same psychological technique that he used in Sonnet 29. He describes a painful state of feelings that is overcome, late in the poem, by the power of love. It is an emotional state familiar to many and prone to overtake us when we are lonely—a state in which past love relationships re-emerge and become conscious, and with them, the pain these relationships have inflicted. In

Sonnet 29, love was the antidote to envy. In Sonnet 30, it is experienced as a remedy against mourning.

Sonnet 30 raises important questions in the psychology of loving. Many men and women fear a new love because it could reactivate the pain of earlier loves, especially if they have suffered the pain of unrequited love, the loss of a lover, or other traumatic experiences in previous love relationships. The sonnet explores this unknown terrain between new love and old love. What happens to the memories of earlier loves when one falls in love once more? Does an intense recall of previous loves reactivate the mourning process? When is the work of mourning done? Is it ever complete? Some people report the end of mourning suddenly and sharply. A widow undergoing psychoanalysis suddenly realized, "I am not a widow anymore." On the other hand, we are familiar with the image of the women in Sicily or Greece, who are known to wear only black when they reach a certain age as they go into a permanent mourning for an unending series of lost family members.

Turning to the language of the text we find the alliteration—"sessions of sweet silent thought," followed by two "s" sounds in the second line ("summons" and the final syllable of "remembrance")—imprints itself strongly on our minds. This poetic tool is employed with success throughout the poem. The third line follows with "sigh" and "sought." In the fourth line the "s" gives way to "w" "woes," "wail" and "waste." Then line 4's, "dear time's waste" evokes a series of Ds: "drown an eye," line 5, and the beautiful; "death's dateless night," line 6. The "w" returns in line 7 in the form of "weep" and "woe," with "woe" repeated twice in line 10, and "while" appearing in the couplet. These repetitions subtly support the poem's theme of the repetition of feelings, contributing to making this sonnet memorable.

In the first line, the Poet is not unhappy. He seems alone, absorbed in "sweet silent thought." However, the word "sessions" implies the presence of at least one more person, but typically is used only when a number of people are deliberating. (The word "sessions" was used by Shakespeare four times but only once metaphorically, in this sonnet.) The possibility of some guilt may be implied. The phrase "I summon" in line 2 may well reinforce the feeling of standing before some imaginary psychological court. The second line will have a familiar ring for many readers, because Scott

Moncrief, Marcel Proust's English translator, borrowed "remembrance of things past" as a title for the English translation of Proust's *A la recherche du temps perdu*. Line 4 is poetically satisfying line: "And with old woes new wail my dear time's waste." The Poet has skillfully used his "w" sounds to convey that investing "new wail" in "old woes" is "dear time's waste." Time is experienced as dear in the sense of precious and valuable, as it is often thought of in a state of nostalgia for the past. Yet just as the thoughts experienced in the first line were labeled sweet, so also in the fourth line the application of "dear" implies that the time spent remembering past loves was endearing for the Poet. In the fifth line, the Poet is so deeply immersed in his own memories that he begins to cry, even though his eyes are "unused to flow." The resistance to crying is familiar; there are many men who, under the pressure to be masculine, have struggled against crying. When they love, the possibility of deep feelings finding expression in tears evokes their fear of femininity.

Without any external cause, the Poet is capable of creating a state of mourning not for a specific person but for a host of non-specified "precious friends." This is not a capacity most people have, but it may be typical of creative individuals. They may more powerfully remember not the loss of a specific person but their love for a quasi-abstract collection of lost lovers.

In line 6, "death's dateless night" is a strong phrase not only because of the alliteration, but more relevantly because it conveys that time can be experienced only by the living. Those who have died live in a perpetual "dateless night." The idea that death is dateless is an original association of the Poet of the Sonnets. The word "dateless" appears in Shakespeare's work only four times. In *Richard II* there is "the dateless limit of thy dear exile (I.iii.151)" and *Romeo and Juliet* contains "a dateless bargain to engrossing death! (V.iii.115)." The word "dateless" also appears in line 6 of Sonnet 153: "a dateless lively heat." In that sonnet the word is associated with "lively heat," a markedly inferior association than "dateless night," and in our opinion this is further evidence that Sonnet 153 is not by Shakespeare. If the Poet understood the word "dateless" so profoundly in Sonnet 30, it seems to us unlikely that he would use the same word so superficially in another sonnet.

In line 7, the Poet found a striking way to express the idea that the mourning process for old loves, the "long since cancelled woe," can be reactivated in a new love relationship. Line 9—"Then can I grieve at grievances forgone"—powerfully expresses mourning again for what has already been mourned, as does "fore-bemoanéd moan (line 11)." The same idea is expressed once more by "I new pay as if not paid before" in line 12. In these six lines the same idea of repeating past injuries is expressed in six ways:

1. "weep afresh love's long since cancelled woe"
2. "moan th' expense of many a vanished sight"
3. "grieve at grievances foregone"
4. "from woe to woe tell o'er"
5. "fore-bemoanéd moan"
6. "new pay as if not paid before"

Since the concept of the resumption of mourning was not part of the Elizabethan vocabulary, repeating it in six different ways powerfully drives this concept home. And the same objection that we raised to the couplet in Sonnet 29 applies to this sonnet. To our ear, the couplet, which offers consolation and in which love triumphs, is too weak to convince us that the dangers of loving anew have been safely overcome. One may well ask when a new love will evoke the joyful memories of old loves and when will the same love reactivate past woes. We may assume that if the previous loves ended traumatically the danger of the reactivation of past pains will be greater.

Meditation on the nature of mourning in this sonnet yields astonishing combinations of words. One example is "cancelled woe" in line 7. Debts can be cancelled, but can woes, ever? The Poet uses the term to show us that we have erroneously believed that we have overcome, forgotten or healed from old woes only to discover that a new love has re-awakened them from repression. "Cancelled woe" refers to what we call, in our current language, past traumatic memories. The same is true for "grievances foregone." The word forego means to go past or overlook, but the word "grievances" is so powerful that it is hard to believe that they are really foregone, an ambiguity that allows two contrasting interpretations, both valid. It is also possible that the Poet refers to grievances he had "forgone" to grieve over, that is, not worked through during the mourning process. The couplet, however, attempts to annul what the 12 previous lines so beautifully impressed on us. The Poet lets the new love triumph over the remembered objections raised by the old loves.

Sonnet 30 has the rare distinction of having been selected by all six anthologies. It is unique in its subject matter—the activation of past loves and the resumption of interrupted mourning—as well as in being endowed with magnificent alliterations.

SONNET 31

Thy bosom is endearéd with all hearts,
Which I by lacking have supposéd dead,
And there reigns love and all love's loving parts,
And all those friends which I thought buriéd.
How many a holy and obsequious tear
Hath dear religious love stolen from mine eye
As interest of the dead, which now appear
But things removed that hidden in thee lie.
Thou art the grave where buried love doth live,
Hung with the trophies of my lovers gone,
Who all their part of me to thee did give;
That due of many now is thine alone.
    Their images I loved, I view in thee,
    And thou (all they) hast all the all of me.

Sonnet 31 deals with the same theme as Sonnet 30, the relationship between the current love and past loves. But this sonnet is more radical and significantly closer to the unconscious than Sonnet 30, for now the Poet claims that all his past loves live in the bosom of the man he loves currently.

This sonnet is rich in bold ideas and striking metaphors. Perhaps the boldest is the celebration of the feeling that all previous love for others has been successfully transferred to the new lover. The idea is bound to have a new meaning after Freud's discovery of transference, which means that the love of the child for one or both parents can be transferred to a new person in adulthood. Although Freud spoke of an unconscious process, the Poet's experiences in Sonnet 31 are fully conscious; he has succeeded in transferring his love from all his old lovers to the new one.

This basic idea, to our knowledge, is to be found nowhere else in the poetry and literature on love. Nor is it repeated in other sonnets, remaining unique to this one. There is something frightening about the idea of this sonnet, and so far as we can tell, commentators have shied away from interpreting it. Vendler commented on the somber quality of this poem. To her, it is "as much of a *Liebes Tod* as a love poem." She noted that the word "love" (or forms of it) appears in line 3 (three times) and then in lines 6, 9 (where it is further emphasized by the word "live"), 10 and 13, and the word "all" in lines 1, 3, 4, 11 and 14, where it appears three times. That there is a close affinity between "love" and "all" is familiar from the expression "All my love." In our view, Vendler denies the frightening quality of this sonnet by focusing solely on the repetition of these two words.

The first line is already frightening; it proclaims that the bosom of the lover has become "endearéd," or rendered more valuable, by all the hearts of previous lovers long supposed dead. The second line contains a complex idea highly condensed: "Which I by lacking have supposéd dead." It was the Poet's inability to keep alive within himself the memory of previous loves that made him suppose that these lovers were dead, but now that he has fallen in love again, he knows that the hearts of earlier lovers are still alive, for he experiences them as transferred to the new lover. In that new bosom "there reigns love and all love's loving parts." This is indeed a bold idea, for not only the love was transferred but also what we call today the erogenous zones, the parts of the body that participate in lovemaking, to the man the Poet loves. This is a daring idea that not many people will be able to tolerate, but the Poet feels more in love when he has transferred not only the love, but also the sexual organ that participated in the lovemaking, from his earlier lovers to his new one.

In the second quatrain, religion is introduced. It is called "dear religion" in the sense of being expensive and is accused of stealing many a tear from the Poet's eyes. We note that the tears of the Poet, not religion, are labeled "holy," and also "obsequious," meaning obedient and willing to serve and please. We find this term in Sonnet 125, "let me be obsequious in thy heart," and from Laertes at Ophelia's grave, demanding further "obsequious gestures." "Religious love" is accused of stealing tears from the

Poet's eyes as "interest of the dead." The line is not easy to comprehend and the traditional interpreters tend to gloss over its meaning. To us the Poet seems to imply that "religious love" made him believe that the previous lovers were dead and therefore were owed his tears (and took an interest in them), but now he realizes that his previous lovers did not die but were transferred to the current lover.

In the first two quatrains, a special kind of resurrection is celebrated. Earlier loves long regarded as dead had been successfully transplanted like bulbs into the bosom of the new lover, and are once more alive there. The third quatrain changes course and melancholic imagery triumphs. Instead of being the resurrection of the previous lovers, the new lover himself becomes the grave "where buried love doth live." In line 9, death triumphs over love. The former lovers have not really come to life and are described both as trophies hung and on display and as bodies living beneath trophies they have won from the Poet, which they in turn have given to his lover. To understand this complex trend of thought we have to assume that the Poet's first feeling when he fell in love was an optimistic one. The Poet makes us understand that when he fell in love there was a moment of elation when all previous lovers came to life, residing within the new beloved, but he could not sustain that feeling for long. In the third quatrain the opposite feeling prevails: the previous loves have overwhelmed the new relationship and therefore the new love has become the tomb in which the old loves are buried.

Trophy is a term associated with war, not love; trophies consist of things of value captured from the enemy. Shakespeare used the word "trophies" seven times and the singular "trophy" five times, and usually associates it with death: "Thus trophies do adorn thy tomb (*Titus Andronicus*, I.i.388);" Ophelia drowns with "weedy trophies (*Hamlet*, IV.vii.174)." The couplet attempts to restore the earlier elation: "Their images I loved, I view in thee,/And thou (all they) hast all the all of me." The Poet repeats the assertion that he can view all the images he ever loved in the lover, and that the lover has all of him by having all of them. However, the description of the grave and the trophies feels stronger than the more optimistic lines of the couplet. What on the surface seemed to be a poem celebrating the transfer of love becomes on a deeper level an homage to the power of death.

Paranoid elements appear and are transformed into poetic images. Thus in lines 5 and 6, "dear religion" is accused of having "stolen" a tear. The word "stolen" has paranoid connotations, as does "trophies" in line 10, implying some unspecified war between the earlier lovers of the Poet.

Implicit in the sonnet is the idea of two kinds of death, physical death and psychic death. Psychic death takes place when the lover is forgotten. Remembrance is an antidote to psychic death. This idea is not original to Shakespeare, for it is expressed in many religious rites and secular commemorations. What is new in this sonnet is that long forgotten and therefore seemingly dead loves can be remembered, resurrected and transported into the new love relationship, but then the new love becomes the mere tomb where previous loves' trophies hang. The bold attempt to transfer old loves regarded as dead to the new lover fails and they remain dead, eventually transforming the lover himself into a grave.

Only Auden selected this sonnet in his anthology. The sonnet offers a unique opportunity for reflection on how using a bold idea that no one before had dared to verbalize can make a great sonnet. It is the concreteness of the imagery that many readers may find difficult to accept. In our opinion, this sonnet should be counted among the Poet's most original ones, but the topic is so frightening that only Auden dared put it among the greatest.

SONNET 114

Or whether doth my mind, being crown'd with you,
Drink up the monarch's plague, this flattery?
Or whether shall I say, mine eye saith true,
And that your love taught it this alchemy,
To make of monsters and things indigest
Such cherubins as your sweet self resemble,
Creating every bad a perfect best,
As fast as objects to his beams assemble?
O! 'tis the first; 'tis flattery in my seeing,
And my great mind most kingly drinks it up:
Mine eye well knows what with his gust is 'greeing,
And to his palate doth prepare the cup:
    If it be poison'd, 'tis the lesser sin
    That mine eye loves it and doth first begin.

In this sonnet the Poet explores a very painful state of feelings in which he mistrusts that what his eyes are seeing may not be reality but a falsification brought about by being in love. As a metaphor this state may be tolerable, but when it becomes real, the loss of faith in what the eyes see becomes painful. The sonnet expresses deep disappointment in love which the Poet then turns inward, mistrusting his capacity to judge reality: a state akin to madness. This no doubt causes a great deal of anxiety which is evident in the use of "Or whether" beginning the first and third lines. Through this we can see the Poet struggling to determine which of his faculties to trust.

The first two lines are rich in ideas. The Poet in love feels with and by the lover: love makes him a king. Having become a king, the Poet feels he must "Drink up the monarch's plague," which is flattery. That flattery is the plague of kings is by itself a very interesting idea. In *Coriolanus* Shakespeare coined another remarkable metaphor for flattery, "He watered his new plants with dews of flattery." Sonnet 138 concludes that "in our faults by lies we flattered be." The lover shares with the king the difficulty of discovering the truth. When composing this sonnet, the Poet must have been aware of his own capacity to flatter his lover by overpraising his beauty; in this sonnet he wonders whether he himself has succumbed to flattery. The Poet questions whether he can trust his eyes and subsequently blames the lover's love for teaching him to transform "monsters and things indigest" into cherubim the way alchemy transforms base metals into gold. "Indigest" things are ill-formed objects, crude and shapeless; the term goes back to Ovid's *rudis et sine imagine* (crude and devoid of imagination). In this sonnet, the word "alchemy" is employed in a very different sense than it was in Sonnet 33, when the Poet spoke of "Gilding pale streams with heavenly alchemy." There, "heavenly alchemy" had a positive connotation of magic transformation; in this sonnet alchemy has a negative connotation of destroying the truth. In the seventh and eighth lines the comparison with alchemy is continued; the Young Man is said to be capable of creating or transforming "every bad" into a "perfect best/As fast as objects to his beams assemble," meaning that the transformation takes place as soon as he gazes at an object. The magic resides in the beam of light of the Young Man's eyes.

In the third quatrain the "O" in line 9 stands for "or;" the Poet now suspects that there may be "flattery in my seeing," that is, that his eyes are no longer reliable judges of reality. The Poet's "great mind drinks up" the monarch's plague, flattery. Because the mind is really deceived by the eyes, the reference to the "great mind" is sardonic. The eye well knows what the mind's "gust," meaning taste, is "greeing," and prepares a palatable version of reality. (The word " 'greeing," now obsolete, survives as "agreeing"). The ending couplet is written in a lighter mood. Flattery, the monarch's plague, may be poison, but even so it is "the lesser sin" because the eye started the whole process of falling in love; "doth first begin" means it all began with the eyes. Perhaps because this sonnet is so difficult to understand or because it is such a severe attack on the Poet's loving, no anthology selected it.

SONNET 23

As an unperfect actor on the stage,
Who with his fear is put besides his part,
Or some fierce thing replete with too much rage,
Whose strength's abundance weakens his own heart;
So I, for fear of trust, forget to say
The perfect ceremony of love's rite,
And in mine own love's strength seem to decay,
O'ercharged with burden of mine own love's might.
O, let my looks be then the eloquence
And dumb presagers of my speaking breast,
Who plead for love and look for recompense
More than that tongue that more hath more expressed.
    O learn to read what silent love hath writ;
    To hear with eyes belongs to love's fine wit.

This sonnet raises the question many lovers have struggled with: can love be expressed by words? Mystics and lovers have traditionally complained that they are unable to put their feelings into words, but paradoxically they have spoken a great deal about the inability to verbalize their emotions. We read this sonnet differently than the traditional commentators on Shakespeare's sonnets, as a veiled confession of the Poet's sexual impotence. Silence between lovers can have many meanings. It can be an expression of bliss, a preverbal harmony that makes words unnecessary. However, silence can also mean that something has happened between the lovers that they are afraid to verbalize. In this sonnet the Poet is under pressure to talk but for reasons not specified he feels he cannot do so. We surmise that what cannot be spoken are the infidelities committed by either or both partners. There is something strange about a poem in which the greatest wordsmith the world has known complains that he is at a loss for words.

The sonnet opens with the simile of the imperfect actor, who, because of his fear, forgets his lines. Blackmore Evans cites at this point Shakespeare's *Coriolanus* (V.iii.40-42): "Like a dull actor now—I have forgot my part, and I am out—even to a full disgrace." The possibility that there is a hint of impotence in these lines cannot be excluded.

This simile is followed in line 3 by a metaphor comparing the Poet to a fierce "thing" full of rage, whose abundant strength only weakens his heart. The theme of impotence is more explicit here: rage has rendered him impotent. There is nothing in line 1's imperfect actor to prepare us for this line. "Fierce thing" refers to a wild animal, while "replete" means filled, but the psychoanalytic ear may connect these, implying that the imperfect actor forgot his lies because he was "replete with rage." We hear how the actor's "fear" becomes "fierce." When inhibited actors undergo psychoanalysis, one often discovers that their acting inhibition is based on repressed rage. That Shakespeare knew this connection and could express it in a sonnet remains astonishing. The reasons for this rage remain unspecified. One often hears lovers complain that they have nothing to say to each other and in many cases it turns out that this "nothing" is due to unexpressed rage.

The use of the word "rage" in the third line should make us pause. In Sonnet 13 we encounter the "barren rage of death's eternal cold." In Sonnet 17 the Poet used the term "poet's rage" to imply exaggeration. In this sonnet the Poet explores the ways rage weakens his heart and his love. In line 5, the Poet goes back to the imperfect actor, who "for fear of trust, forget[s] to say/The perfect ceremony of love's rite." "Fear of trust" has usually been interpreted as not being able to trust himself to speak, but it could also be read as a fear that he does not trust the lover. The phrase "The perfect ceremony of love's rite" picks up, echoes, and is directly opposed to "the unperfect actor" in the first line.

What is this "perfect ceremony of love's rite" if not sexual union? The Poet feels overcharged, that is, overwhelmed, by "mine own love's might;" he feels awed by the magnitude of his love, or at least claims to be awed. The phrase may refer to the Poet's own love being experienced by him as overwhelming, but it can also be read as a reference to premature ejaculation, which for centuries, until psychoanalysis proved it to be otherwise, had been considered as due to overwhelming desire, rather than an unconscious wish to deny sexual satisfaction to the partner and a symptom of repressed rage.

In the third quatrain, the word "looks" in line 9 is controversial since the 1609 quarto printed "books" and there is a reference to reading and writing in the couplet. However, most critics accept "looks." Thus the Poet, denied speech, urges his lover to examine his looks rather than his words. We note once more the prominent role given to the eyes as the main organ of the relationship.

Duncan-Jones noticed that in *Venus and Adonis*, when Adonis blushes it is an "ill presage" of the words he is about to utter. What was an "ill presage," an unfortunate precursor, becomes in this sonnet "dumb presagers" of the Poet's "speaking breast." Thus "dumb presagers" can be interpreted as non-speaking messengers of the Poet's verbal incapacity. By contrast to these silent presagers, the Poet's breast is a speaking one. In *Romeo and Juliet* we find "My dreams presage some joyful news (V.i.2)" and Sonnet 107 contains the line "and the sad augurs mock their own presage."

The sonnet ends with a couplet that we have adopted as the title of this book:

> O, learn to read what silent love hath writ;
> To hear with eyes belongs to love's fine wit.

The eyes are usually experienced as active, piercing and therefore masculine, while the ear is experienced as receptive, passive and therefore feminine. To hear with eyes means to use the eyes passively and take in the beauty of the other. The sonnet is resolved into a moving plea that the lover pay less attention to what is being said and look more intently into the Poet's eyes. The sonnet moves from the verbal realm of the actor, who was an imperfect one, to an acceptance of the developmentally earlier preverbal period in a child's life when love was felt, but not expressed in words. It is a verbal plea for a return to the preverbal realm.

In other sonnets not included in this book, Shakespeare expressed a similar attitude that silence is preferable to words, such as in Sonnet 83:

> This silence for my sin you did impute,
> Which shall be most my glory, being dumb;
> For I impair not beauty, being mute,

The situation is similar to Sonnet 23; the lover regards the Poet's silence as a sin. The Poet feels that words can "impair," or damage, beauty, while muteness keeps beauty intact. And again in Sonnet 85:

> Then others for the breath of words respect,
> Me for my dumb thoughts, speaking in effect.

In a subtle way, the Poet diminishes the value of words by calling them "breath of words" while "dumb", unverbalized thoughts are actually effective. In Sonnet 106 (Chapter 2) we find:

> For we which now behold these present days
> Have eyes to wonder, but lack tongues to praise.

Frequently in the sonnets, the Poet creates conflicts between two organs to express intrapsychic conflict. In Sonnet 106, the conflict is between eyes and tongue. Strictly speaking, Sonnet 23 is a plea for love that cannot be adequately put into words. Even if we assume that the sonnet contains a veiled reference to the Poet's impotence, it will continue to move us because the Poet's explanation that he is an imperfect actor and cannot say his lines will remind many lovers of a state of near muteness which is experienced when the full power of love takes hold. This sonnet was cited in only one of the anthologies we consulted.

SONNET 36

Let me confess that we two must be twain,
Although our undivided loves are one:
So shall those blots that do with me remain,
Without thy help, by me be borne alone.
In our two loves there is but one respect,
Though in our lives a separable spite,
Which though it alter not love's sole effect,
Yet doth it steal sweet hours from love's delight.
I may not evermore acknowledge thee,
Lest my bewailed guilt should do thee shame,
Nor thou with public kindness honour me,
Unless thou take that honour from thy name:
    But do not so, I love thee in such sort,
    As thou being mine, mine is thy good report.

The idea in this sonnet, that lovers desire to give up their separate existence and become one, has deep literary as well as psychological roots. In Plato's *Symposium* Aristophanes states:

> For the intense yearning which each of them has towards the
> other does not appear to be the desire of lover's intercourse,
> but of something else which the soul of either evidently desires
> and cannot tell, and of which she has only a dark and doubt-
> ful presentiment. Suppose Hephaestus, with his instruments,
> to come to the pair who are lying side by side and to say
> to them, "What do you people want of one another?" they
> would be unable to explain. And suppose further, that when
> he saw their perplexity said: "Do you desire to be wholly one;
> always day and night to be in one another's company? for if
> this is what you desire, I am ready to melt you into one and let
> you grow together… (*Symposium* 192, Jowett translation)"

In Genesis 2:24 God says: "Therefore shall man leave his father and his mother, and cleave unto his wife; and they shall be one flesh." This sentence is repeated in Ephesians chapter 5 and found its way into the marriage ceremony. In Sonnet 36 the Poet confesses why he and his lover could not merge and reach this state of oneness.

The Poet says that although he and his lover are undivided in their love they must nevertheless be "twain," meaning two. The rest of the sonnet is devoted to the Poet accepting their separateness from each other. We are told that the Poet did not wish to share his own faults or weaknesses and preferred to keep them to himself. He was to blame, and the lover, being idealized, is to be exonerated and kept free of the Poet's blemish. The psychological miracle of love as a cure for envy in Sonnet 29 is not available to the Poet as he writes this sonnet. Both shame and guilt over some unspecified misdeeds prevent him from feelings of being one with the man he loves and causes him to feel the pain of being "twain."

In the third quatrain the Poet reassures us that the "spite," meaning anger and grudges, did not alter their love but stole many "sweet hours from love's delight." Many couples who fight will understand what is meant by this phrase. In the last quatrain we learn that the two dare not make their love public. The Poet's own "bewailed guilt" (perhaps because he was married) could put the lover to shame. The Poet is resigned to not expecting the honor of public recognition from the lover, perhaps because the lover is a person of higher social status. If their love were to be publicly acknowledged it would take honor away from the name of the lover, and this the Poet does not wish. We thus learn from this sonnet that too much respect for the narcissistic feelings of the partner can impose a restriction on the capacity to love. This is an interesting psychological idea, but it did not create a significant poem. For this reason we agree with the verdict of the anthology authors, none of whom included this sonnet.

SONNET 96

Some say thy fault is youth, some wantonness,
Some say thy grace is youth and gentle sport;
Both grace and faults are loved of more and less;
Thou mak'st faults graces that to thee resort.
As on the finger of a thronèd queen
The basest jewel will be well esteemed,
So are those errors that in thee are seen
To truths translated, and for true things deemed.
How many lambs might the stern wolf betray,
If like a lamb he could his looks translate;
How many gazers might'st thou lead away,
If thou wouldst use the strength of all thy state!
    But do not so; I love thee in such sort
    As, thou being mine, mine is thy good report.

Like Sonnet 36, this sonnet deals with the subtle border between love, and admiration for the self-love exhibited by the Young Man so dear to the Poet. That this poem was not written in a moment when love is at its height is indicated by the fact that the opinions of others use up the first lines. The Poet does not experience the protective tendencies that make lovers immune to the evaluation of others.

The Poet has to deal with some misgivings aroused in him by the lover's infidelities, but he does not choose to speak of his own feelings. Instead, he quotes others' criticisms and excuses. "Youth" cannot be at fault and even if so designated it can be excused. "Wantonness" is more critical, for it implies that the Young Man is spoiled, self-indulgent, reckless and insolent, but even so, the word wantonness is closely associated in Shakespeare's mind with youth. In the third line the Poet states that whether one judges these behaviors as "faults" or graces is based on whether one loves the Young Man more or less.

The second quatrain introduces a new metaphor. In the way in which a jewel may gain in value from the status of its wearer, the youth's "errors" will be translated into "truths" and seen in a better light than they deserve. Those who think in psychoanalytic terms will note that the Young Man is here compared to a "thronèd queen," stressing his feminine qualities. In the third quatrain the Poet attempts to reconcile the two ways of looking at the Young Man into one, expressed in line 8 as "To truths translated and for true things deemed." The Poet is trying to reach an unambiguous truth, but subsequent lines show that he is not successful. In line 9 he makes use of the metaphor of the wolf in sheep's clothing to suggest that the Young Man is really a "stern wolf"—stern here means hard or grim—who would betray many lambs if he could only look like a lamb. This may be difficult for a wolf, but was done easily by the youth. Line 11 once more emphasizes the good looks of the beloved by converting the lambs into "gazers" looking upon him. The Poet agrees that the beloved can do all this because his "state" has such "strength," but in the couplet the Poet advises him not to betray so many "lambs" or lead astray so many "gazers." In the last two lines (which are exactly the same as the couplet of Sonnet 36), the Poet asks the Young Man not to use the power he has to mislead others, since the Poet feels that the good reputation of the Young Man is also a part of the Poet's reputation. The Poet asserts that a "good report" of the lover applies to the Poet as well. As we observed in Sonnet 36, here too the lovers seem too dependent on the judgment of the outside world, and too disturbed by what the others think to be able to enjoy their love.

No anthology selected Sonnet 96. Like Sonnet 86, it is psychologically of interest but the alchemy that transforms the ambivalence of the Poet into a significant work of art did not succeed in this poem.

THE ERUDITE SONNETS: SONNET 53, SONNET 99

In this category come sonnets that require some knowledge of the classical past for full enjoyment. Here part of the pleasure is the recognition that the reader feels on being part of the select group who understand what the author is subverting. The two sonnets can be enjoyed without any awareness that they are poetic derivations of Platonic thought, but knowing their cultural background enhances the pleasure of reading them.

SONNET 53

What is your substance, whereof are you made,
That millions of strange shadows on you tend?
Since every one hath, every one, one shade,
And you, but one, can every shadow lend:
Describe Adonis, and the counterfeit
Is poorly imitated after you;
On Helen's cheek all art of beauty set,
And you in Grecian tires are painted new;
Speak of the spring and foison of the year:
The one doth shadow of your beauty show,
The other as your bounty doth appear,
And you in every blessèd shape we know.
    In all external grace you have some part,
    But you like none, none you, for constant heart.

Strictly speaking, this sonnet is not a sonnet about love but a sonnet of praise, a praise so extravagant that it is hard to take it seriously. Shakespeare calls the Platonic distinction between reality and appearance in this sonnet "substance" and "shadow." Substance is what endures, the permanent sub-stratum of things. Plato taught that what we perceive with our senses is not the ultimate reality, but only shadows or reflections of that higher reality. The particulars we perceive are transients and ever changing, while ultimate reality, called "substance" by the poet, is permanent. Substance is also indivisible, and being indivisible it is a metaphor for the constant heart. A beautiful young man would, in Plato's thinking, be a mere shadow of beauty, a particular example of the ideal of beauty. We might even say that Sonnet 53 and a number of others are anti-Platonic, since the Poet refuses to accept the fact that his Young Man's beauty is only a shadow of true beauty. On the contrary, he is elevated to the substance of beauty and all other past beauties are merely his shadow. The Poet of the Sonnets subverts Plato to make his beloved the very ideal and the very substance of beauty. Taking full poetic license, Plato's philosophy was to him merely the raw material out of which to construct a poem of praise.

The uniqueness of the Poet's lover gives rise to "millions of strange shadows" that "tend," that is render, service to him. This is confirmed in line 4 when the Poet informs us that although the Young Man is only one, he can bestow shadow to many. In Ovid, Adonis was the most beautiful youth, so beautiful that he succeeded in making the goddess of love herself fall in love with him. In line 5, the Poet inverts the myth and makes Adonis only a "counterfeit," a copy or an imitation, of the Poet's lover. Similarly, Helen of Troy, the great beauty of Homer's *Iliad,* is only the feminine equivalent of Adonis, and she too derives her beauty from the Poet's Young Man.

At this point, the Poet's bisexuality reappears. His lover contains in his essence the beauty of both genders, exemplified by Adonis and Helen. The term "Grecian tires," meaning Greek costumes, is another example of how the Poet reverses history to claim that were the lover dressed in Greek clothing he would not be a reproduction but would appear "painted new." In line 9, the Young Man is compared to "the spring and foison of the year;" the word foison means abundance or the richest part of the year. Even the spring is merely the shadow of the youth's beauty. If Plato's philosophy were a religion, then line 12 could be called blasphemous, because the lover is elevated to the substance of "every blessèd shape we know." The lover has some part in every "external grace," but no one can be compared with him because no one has a comparable "constant heart." The rest of the sonnets, however, do not support this claim, for, as the story of their love unfolds, it is anything but constant.

The same poetic license, used to describe the lover as the "substance" of beauty in this sonnet, is found in the Platonic metaphor of shadow and substance in Sonnets 98 and 101. In the former, the Poet writes:

> Nor did I wonder at the lily's white
> Nor praise the deep vermilion in the rose;
> They were but sweet, but figures of delight,
> Drawn after you, you pattern of all those (Lines 9-12).

The equation of truth and beauty in Sonnet 101 is also Platonic; there the Poet wrote of truth dyed in beauty:

O truant Muse, what shall be thy amends
For thy neglect of truth in beauty dyed?
Both truth and beauty on my love depends (Line 1-3);

In this sonnet the Poet complains that his "truant Muse" neglected the truth of his lover's excellence. That any poet can accuse his muse of neglecting truth when it is "dyed" in beauty is an astonishing variation on the Platonic theme that equates truth and beauty. Both Sonnet 98 and Sonnet 101 were selected by only one of the anthologies.

Two anthologies cited Sonnet 53, no small achievement.

SONNET 99

The forward violet thus did I chide:
'Sweet thief, whence didst thou steal thy sweet that smells,
If not from my love's breath? The purple pride
Which on thy soft cheek for complexion dwells
In my love's veins thou hast too grossly dyed.'
The lily I condemned for thy hand,
And buds of marjoram had stol'n thy hair;
The roses fearfully on thorns did stand,
One blushing shame, another white despair;
A third, nor red, nor white, had stol'n of both,
And to his robb'ry had annexed thy breath;
But for his theft, in pride of all his growth,
A vengeful canker ate him up to death.
    More flowers I noted, yet I none could see,
    But sweet, or colour, it had stol'n from thee.

We believe that the Poet greatly enjoyed the idea, presented in Sonnet 53, that his lover is the true origin of all other beauties, for he essentially repeated the same idea in Sonnet 99. This is the only 15-line sonnet, and has therefore given rise to a great deal of speculation.

It has also been argued by Kerrigan that this sonnet is too close to a poem by Henry Constable, "Diana," which appeared in 1592. Blackmore Evans quotes that poem, which we will cite only in part.

> My ladies presence makes the roses red,
> Because to see her lips they blush for shame.
> The lilies leaves, for envy, pale became,
> And her white hands in them this envy bred.
> The marygold abroad the leaves did spread,
> Because the suns and her power is the same
> The violet of purple coloure came,
> Dy'd with the bloud she made my heart to shed.

But if Shakespeare was indeed influenced by another poet, he transformed what he took the way Picasso often copied other painters yet transformed what they had done into something uniquely his. The idea behind Constable's poem is a simple one: nature envies the woman the Poet loves. Roses blush out of shame because they cannot compete with the redness of his lady's lips. The leaves of lilies pale out of envy because the lady's white hands are far more beautiful. The marigold, mistaking her for the sun, opens up for her. Finally, and more aggressively, the violet gets its purple color from the bleeding heart of the Poet. Shakespeare's idea is bolder and contains more aggression. Nature stole its sweet smells and its colors from his lover. Variations of the word "steal" appear four times, as well as "thief," "theft" and "robb'ry" (robbery). We suggested earlier that the emphasis on theft may well express a tendency towards unconscious paranoid ideas.

In the first line, the Poet claims that he chided the violet for being too presumptuous, stealing its sweet smell from the breath of the Poet's lover and its purple color from his veins. In the second quatrain the lily is condemned for stealing its whiteness from the Young Man's hands and marjoram for stealing the color or texture from his hair. In the third quatrain, the flowers begin to exhibit anxiety, standing ready to be accused. Red roses blush with shame and others are pale and white with despair, while a third rose "had stol'n of both" and is therefore pink. Because in addition the rose stole sweetness from the lover's breath, a vengeful canker will devour the flowers. The poem concludes with a couplet in which the Poet assures us that all the flowers he can see have stolen their color and their smell from the man he loves.

The sonnet is a paean to the Young Man's beauty. We sense an artifice and a coldness in the Poet's capacity to show all nature as stealing his lover's beauty for its own purposes. This metaphor of the Poet's is so daring that his possible lack of sincerity does not seem to matter. In Platonic philosophy the concrete flowers in nature reflect one ideal flower. The Poet subverts Plato in two ways. First, the flowers' beauty is not derived from an ideal flower but from the Young Man's beauty. Second, this transference of beauty did not proceed harmoniously; the flowers stole from his lover. We can feel the Poet's pleasure in himself, stealing from and transforming Plato. Only Harold Bloom included this sonnet in his anthology.

SONNET 112

Your love and pity doth th'impression fill
Which vulgar scandal stamped upon my brow;
For what care I who calls me well or ill
So you o'er-green my bad, my good allow?
You are my all-the-world, and I must strive
To know my shames and praises from your tongue;
None else to me, nor I to none, alive,
That my steeled sense o'er-changes right or wrong.
In so profound abysm I throw all care
Of others' voices, that my adder's sense
To critic and to flatterer stopped are.
Mark how with my neglect I do dispense:
    You are so strongly in my purpose bred
    That all the world besides me thinks you're dead.

This sonnet has been regarded as difficult to decipher by many commentators (note the 10-page commentary by Stephen Booth). Indeed, Sonnet 112 contains rare phrases like "adder's sense" and strained grammatical constructions. But in our opinion the difficulties lie elsewhere. The love aimed at in this sonnet is frighteningly close to death and this proximity may have been difficult to befriend. What is frightening is that the beloved has become the Poet's whole world; nothing matters except what the beloved thinks. His withdrawal from the world did not result in a happy, self-sufficient union, but in a kind of depressive love.

Logically, lines 1 and 2 should be reversed, but poetically the prominence of love and pity adds power to the poem. The third and fourth lines are exuberant. The Poet need not be concerned with the opinions of others as long as the man he loves "o'er-green my bad, my good allow." The word "o'er-green" has been coined by the Poet for this occasion; it does not appear anywhere else in his work. The second quatrain contains the familiar declaration of love: "You are my all-the-world." The Poet now promises to teach himself to receive praise and shame only from his lover. No one else will be alive to him, nor will he be alive to anyone else.

The lovers are alive only to each other, but dead to the world—a secular variant on the monastic ideal. The phrase "steeled sense" in line 8 has been interpreted by commentators as implying "stubborn resolution," "resolute perception," and "hardened sensibilities." All have approximately the same meaning: that the Poet is resolved to let no one but his lover matter to him. Furthermore, in this abandon, moral judgments are dispensed with.

In line 10, the term "adder's sense" is difficult to decipher. An adder, meaning viper or dragon, was thought to be endowed with an extraordinary sense of hearing, but was also believed to be capable of turning a deaf ear. In line 12, the Poet's promise to hear only the lover is reiterated and "I do dispense" can be interpreted as "I excuse myself if I listen to no other voices."

Some commentators spell "me thinks" (in the last line) as two words, while others combine them into one. Both interpretations are possible. In the two-word version, the whole world except the Poet thinks the lover is dead. In the one word version, the Poet himself, perhaps unconsciously, regards his lover also as dead. In spite of the powerful wish of the lovers for an exclusive universe, the last line betrays the Poet's hostility towards his lover. In line 7 the Poet felt that he was dead to anyone besides his lover; in line 14 it is the lover who is regarded as dead by the whole world except by the Poet. The interpretation of the last line is further complicated by the Quarto spelling "me thinkes y'are dead" and the generally accepted reading "me thinks th'are dead" (th' standing for "they." The cutting off of the rest of the word emphasizes the death). In the Quarto spelling the rest of the world thinks the lover is dead; in the corrected spelling the rest of the world is dead. In either case by the end of the sonnet what began as a hymn to the lovers' independence from the world has begun to give way to a powerful awareness of death.

In the extremity of the wish to create a psychic world in which only the two of them exist for each other and the rest of the world appears dead, Sonnet 112 can be read as desiring the most radical version of love. In this poem we hear how strong the wish of the Poet was to create a joint world with the lover where no one else will matter, but we also hear clearly that this wish will never materialize. The outside world retained its power over the two. We should also note that this love must be called pathological because it is built on hostility towards the whole outside world.

The wish to create a universe in which only the Poet and lover exist will seem familiar to some lovers. Psychoanalytically, it represents the wish to recreate infancy, the time when the mother represented the whole universe. When this wish becomes powerful in adult love it makes the couple antisocial because it can only be achieved if the couple withdraws from the world and even hates it. Yet, if our reconstructions are correct, the social reality of the Poet and his lover was such that even the ordinary opportunities for the lovers to be alone together were barred.

The sonnet explores a territory which only a few writers have dared enter, in which a love relationship can be so all-consuming that it brings about total withdrawal from the outside world. Reading this sonnet in the way we are proposing may throw a different light on *Romeo and Juliet,* although there the death of the lovers is ascribed to all kinds of errors and mishaps created by external forces. The heart of the play may be a dim presentiment on the part of the Poet that love, carried to its extreme, endangers not only social existence but life itself. Three centuries later Wagner, in *Tristan and Isolde,* will make the same discovery: that love can be at war with life. Sonnet 112 was selected by one anthology. It may not be an accident that this sonnet of withdrawal from the outside world was written in a language inimical to life and difficult to decipher.

SONNET 121

'Tis better to be vile than vile esteemed,
When not to be receives reproach of being,
And the just pleasure lost, which is so deemed,
Not by our feeling but by others' seeing.
For why should others' false adulterate eyes
Give salutation to my sportive blood?
Or on my frailties why are frailer spies,
Which in their wills count bad what I think good?
No, I am that I am, and they that level
At my abuses, reckon up their own;
I may be straight though they themselves be bevel;
By their rank thoughts, my deeds must not be shown,
   Unless this general evil they maintain:
   All men are bad and in their badness reign.

This sonnet is thematically close to Sonnet 112. It also deals with the relationship of the lovers to the outside world, but unlike Sonnet 112 it is defiant rather than depressed. Sonnet 121 is not a love poem. One could easily mistake the sonnet for an adolescent poem wherein a young man regrets that he was not nearly as vile as he is accused of being.

The most surprising and strongest phrase in this sonnet occurs in line 9, "I am that I am." The phrase is taken verbatim from Exodus, when Moses stood before the burning bush and was told to take off his shoes because the ground upon which he was standing was holy ground. He asked God for his name. "I am that I am," was the reply. (In the original Hebrew this is expressed in three words: "Eye Asher Ehye.") Here the Poet applies these words to himself, asserting his identity in a way many would consider blasphemous. We may go further and say that this line exemplifies the difference between the Middle Ages and the Renaissance, when men usurped for themselves certain attributes of the deity.

The Poet is protesting some false accusation by asserting that it is "better to be vile" than being innocent and accused of being vile. The second line reiterates the same idea: "When not to be, receives reproach of being." Line 2 may have later on given rise to the famous "To be or not to be" in

Hamlet's soliloquy. What the Poet is accused of is left unspecified. However, the phrase "just pleasure lost" in the third line suggests that the reference is to some sexual activity that was not consummated but is the basis of an accusation; a pleasure the Poet did not allow himself is deemed by others to have been taken. Today it is difficult to read this veiled language without thinking that the accusation was homosexuality. If our interpretation is correct, the Poet loved the Young Man but had no sexual relationship with him. He was nevertheless accused of homosexuality, and now feels it would have been better to have consummated the sexual relationship, fulfilling the implied accusation. In clinical work, we encounter men who are in love with another man and yet claim that this love does not make them homosexual. So the Poet could have loved his Young Man without feeling that he is "vile."

From Sonnet 121 the Poet emerges as both a sexual sinner and one who did not sin enough out of fear of social criticism. The Poet sees himself as no worse than his detractors, and since there is no man free of sin, no one should cast the first stone against him. The sonnet was included by four anthologies. Since we did not find anything remarkable or beautiful in the way the Poet described his state, we assume that many agree with the Poet that it is better to be "vile" than to be accused when one is free of sin, and therefore many readers would have found that the sonnet appealed to them.

*

Unlike philosophers and psychoanalysts who have attempted to create a coherent theory of love, the sonnets we assembled in this chapter do not present a coherent view of the nature of love. However, taken together they present an astonishing wealth of original ideas about this emotion.

CHAPTER 4: AS LOVE DECLINES

SONNETS 33, 34, 35, 86, 93, 94, 39, 49, 56, 75, 87, 88, 90, 95, 110, 111, 120

It takes a greater artist to record love's slow decline than to record its appearance. The moment of falling in love is dramatic and exhilarating. It has often been recorded in song, music and literature. The end of love may also be dramatic, as when one discovers in a traumatic moment that the partner has been unfaithful, or that he or she has a different sexual orientation than expected. But love often declines slowly over a longer period and the decline is associated with many emotions: regret, rage, despair, fear and guilt. The 17 sonnets that make up this chapter deal with a love that has passed its prime, and with how to deal with this loss. The sonnets in this chapter can be read as a fulfillment of the curse that Venus, in *Venus and Adonis,* imposed on love: "Find sweet beginning but unsavory end." When Shakespeare's sonnets are regrouped thematically, as we have done in this book, the reader is asked to relate the sonnets to each other the way a composer combines themes into melodies. The reader may combine them in a different sequence and perhaps obtain a different melody.

SONNETS IN WHICH THE POET ATTEMPTS TO TEACH HIMSELF TO ACCEPT THE INFIDELITY OF THE LOVER: SONNETS 33, 34, 35, 86, 93 AND 94.

SONNET 33

Full many a glorious morning have I seen,
Flatter the mountain tops with sovereign eye,
Kissing with golden face the meadows green;
Gilding pale streams with heavenly alchemy:
Anon permit the basest clouds to ride,
With ugly rack on his celestial face,
And from the forlorn world his visage hide
Stealing unseen to west with this disgrace:
Even so my sun one early morn did shine,
With all triumphant splendour on my brow,
But out alack, he was but one hour mine,
The region cloud hath masked him from me now.
    Yet him for this, my love no whit disdaineth,
    Suns of the world may stain, when heaven's sun staineth.

Many women and men have to face the task of forgiving a partner's disloyalties, if the relationship is to survive. This sonnet will have a special appeal to a couple facing such an event. In this sonnet the dreaded event has already happened and the Poet is engaged in finding a "balm for the wound." Shakespeare calls upon nature herself for help. In the beauty of its language, and the brilliance of the metaphors employed, Sonnet 33 is one of the strongest. It was selected by three anthologies.

The dazzling language of the first quatrain is a hymn to the splendor of the sun's impact on nature. The second quatrain is a lament over the staining of this splendor by clouds. The third quatrain compares the dangers of staining in nature to the dangers of infidelity in a love relationship; because it happens in nature, what happens to love should be bearable.

The secret of the beauty of the poem may be found in its anthropomorphization of nature. Because the sun with its golden face is kissing the meadows green, and because it can gild pale streams with "heavenly alchemy," nature itself is experienced as capable of falling in love.

The first quatrain is a hymn to the majesty of the sun without the word sun being mentioned. Describing without naming heightens the effect of this metaphor, as the sun is treated like a god whose name should not be taken up in vain. While it is not named directly, its effects are far-reaching. The mountaintops are described as happy to be flattered by the sovereign eye of the un-named sun. The word "flatter" had to the Elizabethan a wider meaning than it has to us today, including encouraging with hopeful signs. It also had the connotation that we give to the words beguiling or deceiving. The streams become gilded—that is, transformed—into gold by the sun's alchemy. The sun accomplishes a transformation of the meadows and streams that the alchemists failed to do when they tried to transform base metals into gold.

Vendler noted that the Poet suppressed the analogical signal "just as" in the opening of the poem and suggested that "Shakespeare lets us see the octave as pure and literal landscape (p. 176)." We agree but would add that words like "just as" are concessions to logical thinking, what Freud called secondary process thinking, while omitting "just as" heightens the direct connection between the sun and lovers' kisses. It is well known that words such as "just so" are omitted in dreams. Vendler correctly observed that the poem becomes analogical in the third quatrain with the words "even so," but by that time the magic of the love affair between the sun, the mountains and the stream is over. By anthropomorphizing the first two quatrains, the Poet enabled us to see love at its most glorious, a love not yet stained by infidelity.

The sun in not mentioned by name even in the second quatrain. But the quatrain introduces a catastrophic change. "Anon," meaning almost immediately, a license was given to the basest clouds to stain the sun. Who gave this permission is left unclear. By implication however, since the sun was described as sovereign, we assume that the sun itself allowed the clouds to obscure it. The clouds are now allowed to rise and cover his face. The

Poet lets us know by using the word "basest" how strongly he participates in the change taking place in nature. The word rack in the sixth line means a cold mass of clouds "to drive before the wind." We find the metaphor "from the forlorn world his visage hide" noteworthy. It is only recently that psychologists discovered how important the face of the mother is for the baby and what it expresses or fails to express; in this sonnet Shakespeare knew how painful it is when the face is not available. Nature, like the baby, is forlorn when the visage becomes hidden. In line 8 the sun, now experienced as disgraced by the rack of clouds, is stealing unseen to the west, where it will set.

In the third quatrain the word "sun" finally appears and a comparison is drawn between the individual fate of the Poet and nature. The dramatic changes in nature are used by the Poet to teach himself forgiveness. It is only in the last quatrain that we learn that the first two were metaphors for the Poet's fate as a lover. Lines 9 and 10 are a poignant reminder of the transience of love. For a short time, the Poet, like nature, felt flattered by the kisses of his lover's sun-like face. The morning glory was short-lived, for the lover belonged to the Poet "but one hour." In the couplet, the Poet is resolved not to disdain the lover. He will not think less of him. If the sun is allowed to be stained by clouds, "suns of the world," meaning mortal men, may also stain by their infidelity.

The sonnet brings out one of the less obvious characteristics of love: to enable us to experience nature more vividly and in a more personal way. Love can bring us closer to the time when nature was experienced as alive. It may be useful to remember that Robert Burton, the author of *The Anatomy of Melancholy*, who was Shakespeare's contemporary, saw love as not confined to human beings alone. He could describe the moon as lamenting that she is besotted with Endymion. Palm trees could be experienced as fervently in love when they bend their branches towards each other. Burton also reported that trees are known to marry one another, and fish to pine away for love. Shakespeare, unlike Burton, knows the difference between the world of nature and the human world, but he can powerfully evoke changes in nature as a metaphor for human change.

SONNET 34

Why didst thou promise such a beauteous day
And make me travail forth without my cloak,
To let base clouds o'ertake me in my way,
Hiding thy brav'ry in their rotten smoke?
'Tis not enough that through the cloud thou break,
To dry the rain on my storm-beaten face,
For no man well of such a salve can speak
That heals the wound and cures not the disgrace;
Nor can thy shame give physic to my grief;
Though thou repent, yet I have still the loss;
Th'offender's sorrow lends but weak relief
To him that bears the strong offence's cross.
    Ah, but those tears are pearl which thy love sheds,
    And they are rich, and ransom all ill deeds.

In Sonnet 34 the great psychological discovery comes in the 8 lines in which the Poet differentiates between a wound inflected upon him by the lover's infidelity and the disgrace it caused him. In the vocabulary that psychoanalysis puts at our disposal, the "wound" refers to the love relationship as it exists between two people, while curing "the disgrace" refers to the injury to the Poet's narcissism. The Poet tells us that the relationship wound is easier to cure than the narcissistic injury. The very fact that the Poet can make such a distinction is a contribution to the understanding of the nature of love.

The sonnet is based on an inner dialogue between the Poet and an inner warning voice to which the Poet had neglected to pay attention; this device was already used in Sonnet 33. This sonnet uses a felicitous metaphor of the coat taken not because it is raining but because it may rain. It is foolish to trust the "beauteous day" and not take the coat as protection. Implied is the idea that it is foolish to trust the lover and not remember that the weather of love is subject to change. Once more the metaphor of the "base cloud" is used for the lover's infidelity.

The second quatrain introduces a subtle psychological distinction. The lover must have done something by way of apology to the Poet, which the Poet compares to the sun breaking through the clouds and drying the rain on the Poet's "storm-beaten face." The apology is said to have healed the wound but not the disgrace. The Poet goes on to argue that the fact that the lover was shamed by what he did was no "physic," that is no helpful medicine, to the Poet's narcissistic injury. The Poet continues to be unforgiving, and tells his lover that even though he repented, the Poet's loss was not overcome, and that the lover's sorrow did not erase the loss. It proved to be a weak relief to the Poet, who in line 12 "bears the strong offence's cross," comparing himself to Christ on the Via Dolorosa when he is forced to carry the cross on which he will be crucified. It seems to us that the Poet's petulance and inability to forgive alienates him from us. But if we stop and notice the subtle differentiation between the wound to their love and the wound to the Poet's self-esteem, our appreciation of the Poet's self-analytical capacity is enhanced.

The couplet, in contrast to the body of the poem, conveys the opposite message: the tears of the lover are precious. They are accepted by the Poet as a "rich ransom" that redeems all the previous deeds. We the readers are left to decide whether we believe the body of the sonnet or the couplet. The ambiguity forces us, the readers, to come down on one side or the other or at least face the problem.

Lovers who quarrel and wish to make up can learn from this sonnet, if they can learn to differentiate between the wound inflicted on their love from the wound inflicted on their self-esteem. And if they can concentrate only on the pain inflicted on their love and disregard the narcissistic injury, their capacity to heal will be enhanced. This sonnet was not selected by any anthology. We conclude that subtle psychological distinctions may not be what matters in the popularity of a sonnet.

SONNET 35

No more be grieved at that which thou hast done,
Roses have thorns, and silver fountains mud,
Clouds and eclipses stain both moon and sun,
And loathsome canker lives in sweetest bud.
All men make faults, and even I in this,
Authorizing thy trespass with compare,
My self corrupting salving thy amiss,
Excusing thy sins more than thy sins are:
For to thy sensual fault I bring in sense,
Thy adverse party is thy advocate,
And 'gainst my self a lawful plea commence:
Such civil war is in my love and hate,
> That I an accessory needs must be,
> To that sweet thief which sourly robs from me.

A love relationship is doomed unless the partners develop a capacity to forgive each other's transgressions. But how is such a forgiving attitude to be achieved? Religion would advocate identification with a merciful deity that forgives all sins. Psychoanalysis would advocate the discovery of the unconscious roots of conflict that made forgiving impossible. Sonnet 35, like Sonnet 33, represents an attempt on the part of the Poet to teach himself forgiveness by using nature as a model.

In the first quatrain, the Poet attempts to persuade his partner not to feel guilty or to grieve over what he has done to the Poet, because nature itself, the sovereign power, is replete with fault. Roses have thorns, and "silver fountains," meaning fountains with a clear surface, have mud underneath the water. Clouds as well as eclipses "stain," meaning darken or blot, both moon and sun. Finally and most powerfully, canker in the fourth line refers to a canker worm that consumes a bud from within. The Poet uses four different metaphors, all taken from nature, to forgive the lover's trespasses. Since there is no evidence that the lover was grieving over what he has done to the Poet, it is likely that the Poet attempts to teach himself forgiveness.

In the second quatrain the Poet goes from nature to the nature of man. Since nothing in nature is free from fault, infidelities should be forgiven. We are not sure that many readers will be able to emulate the Poet and find comfort for infidelity in the imperfections of nature. Nor are we sure that the Poet was entirely successful in comforting himself. The contemplative attitude required to achieve this kind of objectivity is not usually available to wounded and jealous lovers. The sonnet can be read as an attempt to come to terms with the imperfection that many love relationships have to endure.

The second quatrain contains a genuine insight. The Poet has realized that the metaphor of nature's imperfection has turned into self-accusation. He realizes that his technique of self-soothing forgiveness and his excusing the lover by making metaphors may have authorized the Young Man to go on trespassing. This is expressed in line 6 as "authorizing thy trespass with compare." The Poet continues to accuse himself. He has used "self corrupting salving," that is, a medicine that corrupted him while soothing the pain of the lover's transgression. Line 9 is of special interest because the Poet realizes that the lover is the more sensual of the two, while he himself was trying to examine the transgressions logically. This is expressed as "I bring in sense." This rational approach forced him to become the lover's advocate, when in fact he was the injured party. The Poet realizes that he was arguing against himself. In contemporary psychological vocabulary, we would understand that such an approach is a sign of unconscious guilt transformed into a masochistic tendency. Through a masochistic reversal, he who should have been the accuser became the partner's advocate. As long as the Poet was trying to forgive the lover's trespasses, he drew upon nature for metaphors. But now that he is accusing himself, the scene shifts to a court of law:

> Thy adverse party is thy advocate,
> And 'gainst my self a lawful plea commence

Only humans can accuse themselves. Nature offers no metaphors for self-blame.

The inner conflict of the Poet arises from the juxtaposition of the wish to exonerate and the realization that he has cause to feel injured. The metaphor of civil war in line 12 is Shakespeare's poetic conceptualization of what we call intra-psychic conflict, conceived long before Freudian psychology had made us familiar with this term. The Poet also realizes that by going over to the side of the Young Man who injured him, he became an accessory to his behavior, again metaphorically. He cooperated with the "sweet thief" who robs him.

Within 14 lines, four insights are presented. First, the Poet calls upon nature to help him forgive the infidelities of his lover. Second, exoneration turns into a self-accusation. Third, the Poet becomes aware of the civil war within himself, between his love and his hate. Fourth, the Poet recognizes his own contribution to the infidelities of his partner. Only one of the anthologies we consulted selected this poem. We conclude that a remarkable description of inner conflict did not result in a popular appeal.

SONNET 86

Was it the proud full sail of his great verse,
Bound for the prize of all too precious you,
That did my ripe thoughts in my brain inhearse,
Making their tomb the womb wherein they grew?
Was it his spirit, by spirits taught to write
Above a mortal pitch, that struck me dead?
No, neither he, nor his compeers by night
Giving him aid, my verse astonished.
He, nor that affable familiar ghost
Which nightly gulls him with intelligence,
As victors of my silence cannot boast;
I was not sick of any fear from thence:
    But when your countenance fill'd up his line,
    Then lack'd I matter; that enfeebl'd mine.

Sonnet 86 is the last and most popular sonnet in the series of the so-called rival poet sonnets, having been selected by three of the six anthologies. Its theme, jealousy, stimulated Shakespeare to write one of his great plays, *Othello*. As is often the case, a sonnet is written to bring about a resolution of two contradictory emotions. On one hand, the Poet feels confident in his power to meet any competition by the rival poet. On the other hand, he feels inhibited by the presence of the rival poet. We have to wait until the couplet to learn that it was not the excellence of the rival that subdued the Poet's capacity, but the fact that the lover or, in this case, the benefactor, derived pleasure from the rival's poem. The poem ends on a subtle distinction: neither rivalry nor jealousy created the working inhibition, but only the fact that the Poet cannot tolerate that the countenance of the lover filled up the rival's lines. The sonnet conveys both the Poet's self-confidence and his utter dependence on the "countenance," or face, of the lover. When the lover looks elsewhere for satisfaction, the Poet becomes enfeebled. Vendler has pointed out the echoes among "full" in the first line, "affable" in the 9th, "fear" in the 12th, "fill'd" in the 13th and "enfeebl'd" in the 14th.

The sonnet contains two words that the contemporary reader cannot be expected to know: "inhearse" in line 3, meaning to shut up into a hearse (it is the only place in Shakespeare's work that this word appears) and "gulls" in line 10, meaning to trick with false information, here used as a verb but familiar to us as the adjective gullible.

The Poet compares the rival's poetry to a "proud full sail" bound for the prize of capturing the "all too precious" Young Man. We know that the "proud full sail" represented a proud pregnant woman, to Shakespeare. By implication, therefore, the lover impregnated the rival poet and the result is the rival's poem. The Poet is asking if this competition created his writer's block. The inhibition itself is expressed in line 3's metaphor, "my ripe thoughts in my brain inhearse." The pregnancy image is extended as the Poet thinks of his thoughts as "ripening," but instead of being born, the inhibition "inhearses" these thoughts. This analogy of birth and death is stated even more fiercely in the fourth line, where the nursing womb becomes the tomb of the poems he wished to write. Equating the rhyming opposites womb and tomb with each other evokes a shudder. Shakespeare used the idea in *Romeo and Juliet:*

> The earth that's nature's mother is her tomb;
> What is her burying grave that is her womb (II.iii.9-10).

In the case of Sonnet 86 the unconscious message conveyed is that the two rivals, like sails impregnated by the wind, were made symbolically pregnant by the "all too precious you," but the Poet did not deliver the poem.

We have inferred from the language of several other poems that the Poet sometimes regards his ability to write poems in praise of his lover as a successful way to compete with women, because his poems offer an immortality that is more secure than the extension of life beyond the grave which a woman can offer by having the Young Man's child. The imagery of Sonnet 86 lends much support to this idea.

The second quatrain is given to another metaphor. The Poet assumes that the rival has at his command spirits that teach him how to write "Above a mortal pitch," meaning at a height not obtainable by mere mortals. The Poet asks whether this had "struck me dead?" He answers: neither the rival Poet nor his nocturnal companions and advisors evoked enough awe in him to kill his desire or ability to work.

The term "affable familiar ghost" in line 9, meaning civil or courteous ghost, has been interpreted by scholars as a reference to Chapman, one of the chief candidates for the rival poet, who claimed to be on a familiar relationship with Homer's ghost. In the tenth line the Poet claims that this ghost deceives the rival with faulty intelligence. In line 11 the rival and the ghost are not entitled to boast that they were victorious in silencing the poet. The Poet tells us that at no time was he awed by the competition, but what he could not stand, and developed a working inhibition over, was that the man he loved turned his "countenance" to the rival. Then the Poet became incapable of writing poetry. The word "countenance" is of biblical origin, for it is God that turns his countenance upon us when he gives us his blessing and gives us peace. In *Hamlet* we find the paternal ghost has "A countenance more in sorrow than in anger (I.ii.232)."

This sonnet, like Sonnet 33, powerfully mirrors a baby's dependence on the expression on its mother's face. If we follow the sonnets in the order in which they were printed, we will note that after Sonnet 86 the relationship between Poet and lover becomes more strained. The relationship seems never to have recovered from the blow of the benefactor's countenance turning to a rival.

SONNET 93

So shall I live, supposing thou art true,
Like a deceived husband; so love's face
May still seem love to me, though altered new,
Thy looks with me, thy heart in other place;
For there can live no hatred in thine eye,
Therefore in that I cannot know thy change.
In many's looks, the false heart's history
Is writ in moods and frowns and wrinkles strange;
But heaven in thy creation did decree
That in thy face sweet love should ever dwell;
Whate'er thy thoughts or thy heart's workings be,
Thy looks should nothing thence but sweetness tell.
   How like Eve's apple doth thy beauty grow,
   If thy sweet virtue answer not thy show.

Sonnets 93 and 94 are thematically connected, but they are also psychologically related in a disturbing way. The Poet suspects that the lover has changed, that he no longer loves the Poet, but that his features do not betray the change. This sonnet is disturbing because it raises the possibility that the whole change alluded to has only taken place within the Poet's own world of feeling, and that no change has taken place in the lover. As poems, the two are very different. Sonnet 94 has been selected by five of the six anthologies, a very high rating, and Sonnet 93 by none of them. Since they are thematically connected, the fact that one was preferred over the other raises interesting questions.

The Poet suspects that his lover no longer loves him and asks himself whether he should, like a deceived husband, pretend that nothing happened and accept "love's face." What is meaningful to us, but probably unconscious to the Poet, is that he sees himself as the deceived husband and he sees the lover as the faithless wife. There is a hint of paranoia in the fourth line: the Young Man's looks are still with the Poet but his heart is elsewhere. Thus once more the difference between "looks" and "heart" are used as an expression of what appears to the outside world and what is really so. We are not sure we can trust the Poet's capacity to read reality correctly; the Poet may be obsessed by his suspicion. The second quatrain explains, in terms flattering to the Young Man, that the change of heart does not register on his face. "For there can live no hatred in thine eye." Other people's eyes, frowns and grimaces betray their "false heart's history."

In the third quatrain, the praise of the Young Man is resumed. When the Young Man was created, it was decreed that "in thy face sweet love should ever dwell." Regardless of what he feels or thinks his face will never change. His looks "should nothing thence but sweetness tell." In other poems the Poet has rejoiced in the fact that Young Man's face does not change with age and in Sonnet 94 he admires him for being the "lord and owner of his face." In this poem, these admirable qualities combine to make the Poet unable to trust what he sees expressed on the face of the Young Man.

In the couplet the Poet compares himself to the biblical Adam, the deceived husband, and his lover's beauty is compared to Eve's apple, which was beautiful but treacherous. In the last line the Poet is unsure of the truth, but says that the Young Man's beauty will become more like Eve's apple if he is unfaithful to the Poet, expressed as "thy virtue" not matching "thy show." The Poet thus compares his lover's infidelity to the Fall of Man, the greatest catastrophe in the history of the world.

SONNET 94

That they have pow'r to hurt and will do none,
That do not do the thing they most do show,
Who, moving others, are themselves as stone,
Unmovèd, cold, and to temptation slow;
They rightly do inherit heaven's graces
And husband nature's riches from expense;
They are the lords and owners of their faces,
Others but stewards of their excellence.
The summer's flower is to the summer sweet,
Though to itself it only live and die;
But if that flower with base infection meet,
The basest weed outbraves his dignity:
    For sweetest things turn sourest by their deeds;
    Lilies that fester smell far worse than weeds.

Sonnet 94 is one of Shakespeare's most popular sonnets; it was cited in five of the six anthologies. The sonnet is unusual because the break between the first two quatrains and the third is greater than usual and the couplet carries far more weight than is customary. In this sonnet, men who "are themselves as stone" replace the Young Man of Sonnet 93. The greater appeal of this sonnet, by comparison to the earlier one, is in our opinion explained by the fact that in this poem the Poet no longer complains but praises those men, including his lover, who remain "Unmovèd, cold, and to temptation slow." If in Sonnet 62 the Poet condemned self-love, Sonnet 94 is a subtle glorification of self-love.

In the first two quatrains, the Poet heaps praise on men who do not express what they feel. He does so for two reasons: first, because they "husband nature's riches from expense." By not expressing what they feel, they keep their feelings to (and for) themselves, and do not spend the riches with which nature has endowed them on loving someone else. In line 7 they are praised for being "lords and owners of their faces," meaning that they do not give away what they feel. In line 8 we are told that their excellence makes others their stewards, which we might interpret as meaning that their narcissism makes others serve them.

If the two sonnets are read in succession, these men are praised for the very character trait the lover was condemned for in the previous sonnet. A contradictory attitude is at the very core of ambivalence. In this case, however, the contradiction can be reconciled as follows: insofar as the Poet feels that he cannot trust the lover because his face does not register his feelings, the Poet hates the deception; but insofar as he admires this capacity as a sign of independence, even if this means independence from the Poet himself, he praises this capacity as a kind of superior self-sufficiency.

The third quatrain introduces a radical change. The unmoved men are compared to "summer's flower," who, like these men, "live and die" only for themselves. Even so, these flowers contribute to the "summer's sweet." In line 11 the Poet's anger at the self-sufficiency of his lover breaks through. If the summer's flower should "with base infection meet," the "basest" or humblest weed will "outbrave" or surpass the flower in dignity. The last line—"Lilies that fester smell far worse than weeds"—is the most powerful metaphor in the whole poem, meaning that a fault in the best of men appears more glaring than in the mediocre man. However, critics of Shakespeare have discovered that the metaphor and even the line were not original. The metaphor of the lily, as Booth has pointed out, was taken from the Sermon on the Mount:

> Learne, how the lilies of the field do growe: they labour not, nether spinne,

> Yet…even Solomon in all his glorie was not arrayed like one of these.

According to Duncan-Jones, the last line appears in the anonymous *The Reign of King Edward III,* published in 1596. The Countess of Salisbury rebuffs the king's sexual advances with: "Darke night seems darker by the lightning flash;/Lillies that fester smell far worse than weeds (Booth p. 308 and Jones p. 94)."

The couplet combines the three quatrains. In the couplet, "deeds" rhymes with "weeds," but deeds can also be understood as the plural of "do," which appears several times in the body of the poem: once in the first line, three times in the second, and once in the fifth.

Vendler emphasized the relationship between "power" in the first line and "flower" in lines 9 and 11. In Vendler's analysis, the third quatrain moves from the world of men to the vegetable kingdom with the contrast between weeds and flowers replacing the contrast between two types of men. The couplet, for her, remains split between the two realms. Shakespeare's commentators have complained that this sonnet is one of the most enigmatic ones. In our view, we can understand it if we keep in mind the Poet's ambivalence about self-love as well as his need to keep all aggression repressed. We can discern the Poet's aggression in the most powerful accusing metaphor: "Lilies that fester smell far worse than weeds."

SONNETS WHERE THE POET
TEACHES HIMSELF TO ACCEPT SEPARATION

SONNET 39

O how thy worth with manners may I sing,
When thou art all the better part of me?
What can mine own praise to mine own self bring,
And what is't but mine own, when I praise thee?
Even for this, let us divided live,
And our dear love lose name of single one,
That by this separation I may give
That due to thee which thou deserv'st alone.
O absence, what a torment wouldst thou prove,
Were it not thy sour leisure gave sweet leave
To entertain the time with thoughts of love,
Which time and thoughts so sweetly dost deceive,
    And that thou teachest how to make one twain
    By praising him here who doth hence remain.

Sonnet 39 cannot be called a significant poem. Its central idea is banal, its metaphors lack luster and are strikingly unoriginal. It has not been selected in any anthology. In spite of these defects we find it worth reproducing because in it we can see how narcissism and love can be at war with each other and how narcissism eventually wins over love.

In this sonnet, the Poet is attempting to defend himself against the pain of separation. In the first quatrain he tried, not very convincingly, to claim that separation is necessary between the two because otherwise the praise of the other is only self-praise. The third quatrain proclaims that absence can be made tolerable by entertaining thoughts of love. What can "thoughts of love" be except fantasies? The Poet therefore tries to substitute fantasies to compensate him for the reality of separation. The question of whether the Elizabethans were convinced by this sonnet that the Poet and lover must be separated, because only when they are twain and not one can the Poet praise his lover, is problematic, but contemporary readers are not likely to agree.

Below the surface, we discern another conflict: the Poet has argued that in a state of oneness, all praise is self-praise. True enough. Is praise so important? Is not the very centrality of praise a sign that the love relationship has deteriorated? The Poet seems to have sacrificed the relationship so that praise can be bestowed. If praise is indeed so crucial, what is being celebrated in this sonnet is the victory of narcissism over love.

In the first two lines, the Poet asks by what means and in with what manners, meaning in conventionally acceptable ways, can he praise the lover's worth. Since the Poet and the lover are one and the lover is the conventional "better" part of the Poet, to praise the lover is only self-praise. When we read this poem, we feel that such thoughts would never occur to those deeply in love, and that they can come only when the ardor of love has abated.

The third quatrain is even further removed from any passion. Absence could have proven to be a torment, but fortunately "sour" or bitter leisure can be transformed into "sweet leave" to "entertain the time with thoughts of love." Lovers who can tolerate separation in this way and prefer fantasy to the reality of being together do not appear to us as being in love. Suffering when separated has often been taken to be an experience at the very core of love. In the couplet, the Poet credits the lover as teaching him "to make one twain," that is, to break up the sense of oneness of the lovers, and assure the separate existence of the lover through the Poet's praise, which is in turn based on separation.

Many commentators have mentioned *Antony and Cleopatra* (1.3.102-3), when Antony, leaving, says to the queen: "That thou residing here goest yet with me, and I hence fleeing here remain with thee." In our reading, the sonnet and Antony are at opposite poles. The Poet affirms their separation, but Antony leaves affirming their union.

SONNET 49

Against that time (if ever that time come)
When I shall see thee frown on my defects,
When as thy love hath cast his utmost sum,
Called to that audit by advised respects,
Against that time when thou shalt strangely pass,
And scarcely greet me with that sun thine eye,
When love converted from the thing it was
Shall reasons find of settled gravity;
Against that time do I ensconce me here
Within the knowledge of mine own desert,
And this my hand, against my self uprear,
To guard the lawful reasons on thy part,
    To leave poor me, thou hast the strength of laws,
    Since why to love, I can allege no cause.

When a person is traumatized by a previous separation, he or she will anticipate the return of the trauma, and often without intending to do so bring the separation about. In Sonnet 49 the return of the trauma is anticipated with such certainty and vividness that we are left wondering whether the Poet will not bring about the very separation he fears so vividly. The situation is familiar in the psychoanalyses of neurotic men and women, when the fear of being deserted is so great that one prefers to bring the separation about actively rather than fear its coming passively. It is also possible to read the anticipated calamity as belated prophecy, namely that the calamity has already happened.

The first and the second quatrains are written like prophecies; the Poet anticipates a time when he will be deserted. In the third quatrain we are told how he will react to this desertion. He will be left bereft and helpless, and will not blame the lover.

Not all commentators put "(if ever that time come)" in parentheses. With or without the parentheses, the Poet would not have phrased the first line the way he did if he did not in some way have the insight that this preparation may not have been necessary. The second, third and fourth lines tell us what the Poet fears: the lover will, at some future date, frown upon the Poet's defects. The Poet compares love to money and loving to a business deal, perhaps a criticism of the character of the man the Poet loves. Love is seen as an investment and the lover will conclude that he already "cast his utmost sum," meaning that he has already invested the maximum that he should in the relationship. The lover is not expected to be rash in bringing about a separation but to conduct an "audit," or careful evaluation. The term "advised respects" emphasizes the sober nature of the calculations as to whether the relationship is worth continuing.

In the second quatrain the Poet has dropped the attempt to speak of love in monetary terms. He now anticipates the time when the lover will "strangely pass" him by "and scarcely greet [him] with that sun thine eye." By evoking the equation of eyes with the sun the Poet lets us know that he is still in love. For readers familiar with these sonnets, the association between the lover's eyes and the alchemy that the sun can bring about when it "kisses the meadows green" is so familiar that contrary to the dire prophecy in this sonnet, we surmise that the Poet is still in love. In line 7, the theme of the sonnet is resumed: "Love is converted from "the thing it was" and is now under scrutiny of "settled gravity," meaning unemotional evaluation.

The third quatrain opens with the Poet's wish to ensconce himself, meaning to establish himself firmly, to fortify himself, to dig in his heels. In *The Rape of Lucrece* Shakespeare used the phrase "And therein so ensconc'd his secret evil (line 1515)." The Poet is resolved not to let the lover affect his own self-esteem. However, in line 11 the masochism of the Poet gains the upper hand. He will raise his hand as a witness in court, testifying against himself and siding with the lover's criticism. Masochism also triumphs in the couplet: the lover has the law on his side when he decides to break off the relationship because the Poet can find no reason why the relationship should go on, or even why he should be loved at all. One can read this sonnet as an interpersonal statement between the Poet and his lover, but one can also read it as the Poet's inner dialogue on the perils of a commitment to loving, and thus see masochism as the enemy of love. The sonnet was selected by one anthology.

SONNET 56

Sweet love, renew thy force; be it not said
Thy edge should blunter be than appetite,
Which but today by feeding is allayed,
Tomorrow sharpened in his former might;
So, love, be thou; although today thou fill
Thy hungry eyes even till they wink with fullness,
Tomorrow see again, and do not kill
The spirit of love with a perpetual dullness;
Let this sad interim like the ocean be
Which parts the shore, where two contracted new
Come daily to the banks, that when they see
Return of love, more blessed may be the view;
    Or call it winter, which being full of care
    Makes summer's welcome thrice more wished, more rare.

In Sonnet 56 the Poet deals with an anxiety of loving that, to our knowledge, has not been dealt with elsewhere in the poetry of love. This sonnet has not been selected by any of the six anthologies, which we take to mean that is was not an anxiety that many readers share. The sonnet deals with the anxiety of love ending in the unhappy state of satiety. That this anxiety meant much to Shakespeare gains support from the following passage from *Venus and Adonis,* in which the goddess of love promises Adonis:

I'll smother thee with kisses
And yet not cloy thy lips with loath'd satiety,
But rather famish them amid their plenty (lines 18-20),

One of the highest compliments that could be given to a woman was given to Cleopatra:

other women cloy
The appetites they feed, but she makes hungry
Where most she satisfies (*Antony and Cleopatra*, II.iii.242-244).

Sonnet 56 can be read as a secular prayer to love, asking that it not depart. "Sweet love" could be addressed to the lover, but also abstractly to Amor, the god of love, to not desert the Poet and his lover. It could also be read as a plea for the renewal of love which has already begun to fade. The specific sexual anxiety is best expressed in lines 7 and 8: "Do not kill/the spirit of love with perpetual dullness."

Something unspecified happened to the lovers that alarms the Poet; their love lost force and is in need of renewal. In the second through fourth lines, two comparisons are introduced, that of the knife and that of appetite. The word knife is not mentioned but the term is implied in "be it not said/ Thy edge should blunter be than appetite." Sexual hunger is implicitly compared with a knife whose edge can be blunted. In the third line this comparison is dropped and the Poet speaks directly about appetite, which can be allayed by feeding today but tomorrow can be relied upon to be "sharpened" and returned to "his former might."

In the second quatrain, the hunger is transferred to the eyes. They can "wink with fullness" one day and tomorrow see again, meaning becoming hungry once more.

In the third quatrain, there is a shift in metaphor to the relationship between waves and shore. This relationship is described by the Poet as "more blessed" since ocean and shore renew their contact daily, a highly original metaphor. Ocean and shore, in the Poet's imagination, never reach satiety and are therefore in a perpetually alive love relationship. The waves meet the shore continuously with the same energy and without the danger of dullness because tides are always changing. The Poet uses the ever-vital relationship between waves and shore to help them overcome the "sad interim" of the dullness that has set into their love relationship. If the waves never tire, the Poet argues, the lovers too should not succumb to satiety. The couplet is given to a more familiar metaphor, in which winter, "full of care/Makes summer's welcome thrice more wished, more rare." Like the seasons of the year, the lovers should be able to renew the force of their love.

SONNET 75

So are you to my thoughts as food to life,
Or as sweet seasoned showers to the ground;
And for the peace of you I hold such strife
As 'twixt a miser and his wealth is found:
Now proud as an enjoyer, and anon
Doubting the filching age will steal his treasure;
Now counting best to be with you alone,
Then bettered that the world may see my pleasure;
Sometime all full with feasting on your sight,
And by and by clean starved for a look,
Possessing or pursuing no delight
Save what is had, or must from you be took.
    Thus do I pine and surfeit day by day,
    Or gluttoning on all, or all away.

Auden was the only anthologist to include Sonnet 75 among those he selected. We share his view. The sonnet describes well the anxieties associated with loving. Psychologically speaking, Sonnet 75 is an important poem, because it describes in poetic terms a special kind of unhappiness experienced by lovers if their own store of narcissism is so depleted that all they can do is wait upon the lover's return. Even when he comes back, happiness does not return because of anxiety that the lover will again be taken away.

This sonnet describes an inner conflict of the Poet in love. The Poet admits his dependence on the lover, but on the other hand he is afraid that if they are together too often they will blunt the edge of their love. In the third line the Poet admits that for the "peace of you," that is, in order to be happy with his lover, the Poet will have to "hold such strife," or in current language, create such inner conflict "As 'twixt a miser and his wealth is found." Sonnet 52 also employs the metaphor of the miser and introduces a new term "seldom pleasure;" in that sonnet the miser can look at his "up-locked treasure" only at rare intervals, fearing to blunt "the fine point of seldom pleasure." We see that here in Sonnet 75 the paranoia is stronger; the miser can allow himself to be "proud as an enjoyer" only seldom,

"Doubting the filching age will steal his treasure." In other words, if the Poet permits the two of them to be together more frequently, someone else will filch the lover away.

In line 7 the Poet feels like the miser "counting best to be with you alone." This line contains an expressed dyadic wish and a repressed exhibitionistic wish that asserts itself in lines 8 and 9. In line 8 the Poet feels he will be "bettered," or feel even better, if the "world may see my pleasure." When this happens the dyadic wish expressed in line 7 is lost in favor of the repressed exhibitionistic wish for others to admire their relationship. Line 9 reinforces this new hope. The Poet now desires to be seen or looked upon at his pleasure, and what the onlooker will see is the Poet "feasting on your sight." Feasting is usually connected with eating, but in this sonnet, the eyes do the feasting. The sexual urge has been transformed into looking. The Poet realizes that his voyeuristic wish to look has become transformed into the opposite, the wish to exhibit.

Seeking but not finding a compromise, the Poet expresses his inner conflict between longing and satiety by contrasting the word "feasting" in the last quatrain with the word "surfeit" in the couplet. This surfeit is then condemned by the term "gluttoning" in the last line. Psychologically speaking, the last quatrain is the most complex. The Poet complains that sometimes he feels oversated while at other times he feels "clean starved for a look." Both surfeit and starvation are experienced as suffering.

In line 12 the Poet tells us that both possessing and pursuing offer him no delight except what he can take from the lover, expressed as "Save what is had, or must from you be took." This introduces another conflict: he is faced with the choice of what is available to him, and what becomes available only when it is taken away from the lover against his wishes. Therefore the Poet must live in the paradoxical state of both pining away and surfeit expressed in the couplet, "or all away."

SONNETS ACCEPTING THE END
OF THE RELATIONSHIP

SONNET 87

Farewell, thou art too dear for my possessing,
And like enough thou know'st thy estimate;
The charter of thy worth gives thee releasing:
My bonds in thee are all determinate.
For how do I hold thee but by thy granting,
And for that riches where is my deserving?
The cause of this fair gift in me is wanting,
And so my patent back again is swerving.
Thy self thou gav'st, thy own worth then not knowing,
Or me, to whom thou gav'st it, else mistaking;
So thy great gift, upon misprision growing,
Comes home again, on better judgment making,
    Thus have I had thee as a dream doth flatter,
    In sleep a king, but waking no such matter.

Sonnet 87 is among Shakespeare's most popular sonnets; five out of the six anthologists selected it. Letting go of a lover one still loves is difficult. The popularity of the sonnet suggests that many readers find solace in the way the Poet responded to this painful moment.

"Farewell, thou art too dear for my possessing" has a double meaning. The word "dear" supported by the word "estimate" in line 2 and "worth" in line 3 implies that dear is meant as expensive. But unconsciously another message may be transmitted. "Dear" could also mean I love you more than I am permitted to love, and you have become too dear in the sense of too precious or too important for my possession. If this interpretation is accepted, then Shakespeare, at least metaphorically speaking, realized that for him when love that increased beyond a certain point it became urgent to break the relationship off. In psychoanalytic work, we often discover that men and women have a limit beyond which they are not permitted to love and if that limit is exceeded, the relationship has to be terminated. The word "estimate" and the phrase "gives thee releasing" re-introduce the world of commerce and contractual obligation. The word "determinate" in line 4 is also taken from the world of commerce, meaning that all claims to ownership have expired. In Sonnet 13 there is a similar comparison of love to commerce in "that beauty which you hold in lease/Find no determination."

In the second, more obsequious quatrain, the Poet feels that he must grant the lover release because he does not deserve this relationship. The Poet sees their love as entirely granted by the lover. The Poet cannot find any reason for deserving the love he had. In line 8 the language of commerce is resumed; the patent he enjoyed is "swerving" back, meaning reverting back to the lover, implying that love, like money, can be quantified and refunded. The term "patent," in Shakespeare's day, had almost the same meaning it has for us, namely, license and exclusive possession. The self-deprecation in the second quatrain implies considerable masochism in the relationship.

In the third quatrain, the masochism is even stronger. It was only because the lover did not know his own worth that he entered into their relationship. Line 10 further increases the differences between the two. The love the lover gave the Poet grew upon "misprision," and was the result of a mistake or false estimate. In line 12, the Poet takes the side against himself and deems the separation "better judgment."

The couplet really drives home the disillusionment and masochism of the Poet. He wants to relegate the whole relationship to the realm of a dream that flatters, that is, beguiles with false illusions, as if the whole relationship had never really taken place. It was but a dream, with himself awakening from the dream of love and realizing it was all nothing but a mistake.

In this sonnet, as in *Midsummer Night's Dream,* Shakespeare once more equates love with dreaming, and awakening with realizing that the union that lovers desire was an illusion. Psychologically speaking, Sonnet 87 is a striking confirmation of the fact that the self can be depleted in a love relationship, particularly in a narcissistic love.

It has been assumed that the great difference in rank was the cause of the separation. In this sonnet the Poet adopts a deferential attitude towards the man he loves, finding no value in himself and saying he deserves to be abandoned. In psychoanalytic terms the Poet suffers from a narcissistic deficiency, that is, an insufficient amount of self-love, which makes him feel that his abandonment is deserved. Because of the difference in rank, the Poet releases the lover from love's bondage. In this sonnet, as well as in the next, one cannot fail but recognize a masochistic element to the Poet's love. Many love relationships transgressed social boundaries; a homosexual love was particularly frowned upon, regardless of class distinction.

When we analyzed Sonnet 62 in chapter two, we emphasized self-love as setting limits on the capacity to love. Sonnet 87 teaches the opposite lesson: love can deplete the necessary narcissistic reservoir, and when that happens the person feels unworthy of being loved. Both narcissistic depletion and excess self-love are inimical to a capacity to love.

SONNET 88

When thou shalt be disposed to set me light
And place my merit in the eye of scorn,
Upon thy side, against myself, I'll fight,
And prove thee virtuous, though thou art forsworn:
With mine own weakness being best acquainted,
Upon thy part I can set down a story
Of faults concealed, wherein I am attainted,
That thou, in losing me, shall win much glory;
And I by this will be a gainer too,
For bending all my loving thoughts on thee,
The injuries that to myself I do,
Doing thee vantage, double vantage me:
    Such is my love, to thee I so belong,
    That for thy right myself will bear all wrong.

As in Sonnets 49 and 87, the Poet once more felt the need to protect himself against the time when his lover would scarcely greet him and strangely pass him by. Sonnet 88 shows the same submission towards the lover, the same censorship of any anger, and the same siding with the aggressor as we saw in Sonnet 87, giving these sonnets their masochistic cast.

"When thou shalt be disposed to set me light"—when you will be inclined to put little value on me—is how Sonnet 88 opens, indicating that the Poet has no doubt this will happen. The Poet assures the lover that he will fight on the side of the rejecter against himself. The fourth line, as Vendler pointed out, contains the crucial phrase "And prove thee virtuous, though thou art forsworn," that is, the Poet will prove the lover virtuous even though he knows that the lover was unfaithful to the Poet.

In the second quatrain, the self-accusation of the Poet continues. He is well acquainted with his own faults, and experiences the break in their relationship from the lover's point of view. The Poet goes on to castigate himself, and suggests that the lover will "win much glory" by "losing me." The logic of the next line is tortured. The Poet too will gain, but how? At this point, his masochism reaches the highest point. He will gain because at the moment of desertion he will be "bending all my loving thoughts on thee" and thus do himself injuries. The couplet "Such is my love, to thee I so belong/That for thy right myself will bear all wrong" can be cited as a declaration of masochistic love.

The difference between Sonnets 87 and 88 deserves our interest. The two sonnets are similar in content and their masochism is of similar strength. Why then was 87 chosen by four anthologies and 88 by none? Sonnet 87 is a sonnet of active renunciation. The Poet does not feel he deserves the lover's love; the whole love relationship was based on a mistake, a false dream. In Sonnet 88, the masochism extends over this whole sonnet. It lacks the tension and therefore the beauty of Sonnet 87.

SONNET 90

Then hate me when thou wilt, if ever, now,
Now, while the world is bent my deeds to cross,
Join with the spite of fortune, make me bow,
And do not drop in for an after-loss.
Ah, do not, when my heart hath 'scaped this sorrow,
Come in the rearward of a conquered woe;
Give not a windy night a rainy morrow,
To linger out a purposed overthrow.
If thou wilt leave me, do not leave me last,
When other petty griefs have done their spite;
But in the onset come, so shall I taste
At first the very worst of fortune's might;
  And other strains of woe, which now seem woe,
  Compared with loss of thee, will not seem so.

Sonnet 90 is another sonnet in which the Poet anticipates the end of the love relationship. In this sonnet, the Poet believes that he can at least choose the time of the breakup. He asks the lover to do so sooner rather than later, with the mistaken belief that it will hurt less.

The music of the poem is determined by the word "now" in the first and second lines, "now" in the third, "woe" in the sixth, "morrow" in the seventh, "throw" in the eighth and "thou" in the ninth. The final couplet uses these words three times, with two occurrences of "woe" and one of "now." What remains ringing in our ears is "now woe," making the sonnet one arc of lamentation.

In the first line the Poet asks the lover to hate him now, when the world is at cruelly oppressing the Poet's wishes. With considerable masochism, he asks the lover to "join with the spite of fortune" and make the Poet bow, meaning that at the very time when the Poet is abandoned by fortune, the lover should desert him also. This grandiose debasement is the effect of the inversion of self-esteem. We saw it when the Poet compared himself to Christ in Sonnet 34 and here when he claims the whole world is against him. In the fourth line, the Poet asks that the lover not come to him after other sorrows are over, wonderfully expressed as "do not drop in for an after-loss." The Poet asks that the separation should not take place after he escaped this sorrow, that is, after he had already begun to heal. In lines 5 and 6 is the implied accusation that the lover could be cruel and inflict new pain when the Poet was already healing. This is expressed as coming in the "rearward of a conquered woe." "Give not a windy night a rainy morrow," is a beautiful and memorable metaphor, even if the rest of the sonnet has been forgotten.

Fearing the coming breakup, the Poet may well help to bring it about. He is unable to fully suppress the burgeoning anger and bitterness that seeps into the last quatrain and couplet. Other "petty griefs" have mutated ominously into "other strains of woe." The sonnet appears in two of the six anthologies.

SONNETS EXPRESSING THE AMBIVALENCE IN THE RELATIONSHIP

SONNET 95

How sweet and lovely dost thou make the shame
Which like a canker in the fragrant rose
Doth spot the beauty of thy budding name:
O in what sweets dost thou thy sins enclose!
That tongue that tells the story of thy days,
Making lascivious comments on thy sport,
Cannot dispraise; but in a kind of praise,
Naming thy name, blesses an ill report.
O what a mansion have those vices got,
Which for their habitation chose out thee,
Where beauty's veil doth cover every blot,
And all things turns to fair that eyes can see!
  Take heed, dear heart, of this large privilege;
  The hardest knife ill used doth lose his edge.

When one is angry with someone whom one also loves, if one wants to condemn but also to flatter, what kind of a poem will emerge? The answer could be Sonnet 95, a poem of ambivalence where love and hostility are expressed in equal measure.

The metaphor of the canker that eats the rose must have had a special appeal for Shakespeare, expressing for him the hungry nature of death. In Sonnet 35 he spoke of a "loathsome canker" that "lives in sweetest bud." In Sonnet 70 "For canker vice the sweetest buds doth love" appears, and, more ominously, in Sonnet 99 we find the line "A vengeful canker eat him up to death." The last example shows most clearly the cannibalistic drive behind the frequent use of this metaphor. In this sonnet, the canker is the shame, here left unspecified, that makes a spot on the "budding name" of the Young Man. The choice of the word budding refers to the youth of the lover but also to the fact that cankers live "in the sweetest bud." The sins of the lover are real, but they are hidden in the Young Man's sweetness. In the second quatrain, someone is "making lascivious comments" on the Young Man's "sport;" by calling their love relationship "sport" the Poet diminishes its importance. In Sonnet 40, line 13, Shakespeare used the phrase to express the same contradictory feeling: "Lascivious grace, in whom all ill well shows."

In the couplet, the Poet warns his lover against the privileges he is taking. He suggests that even "the hardest knife ill-used," meaning used wrongly or too often, can lose its edge—a veiled reference to the fact that the Poet's love, although like the hardest knife (suggesting perhaps an erect penis), should nevertheless not be "ill used" because it might lose its edge, or erection. We recall that in Sonnet 56 the Poet used the analogy of the knife in the second line: "Thy edge should blunter be than appetite." In that sonnet, blunting the knife's edge was a metaphor for the satiation of love. What was feared as a calamity in Sonnet 56 has become, in this sonnet, the accusation that the Young Man's beauty and grace, if ill-employed, may wear out.

In this sonnet, the relationship between the body of the poem and the couplet seems strained. The warning seems to be an afterthought designed to salvage the Poet's pride. It lacks conviction. Only Untermeyer selected this sonnet.

SONNET 110

Alas 'tis true', I have gone here and there,
And made my self a motley to the view,
Gored mine own thoughts, sold cheap what is most dear,
Made old offenses of affections new.
Most true it is, that I have looked on truth
Askance and strangely: but by all above,
These blenches gave my heart another youth,
And worse essays proved thee my best of love.
Now all is done, have what shall have no end,
Mine appetite I never more will grind
On newer proof, to try an older friend,
A god in love, to whom I am confined.
    Then give me welcome, next my heaven the best,
    Even to thy pure and most most loving breast.

Psychoanalytic experience has taught us that feelings of guilt are not usually helpful in checking promiscuity. They only make the person feel less worthy and more deprived, and the anxiety and feelings of inferiority thus generated may compel the person to seek new sexual conquests to counteract the feelings of inferiority.

The first line contains a confession of promiscuity: "I have gone here and there" implies that the Poet has been disloyal in many places. The word motley in the second line refers to the colored dress of professional clowns, and therefore equates the Poet's infidelity with making a fool of himself, and conveys to us the Poet's shame. (We encounter a very different clown in *King Lear*). The phrase "gored mine own thoughts" in line 3 is a savage metaphor. The use of the word "gored" has a double meaning. It means being wounded, with special reference to the wounds bulls or wild animals can inflict, but in context with "motley" can also mean to furnish with gores, triangular pieces of cloth, creating a motley effect. In its usual meaning gored recalls Oedipus goring his own eyes. Another accusation follows—he sold cheap what was most dear to him. In line 4, "Made old offenses of affections new," the Poet reprimands himself for repeating actions he had committed earlier, perhaps in other relationships.

He accuses himself of lying. Line 7 contains a confession. His "blenches," meaning sidelong glances or disloyalties, gave him a new feeling of youth. The term "worse essays" in line 8 refers to bad deeds or mistakes, acts that only proved that his lover is "my best of love."

In line 9 the Poet promises that these disloyalties are behind him: "now all is done." "Have what shall have no end" means the lover can now have the Poet's love without fear of it ending. In line 10, the Poet promises that he will not grind, that is, sharpen, his sexual appetites. He promises not to be promiscuous just in order to test his lover's loyalty, expressed as "to try an older friend." The Poet implies that the infidelity was no more than a test of loyalty. This is an important insight, for in many promiscuous relationships the real aim of infidelity is not the new sexual experience but the arousal of the original partner's jealousy as a way of testing the strength of the love. In line 12 he will confine himself to the lover whom he calls a "god in love." The expression can be read as a worshipful attitude towards the lover; it could also be a comparison to Cupid, the god of love. "Confined" here means wholly devoted. In Sonnet 105 Shakespeare used the phrase "my verse, to constancy confined," in which the word also meant devoted. Repenting of his infidelities, the Poet asks his lover to "give me welcome." The sonnet ends with praise; the lover's breast is "pure and most most loving" and, poignantly, "next my heaven," also implying that this relationship will be indeed the Poet's last. The sonnet was chosen by one anthology.

SONNET 111

O, for my sake do you with Fortune chide,
The guilty goddess of my harmful deeds,
That did not better for my life provide
Than public means, which public manners breeds;
Thence comes it that my name receives a brand,
And almost thence my nature is subdued
To what it works in, like the dyer's hand;
Pity me, then, and wish I were renewed,
Whilst like a willing patient I will drink
Potions of eisel 'gainst my strong infection;
No bitterness that I will bitter think,
Nor double penance to correct correction.
    Pity me then, dear friend, and I assure ye,
    Even that your pity is enough to cure me.

Sonnet 111 implies that the Poet's lover belonged to a higher social stratum, and some social act left unspecified was committed by the Poet prior to the love relationship of which he is now ashamed because it may embarrass the partner. One of the dangers of falling in love, as Freud has pointed out, is that all narcissistic self-feelings flow to the partner. That may leave the lover idealized and the self impoverished. This seems to have happened to the Poet in Sonnet 111. It is a painful sonnet to read, because being in love has so lowered the Poet's self-esteem.

When lovers form a unit and create a new relationship, their ties to the world beyond their union undergo transformation. Ties to parents, siblings, friends, and the whole surrounding world change and have to be reworked. When, for psychological reasons, the other ties remain too strong, this reworking cannot fully take place; one then can expect difficulties in the love relationship. We often hear one partner complain that the other has remained too attached to his or her original family. When the lovers belong to a different social strata, different race or different religion, the realignment that must take place can be a painful one. Romeo and Juliet have become the classic example of a couple whose love takes place in opposition to parental hostility.

In the Poet's mind, the lover chides Fortune as a kind of goddess responsible for the Poet's "harmful deeds." These deeds bring dishonor on the Poet's lover, or his patron. The Poet seems ashamed of his "public means," which is probably a reference to his behavior as an actor. These "public means," in turn, bred in him "public manners," a likely reference to the vulgar behavior of actors who were often assumed to be more promiscuous than members of other professions. He asks his lover to excuse his character for being overwhelmed by his profession. In line 7, the Poet compares the effect of his profession on him as equivalent to what happens to a dyer's hand, which becomes discolored by the continuous use of dyes. It is an original and powerful metaphor for the effect a profession eventually has on the formation of character. Based on this line, W. H. Auden called his inaugural lecture as professor of poetry at Oxford University "The Dyer's Hand," an apt reference to some characteristics acquired in the pursuit of poetry as a profession that had become a permanent part of his identity, marking him for life.

In the last quatrain, the Poet compares himself to a willing patient who will drink potions of eisel, meaning vinegar, a remedy that was considered beneficial in Elizabethan times. The Poet ends, however, with the declaration that the lover's or patron's pity is all he needs for his cure. A masochistic note of submission enters this sonnet, making it difficult to enjoy it or even empathize with the Poet. The sonnet seems so private that we have difficulty in identifying ourselves with its obsequious tone. No anthology cited it.

SONNET 120

That you were once unkind befriends me now,
And for that sorrow, which I then did feel,
Needs must I under my transgression bow,
Unless my nerves were brass or hammered steel:
For if you were by my unkindness shaken,
As I by yours, you've passed a hell of time,
And I, a tyrant, have no leisure taken
To weigh how once I suffered in your crime.
O that our night of woe might have remembered
My deepest sense how hard true sorrow hits,
And soon to you, as you to me then, tendered
The humble salve which wounded bosoms fits!
    But that your trespass now becomes a fee;
    Mine ransoms yours, and yours must ransom me.

A major quarrel has taken place; it was a culmination point of sorrows the two inflicted upon each other. They were both guilty of transgressions at different times and the Poet may well have been the first offender, but now the Poet is asking that each one forgive the other.

We follow Vendler's lead in assigning "our night of woe" in line 9 to the central position in this sonnet. The central word is "woe;" it is anticipated in the first line by "now," by "sorrow" in line 2, and "bow" in line 3. The content of the poem is mirrored in the verbal structure. "You" and "I" alternate, with "you" in the first line and "I" in the second and third, "you" in the fifth, "I" and "you've" and "yours" in the sixth, "I" in lines 7 and 8. Then finally, in line 9, the word "our" appears, reconciling the opposites "I" and "you." After line 9 the "I" no longer appears. Line 11, like line 9, is also a line of reconciliation; "soon to you" is balanced by "you to me." The reconciliation is maintained in the last line; "Mine ransoms yours" is balanced by "yours must ransom me."

From the first line to the last, the sonnet retains an ambiguity. Is the Poet asking for reconciliation? For the resumption of the relationship after the two have injured each other? Or is he not asking for a resumption but only for a different and kinder evaluation of what happened between them? In one case the sonnet is directed towards the lover; in the other to the Poet's remembrance of the lover. We favor the second interpretation because there is no mention of their meeting again. The ambiguity is not accidental but was intended by the Poet.

The first quatrain deals with the Poet's transgressions. He experienced great sorrow but now refuses to bow under his transgressions, that is, he refuses to be overwhelmed by his guilt. The word "nerves" in line 4—"Unless my nerves were brass or hammered steel"—is unusual because the modern term "nerves" was not part of Elizabethan vocabulary. It meant sinews that give the body its strength. The Poet recognizes that only something inhuman—a statue or a suit of armor—could have withstood the pain of his lover's abuse. Having achieved this insight, in the second quatrain he can turn his attention to the partner. He recognizes that the other, too, must have "passed a hell of time." Only the first two lines of the second quatrain are devoted to the other before the Poet returns to his own suffering. He now chastises himself because he did not allow himself to recognize the extent of his suffering.

The first eight lines are necessary for the Poet to recognize that they both suffered and then in the third quatrain a "we" can emerge in "our night of woe." The Poet wants both of them to recognize "how hard true sorrow hits." The word "remembered" (in line 9) was used by Shakespeare in the way we use "reminded;" thus in *The Tempest* (I.ii) "Let me remember thee what thou hast promised." In line 10 we find "my deepest sense," indicating that it required a deeper reflection for the Poet to realize the depth of their injuries. Consulting the Concordance, we see that Shakespeare used the word "sense" 139 times, but this combination, "deepest sense," occurs only in this sonnet. The line implies that the Poet had to find a new term to describe what was not immediately consciously available to him.

Then the sense of mutuality returns. They are not as separated if they can see how they both were at fault. To heal the wound inflicted on the night of woe they should "tender" each other "The humble salve which wounded bosoms fits!" Many lovers have known such nights of woe; once the hostility has been spent, the tender wish for reconciliation returns. We recall that the idea of a salve occurred in Sonnet 34:

For no man well of such a salve can speak
That heals the wound and cures not the disgrace (lines 7-8);

The same salve that was rejected in Sonnet 34 because it did not cure the narcissistic wound is now offered as "the humble salve." The lover's "trespass" is not forgiven; it still demands a fee but the Poet is willing to pay for the lover's transgression against him if he will do the same and ransom the Poet. The relationship will be ransomed by a mutual forgiveness.

CHAPTER 5:
THE PROCREATION SONNETS

SONNETS 1, 2, 3, 4, 5, 6, 7, 8, 9, 10, 11, 12, 13, 14, 16, 17

The first 17 sonnets have been called the procreation sonnets, because in them the Poet, adopting a pedagogical attitude toward a young man reluctant to procreate, cajoles him to become a father. The Poet uses a variety of ingenious arguments to persuade the Young Man to beget children, but the reason that most easily occurs to most people is notably absent: the love between a man and a woman and a wish for parenthood growing out of that love. Within the context of this book, we would say that the Poet is urging the Young Man he loves to have children without violating the compromise set forth in Sonnet 20 (Chapter 1).

For 15 sonnets out of the first 17 of the traditional printed sequence (Sonnets 5 and 15 are the exceptions), the Poet urges the Young Man to protect himself against the inevitability of aging by begetting a son. Commentators, puzzled by these sonnets, believe that Shakespeare was hired by an aristocratic family to persuade a young man to marry. Whatever the plausibility of this idea may be, historically, (whatever the odds of the family's success in such a ploy) these poems are united by a disturbing implication—that the Poet may be able to transfer his love once again and love the Young Man's son when age has made the Young Man unlovable. This idea is never stated explicitly in the text and is suggested only once, in line 13 of Sonnet 10: "Make thee another self for love of me." If we consult the table in chapter one, we will note that these sonnets are not among Shakespeare's most popular ones. Sonnets 2 and 12 appear in two anthologies only; Sonnet 15, an exception to the procreation series, was selected by three, while none of the rest has been selected by anthologies. To us the procreation sonnets were of interest for two reasons: they continue the battle against narcissism that we stressed in connection with the analysis of Sonnet 62 (Chapter 1) as well as the Poet's battle against death, dealt with in Chapter 2. We therefore included all of the procreation sonnets in this chapter except Sonnet 15, which, strictly speaking, is not a procreation sonnet and was discussed as part of our *love at war with time and death* theme in Chapter 2. These sonnets acquire new relevance when understood as the Poet's battle against his own narcissism. Yet the deeper relevance and beauty of the procreation sonnets can be discovered in the underlying fear of death that pervades them.

The reluctance to procreate is also found in Shakespeare's *Venus and Adonis*. But in that poem it is Venus, the mature goddess of love, pleading for a child from Adonis, who is still a mere youth and unresponsive to her wishes. The difference between Venus and Adonis is captured in two lines:

> She red and hot as coals of glowing fire
> He red for shame, but frosty in desire (lines 35-6)

The Poet leaves us in no doubt that we are dealing with an older woman seducing a younger man. Were the relationship taking place today, the term "molestation" would be considered appropriate.

Venus pleads:

> The tender spring upon thy tempting lip
> Shows thee unripe, yet may as thou well be tasted
> Make use of time and let no advantage slip (lines 127-9)

These words are followed by a metaphor that will be used frequently in the sonnets.

> Beauty within itself should not be wasted:
> Fair flowers that are not gathered in their prime
> Rot and consume themselves in little time (lines 130-132)

Venus launches an attack on the narcissism of Adonis in a way the Poet will use in the procreation sonnets:

> Narcissus saw himself forsook
> And died to kiss his shadow in the brook (lines 150-1).

> Is thine own heart to thine own face affected? (line 157)

> Things growing to themselves are growth's abuse
> Seeds spring from seeds and beauty breatheth beauty
> Thou was begot; to get it is thy duty (lines 166-8).

> By law of nature thou art bound to breed
> That thou may live when thou thyself are dead
> And so in spite of death thou dost survive
> In that thy likeness still is left alive (lines 171-4).

When a woman pleads for the right to reproduce the man's beauty, we know well what she means: she desires a child by the man. But when the Poet, a man, repeats the argument, we have a right to be puzzled. Comparing *Venus and Adonis* to the sonnets, we may conclude that the Poet had identified himself with Venus.

Eventually a boar will gore Adonis and death will occupy center stage, but in the pleading of Venus, unlike the pleading of the Poet of the procreation sonnets, death is not in the shadows when Venus is trying to seduce Adonis.

Romeo and Juliet contains the wonderful line, spoken by Romeo: "Love is a smoke made with the fumes of sighs (I.i.196)." But then come lines, describing Rosaline, that parallel this chapter:

> *Romeo:* … she'll not be hit
> With Cupid's arrow; she hath Dian's wit;
> And, in strong proof of chastity well arm'd,
> From love's weak childish bow she lives unharm'd.
> She will not stay the siege of loving terms,
> Nor bide the encounter of assailing eyes,
> Nor ope her lap to saint-seducing gold:
> O! she is rich in beauty; only poor
> That, when she dies, with beauty dies her store (I.i.214-222).

In Ovid's tale, Venus fell in love with Adonis as a result of an accident that happened to her son Cupid: Cupid was kissing his mother with his quiver on his shoulder when one of his arrows grazed her breast. As a result of being wounded by Cupid's arrow, she fell in love with the mortal Adonis. However, in Ovid's tale Adonis was a full-grown man. Shakespeare changed him to a boy. In our view, this supports our interpretation of Sonnet 104 in Chapter 2. In addition to Ovid, the procreation sonnets show the influence of Plato. In the *Symposium*, Diotima instructs Socrates:

> There is a certain age at which human nature is desirous of
> procreation—procreation which must be in beauty and not
> in deformity; and this procreation is the union of a man and
> woman, and is a divine thing; for conception and genera-
> tion are an immortal principle in the mortal creature…a
> sort of eternity and immortality (*Symposium*, 206-7, Jowett
> translation).

Plato envisioned that young men and women should divert their sexual drive, at a time in their life when sexuality is making particularly strong demands upon them, to higher aims. The idea that love can be desexualized and sublimated appears for the first time in Plato's *Symposium*, when Plato lets Diotima teach Socrates the following "wisdom:"

> "…to the mortal creature, generation is a sort of eternity and immortality," she replied; "and if, as has been already admitted, love is the ever-lasting possession of the good, all men will necessarily desire immortality together with the good: wherefore love is of immortality."

We may question Diotima's logic, but there is no question that this passage has impressed many future writings on love. Almost two thousand years separate Plato from Shakespeare, and yet the procreation sonnets can be read as a commentary on this passage in the *Symposium*. Shakespeare, however, neglects another aspect of Diotima's teachings to Socrates.

> What is the cause, Socrates, of love, and the attendant desire? See you not how all animals, birds, as well as beasts, in their desire of procreation are in agony when they take the infection of love which begins with the desire of union; whereto is added the care of offspring on whose behalf the weakest are ready to battle against the strongest even to the uttermost and die for them, and let themselves be tormented with hunger or suffer anything in order to maintain their young (*Symposium*, 207, Jowett translation).

The Poet in the procreation sonnets echoes Diotima's teachings, but knows what Socrates and Plato may not have known: that self-love can override the wish to beget a child. Unlike Socrates, the Poet was obsessed with the fear of death and likened procreation to a battle against death. It will be recalled that at the end of the Apology, Socrates expressed no fear of death, for death is either a dreamless sleep, the best possible sleep available, or it will take him to another place, where "I shall be able to continue my search into true and false knowledge." The Poet's attitude towards death was more complex and less settled one than that of Socrates.

SONNET 1

From fairest creatures we desire increase,
That thereby beauty's rose might never die,
But as the riper should by time decease,
His tender heir might bear his memory:
But thou contracted to thine own bright eyes,
Feed'st thy light's flame with self-substantial fuel,
Making a famine where abundance lies,
Thy self thy foe, to thy sweet self too cruel:
Thou that art now the world's fresh ornament,
And only herald to the gaudy spring,
Within thine own bud buriest thy content,
And tender churl mak'st waste in niggarding:
 Pity the world, or else this glutton be,
 To eat the world's due, by the grave and thee.

Aware of what we said about narcissism in the analysis of Sonnet 62, we read the first sonnet with its powerful indictment of the Young Man's narcissism as a displacement from the Poet's own narcissism to the Young Man.

The sonnet opens with the imperial "we." The first line modifies Genesis where God the Creator commanded the animals, including Adam and Eve, to be fruitful and multiply. The Poet, unlike God in the Bible, desires the increase of only the "fairest" creatures, and we find ourselves squarely in the world of the Renaissance, where man tended to assume the prerogative of deity. In the spirit of the Renaissance, the basic idea expressed in line 1 owes much to Plato's *Symposium,* in which Diotima teaches Socrates that the fairest creatures owe it to the world to reproduce themselves. Here, as in many other places, the Poet is shaping Classical ideas to suit his own purposes.

Line 2, "thereby beauty's rose might never die," echoes Diotima's dictum with greater awareness and anxiety over death. Youth gives way to ripeness and maturity, which in turn yields to death. This is expressed in line 3: "But as the riper should by time decease;" he will continue to live in his offspring.

The second quatrain is accusatory in tone. The Young Man is "contracted," that is engaged or married, to his "own bright eyes," a striking metaphor for the expression of self-love. In line 6 we encounter: "Feed'st thy light's flame with self-substantial fuel." The line refers to the candle that consumes itself as it burns, as the Young Man does by refusing to procreate. The youth makes "famine" by not reproducing where otherwise "abundance lies." In the third quatrain the accusation goes deeper. He is his own enemy and cruel towards himself. What follows is the insight that self-love is really self-hate: "Thy self thy foe." Line 11 is a beautiful metaphor for the self-destructive aspects of self-love: "Within thine own bud buriest thy content," a disguised accusation that the Young Man prefers masturbation to heterosexual intercourse, burying his content (semen) within his own bud.

In line 12 the Poet calls the Young Man "tender churl." We note that he called the Young Man's prospective child his "tender heir" in line 4. Tender means young with an implication of soft, so the epithet moderates the accusing tone of the preceding lines. "Churl" means a rustic bore or a low-bred fellow; in Sonnet 32, line 2, the Poet will apply the term "churl" to death himself, "When that churl death my bones with dust shall cover," and in Sonnet 69 he uses the term as a verb, "Then churls their thoughts" (line 11). Also interesting is the phrase, "To make waste in niggarding." Usually, stinginess or niggarding is opposed to waste. But here the youth is accused of being wasteful by being niggardly.

The couplet is obscure. Some commentators have appealed to a passage in *Venus and Adonis* for help:

> What is thy body but a swallowing grave,
> Seeming to bury that posterity
> Which by the rights of time thou needs must have,
> If thou destroy them not in dark obscurity (756-760)?

The world should be pitied because the Young Man did not provide it an heir. The world is said to be deprived twice: by the "grave," meaning by his death, and by "thee," meaning by his failure to reproduce while still alive. This failure to reproduce is experienced by the Poet as a form of gluttony, a sin, as if the unborn child was eaten up by the reluctant father and the father himself will, after his death, be devoured by his grave. The language is awkward because the Poet has ventured into the forbidden world of cannibalism. If we want to understand him, we have to accept cannibalistic impulses among the unconscious impulses that ordinarily remain repressed. The Poet of the Sonnets makes a dramatic transition from a candle that feeds on its own self as it burns to the more frightening image of a father who eats his own child by his failure to reproduce.

We come now to the difficult task of evaluating this sonnet. We note that only one anthology included it, and yet if we look upon it strictly from an aesthetic point of view it contains some very original and striking metaphors: "contracted to thine own bright eyes" and "Feed'st thy light's flame with self-substantial fuel," to name just two. However, ultimately what makes us pause is the savage quality of the attack on what seems to be a very young man who is not yet ready to assume the obligation of parenthood. Why so savage an attack? In our view the beauty of this sonnet can only be appreciated if we recall what we said in Chapter 1: the Poet himself loves the Young Man but is afraid that he will age and die. Addicted as the Poet is to loving only very young men, he feels the danger of losing his love. As he himself suffers from the excessive burden of self-love, he projects his hatred of his own self-love on the Young Man. If we can understand and tolerate the intrapsychic strain within the Poet of the Sonnets we will be able to appreciate the inherent beauty of this savage poem.

SONNET 2

When forty winters besiege thy brow,
And dig deep trenches in thy beauty's field,
Thy youth's proud livery so gazed on now,
Will be a tattered weed of small worth held:
Then being asked, where all thy beauty lies,
Where all the treasure of thy lusty days;
To say within thine own deep sunken eyes,
Were an all-eating shame, and thriftless praise.
How much more praise deserved thy beauty's use,
If thou couldst answer 'This fair child of mine
Shall sum my count, and make my old excuse'
Proving his beauty by succession thine.
    This were to be new made when thou art old,
    And see thy blood warm when thou feel'st it cold.

The first quatrain poetically expresses the "horror" of becoming forty. The Poet animates the forty winters and made them into an army that beseeches the brow; they dig deep trenches in the lover's forehead. In the third line, the Young Man's youth is seen metaphorically as a "proud livery," a kind of uniform that destructive time will eventually transform into "tattered weed of small worth." As in Sonnet 1, the second quatrain addresses the Young Man in accusatory tone. "Where all thy beauty lies?" and what happened to "the treasure of thy lusty days?" All of this, the harsh interrogator will say, has disappeared "within thine own deep sunken eyes." The Poet prophesizes that an "all-eating shame, and thriftless praise" is all that will belong to the Young Man at 40 if he fails to reproduce.

In psychoanalytic language, we are inclined to believe that the Poet prophesizes a kind of superego attack when the Young Man reaches 40, but that this is not a moral superego that punishes moral transgressions but a psychic structure that the Poet invented, which demands that beauty is entitled to reproduction. Like "waste in niggarding" in Sonnet 1, "thriftless praise" is not a usual association of these two words. When words that are not usually associated with each other in our preconscious are suddenly brought together by the Poet, their unexpected combination has a special impact.

It is only the third quatrain that makes this sonnet a procreation sonnet. "Beauty's use," like "love's use" in Sonnet 20, is a reference to sexual intercourse. We are standing before an imaginary judge. The Young Man seems to have been accused of aging and could be excused if he could point to a child. We are in the midst of the Poet's strange inner world, where aging is a crime and having a son is "my old excuse" for this act. This imaginary son will, by "Proving his beauty by succession thine," provide testimony and legitimize the father's beauty. Only a "fair child" can "sum" my "count," that is, present the balanced audit and thereby counteract "deep-sunken eyes" of old age by a positive balance. The Poet implies that old age is a kind of offense against nature that demands atonement. The child is idealized as warming the old man's blood. It is fitting that in this sonnet shame is the central emotion, because it is the emotion that we closely associate with narcissism. We note also that shame is expressed in oral terms, it is "all-eating." If the Young Man fails to reproduce, death will cannibalize him, and a fear that is developmentally very early, the fear of being eaten up, is pressed into the service of reproduction.

There is something new in this sonnet that we should not overlook: a cult of beauty and an almost religious obligation to perpetuate beauty. One cannot imagine a medieval writer making the perpetuation of beauty an obligation.

Two of the six anthologies included this sonnet. Comparing Sonnet 1 and Sonnet 2 is of interest. The first is addressed to the Young Man as he is now; the second is addressed to him in the future. Of the two, the first seems to us the stronger poem, but the anthologizers find the second superior. We should note also that Untermeyer, who voted for Sonnet 1, did not include Sonnet 2.

SONNET 3

Look in thy glass and tell the face thou viewest,
Now is the time that face should form another,
Whose fresh repair if now thou not renewest,
Thou dost beguile the world, unbless some mother,
for where is she so fair whose uneared womb
Disdains the tillage of thy husbandry?
Or who is he so fond will be the tomb
Of his self-love to stop posterity?
Thou art thy mother's glass and she in thee
Calls back the lovely April of her prime,
So thou through windows of thine age shalt see,
Despite of wrinkles this thy golden time.
  But if thou live remembered not to be,
  Die single and thine image dies with thee.

The mirror that in Sonnet 62 brought about a change in the Poet from self-love to a narcissistic love for the Young Man is used in this sonnet to urge the Young Man to curb his own narcissism and reproduce.

The obligation to perpetuate beauty is even stronger than in the previous sonnets. Like Narcissus, the Young Man is urged to look into the mirror, but unlike Narcissus, the encounter should not cause him to fall in love with his own face, but rather, to make him anticipate and avert the catastrophic experience the Poet described in Sonnets 2 and 62.

In this sonnet the Poet is subverting Ovid's legend of Narcissus, urging the Young Man not to fall in love with his mirror image, but to recognize that his beauty is transitory. The future child's face is to the Poet a "fresh repair" of the lover's aging face. If the Young Man should fail to procreate, he will deceive the world and deny a blessing to some potential mother.

The second quatrain is also under the spell of self-love. The first two lines suggest that no woman is so beautiful that she would disdain to have the Young Man's child. "Tillage of thy husbandry" is a beautiful metaphor, equating procreation with the work of the farmer. The metaphor of tillage, or plowing, fuses sexuality with aggression just below the level of our conscious awareness. The other two lines in the second quatrain are harshly addressed to the man who is so fond of himself that he is in danger of becoming the tomb of his self-love. Describing the woman as "fair" in line 5 and the man as "fond" in line 7 is an appealing play of words. The Poet would never imply there could be another man "so fair" because the Poet will never admit that there is any limit on the Young Man's beauty.

Self-love as a tomb is a powerful metaphor. By rhyming "tomb" with the "uneared womb" the Poet brings the fear of death into the service of procreation. The rhyme juxtaposes the womb, which is dead when empty (uneared, meaning devoid of kernels or seed), with the tomb, which is filled with the dead.

In lines 9 and 10 the Poet attempts to evoke the Young Man's gratitude towards his mother.

> Thou art thy mother's glass and she in thee
> Call back the lovely April of her prime.

It is now his turn to do the same as the mother did. We should note, however, that the mother herself is also experienced as narcissistic, seeing a reflection of herself in her son. There is no sense that the Young Man's mother had a child because she loved her son or his father. She looks upon the Young Man and comforts her fear of death by seeing herself fresh and new, in spring. In this sonnet as in Sonnet 1, the Poet introduces an obligation to try to set limits to the power of self-contained love.

After Sonnets 1 and 2, which were heavy with condemnation of the Young Man, this one seems lighter in tone. It is also, refreshingly, less narcissistic and more heterosexual. The woman and her own feminine interest in reproduction, which was so conspicuously absent in the first two sonnets, plays a major role in this one. No anthology included this sonnet.

SONNET 4

Unthrifty loveliness why dost thou spend,
Upon thy self they beauty's legacy?
Nature's bequest gives nothing but doth lend,
And being frank she lends to those are free:
Then beauteous niggard why dost thou abuse,
The bounteous largess given thee to give?
Profitless usurer why dost thou use
So great a sum of sums yet canst not live?
For having traffic with thy self alone,
Thou of thy self thy sweet self dost deceive,
Then how when nature calls thee to be gone,
What acceptable audit canst thou leave?
    Thy unused beauty must be tombed with thee,
    Which usèd lives th' executor to be.

This sonnet's metaphors are taken from the world of commerce. After reading the first three sonnets, one may notice a slackening of inspiration in this one. Had the Poet already said all he had to say on this topic, but from inner compulsion or for commercial reasons needed to write more? Is that the hidden reason why the language of commerce is so prominent in this sonnet?

The sonnet it is well written, and we enjoy the contradictory adjectives "unthrifty loveliness" and "beauteous niggard" as well as "profitless usurer." Furthermore, "spend upon thyself thy beauty's legacy" and "having traffic with thyself alone" are original metaphors that express the essence of narcissism. Noteworthy also is the description of death in lines 11 and 12. To phrase dying as "nature calls thee to be gone," without a trace of the personification of death as a cannibal, is also to remove any suggestion of an afterlife.

In lines 10-11, nature appears as a kind of district attorney, who demands an "acceptable audit" after death, during which the obstinate Young Man will not be able to justify his failure to reproduce. This the second time in the sonnets that the vocabulary of accounting is introduced by the Poet; in Sonnet 2 he used "shall sum my count." Not every reader will find this intrusion appropriate, but it is a poetic reference to the psychological fact that we experience our morality or, in psychoanalytic language, our superego, as surviving our own death, implying that our reputation survives our death and we must be concerned with the impression we leave behind us.

Sonnet 4 is even more accusing than Sonnets 1 and 2. The Young Man is charged with "unthrifty loveliness," implying that loveliness becomes thrifty when reproduction takes place and wasteful when someone refuses to procreate. The same contrast is expressed in the fifth line by "beauteous niggard," meaning a beautiful miser, in contrast to "bounteous largess." Evans pointed out that this is a tautology, where the Poet may have sacrificed meaning for the play of words. Shakespeare must have enjoyed contrasting beauteous with bounteous but he achieved more than just a play on words. It enabled him to soften niggard by calling it beauteous or strengthen largess by calling in bounteous. In line 7, the contrasting words "profitless usurer" form a paradox; usury is a sin, but a "profitless usurer" is a contradictory term since the usurer, by definition, charges high interest rates.

"Unused beauty" in the couplet means beauty that neglected to reproduce itself. It must go into the tomb, while beauty that procreates survives death, producing an heir to and "executor" of that legacy of beauty. The sonnets in praise of the Young Man are noteworthy for their lack of any specific traits or identifying qualities, but Sonnet 20, by comparison, praises aspects of the Young Man's character as well as his beauty. This sonnet is written as if to a painted portrait: nothing is available to the Poet except the subject's beauty.

SONNET 5

Those hours that with gentle work did frame
The lovely gaze where every eye doth dwell
Will play the tyrants to the very same,
And that unfair which fairly doth excel:
For never-resting time leads summer on
To hideous winter and confounds him there,
Sap checked with frost and lusty leaves quite gone,
Beauty o'er snowed and bareness every where:
Then were not summer's distillation left
A liquid prisoner pent in walls of glass,
Beauty's effect with beauty were bereft,
Nor it nor no rememberance what it was
> But flowers distilled though they with winter meet,
> Leese but their show, their substance still lives sweet.

Unlike the preceding sonnets, Sonnet 5 does not deal with procreation directly, but rather through the strange metaphor of the distillation of flowers into perfume. Although it is a sonnet of great beauty, it is rooted in the Poet's strange conviction that time is on the side of youth until manhood and then changes sides, working against the aging man. This idea is related to changes in the seasons, with winter experienced as attacking the aging summer. This idea of time as vengeful is also expressed in Sonnets 73 and 97 (Chapter 2, Chapter 6).

The Poet tells us that the Young Man was framed by gentle and propitious hours, so that every eye dwells on him. We note the prominent role of the eye in the sexuality of the Poet. The man he loves has a "lovely gaze" and every eye, in turn, dwells on him.

The next two lines reverse time's attitude: gentle time now will play the tyrant to the same young man. "Unfair" is used here as a verb, meaning to remove fairness, and time's hours excel at removing what they had earlier gently framed.

The second quatrain is dominated by a metaphor of the seasons of the years. "Never-resting time" is experienced as very powerful as it "leads summer on/To hideous winter and confounds him there." The metaphor is a beautiful one, but it is based on a paranoid sensitivity. "Never-resting time" is personified here as a treacherous person that directs summer to a dangerous place ("hideous winter") and overcomes him there. One of the many rewards that these sonnets yield is the way in which paranoid ideas can become original poetic metaphors of striking power. In line 7, "the flow of the sap of trees," a metaphor for human blood, is checked by frost, and leaves that were once lusty are now "quite" gone. To see leaves as having been lusty, a term usually reserved for sexual desire, is one of those breathtaking combinations of words characteristic of Shakespeare. The leaves can be read as part of the anthropomorphized tree, as fingers or a youthful head of hair, or as pages of love poems.

The final quatrain is built around an odd metaphor which Shakespeare seems to have borrowed from the poet Sidney. In the ninth line a new metaphor takes over; it is not easy to follow. The Poet compares the begetting of a child to distilling summer flowers to make perfume. The bareness the Poet spoke of in line 8 is somewhat redeemed by the flowers' "summer's distillation." In the 10th line the Poet compares a child in the womb to the flowers' perfume distilled and held prisoner in a vial of glass. An anti-feminine whisper is introduced because the child is "imprisoned" in the mother. Line 11 means that the both the effect of beauty, which is the way everyone looks at the Young Man in line 2, and the Young Man himself, here called "beauty," will be bereft. The Young Man will no longer be beautiful and there will be no perfume (child) to remember him by. Remembrance, in this case, happens through the nose, which replaces the eye in this poem. The difference between show and substance is in the platonic tradition that form may perish but idea is immortal.

SONNET 6

Then let not winter's ragged hand deface
In thee thy summer, ere thou be distill'd
Make sweet some vial; treasure thou some place
With beauty's treasure, ere it be self-kill'd.
That use is not forbidden usury,
Which happies those that pay the willing loan;
That's for thyself to breed another thee,
Or ten times happier, be it ten for one;
Ten times thyself were happier than thou art,
If ten of thine ten times refigur'd thee;
Then what could death do, if thou should'st depart,
Leaving thee living in posterity?
    Be not self-will'd, for thou art much too fair
    To be death's conquest and make worms thine heir.

The distillation metaphor of the previous sonnet carries over into the first quatrain of this next poem. "Winter's ragged hand" cannot deface the Young Man's summer if he agrees to make "sweet some vial." The vial made sweet is the woman's womb sweetened by pregnancy, a tender image of sexual intercourse. All this has to happen before the semen, here referred to as "beauty's treasure," is "self-kill'd" by sexual abstinence.

The fifth line, with the metaphor of usury, is neither appropriate nor logical, so that we assume that it represented a concession to the Poet's unconscious, in which he believed that a woman asking for a child was equivalent to usury. Usury, the lending of money at high interest, was regarded as a sin and forbidden to Christians during the Middle Ages. That was the reason Jews became moneylenders, as Shylock was. But what has usury to do with procreation? "That use" is a reference to the sexual act, as we know from Sonnet 20's phrase "love's use." Usury involves forced exploitation; the borrower is in dire need and the usurer imposes upon the borrower a prohibitive rate of interest. The "willing loan" is the opposite of usury and emphasizes that both man and woman are glad to procreate a child. After the man has given the woman his seed as a "willing loan" he will be rewarded by breeding "another thee."

Why did the Poet have to reassure us that this is not "forbidden usury?" The presence of that metaphor indicates that heterosexual sexuality was experienced by the Poet as forbidden and he had to persuade himself and his readers that it should not be equated with usury. Shakespeare used the word "usury" only four times and the word "usurer" nine times. In Sonnet 134, line 10, we find "Thou usurer that put'st forth all to use." In that sonnet the Dark Lady was called usurer because her beauty had enslaved the Poet's lover.

In the third quatrain, the Poet jumps from suggesting one child to ten offspring; the Young Man will then be ten times happier, becoming "ten times refigur'd." This could also refer to the extended proposition that each of his ten children could beget another ten. The Poet is returning to and redoubling his familiar argument that leaving children, each one a reproduction of the father and capable of continuing the family's beauty, renders death harmless. The term "self-will'd," in the couplet, is Shakespeare's code word for what we refer to as narcissism. If the Young Man does not reproduce he will be "death's conquest;" a word combination that has both warlike and sexual connotations, "and make worms thine heir." The word choice in this line draws out the underlying threat of emasculation in failure to produce an heir, and worse, implies that the Young Man could, as death's "conquest," be penetrated by charnel worms and have them come out of his body as well.

One anthology included this sonnet.

SONNET 7

Lo in the orient when the gracious light
Lifts up his burning head, each under eye
Doth homage to his new-appearing sight,
Serving with looks his sacred majesty;
And having climbed the steep-up heavenly hill,
Resembling strong youth in his middle age,
Yet mortal looks adore his beauty still,
Attending on his golden pilgrimage:
But when from highmost pitch with weary car
Like feeble age he reeleth from the day,
The eyes (fore duteous) now converted are
From his low tract and look another way:
    So thou, thyself outgoing in thy noon,
    Unlooked on diest unless thou get a son.

The first quatrain is a hymn to the rising sun. As the sun rises it becomes a burning head, evoking homage in each "under eye," meaning the eyes below that look up to the sun. By looking up at the rising sun, the Poet feels he is "serving" the "sacred majesty" of the sun.

The second quatrain follows the sun until it reaches its zenith, climbing with it up the steep "heavenly hill." At this point, the sun resembles "strong youth in his middle age." He still draws adoring looks from the eyes of men, "mortal looks" that follow his "golden pilgrimage."

In the third quatrain, the decline begins. Now the chariot of Helios, the sun god, is experienced by the Poet as a "weary car" that staggers or wobbles down from the zenith. Line 10 makes this simile explicit: the sun, like "feeble age," is no longer steady but "reeleth from the day." Even accustomed as we are to the Poet's attitude toward old age, we cannot help being astonished that he can see the frailty of an old man's unstable walk reflected in the setting of the sun.

The mortal eyes that earlier paid homage to the sun and served it dutiously with looks are now "converted," or turned away. As sunset is moving closer, the man that worshiped the sun in the morning is now looking "another way," perhaps at other heavenly bodies. Only the couplet, rather jarringly, tells us that Sonnet 7 is a procreation sonnet because the Young Man has reached his noon and he will remain "unlooked on" unless he begets a child.

The key word of his sonnet, as Vendler has pointed out, is the word "look." As "looks" it appears in lines 4 and 7, as "look" in line 12, and as "unlooked for" in line 14. In lines 4 and 7 the word look has a positive connotation, being associated with "sacred majesty" and being adored by "mortal looks." However, the juxtaposition of sacred and mortal hints at the reality that mortal looks are not lasting. For the Poet, when one is no longer looked on one is no longer loved. The solution is to create a self in your image. In line 12, "look" has a negative connotation, while in the last line the transformation into its opposite is complete and we have "unlooked for." Within the metaphor of the sun, the sonnet confirms the role eyes play as the dominant sexual organ in this love relationship. No anthology selected this sonnet.

SONNET 8

Music to hear, why hear'st thou music sadly?
Sweets with sweets war not, joy delights in joy;
Why lov'st thou that which thou receiv'st not gladly,
Or else receiv'st with pleasure thine annoy?
If the true concord of well-tuned sounds
By unions married, do offend thine ear,
They do but sweetly chide thee, who confounds
In singleness the parts that thou shouldst bear:
Mark how one string, sweet husband to another,
Strikes each in each by mutual ordering,
Resembling sire, and child, and happy mother,
Who all in one, one pleasing note do sing:
    Whose speechless song being many, seeming one,
    Sings this to thee: 'Thou single wilt prove none.'

Sonnet 8 is in many ways an exceptional sonnet in this series. The attitudes toward women and family are far more positive than in the other procreation sonnets. Music is the leading metaphor through which the

Poet addresses the Young Man. Until now, the Poet spoke mainly about the Young Man's need to reproduce himself as an antidote to aging and death. But in this sonnet the Poet compares matrimony to music, and by appealing to the Young Man's love of music hopes to persuade him to procreate.

The Young Man is asked why he hears music sadly. The Poet claims that to be saddened by music suggests an inner disharmony. Sweets, presumably sweet tones, should not be at war with other sweet tones, and harmony should reign. The Young Man is accused of being pleased with what should annoy him and make him unhappy. Throughout the first quatrain the man is both flattered and chided.

In lines 5 and 6, the equation is made explicit between musical harmony and happy marriage. The third quatrain takes the analogy to its crescendo. After one string is said to be "sweet husband to another," we get Line 10's "strikes each by each in mutual ordering," which may allude to sexual intercourse. The next line expands the metaphor to include not only the couple but the whole family: sire, child, and happy mother. A psychoanalyst interested in the unconscious would note the sequence: sire first, child second, and happy mother third, the three of them singing in "one pleasing note." In line 13 the Poet asserts that father, mother and child seem one. The image of the happy family then becomes more ominous as our "speechless" model family choir issues the traditional warning that to die single is as if one has not existed, expressed as "prove none." This alludes to the proverb that "one is none" or that one is not yet a number. The last three lines introduce the word "sing" twice, clearly pairing "single" and "singing" in the musically alliterative last line: "Sings this to thee: 'Thou single wilt prove none'." We note that this sonnet was not selected by any anthology, suggesting to us that the metaphors did not carry conviction.

SONNET 9

Is it for fear to wet a widow's eye
That thou consum'st thyself in single life?
Ah! If thou issueless shall hap to die,
The world will wail thee, like a makeless wife;
The world will be thy widow, and still weep
That thou no form of thee hast left behind,
When every private widow well may keep
By children's eyes her husband's shape in mind.
Look! What an unthrift in the world doth spend
Shifts but his place, for still the world enjoys it;
But beauty's waste hath in the world an end,
And, kept unus'd, the user so destroys it.
    No love toward others in that bosom sits
    That on himself such murderous shame commits.

Examined superficially, Sonnet 9 is one of the weakest. How likely was it that a young noble man just reaching maturity would refuse to procreate because the woman would at some future time become his widow? The rejoinder of the Poet is equally facetious: will the whole world become his widow if he fails to procreate? Structurally, the poem is held together by a judicious use of the W. The word widow is felicitous because it begins and ends with a W. It appears three times in the sonnet. The word world is repeated five times and we observe wet, will, wail, and wife all in the fourth line, and world, will, widow, and weep in the fifth. After this onslaught of W's the word makeless in line 4 gives us pause. This is the only place in Shakespeare's work where this word appears. It means matchless, without peer, and mateless or widowed. The Poet asserts that the whole world has no match or mate but the Young Man. He further implies that the world will mourn the Young Man as if he had been a matchless wife, and that if a man fails to procreate he will not be remembered as a man; a peculiar post-mortem castration anxiety. The term private widow in line 7 is also puzzling, since in a monogamous society every widow is, strictly speaking, a private widow until one contrasts it with the idea that the world will be the Young Man's widow. The sonnet makes more sense if we allow a psychoanalytic interpretation. The Poet has identified himself with the supposed widow pleading for a child. The fact that the feminine wish to bear a child to reproduce the lover has to remain unconscious gives this sonnet its enigmatic quality. One anthology included this sonnet.

SONNET 10

For shame deny that thou bear'st love to any,
Who for thyself art so unprovident;
Grant, if thou wilt, thou art beloved of many,
But that thou none lov'st is most evident:
For thou art so possessed with murd'rous hate,
That 'gainst thy self thou stick'st not to conspire,
Seeking that beauteous roof to ruinate
Which to repair should be thy chief desire:
O change thy thought, that I may change my mind;
Shall hate be fairer lodged than gentle love?
Be as thy presence is, gracious and kind;
Or to thyself at least kind-hearted prove,
    Make thee another self for love of me,
    That beauty still may live in thine or thee.

It was only recently that the psychoanalyst André Green (2001) differentiated between life-affirming narcissism and narcissism that leads to death. Shakespeare seems to have intuitively sensed this difference in Sonnet 10. As a poem, it does not rank highly. Its images and metaphors are not striking. Its disturbing tone is severely condemnatory. If, however, we disregard its tone, we will note that it contains a significant new idea.

In Ovid, Narcissus merely fell in love with himself; he was indifferent to the love of others. Shakespeare's insight goes deeper. Narcissism will result in "ruination" when repair should be the main concern. Extreme self-love is not only a deficiency in loving others, but it is based on "murd'rous hate."

The Young Man is urged to grant that he is "beloved of many" but loves no one. The hatred of others turns into self-hatred in line 6, " That gainst thyself stick'st not to conspire" meaning that the Young Man doesn't hesitate to plot his own destruction. Line 7 continues the accusation. The Young Man refusing to beget a child will "ruinate" his own "beauteous roof," his protection (from old age) and literally his head, meaning his sense, his looks and his estate—which his chief desire should have been to repair. Having admonished in the first two quatrains, in the third the Poet pleads "change thy thought, that I may change my mind." Continuing the metaphor of the roof, he asks in line 10 "Shall hate be fairer lodged than gentle love?"

It is in the couplet that the Poet becomes most intimate, explicitly asking the Young Man to make another self "for love of me." In this sonnet, the Poet drops the pretense of being an observer-critic of the Young Man, and openly admits that he loves him. The Young Man is asked to procreate and beget a child, not because he loves the woman, but for love of the Poet. The last line refers to the now familiar argument that procreation is necessary for beauty to "live in thine or thee" meaning that the Young Man will survive only in the reflected beauty of his offspring. This suggests a rather beautiful symbiotic relationship between parent and child. Still, a more ominous interpretation cannot be excluded: now that the Young Man has begun to age, he should procreate in order to give the Poet a fresh copy of himself to love.

Many a love relationship has suffered shipwreck because one or both partners demanded of the other to "make thee another self for love of me." The wish to change the partner was too self-centered to be conducive to memorable poetry, and this sonnet does not appear in any of the six anthologies.

SONNET 11

As fast as thou shalt wane, so fast thou grow'st,
In one of thine, from that which thou departest,
And that fresh blood which youngly thou bestow'st
Thou mayst call thine, when thou from youth convertest:
Herein lives wisdom, beauty, and increase,
Without this, folly, age, and cold decay;
If all were minded so, the times should cease,
And threescore year would make the world away.
Let those whom Nature hath not made for store,
Harsh, featureless, and rude, barrenly perish:
Look whom she best endowed she gave the more;
Which bounteous gift thou shouldst in bounty cherish:
    She carved thee for her seal, and meant thereby
    Thou shouldst print more, not let that copy die.

We are struck by the word wane. We all know that the moon can either wax or wane, but the Poet's lover can achieve both at the same time. We will see that he achieves the same feat in Sonnet 126, when the lover is "by waning grown." In *The Taming of the Shrew* a woman can be "in this waning state." But this miracle of growing while one is waning can only be achieved if "one of thine," meaning a child, takes over "from that which thou departest." In line 3 the blood of the child is described as "fresh" because it was bestowed "youngly," meaning that the father was still young when he fathered the child. Lines 7 and 8 emphasize that if no one reproduced himself the world would end, expressed as "make the world away," in three scores, the average life expectancy in the Old Testament.

The third quatrain is reminiscent of a special kind of survival of the fittest. Those who are "harsh, featureless, and rude" can "barrenly perish," while the "best endowed" are under obligation to reproduce. Line 9 also gives us our third list of three states, echoing the opposed "wisdom, beauty, and increase" and "folly, age, and cold decay," and re-enforcing the Poet's argument by repetition. In lines 11 and 12, the Young Man is reminded of nature's "bounteous gift" and admonished to express his gratitude towards nature by reproducing himself "in bounty," implying many children.

In the couplet we find the same idea we stressed earlier, when we discussed sonnet 20. Nature, too, is basically narcissistic; she "carved" the Young Man "for her seal," to represent her. Being nothing but her seal, or stamp, he should "print more" and not let the only copy be destroyed. Once more the narcissistic nature of the sonnets is striking. Wisdom and beauty, the terms so dear to Greek philosophy, demand increase; otherwise "folly, age, and cold decay" will win the day. This is not a world where love reigns; only frosty narcissism holds sway. One anthology cited this sonnet.

SONNET 12

When I do count the clock that tells the time,
And see the brave day sunk in hideous night,
When I behold the violet past prime,
And sable curls all silvered o'er with white:
When lofty trees I see barren of leaves,
Which erst from heat did canopy the herd
And summer's green all girded up in sheaves
Borne on the bier with white and bristly beard:
Then of thy beauty do I question make
That thou among the wastes of time must go,
Since sweets and beauties do themselves forsake,
And die as fast as they see others grow,
    And nothing 'gainst Time's scythe can make defence
    Save breed to brave him, when he takes thee hence.

Were it not for the last line, this very beautiful sonnet would appear in our chapter on the "war against time." Sonnet 12 contributes no new insight, but it is a beautiful sonnet of mourning over the transience of beauty. Reading this sonnet, we feel the absence of mourning in the previous procreation sonnets and how strikingly mourning can add beauty even to the theme of procreation. If we correctly interpretated Sonnet 104 (Chapter 1), that the Poet's capacity to love was restricted to a lover in the years preceding puberty, in this sonnet he found compensation in his ability to transform his loss into a magnificent poetic mourning.

Just as the Poet, in the previous sonnets, experienced the seasons of the year in conflict with each other, he now experiences the passage of time as a battle in which "brave day" is overcome and "sunk in hideous night." The first quatrain contains the familiar lament over the impossibility of remaining forever young. In the second quatrain the metaphor is carried over to seasonal changes, where "lofty trees" become "barren of leaves." The very same trees, now barren, in the summer did provide "canopy," that is, a shade for herds. One can feel the heat of the summer in the animals seeking the cooler shade. It is also a tender, motherly image of a brood enfolded in the shelter of the trees' fertile branches. By contrast, "barren" suggests a loss of fertility, but that is not true for trees, for they will bloom again.

The first two quatrains are rich with illustrations of the passage of time. These are: 1) the clock, 2) the metaphor of brave day overcome by hideous night, 3) the violet who passes her prime, 4) the sable curls silvered with white, 5) trees that have lost their leaves, 6) the loss of summer's heat, 7) the harvesting of the wheat, and 8) the metaphor of the harvest bier as a funeral procession. All of them are vibrant with life, even though the Poet is describing the coming of death.

In the ninth line the beauty of the Young Man is called into question because he must go "among the wastes of time." "Sweets and beauties" cannot stand up to time, and die as if out of envy when they "see others grow." The equation of harvest with death is reinforced in the couplet: "And nothing 'gainst Time's scythe can make defence." Once more we are told that only an offspring can "brave" death. We should note the poetic repetition of the word brave. In line 2 it is used to designate the struggle of day against night, and in line 14, it is used against time's scythe. Only the last line makes us aware that we are still in the procreation sonnets, because the word "breed" means that begetting children is the only weapon mortal men have against time. Two anthologies included this sonnet.

SONNET 13

O that you were yourself! But, love, you are
No longer yours, than you yourself here live;
Against this coming end you should prepare,
And your sweet semblance to some other give:
So should that beauty which you hold in lease
Find no determination; then you were
Yourself again after yourself's decease,
When your sweet issue your sweet form should bear.
Who lets so fair a house fall to decay,
Which husbandry in honour might uphold
Against the stormy gusts of winter's day
And barren rage of death's eternal cold?
    O none but unthrifts, dear my love you know:
    You had a father; let your son say so.

In this sonnet the pretense of objectivity has been given up; the Young Man is directly addressed as "love." However, the Poet then argues that the loved Young Man is no longer himself because he is destined someday to die. The Poet uses death as an antidote to narcissism. Because the Young Man is mortal, he cannot be and should not see himself as the final aim of creation. He must make sure that his "sweet semblance" is perpetuated.

The use of the word "determination" in line seven is taken from legal language as a reference to the expiration of a lease. It implies that to the Poet the Young Man's beauty was only held as a short-term lease, not as a permanent possession.

In the third quatrain the Poet shifts the argument to another favorite metaphor: the Young Man as a fair house or "beauteous roof." If the Young Man fails to reproduce, he will let his house fall into decay. Reproduction is here equated with reparation. This house is in need of repair against "the stormy gusts of winter's day," a metaphor for the sensation, in old age, of impending death. When, in line 12, the word "death" is mentioned, it has become more frightening by being described as "barren rage" and "eternal cold." We see, perhaps more clearly than we saw before, how frightened the Poet is of the Young Man's death, a fear the Young Man may not share to the same extent. It is the fear of death that makes the call for reproduction so urgent in this sonnet.

As in other sonnets, the impact of the ideas is the strongest after line 12, and the couplet softens the impact. The fear of death is reduced to mere "unthrifts." We rank the sonnet higher than the anthologizers who did not include it. The Poet says nothing new, nothing he has not said in the previous procreation sonnets. However, we find that lines 11 and 12 are exceptionally beautiful. The "barren rage of death's eternal cold" will stay with us.

SONNET 14

Nor from the stars do I my judgement pluck;
And yet, methinks, I have astronomy,
But not to tell of good or evil luck,
Of plagues, of dearths, or seasons' quality;
Nor can I fortune to brief minutes tell
Pointing to each his thunder, rain and wind;
Or say with princes if it shall go well
By aught predict that I in heaven find;
But from thine eyes my knowledge I derive,
And, constant stars, in them I read such art
As truth and beauty shall together thrive
If from thyself, to store thou wouldst convert:
 Or else of thee this I prognosticate,
 Thy end is truth's and beauty's doom and date.

One can read this sonnet without realizing that it is a procreation sonnet, for procreation is not referred to until line 12, where the traditional conversion from self-love to procreation is, in a veiled way, added as "If from thyself, to store thou wouldst convert." The word "store" was used in line 9 of Sonnet 11, meaning to prepare food for the future. In this instance a child is required to protect against losses.

The first two lines convey a contradictory message regarding astronomy. Today we would say that the reference was to astrology. The Poet does not claim that he does not believe in astrology, but he does not "pluck" decisive judgment from the stars. Mockingly, the Poet promises that he will not use his "astronomy" to predict good or evil luck, plagues, dry seasons or the seasons' "quality." Nor will he "fortune to brief minutes tell." It is only in lines 8 and 9 that the puzzle of the first two lines is solved: "But from thine eyes my knowledge I derive." Unlike the stars of heaven that move through the zodiac, the lover's eyes are "constant stars." In the age that still believed in astrology, this line was high praise for the man the Poet loved. In his the Poet reads what he calls "such art" as to make truth and beauty grow, but only if the Young Man will agree to procreate. The Poet's sole prediction is that if the Young Man will not "convert," meaning change his mind and provide for the future by storing his truth and beauty in his children, those qualities will die. The Poet establishes truth and beauty as exceptionally higher ranking than the list of 'good or evil' things that precede them. In the couplet the Poet subverts Plato, as we have seen him do in previous sonnets, by saying that truth and beauty are not eternal ideas but will be extinguished once the Young Man is no longer here to give them expression. Only one anthology included this sonnet.

SONNET 16

But wherefore do not you a mightier way
Make war upon this bloody tyrant Time?
And fortify your self in your decay
With means more blessed than my barren rhyme?
Now stand you on the top of happy hours,
And many maiden gardens yet unset,
With virtuous wish would bear your living flowers,
Much liker than your painted counterfeit,
So should the lines of life that life repair
Which this, time's pencil or my pupil pen,
Neither in inward worth nor outward fair
Can make you live yourself in eyes of men.
    To give away yourself, keeps your self will
    And you must live drawn by your own sweet skill

In the first quatrain the Poet invites the Young Man to use a stronger weapon against "this bloody tyrant Time" than these sonnets. The Poet's attempt to give him immortality is negated when the Poet experiences his own poetry as "barren rhyme."

The Poet's self-reference exposes his envy of the woman's capacity to beget children. In happier moods, the Poet could conceal his envy of women's capacity to bear children behind the assertion that his lover will live forever through his verse (as in Sonnets 18 and 55). Now his rhymes appear to him as not just mortal and finite, but infertile—"barren." The choice of the word "barren" is of psychological interest because it conveys the Poet's identification with woman. However, it is a painful identification since the Poet cannot bear children to his lover, and his poetry cannot compete. What a woman can do by creating a child is "much liker," meaning more like the lover than what the Poet's "painted counterfeit" can achieve. "Painted counterfeit" is a particularly harsh condemnation of the Poet's effort at making the lover immortal, but it is an original metaphor for his poem.

In line 6, women not yet impregnated are referred to as "gardens yet unset," and the children these women can bear are called the Young Man's "living flowers." The Poet calls the wish of these maidens to be impregnated "virtuous," a direct challenge to Christian morality and St. Paul's famous anti-sexual dictum that it is better to marry than to burn.

In line 8 the Poet introduces a painted portrait of the Young Man ("your painted counterfeit") which leads him to use the word "time" differently in line 10, when he refers to the portrait as "this time's pencil" because the picture can only be drawn right now, right at this time. The picture, however, is as helpless as the Poet's praise to make the Young Man come alive in the eyes of others. In Chapter 2, we saw that Time is often referred to as drawing lines of age in the Young Man's forehead with his pen, but that does not seem to us to have happened here. We are struck, however, by the symmetry of lines 10 and 11:

> Which this, time's pencil or my pupil pen,
> Neither in inward worth nor outward fair

The implication of the sequence of words in these lines is that the picture is concerned with the Young Man's character and inner life (inward worth) and the poem is concerned with his outer beauty (outward fair). It is accurate to say of the sonnets that they praise the Young Man's beauty without concerning themselves with his inward worth, but it is noteworthy that the Poet knows this and finds it natural and tells us so in Sonnet 16.

The Poet's abdication becomes even stronger in the couplet when the Poet describes the activity needed to beget a child as the Young Man's "own sweet skill," implying that writing the sonnets requires far less (or less important) skill.

Even when the Poet is feeling inadequate, he is not angry or depressed. The unset gardens and the Young Man's sweet skill create, in this poem, a rather delicate and appealing picture of the heterosexual pleasure that await the Young Man who will procreate. However, no anthology selected it.

SONNET 17

Who will believe my verse in time to come
If it were filled with your most high deserts?
Though yet heaven knows it is but as a tomb
Which hides your life, and shows not half your parts:
If I could write the beauty of your eyes,
And in fresh numbers number all your graces,
The age to come would say this poet lies,
Such heavenly touches ne'er touched earthly faces.
So should my papers (yellowed with their age)
Be scorned, like old men of less truth than tongue,
And your true rights be termed a poet's rage,
And stretched meter of an antique song.
    But were some child of yours alive that time,
    You should live twice in it, and in my rhyme.

Joel Fineman, in his book *Shakespeare's Perjured Eye*, published in 1986, dealt with the sonnets as poetry of praise. We have so far not stressed this aspect of the sonnets. But Sonnet 17 compels us to acknowledge that it is primarily a poem of praise, and being a sonnet of praise what emanates from it is coldness and formality and a lack of deeper feelings. We have shown that insofar as the Poet urges the young lover to procreate, he is trying to evoke in him a fear of death to combat the Young Man's love of himself, but when he praises the Young Man so highly he is doing the opposite, and fortifying the Young Man's self-love.

In the first quatrain, the Poet adopts a humble attitude. No one in times to come will believe his praise—his lover is so beautiful as to be unbelievable. But even this extraordinary praise, by the third line, appears to the Poet to be only the lover's tomb and does justice only to "half your parts." On the surface lines three and four only continue the praise, but if we take into account the reference to a tomb we are justified in assuming that death wishes towards the lover have become activated. The tomb was created by the Young Man's self-love and his failure to beget a child, but to call his own verse a tomb connotes an attack by the Poet against his own creativity.

The third quatrain elaborates this theme. No one will believe that such beauty existed, and the age to come will accuse the Poet of lying or madness. This prophecy has come to pass: it is very difficult for a modern reader to believe that the Young Man was worthy of the praise heaped on him in the sonnets. We are indeed inclined to attribute the extent of the praise to the very madness that Shakespeare often attributes to lovers who "see Helen's beauty in the brow of Egypt."

We may wonder: why should a writer as confident as the Poet fear that future generations will not believe him? Is it not the function of the Poet to write in such a way that he will compel belief? Two possibilities come to mind. One is that the Poet is growing disillusioned with the Young Man and is avoiding that feeling by projecting his disbelief on the age to come. The other is that the Poet feels unable to compete effectively with a woman who can have the Young Man's child. Both feelings could co-exist.

This sonnet can easily be read as nothing more than a poem of exaggerated praise. However, if the disbelief in future readers' reactions is read as a projection of the Poet's own disbelief in what he is saying, the sonnet becomes a sonnet of ambivalence. Ambivalence that is based on the denial of one's real feelings is difficult even for Shakespeare to convert into a significant poem. One anthology included this sonnet.

If our analysis of the procreation sonnets was persuasive, we have shown that they were more than just poems written to persuade an aristocratic young man to become a father. We believe their aim was to persuade the Poet to combat his own self-love, and that they were written to combat the fear the Poet felt that the time would come when he would lose his love for the Young Man.

CHAPTER 6:
LONGING AND INTERNALIZATION

SONNETS 27, 28, 43, 44, 45, 46, 47,
113, 50, 51, 52, 57, 58, 97

The pain of enforced separation between lovers seems to be the oldest theme in love poetry. It is already prominent 1,500 years before the Christian era. We quote a love poem written in Egypt between 1300 and 1100 BC.

Seven days since I saw my sister,
And sickness invaded me;
I am heavy in all my limbs,
My body has forsaken me,
When the physicians come to me,
My heart rejects their remedies;
The magicians are quite helpless,
My sickness is not discerned.
To tell me "She is here" would revive me (Bergmann 1987 p. 4)!

The metaphor of love as a form of sickness is also found in the Song of Songs (2:5). "Stay with me flagons, comfort me with apples: for I am sick of love (Ibid p. 4)."

Into this ancient theme the Poet of the Sonnets poured images and metaphors never used before. A number of sonnets repeat the same theme but use different metaphors, giving us a theme with variations. Accordingly we have broken these sonnets on longing and internalization into subgroups based on psychoanalytic themes. The first major theme connects the absent lover to insomnia. It extends over Sonnets 27, 28, and 43. Three hundred years before psychoanalysis established that insomnia is connected first with the absent mother and later with the inability of a person to find within her or himself a representation of the good mother. Shakespeare in these sonnets described insomnia as a longing for the absent lover. We observe that in Macbeth he will discover another form of insomnia based on unbearable guilt.

In Sonnets 44 and 45, the traditional four elements were expressed as metaphors to convey the pain of separation. In Sonnets 46 and 47, the pain of separation is developed as a conflict between eyes and heart. This metaphor enabled the Poet to discover the role of what we today call the internalization of the lover's image so as to make his absence bearable. In Sonnets 27, 28, 43 and 44, the Poet created a new vocabulary to describe how, when in love, and the lover unavailable, he succeeds in overcoming his longings by creating at night before his internal eyes the image of the man the Poet loves.

This is an idea that psychoanalysis successfully approached only after World War II, namely the internalization of the image of the mother by the child that enables the child to tolerate her absence. Psychoanalysts have found that the infant's fear of being separated from the mother is at its height during a specific period: from the moment the infant learns to differentiate between mother and stranger and until what is called "object constancy" is established. Separation from the caring mother is a major theme of early childhood. Mothers that never leave their children fail to promote them and mothers who are not maternal and leave the children to others prevent them from becoming capable of loving. At birth and shortly afterwards the infant is "promiscuous," smiling at every caretaker with the same pleasure. Then between six and eight months a "stranger anxiety" sets in; when handed to an unknown person the infant feels deeply unhappy and starts to cry. Eventually, as the inner image of the caretaker is established, the inner image can (up to a point) replace the real person. When this psychological process is successful the infant can tolerate the absence of the mother without becoming desperate (Spitz 1965). One of the unsolved problems of love is why this whole process is repeated and has to be mastered anew when one falls in love. That the process of internalization of the lover has to repeat itself is one psychoanalytic contribution to the understanding of love. The sonnets assembled in this chapter do not solve the problem, but they describe it.

In Chapter 4, Sonnet 49 we saw how a disturbing psychological process takes hold of the Poet as he attempts to teach himself to accept separation. He prepares himself for the permanent end of a love relationship, a kind of psychological preparation that is in danger of becoming a self-fulfilling prophecy. In the last two sonnets of this chapter, 50 and 51, the Poet transfers some of the burden of his feelings to the horse that carries him away from his lover. These sonnets suggest that it was the Poet rather than the lover who initiated the separation.

Because psychoanalysis has made us more aware of separation anxiety in childhood and the various side effects and coping mechanisms for resolving it as it reoccurs in adult relationships, our analysis of the poems in this chapter is different from those of traditional interpreters.

I.   SEPARATION AND INSOMNIA

SONNET 27

Weary with toil, I haste me to my bed,
The dear repose for limbs with travel tired,
But then begins a journey in my head
To work my mind, when body's work's expired.
For then my thoughts (from far where I abide)
Intend a zealous pilgrimage to thee,
And keep my drooping eyelids open wide,
Looking on darkness which the blind do see.
Save that my soul's imaginary sight
Presents thy shadow to my sightless view,
Which like a jewel (hung in ghastly night)
Makes black night beauteous, and her old face new.
    Lo thus by day my limbs, by night my mind,
    For thee, and for my self, no quiet find.

Many artists have drawn inspiration from the differentiation between day and night. We need only think of the "Day and Night" by Michelangelo in the Medici chapel in Florence, where day, a man, looks sternly at us and night, a woman, is entirely self-absorbed. In *Tristan and Isolde,* Wagner contrasts the philosophy of "day" with the philosophy of "night." And in *The Rape of Lucrece* (1571) we find that she "looks for night and then she longs for morrow."

In this sub-grouping of sonnets Shakespeare used the contrast between day and night to deal with the pain of separation.

In the above sonnet the Poet has gone to bed to seek repose for his tired limbs. This repose is labeled "dear" to tell us how highly that rest was valued. However, he cannot sleep. A new journey takes place in the Poet's head as his mind goes to work now that the body is at rest. The second quatrain explains the nature of this nocturnal journey. It consists of "… a zealous pilgrimage to thee," a beautiful metaphor to express longing, containing a hidden comparison between love and religion with blasphemous connotations because the lover has become the object of a pilgrimage. In line 8 the Poet implies, paradoxically, that the blind are capable of "looking on darkness," a metaphor for the imagination's capacity to evoke the image of the lover in his absence. The ability to imagine what is not there enables even the blind to see.

Unexpected in line 9 is the word "save." It suggests to us that the Poet felt that his capacity "to look on darkness" made possible "my soul's imaginary sight." In line 11 the lover's shadow is compared to a "jewel (hung in ghastly night)," which can make "black night beauteous and her old face new." Psychoanalysis has made us particularly aware of the beauty of this 12th line. Night is black and we know that black is not beautiful to the Poet, but the image of the lover on the inner eye of the Poet changed the experience and appearance of night. On psychoanalytic grounds we can add that the "old face" is an unconscious reference to the mother's face and the "new face" is that of the young lover.

The couplet is introduced by the evocative word "lo," with connotations of surprise. It reintroduces the first quatrain's idea that limbs work during the day and the mind is active at night. Here placed together in one line we get a greater sense of the relentless output of energy the Poet dispenses towards the lover. This animation is passed seamlessly to the lover in the duality expressed in the final line, "for thee, and for myself, no quiet find." The sonnet implies that the essence of love is a permanent state of longing and not finding repose.

In a psychoanalytic perspective, Sonnet 27 can be described as celebrating a successful internalization that makes it possible to imagine the lover as present and thus to diminish the longing.

The moment in childhood when the image of the mother is internalized coincides for many people with the first memory. What is amazing is that when we fall in love the same moment returns and has to be mastered once more. Sonnet 27 does not rank among Shakespeare's distinguished sonnets but it is remarkable that the Poet described an important moment in a love relationship when a key moment in childhood development has been recaptured. The sonnet was not included in any anthology.

SONNET 28

How can I then return in happy plight
That am debarred the benefit of rest?
When day's oppression is not eased by night,
But day by night and night by day oppressed.
And each (though enemies to either's reign)
Do in consent shake hands to torture me,
The one by toil, the other to complain
How far I toil, still farther off from thee.
I tell the day to please him thou art bright,
And dost him grace when clouds do blot the heaven:
So flatter I the swart-complexioned night,
When sparkling stars twire not thou gild'st the even.
But day doth daily draw my sorrows longer,
And night doth nightly make grief's length seem stronger.

Both Sonnet 27 and Sonnet 28 are sonnets of longing for the absent beloved, but if we compare them we learn that longing can evoke astonishingly different states of feeling. In Sonnet 27 the fantasy of the lover took over. The sonnet represented, psychologically speaking, the success of internalization. If this process is too successful, fantasy may be preferred over reality.

Unlike Sonnet 27, Sonnet 28 describes the moment when the absence of the mother and the separation from the lover can give rise to paranoid fear. The Poet does not feel deserted; he feels attacked. Day and night, usually enemies to each other, have joined forces to attack him. The attempt to internalize the absent lover is not in evidence. Instead, the separation from the lover evokes in the Poet a paranoid sense of being attacked. Sonnet 28 belongs to an earlier phase of childhood, when the internalization of the absent mother cannot yet take place, giving rise to an overwhelming anxiety.

"Happy plight" in the first line is one more example of Shakespeare's capacity to pair words that contradict each other. Yet what lacks logic is nonetheless psychologically true. We can experience "happy plight" when we experience contradictory emotions at the same time. The Poet finds himself "debarred the benefit of rest," but this restless state is experienced as a "happy plight." In the third line, the Poet reiterates what he said in Sonnet 27: that night offers no relief from the "day's oppression." In the fourth line, both day and night are animated. The day is oppressed by the night and the night by the painful memories of day. Traditionally, they are enemies, but here they declare truce in order to torture the Poet. The day tortures by demanding toil; the night tortures by creating unhappiness, here called "complain."

In the second quatrain the "happy plight" is expressed once more because the Poet cannot internalize the lover, as far as he toils at work he still feels further away from his absent lover. The third quatrain now introduces a new theme. Earlier we were told that both day and night combined their forces to torture the Poet. In this quatrain we learn that he flatters both. He says to the day "Thou art bright,/And dost him grace" even though this is not true because in fact clouds "blot the heaven," a symbolic reference to the lover's absence. The "swart-complexioned night" is also flattered when "sparkling stars twire," that is, when stars move in a dance. "Not thou gild'st the even" implies that the night is credited with brightness it does not deserve. Flattery of both day and night brings no relief; the day makes "sorrow longer" and night makes "grief's length seem stronger." The sonnet was not selected by any anthology.

When most I wink, then do mine eyes best see;
For all the day they view things unrespected,
But when I sleep, in dreams they look on thee,
And darkly bright, are bright in dark directed.
Then thou whose shadow shadows doth make bright,
How would thy shadow's form form happy show
To the clear day with thy much clearer light,
When to unseeing eyes thy shade shines so?
How would (I say) mine eyes be blessed made
By looking on thee in the living day,
When in dead night thy fair imperfect shade
Through heavy sleep on sightless eyes doth stay?
    All days are nights to see till I see thee,
    And nights bright days when dreams do show thee me.

In this sonnet the Poet overcomes the insomnia of longing and the difference between night and day discussed in Sonnets 27 and 28 is put to a new use to differentiate fantasy from reality. In the first line, the Poet introduces a paradox. He sees best when he winks; he thus introduces the difference between day and night. Throughout the day he sees only "things unrespected," unworthy of his attention because his lover is absent, implying that in the absence of the loved one the world around the Poet has lost its significance or is no longer alive for him. Many lovers have experienced a milder version of this feeling when traveling alone and seeing something and wishing their beloved was there to see it with them. But at night, when he dreams, the Poet can look upon his lover's shadow, which by contrast to the sights of the day evokes respect in the Poet. So far, the Poet has re-introduced the ideas of Sonnet 27, namely that the night is darkly bright because the lover's shadow illuminates it in the Poet's dream. The lover can make the dreams appear "darkly bright," as well as "bright in dark;" it is the "shadow" of the lover that brightens up the dreams. This shadow forms a "happy show." It has the power to make night clearer than the clear day, because the lover's "shade shines so." As in Sonnet 27, what is being celebrated in this sonnet is the victory of the inner psychic reality created by the Poet over the dismal reality caused by the lover's absence.

However, in the third quatrain this psychic reality is not allowed victory over outer reality. In spite of the shadow's brightness, the Poet's eyes would be blessed if he could look upon the lover in the living day. He tells us that until that day "imperfect shade" appearing in the dead of night "through heavy sleep on sightless eyes" is what the Poet lives on. The shade is imperfect because it is only an image of the real lover; the vocabulary that Plato introduced in the Western world is used by the Poet to deal with separation from the man the Poet loves. The sonnet conveys a balance between fantasy and reality. The reality of the lover's presence is most gratifying, but in his absence fantasy can make the absence easier to tolerate. The couplet reiterates that until the lover returns, days are nights and nights are days, "when dreams do show thee me." By reversing the role of day and night, and emphasizing the brightness of the lover's shadow, Shakespeare has created a love poem in which waking, longing and dreaming makes the night brighter than the day. This sonnet is happier than Sonnet 27 because the internalization of the lover has been more successful. This sonnet does not appear in any of the six anthologies.

SONNET 44

If the dull substance of my flesh were thought,
Injurious distance should not stop my way;
For then, despite of space, I would be brought
From limits far remote, where thou dost stay;
No matter then although my foot did stand
Upon the farthest earth removed from thee,
For nimble thought can jump both sea and land
As soon as think the place where he would be.
But ah, thought kills me, that I am not thought,
To leap large lengths of miles when thou art gone,
But that so much of earth and water wrought,
I must attend time's leisure with my moan;
  Receiving naughts by elements so slow
  But heavy tears, badges of either's woe.

As in Sonnet 43 the absence of the lover and the wish to undo the separation provides the impetus for this composition but the mood is lighter. Sonnet 44 is a very beautiful one, and it owes its attractiveness to the light touch with which it was crafted.

The sonnet begins with a creative fantasy. If the Poet were not made out of the dull substance of his flesh, injurious distance could not harm him. It is in the combination of the two words "injurious distance" that makes distance come to life, another example of a magnificent combination of words so often encountered in the sonnets. The unique idea of what it would be like to be made of thought rather than composed of flesh extends over the first two quatrains. Had the Poet's substance been thought rather than flesh, he would instantly be brought from "limits far removed" to "where thou dost stay." The poem culminates in a beautiful image in line 7: "For nimble thought can jump both sea and land."

If the first two quatrains represent a happy dream of what could have happened if the Poet were composed of mere thoughts, the third quatrain and the couplet represent the disappointment upon waking to reality. Realizing that he is not made of thought, and therefore cannot jump both sea and land, is said to kill him. The Poet cannot leap "large lengths of miles" in order to stay united with his lover. The Poet is made of the two heavy elements—earth and water, line 11, which ironically are the components of the sea and land that in line 6 separate him. This is in contrast to the two lighter elements—air and fire. Therefore, he must attend "time's leisure." This phrase in line 13, "I must attend time's leisure," should make us pause. Time is here personified and is like a king and the Poet, like a member of the king's court, is at the mercy of time's leisure, but time is attended to by the Poet's moan. What is also implied is that time, having so much leisure, is moving very slowly.

The separation has evoked in the Poet the need to submit and serve. The couplet draws the conclusion that the Poet receives naught by elements so slow, once more a reference to earth and water. These elements are eloquently combined as "heavy tears" in the last line. The tears are the Poet's "badges," his marks of distinction. What the Poet has accomplished is to take ideas traditionally associated with the four elements to express the heaviness evoked by the lover's absence. One anthology included this sonnet.

SONNET 45

The other two, slight air, and purging fire,
Are both with thee, wherever I abide:
The first my thought, the other my desire,
These, present absent, with swift motion slide;
For when these quicker elements are gone
In tender embassy of love to thee,
My life being made of four, with two alone
Sinks down to death, oppressed with melancholy,
Until life's composition be recurred
By those swift messengers returned from thee
Who even but now come back again assured
Of thy fair health, recounting it to me.
  This told, I joy; but then no longer glad,
  I send them back again and straight grow sad.

This sonnet, like the previous one, can be described as a learned sonnet using knowledge current among thinkers of the time to express love's difficulty. The metaphoric use of the four elements we found in Sonnet 44 is employed once more in this sonnet. Sonnet 44 dealt primarily with the two heavy elements, earth and water, because the Poet, made of flesh, could not like nimble thought leap over many miles. Sonnet 45 opens with the two lighter elements, here described as "slight air" and "purging fire." Because these two elements lack corporality, they did not participate in keeping the lovers apart, instead they leave the Poet and join the lover on his journey, serving in "tender embassy." The metaphor enables the Poet to deal with the lover as a kind of king receiving ambassadors. The Poet explains in line 3 that "slight air" represents the Poet's thoughts and "purging fire" represents the Poet's desire. Both thought and desire are so nimble that they abide with the lover.

Air is given the adjective slight and fire is described as purging. Being light they can "slide with swift motion." The addition of the word "purging" to "fire" implies that the Poet's desire had something elevating, or purifying. In the second quatrain we are told that both "slight air" and "purging fire" were sent "In tender embassy of love to thee," serving as the Poet's ambassadors to the absent lover. Deprived of the lighter elements, and now consisting of only the two heavy ones, the Poet "sinks down to death" and is "oppressed with melancholy." He is incurable, unless the two swift messengers return with the lover and make the Poet normal again, expressed as "until life's composition be recurred." When the messengers return, they must assure the Poet of the fair health of his lover. The couplet ends on a variation on the theme: if the messengers return the Poet will be briefly uplifted but will return to sadness without the lover's presence. He will therefore send them back to the lover for further news, and deprived of these lighter elements he will once more sink and "grow sad."

Sonnets 43, 44, and 45 are elegantly constructed, learned in the use of metaphor, where the four elements are used to illustrate the pangs of separation and the need to keep in touch. It is difficult to remember, in this day of e-mail and internationally roaming cell phones, what it was like to be separated from one's beloved without being able to stay in touch. Even Jane Austen's characters could wait for a letter, but in Shakespeare's day keeping in touch by letter was the privilege of royalty who could send ambassadors. So the Poet imagines that the lightest parts of him are so swift that he can use them as ambassadors and be happy when they return to him with the news that his lover is well. The reassurance does not last long, however—analogous to a child who has not yet learned to tolerate a long absence from the mother—the Poet quickly sends the most enjoyable part of him away again for more news. No anthology included this sonnet.

II. LOVE AND INNER CONFLICT

SONNET 46

Mine eye and heart are at a mortal war,
How to divide the conquest of thy sight,
Mine eye, my heart thy picture's sight would bar,
My heart, mine eye the freedom of that right,
My heart doth plead that thou in him dost lie,
(A closet never pierced with crystal eyes)
But the defendant doth that plea deny,
And says in him thy fair appearance lies.
To side this title is impanellèd
A quest of thoughts, all tenants to the heart,
And by their verdict is determinèd
The clear eye's moiety, and the dear heart's part.
    As thus, mine eye's due is thy outward part,
    And my heart's right, thy inward love of heart.

The eyes of the Poet control the sight of the beloved, that is, his visual image, but they bar, that is, prevent the heart from sharing the image. The heart in turn refuses to grant the eyes the freedom to decide the fate of that image, claiming that the beloved resides in the Poet's heart. The quarrel between heart and eye is a metaphor for promiscuity and fidelity. The eyes as organs are more apt to find other lovers; the heart is the organ of fidelity and the combination now becomes metaphor for ambivalence.

The eyes try to bar the lover's picture from entering the heart and the heart disputes their right to withhold his image, expressed as "mine eye, my heart, thy picture's sight would bar." The heart claims that the lover lies in his own heart, expressed as, "My heart doth plead that thou in him dost lie,/Never pierced with crystal eyes." The Poet compares the heart to a closet, a box, in which jewelry is kept, which was never pierced by crystal eyes. The eyes absorb sight and are crystal, while the heart remains opaque. In line 7, the eyes are the defendants in this pretended lawsuit. They claim that the lover resides in them, because they first spotted the Young Man. With irony, the eyes here are referred to as the defendant and they deny the heart's plea.

The word "side" in line 9 has evoked controversy. Some commentators derive it from decide, others from side or to take sides, the equivalent of being involved in a lawsuit. "Impanelléd" is to be compelled to appear in court. Quest of thoughts in line 10 means a jury made up of thoughts. "All tenants to the heart" means that they owe allegiance to the heart. It is the jury that will eventually determine the verdict, but the clear eye in line 12 insists on its "moiety," meaning its part or share. In the couplet, a compromise is reached. The outward part of the beloved will belong to the eye, while the heart will retain the inward part. The heart is constant but the eyes are more likely to be "false in rolling (Sonnet 20)."

In this debate, the eye has the advantage because the eye can evoke infatuation and sexual desire. The eye does not need the heart, and one is therefore reluctant to yield its monopolistic advantage. The heart, however, is dependent on the eye and needs it to initiate falling in love. The eye does not yield to the heart, for it claims that it alone can mirror the beloved. By introducing the eye and heart conflict, the Poet succeeds to transform a dyadic relationship between the two lovers into a triadic relationship consisting of heart, eye and lover. This conflict creates a triangular love.

What looked like a "mortal war" was easily resolved. Both eye and heart can keep what they are entitled to; to understand this sonnet we should assume that part of the Poet wished to reduce the relationship to something closer to flirtation, with the emphasis on bodily beauty; the other part, desiring closeness, aimed at a deeper and more lasting connection. Thus Shakespeare translated into a metaphor of the eye and heart a conflict familiar to many between the transient superficial relationship and a deeper and more permanent one. In this sonnet, the conflict was peacefully resolved, but as the rest of the sonnet shows, only temporarily.

Contemporary Shakespearian scholars have not commented favorably on this sonnet. According to Booth, "this sonnet presupposes a reader familiar with the endlessly reiterated Renaissance distinction between true love—from the heart—and mere infatuation—inspired by the sight of beauty;" Booth quotes from *Romeo and Juliet* "Young men's love, then lies—not truly in their heart but in their eyes." Commenting on the same sonnet, Vendler observes: "The conceit of eye and heart, outer and inner, is a traditional one, and the distributive solution also is traditional (the speaker's heart owns the beloved's inward heart, the speaker's eye, the beloved's outward part) thus reaffirming the dualism of 'inner essence' and 'outward show' (p. 234)."

Strictly speaking, Sonnets 46 and 47 are not separation sonnets and could have been included in the chapter "Meditation on the Nature of Love." We have included them in this chapter because they are related to the previous sonnet in their theme of the internalization process of the lover. By contrast we are suggesting that the traditional academic commentators miss the significance of the process of internalization that take place through the use of this admittedly by now banal metaphor. Although the war between the eye and the heart is described in the first line as a mortal war, the sonnet as a whole treats this subject humorously. No anthology has included this sonnet.

SONNET 47

Betwixt mine eye and heart a league is took,
And each doth good turns now unto the other,
When that mine eye is famished for a look,
Or heart in love with sighs himself doth smother;
With my love's picture then my eye doth feast,
And to the painted banquet bids my heart:
Another time mine eye is my heart's guest,
And in his thoughts of love doth share a part.
So either by thy picture or my love,
Thy self away, art present still with me,
For thou not farther than my thoughts canst move,
And I am still with them, and they with thee.
    Or if they sleep, thy picture in my sight
    Awakes my heart, to heart's and eye's delight.

As so frequently in Shakespeare's sonnets, Sonnet 47 is the counterbalance to the previous one. In Sonnet 46, the eye and the heart were in "mortal war." In this sonnet, the Poet plays with the idea of their cooperation. The aim of their cooperation is to achieve a peaceful and non-conflicting internalization of the loved one. If this can be achieved, the absence of the lover can be tolerated. One can look upon this poem as an ode to the capacity to internalize the lover while apart as a solution to the pain of missing him.

In Sonnet 46, there was a "mortal war" between eyes and heart, in this sonnet there is a "league" between them: each does a good turn to the other. When the eye is in love it is "famished for a look," but when the heart is in love it smothers itself with sighs. Together however neither of them is helpless, because the eye can feast with "my love's picture," and invite the heart to the banquet. The banquet is called "painted" because the lover is not there in person but only imagined. The situation can also be reversed: then the eyes are the heart's guest. The heart, unlike the eyes, lacks the capacity to present a painted image, but it can invite the eyes to participate in the heart's thoughts. The eyes can reflect; the heart can think. If they cooperate, imagination can mitigate the pain of separation.

The Poet has at his disposal two ways of undoing the pain of not always being in the presence of the man he loves, either the picture or the thought can recreate the absent lover. Once internalization has been achieved, the absent lover cannot be further than the Poet's thoughts of him. This is expressed by the Poet in line 10: "Thy self away, art present still with me." If the Poet can join the image of the lover provided by the eyes and the thoughts of him provided by the heart, he can be "still with them, and they with thee." What is acknowledged in this awkward language is that when the two are at odds the pain of separation prevails, but when the two cooperate imagination can recreate the absent lover. In sleep, the picture of the beloved becomes available to the Poet's inner sight. The image awakens the Poet's heart, to both eyes and heart's delight.

SONNET 113

Since I left you, mine eye is in my mind,
And that which governs me to go about
Doth part his function, and is partly blind;
Seems seeing, but effectually is out:
For it no form delivers to the heart
Of bird, of flower, or shape which it doth latch;
Of his quick objects hath the mind no part,
Nor his own vision holds what it doth catch:
For if it see the rud'st or gentlest sight,
The most sweet-favoured or deformed'st creature,
The mountain, or the sea, the day, or night,
The crow, or dove, it shapes them to your feature.
    Incapable of more, replete with you,
    My most true mind thus maketh mine untrue.

The conflict between eye and heart in earlier sonnets is somewhat modified into a conflict between eye and mind; when the two cooperate we speak of "in my mind's eye." The conflict forces the eye to "part his function," becoming "partly blind." The eye no longer "governs me to go about," that is, the eye has abdicated its role of the protector of mobility.

In the fourth line the Poet tells us that he is not literally blind and "seems seeing," but says it is "effectually...out," meaning ineffective.

In the second quatrain we learn that this non-functioning eye delivers "no form" to the heart. The idea that the organs of sight must cooperate with the heart to make internalization of the lover possible is here once more reported. When they fail to function, no form, no image of the loved one is delivered to the heart. Thus in line 6 even the images of birds and flowers, which to the Poet embody spring, are seen but fail to resonate. The same fate meets "Shape" perhaps the shape of the lover, or a general effusive disconnection with living things and objects alike. The word "latch" in line 6 is difficult to interpret; to latch means to pay attention to and to notice. Some interpreters think that latch is a misprint of lack. Quick objects moving rapidly cannot be retained by the mind. Line 7 can be read as saying that even when a vision is caught it cannot be retained.

In the third quatrain the Poet turns to the mind's eye for help but that too suffers an equal but slightly different dysfunction. The Poet now states that to him all nature takes on the features of the loved man: "the rud'st or gentlest sight" (here "rud'st" means most uncivilized), "the most sweet-favoured or deformed'st creature," the mountain as well as the sea, day as well as night, and the crow and the dove—all these diverse creatures are so transformed by the mind's eye that they take on the lovers features. In the couplet the Poet is "replete with you," meaning that the lover occupies all the inner space of the Poet; nothing is real to the Poet except the man he loves. What we hear is that love has totally distorted differences and converted all perception to replicate the man the Poet loves. The mind that is "most true" because it encompasses only the lover makes the Poet's eyes untrue, that is, incapable of seeing what is real.

Since their separation, the eyes have stopped taking in impressions of the outside world. This perceptual indifference toward the outside world is due to the fact that the Poet is entirely preoccupied by the image of his beloved. Many lovers have dimly perceived that their love object occupies an inordinate inner space in their lives, and their love had diminished their interest in the outside world. But we know of no one to have claimed that the landscape itself takes on the features of the beloved. But the Poet of the sonnet has succeeded in putting into words a feeling that usually remains only at the periphery of awareness: he has given this "eerie nothing" a beautiful new verbal habitation.

III. THE HORSE AS A CO-PARTICIPANT IN THE SEPARATION

SONNET 50

How heavy do I journey on the way
When what I seek, my weary travel's end,
Doth teach that ease and that repose to say,
'Thus far the miles are measured from thy friend.'
The beast that bears me, tired with my woe,
Plods dully on to bear that weight in me,
As if by some instinct the wretch did know
His rider loved not speed being made from thee:
The bloody spur cannot provoke him on
That sometimes anger thrusts into his hide,
Which heavily he answers with a groan,
More sharp to me than spurring to his side,
    For that same groan doth put this in my mind:
    My grief lies onward and my joy behind.

Psychoanalysts often have the chance to observe how a disappointment in human beings can cause feelings to be drawn away from people and to be transferred to animals. A pet can become as dear as child would have been, and its death evoke not only mourning but even melancholia. Sonnet 50 is of interest because of the intimate relationship between the Poet and his horse. Its subject matter is once more the separation from the lover. But the relationship to the animal is at the core of the poem.

The sonnet opens with the Poet on a journey. He feels heavy, because when he finally will reach his destination, he will only be many miles further away from his lover. Instead of the expected ease and repose at the end of his journey, he will experience the pain of being further separated. The second quatrain introduces the relationship to the "beast." It too is tired with the rider's woe and "plods dully" on, bearing the weight of the rider. The word instinct in line 7 is striking because we are not prepared to find it in Shakespeare's language. It is the only place the word instinct appears in the sonnets; in Shakespeare's work it appeared 16 times. The most extensive use of the term instinct is in *Henry IV, Part I,* Act II, scene IV, where the word is closely associated with fear. Prince Hal tells his friends, "…you are lions too, you ran away upon instinct (300)" and later, proclaiming that he is not afraid, notes, "I lack some of thy instinct (372)."

The word was just at that time coming into use. It meant an "innate propensity especially in lower animals varying with the species and manifesting itself in acts that appeared to be rational but are performed without conscious adaptation." The term "wretch" in the same line combines pity with affection.

In the third quatrain, even the spur, bloody from how hard the Poet has kicked the horse, fails to drive the horse on. The rider becomes angry with the horse, and thrusts the spurs into the animal's hide. All the animal can do is to groan, and that is all that his rider can do as well. A subtle displacement has taken place. The suffering of the Poet has been displaced onto the horse. In line 12, the Poet tells us that his pain of separation is more sharp than the "spurring to his [horse's] side." The sonnet ends on a sad note, that only grief lies onward and all joy was left behind. The atmosphere in the sonnet suggests that the separation was not a temporary one. By so vividly describing how the horse called "wretch" "plods dully" and can only "groan," with the "bloody spur" thrust into his hide, the Poet has evoked our participation in a journey that only separates him further from the man he loves. By using the metaphor of the journey, the Poet has found another way of expressing the pain of the lovers' separation. No anthology included this sonnet.

SONNET 51

Thus can my love excuse the slow offence
Of my dull bearer, when from thee I speed:
From where thou art, why should I haste me thence?
Till I return, of posting is no need.
O what excuse will my poor beast then find,
When swift extremity can seem but slow?
Then should I spur, though mounted on the wind;
In winged speed no motion shall I know;
Then can no horse with my desire keep pace;
Therefore desire, of perfect'st love being made,
Shall neigh no dull flesh in his fiery race,
But love, for love, thus shall excuse my jade:
    Since from thee going he went wilful slow,
    Towards thee I'll run, and give him leave to go.

Sonnets 50 and 51 are related to each other, and alone Sonnet 51 loses much of its meaning. Both deal with the same feeling state and use the horse as the central metaphor of the narrative. Nevertheless, the relationship between rider and horse is very different in the two sonnets. In Sonnet 50, the horse slowed down by some instinct, as if the beast knew that the rider "loveth not to speed" away from his lover. In Sonnet 51, the horse appears already in the first quatrain (while in Sonnet 50 the horse appeared only in the second quatrain) and plays a greater role in the narrative. What is remarkable when one reads those two sonnets one after the other is that in spite of such marked similarities, the two sonnets express very different states of feeling. In Sonnet 50, the Poet was separating from his lover without any prospect of reunion. In Sonnet 51 the possibility of reunion makes the sonnet an optimistic one.

The Poet asks why he should hasten away from his lover. Until the return journey, no posting is necessary. "Posting" is a reference is to traveling swiftly with important message when, in order to save time, horses were exchanged to avoid fatigue. But this posting technique is pointless when the Poet leaves his lover behind. The second quatrain is a daydream. The Poet imagines how it will feel to travel towards his lover; then even "swift extremity" will be experienced as too slow. The Poet will spur his horse even if he will be "mounted on the wind." No horse can hope to meet the Poet's desire to return to the lover fast enough. In the last quatrain, the race for reunion is described as a "fiery race" and no dull nor heavy flesh will be allowed to impede this imagined reunion. The term "winged speed" refers to the mythological Pegasus, the horse with wings. But even Pegasus will be unable to move as fast as the desire of the Poet dictates. The word "neigh" is not accepted by all commentators, some suggesting that the word "weigh" replace it. In either case, dull or heavy flesh is unfavorably compared to the "fiery race" that thoughts of love are capable of performing a return to the four elements discussed in Sonnet 50. The word "jade" in line 12 means a worn-out or worthless horse. The couplet summarizes the situation once more. Leaving the beloved, the horse was welcome when it was "wilful slow," but now that the Poet rushes toward his lover, the horse is too slow to be of use. The Poet believes that towards his lover he can run faster and therefore will give the horse leave to go. There is something commonplace and uninspired about both sonnets; neither of them was included in any anthology.

IV. THE CONCEPT OF "SELDOM PLEASURE"

SONNET 52

So am I as the rich whose blessed key,
Can bring him to his sweet up-locked treasure,
The which he will not every hour survey,
For blunting the fine point of seldom pleasure.
Therefore are feasts so solemn and so rare,
Since seldom coming in the long year set,
Like stones of worth they thinly placed are,
Or captain jewels in the carcanet.
So is the time that keeps you as my chest,
Or as the wardrobe which the robe doth hide,
To make some special instant special-blest,
By new unfolding his imprisoned pride.
      Blessed are you whose worthiness gives scope,
      Being had to triumph, being lacked to hope.

The sonnet opens with a parable. The Poet compares himself to a rich man who possesses a key to "a sweet up-locked treasure." The key itself this rich man considers blessed because it opens for him the pleasure of looking at his treasure. The man uses this key only on rare occasions, expressed as "will not every hour survey," because he lives in fear of "blunting the fine point of seldom pleasure." "Seldom pleasure" is more than just pleasure experienced rarely; it is a unique pleasure, experienced only because it is rare. The Poet experiences love as a "seldom pleasure" that should not be blunted by lovers being together too often or for too long periods of time. Is the Poet merely trying to transform a bitter necessity into a virtue or does he believe that their love can continue only if it is a "seldom pleasure?" The sonnet invites comparison with Sonnet 75, where the metaphor of the miser was also used, but the concept of "seldom pleasure" was not available to the Poet at that time. We note that in Sonnet 75 the word "miser" was used explicitly, while in Sonnet 52 the term used is "the rich."

The second quatrain introduces the example of feasts they celebrated as solemn because they occur rarely. These holidays are "set" in a long year at long intervals from each other. In line 7 another metaphor is introduced, "stones of worth" thinly placed, meaning placed far apart, to enhance the feeling of their high value. We note that the metaphor of the "stones of worth" belongs to the first metaphor of "up-locked treasure," but the Poet has separated the two by the metaphor of "feasts that occur only rarely." Through a rapid change of many metaphors, monotony was avoided. The second quatrain introduces the metaphor of the carcanet. In a carcanet (a necklace usually of gold and jewels) there is one jewel that is bigger than the others, and this jewel is called "captain jewels." Being bigger it is also isolated from the rest of the jewelry.

The third quatrain introduces the fourth metaphor, of the robe seldom taken out of the wardrobe. In the same way the Poet will keep the lover in his chest, that is, the lovers will meet at rare intervals but when they do their meeting will be "some special instant" and therefore also "special-blest." The special robe is the pride of its owner but because it is so seldom used it is called "imprisoned pride." The sonnet ends on a note of submission. The worthiness of the lover gives scope to the relationship. It is a triumph to have him but if the Poet cannot have him, there is at least hope. The sonnet can be read as a desperate attempt to transform the painful fact that the two are together only rarely into something special. It is difficult to know if this sonnet gives comfort to the many lovers who are in this predicament. The Poet has given us four metaphors—treasure, feasts, captain jewels and robe—all designed to make him, and by implication us his readers, accept long separations between lovers.

In the couplet the Poet resorts to a religious vocabulary to express his feelings about his lover. The word "blessed" (Benedictus) which appeared in the first line is repeated here. The lover is blessed because his worthiness enlarged the Poet's scope. When the relationship was satisfactory, the Poet felt "being had to triumph;" but when the lover was absent, it turned into "being lacked to hope."

Dover Wilson compares this metaphor with *Henry IV, Part I*, III.ii.56:

My presence like a robe pontifical,
Ne'er seen but wond'rd at; and so not many but my state,
Seldom but sumptuous, showed like a feast,
And won by rareness such solemnity,

Poet and playwright used very different words but the idea and even the metaphors have been used twice. Vendler observed that the word "robe" is literally hidden inside the word "wardrobe." If the poem were a logical structure, we could raise an objection at this point. The Poet has already justified the rare meeting with three metaphors. Why another metaphor of the robe in the wardrobe on rare ceremonial occasions? But unlike the previous three metaphors, the robe metaphor is animated "By new unfolding his imprisoned pride." The robe is both proud as well as imprisoned in the wardrobe. The Poet has projected his own feelings of being both proud and imprisoned on the robe. Only through the metaphor of the robe does the Poet express the unfolding of his own imprisoned pride. One metaphor may have been persuasive, but four show that the Poet at least unconsciously remained unpersuaded. Is he protesting too much?

Sonnet 52 deals with an important psychological and philosophical question: is pleasure dependent on scarcity or can it be maintained even if it is always available? The sonnet is noteworthy for creating the term "seldom pleasure." The term never appears again in Shakespeare's writing. The sonnet can be read in two ways. Since the lovers can only meet on rare occasions, the Poet may be trying to make a virtue out of necessity, or the lovers cannot combine love with everyday cares and trivialities. Men and women who cannot combine love with the cares of everyday life consciously or unconsciously select lovers who live far away, or who are for other reasons only available at rare intervals. No anthology selected this sonnet, but in our estimate, because it introduced the concept of "seldom pleasure" and because it summoned three different metaphors in its defense it deserved better than to have gone unnoticed.

SONNET 57

Being your slave what should I do but tend,
Upon the hours, and times of your desire?
I have no precious time at all to spend;
Nor services to do till you require.
Nor dare I chide the world-without-end hour,
Whilst I (my sovereign) watch the clock for you,
Nor think the bitterness of absence sour,
When you have bid your servant once adieu.
Nor dare I question with my jealous thought,
Where you may be, or your affairs suppose,
But like a sad slave stay and think of nought
Save where you are, how happy you make those.
   So true a fool is love, that in your will,
   (Though you do any thing) he thinks no ill.

Like the other sonnets in this chapter, Sonnet 57 deals with what happens when the lovers are separated. However, this sonnet deals with separation from a new perspective. The separation in this sonnet is more than a geographic one; longing for the lover may still be the source, but the Poet not only feels abandoned, he also feels he has no right to object. The pain of the separation goes deeper. The Poet not only lost the man he loves, he also lost a sense of self as a result of the lover's abandonment.

Sonnet 57 describes a state of feeling many lovers dread, when healthy self-love and healthy self-regard have yielded to submission. In this sonnet the Poet coined a splendid metaphor for this passive waiting state of feeling, "the world-without-end hour."

Roland Barthes (1978) described all lovers as "always in a state of waiting." Shakespeare's sonnets confirms Barthes' claim that tortured and prolonged waiting are the hallmarks of masochistic love. This sonnet, like Sonnet 75 and others, can be seen as sonnets of the narcissistic depletion that lovers feel when all their self love has gone into the love of the other, leaving the self impoverished; they are, so to speak, the very opposites of the self-love that dominated Sonnet 62. Here is how Shakespeare treated these themes in Sonnet 57:

The Poet is his lover's slave. He can only "tend upon," that is wait upon, the hours and times when his lovers chooses to be with him. Without the lover his own time has no value. He has "no precious time at all to spend." He is allowed only to wait to render the required services. The Poet has no room to express wishes of his own; all feelings are at the service of the other. In this state of perpetual waiting time passes slowly and seems endless. Line 5 contains the striking "world-without-end hour." Ordinarily in a state of bliss, lovers desire time to stand still, not to pass so quickly, but in this sonnet the Poet expresses the opposite feeling: a world without an end hour is painful, like a life sentence without parole. The Poet is passively watching the clock and waiting. He prohibits himself any bitter thoughts that could make the absence of the loved one "sour." When he was "bid adieu" he did not dare question the separation with jealous thoughts. The Poet lives under the obligation to suppress all hostile feelings.

In the third quatrain we learn how hard the Poet is trying to suppress his jealousy. Instead of experiencing the jealousy, he forces himself to identify himself with the man he loves and think how happy the lover makes other claimants to his affection. In the couplet the Poet sees himself as love's true fool, to follow wherever his will lead him without thinking ill of him. The masochist's inner world mirrors dictatorships where every sign of opposition or even the expression of divergent thoughts are subjected to censorship. The word "will" in the couplet may be a play on Shakespeare's name and the reference to himself in the third person; Will can think no ill.

We have seen that when the lover is away, the Poet can cope with his absence in different ways, and the sonnets assembled in this chapter illustrate the different strategies the Poet adopted. The Poet can try to bring the lover back in fantasy, as he did in Sonnets 27 and 43. The failure of this effort resulted in Sonnet 28. In Sonnets 44 and 45 the Poet uses the metaphor of the four elements to cope with his longing. All these sonnets show an active effort to deal with the pain of separation. Sonnet 57 is the exception. It admits defeat and shows how masochism can emerge when separation is beyond the power to bear. Two anthologies included this sonnet.

SONNET 58

That god forbid, that made me first your slave,
I should in thought control your times of pleasure,
Or at your hand th'account of hours to crave,
Being your vassal bound to stay your leisure.
O let me suffer, being at your beck,
Th'imprisoned absence of your liberty,
And patience tame, to sufferance bide each check,
Without accusing you of injury.
Be where you list, your charter is so strong
That you yourself may privilege your time
To what you will; to you it doth belong
Yourself to pardon of self-doing crime.
    I am to wait, though waiting so be hell,
    Not blame your pleasure be it ill or well.

Sonnet 58 continues the same theme of Sonnet 57 with stronger metaphors. What the Poet achieved is to make waiting the central emotional experience. Since Homer idealized the waiting of Penelope for the return of Odysseus, the capacity to wait has been regarded as the essence of true love. But this sonnet throws doubt on this long-hallowed assumption. Can one still speak of love when every hostile thought or feeling has to be suppressed? Is the Poet still in love or merely addicted to pain? The Poet was convinced that his waiting was a sign of his truthful loving, but we the readers reflecting upon this sonnet may come to a different conclusion.

Vendler has called Sonnet 58 a "sardonic fantasia on the words you and your, with 17 instances in 14 lines." By this heavy bombardment of "you" and "your," the Poet conveys a surrender of himself to somebody else in a way that bypasses our conscious awareness.

In the first two lines, the Poet prays to the very same god, probably Cupid, that made the Poet "first your slave" to extend his tyranny and not allow the Poet "in thought control your times of pleasure." We note that not only verbal complaints are forbidden, but even thoughts are prohibited. In line 3, "Or at your hand th'account of hours to crave," to crave is to ask humbly. As an act of kindness the Poet feels he has no right to control the time his lover engages with others. Masochists often wonder and would like to know in detail the lover's sexual affairs with other people, but this humiliating pleasure the Poet forbids himself from experiencing. Line 6 is one of those memorable lines in which Shakespeare excels, "Th'imprisoned absence of your liberty." The lover is at liberty but the Poet is imprisoned by the lover's absence. Line 7, "And patience tame, to sufferance bide each check," created difficulty for Shakespeare's commentators. "Patient tame" is an example of Shakespeare's way of combining words, which probably means made tame by patience. "Bide each cheek" would then mean endure each limitation imposed upon me. Both patience and sufferance hold each other in check, that is, they tolerate the pain inflicted on the Poet without objecting to the lover's disloyalties. In line 9, "be where you list" means do whatever you feel like, as in *The Merry Wives of Windsor,* "go to bed when she lists, rise when she lists." The lover is given the right to "list," or his own right to behave as he wishes. He is under no obligation to gratify any of the wishes for intimacy expected by the Poet. The lover is sovereign about his own wishes, while the Poet is deprived of any rights. And finally, the Young Man himself retains the right to pardon any of the crimes he committed, here referred to as "self-doing crime." The couplet reinforces the note of submission. The Poet has to wait on the youth's pleasure even though waiting is hell. What the Poet is trying to achieve in this sonnet is a love devoid of any demands for reciprocity. The sonnet therefore idealizes what we would call today masochistic love. No anthology included this extremely masochistic sonnet.

V.   WHEN THE POET'S FEMININE IDENTIFICATION IS REVEALED

SONNET 97

How like a winter hath my absence been
From thee, the pleasure of the fleeting year!
What freezings have I felt, what dark days seen,
What old December's bareness everywhere!
And yet this time removed was summer's time,
The teeming autumn big with rich increase
Bearing the wanton burden of the prime,
Like widowed wombs after their lords' decease:
Yet this abundant issue seemed to me
But hope of orphans, and unfathered fruit;
For summer and his pleasures wait on thee,
And thou away, the very birds are mute;
> Or if they sing, 'tis with so dull a cheer
> That leaves look pale, dreading the winter's near.

This very beautiful sonnet, which three anthologies have included, is at variance with the earlier sonnets in this chapter, where the Poet tried so very hard to keep alive the inner image of the absent lover. The despair that prevails in this sonnet suggests to us that more than a physical separation gave rise to this sonnet. Amazing and not easy to understand are the many references to pregnancy and abandonment in this poem. We note "bareness" in line 4, "teeming autumn" in line 6, "Bearing the wanton burden" in line 7, "widowed wombs" in line 8, "abundant issue" in line 9 and "unfathered fruit" in line 10. We surmise that in this work the Poet's feminine identification was particularly strong.

We have become accustomed to the Poet's loving descriptions of nature as illustrations of his feelings for the Young Man. In Sonnet 97, however, the beautiful summer and autumn that the Poet observes take place while he is away from the Young Man. The Poet has begun—however incongruously—to note the beauty of the world around him even though he is apart from his lover and therefore the winters that frame the poem. There is winter in the first line and another winter in the last line. The first winter may be the desolation he first felt at the beginning of the separation and the dreaded winter in the last line may be the waning of his love.

The first quatrain compares absence to winter; all is like dark December with bareness everywhere. This absence seemed like freezing and the days are dark. The lover was the Poet's "pleasure" in the last year, now gone, expressed as "the fleeting year." Typically we would expect, as in the other sonnets, "your absence from me." The phrase here is reversed to "my absence from thee." Has the Poet initiated the separation? The Poet chooses four ways of describing how the separation is felt: 1) freezing, 2) dark, 3) old December, and 4) bareness everywhere, lines 3 and 4. The word "bareness" evoked in the Poet an identification with abandoned women and that identification determined the second quatrain. In sharp contrast to the desolation of the first quatrain, and very surprising, the second quatrain evokes the imagery of pregnancy. In line 6 the autumn of separation was "big with rich increase," but the Poet could not enjoy the increase.

Line 7, not easily interpretable, is a very interesting line: "Bearing the wanton burden of the prime." The word "wanton" connotes superabundance, or excessive sexual freedom. The word wanton implies pleasurable, frolicsome and amorously sportive, as in *Richard II*—"Four lagging winters and four wanton springs (I.iii.214)." The word "burden" implies a child in the womb, while "of the prime" refers to the youth of the mother. Was the lover attempting impregnation? Line 8 is more explicit; the lover's absence is now compared to "widowed wombs after their lords' decease." That one man's absence should affect the other man like a widowed womb after the husband had died sounds strange to us, but it reveals the depth of the Poet's identification with a deserted woman.

In line 9 the feeling of plentitude is still present, expressed in "abundant issue," but the sense of desolation is also present, expressed in line 10 as "hope of orphans" and "unfathered fruit." Again we see the Poet's feminine identification in this choice wording. It is not easy to grasp and even harder to accept that, deserted by the lover, the Poet speaks of himself first as pregnant in line 7, then like a widowed womb in line 8 and "unfathered fruit" in line 10.

If our reading of this sonnet is accepted, then the feminine identification of the Poet went further than ever before revealed. That men can experience intense identification with women and with the feminine aspect of themselves is encountered in psychoanalysis. It was too difficult for the academic interpreters of Shakespeare's sonnets, but if this identification is not faced this sonnet is very difficult to interpret.

Line 11 explains the contradictions experienced by the Poet: "For summer and his pleasures wait on thee." The line implies that the Poet may have been promiscuous in the absence of the lover but the real pleasures of the summer can be experienced only with the lover.

With the lover away, the birds sing no more and are mute. The couplet mitigates the verdict somewhat to say that if the birds are not mute and still sing it is "with so dull a cheer" that one might as well assume that they are mute. It is still summer, but the leaves "look pale," dreading the coming of winter. In the couplet the Poet implies that the break in their relationship has not in fact as yet taken place, but the Poet dreads its coming.

The sonnet is not easy to understand, but even after all the obscure passages have been illuminated the puzzles of the sonnet remain: namely the Poet's baffling capacity for identification with the pregnant widow. We find this overcoming of the prohibition separating the genders gives this sonnet a strange beauty.

It seems the very same muse whose generosity we praised in Chapter 2 has turned niggardly in this chapter. Separation, unlike the fear of death, did not stir up the Poet to his very depth and yet it would be a loss were we not to have these sonnets. No sonnet discussed in this chapter, except Sonnet 97, can be counted among the best known. The sonnets are clever, the metaphors learned and often original, but the sonnets fail to convince us that the Poet really suffered when his lover was away. The fear of death was very real to the Poet of the Sonnets; the fear of separation impresses us as far less genuine.

CHAPTER 7:
THE HETEROSEXUAL COMPONENT

THE DYADIC SONNETS: 128, 143, 138, 140, 141, 127, 130, 131, 137, 151, 147, 149, 150, 139, 142, 152

One of the striking features of Shakespeare's sonnets is that a break occurs. Beginning with Sonnet 127, the last 27 sonnets are no longer addressed to the Young Man that the Poet so greatly idealized, but to a dark-haired, married, but promiscuous woman referred to as the Dark Lady. Unlike his relationship to the Young Man, the Poet's relationship to this woman is an ambivalent one, strikingly devoid of idealization. Only a few of these sonnets, such as Sonnets 128, 132 and 143, can be described as love sonnets, and none of them is in any way remarkable. In this chapter we will discuss the dyadic sonnets addressed to the Dark Lady, and leave the triadic ones to the next chapter.

On the basis of stylometric work, which consists of comparing rare words used in the sonnets and the same words appearing in the plays, Burrow (p. 105) constructed a likely sequence in which the sonnets were composed:

127-154 composed 1591-1595 (28 sonnets)
61-103 composed 1594-95 (43 sonnets)
1-60 composed 1595-96 (60 sonnets)
104-126 composed 1598-1604 (23 sonnets)

Even if Burrows' argument is convincing, the sequence in which the sonnets were written will not tell us in what sequence the real or imaginary events proceeded. It is possible that the Poet started the heterosexual relationship to fullfill the dichotomy expressed in Sonnet 20 between asexual homosexual love and heterosexual, loveless sex, referred to as "love's use." Later on, either in fact or in the Poet's imagination, his two partners began a sexual relationship with each other, for which the Poet blamed the woman in a series of bitter sonnets.

This sequence suggests that the Dark Lady sonnets were the first to be written, implying that heterosexual disappointment preceded homosexual love. In the introduction, we commented on the fact that Freud's idea of the "flexibility of the libido" helps explain the conflict among self-love, heterosexual love, and homosexual love in the sonnets. The placement of the heterosexual love in the sequence raises the question of whether the order in which the sonnets were written is important. If the heterosexual sonnets were written first, it was the heterosexual disappointment that ushered in the homosexual love. However, if we assume that the Poet unconsciously brought about the triangulation of the affair himself because the homosexual component, although unconscious, was so powerful, then we could say it was ultimately the Poet's love for his male companion that caused the break in the heterosexual relationship. When the heterosexual component is strong and a disappointment takes place, another woman will replace the disappointing one. As Shakespeare described in *Romeo and Juliet,* Rosaline's aloofness paved the way for Juliet. If, however, the heterosexual component is weak and disappointment takes place, the next love object will either be self-love or homosexual love.

Since nothing is known about the sequence in which the sonnets in this chapter were written, we have reclassified them in terms of the feelings the Poet expresses for the woman he believes he loves. sonnets that can be classified as heterosexual love sonnets are 128 and 143. Sonnets advocating accommodation between him and her are 138 and 140. Sonnets expressing ambivalence and inner conflict are many: 127, 130, 131, 127, 141, 147, 149 and 150. Sonnets 139, 142, 148 and 152 express bitter disappointment. The very fact that we find only two sonnets that can be classified as love poems, another two that advocate accommodation, and a further 10 that must be classified as ambivalent or inner conflict sonnets, suggests that the heterosexual chapter was one of intense inner conflict.

SONNET 128

How oft when thou, my music, music play'st
Upon that blesséd wood whose motion sounds
With thy sweet fingers when thou gentle sway'st
The wiry concord that mine ear confounds,
Do I envy those jacks that nimble leap,
To kiss the tender inward of thy hand,
Whilst my poor lips which should that harvest reap,
At the wood's boldness by thee blushing stand.
To be so tickled they would change their state
And situation with those dancing chips,
O'er whom thy fingers walk with gentle gait,
Making dead wood more blest than living lips,
  Since saucy jacks so happy are in this,
  Give them thy fingers, me thy lips to kiss.

We begin with Sonnet 128 because it is the closest to a love poem. It is addressed to a woman, but unlike many of the other sonnets in this chapter it shows no ambivalence and no quarrel, but is a sonnet of longing. This is one of the more pleasant sonnets to the Dark Lady. It is of interest psychologically because it stresses a fetishistic envy on the part of the Poet that we have not encountered before. If we can accept the envy of the musical instrument as a pleasant metaphor then all is well, but in our reading the unpleasant fetishistic implications cannot entirely be excluded.

Scholars have identified the instrument the Poet's mistress is playing as the virginal, an instrument resembling the spinet but without legs. The sound is produced by plucking, rather than by striking. Two paintings by Vermeer, one of a woman standing by a virginal and another of the same woman playing on it, have made this instrument familiar to art lovers. The Poet flatters his lady in the first line that she herself is his music. In the fourth line, "wiry concord" means the harmony produced by the strings of the virginal; "mine ear confounds" is an unexpected and illogical response to the word "concord." That the two contradictory emotions are evoked at the same time by the lady's exquisite playing heightens the Poet's supposed admiration of her. The Poet envies the "jacks" (keys) of the virginal because they have come to life and of their own volition rise "to kiss the tender inward" of her hands. In line 8 we are told that the Poet's lips stand "blushing" to see the impudence of the keys of the virginal. The jacks of the virginal are experienced as "saucy," and "leap" boldly in the expression of their sexual wishes. The Poet offers a humorous compromise, charming but trivial: let the virginal have her fingers and let the Poet have her lips.

In his plays Shakespeare sometimes extended jealousy beyond the human realm, even to inanimate objects. Romeo wished he could be a glove on Juliet's hands and Cleopatra exclaimed "Lucky horse that bears the weight of Antony." Vendler has pointed out that through synecdoche the mistress is reduced to hand and fingers and the Poet to an eye looking at her, an ear listening to her music, and finally to lips desiring her kisses. We would add that synecdoche has a deeper meaning in psychoanalysis, for this process reduces the love for a person to a love for a part of the person. When such a reduction takes place, love is replaced by a sexual yearning for parts of the body, such as the breasts or penis, possibly at the expense of the relationship between two people. The sonnet has been interpreted as only "playing" at jealousy. This may well be so, but we recall a woman in treatment who was married to a musician. She became jealous of his instrument. She was jealous of the fact that he spent many hours practicing and that he loved his instrument. She had to restrain herself from damaging the musical instrument.

Fetishistic jealousy is jealousy of an inanimate object that receives more love than the person who becomes jealous. Shakespeare may have known the pangs of fetishistic jealousy from personal experience. In subsequent sonnets, we will see that the humorous envy of "those jacks" anticipates the more serious envy that will animate the other sonnets to this lady. This sonnet does not appear in any anthology. We suspect that the Poet's fetishistic jealousy confounds the ears of many readers.

SONNET 143

Lo as a careful huswife runs to catch
One of her feathered creatures broke away,
Sets down her babe and makes all swift dispatch
In pursuit of the thing she would have stay:
Whilst her neglected child hold her in chase,
Cries to catch her whose busy care is bent
To follow that which flies before her face,
Not prizing her poor infant's discontent;
So run'st thou after that which flies from thee,
Whilst I thy babe chase thee afar behind.
But if thou catch thy hope turn back to me,
And play the mother's part, kiss me, be kind.
    So will I pray that thou mayst have thy Will,
    If thou turn back and my loud crying still.

Sonnets 128 and 143, in marked contrast to the later ones, are closer to traditional love poetry. In them, the woman receives something of the worshipful attitude the Poet showed to the Young Man.

Sonnet 143 is rare among the dyadic heterosexual sonnets, in that the Poet's love for the lady is stronger than his hostility towards her. It is a sonnet in which a reconciliation between them is envisioned, and for this purpose he has created a new metaphor, that of the careful housewife and mother who only temporarily neglects her babe to run after "feathered creatures." Like the child who has to give up hope of being the sole possessor of his mother and is glad to welcome her when she returns, so the Poet renounces his wish to be the sole possessor of his lady and is willing to share her provided she returns to him. Without saying so explicitly, the Poet hints that he will accept and may unconsciously even prefer a relationship in which the lady runs after other men, who in turn flee from her. A comic note is introduced into this sonnet by the sly reduction of his rival to a chicken soon to be caught and eaten—a "feathered creature."

Sonnet 143 describes a love relationship based on losing and re-finding as a form of loving. The sonnet is noteworthy because the Poet acknowledges in metaphorical language Freud's discovery that all finding is re-finding, meaning that the mother-child love is the basis for all future loves. From a psychoanalytic point of view, the sonnet shows a connection between what the psychoanalyst Margaret Mahler demonstrated takes place in the years of infancy, when toddlers leave the mother to explore their own world, but expect her to be there when they look back. In this sonnet the process is reversed; it is the mother who runs away and returns. In this sonnet, the lovers' relationship consists of reliving that part of childhood. In such a relationship, one of the partners complains of being continuously deserted and the other answers, "But I always come back." No anthology included this sonnet, perhaps because there is no place for the reader in this sonnet. This kind of attempt at reconciliation is too private an endeavor to allow others to identify themselves with the Poet.

The sonnet is the first of the "Will" sonnets. The Poet, as well as his lover, was called William, and the name lends itself to be used as will in the sense of willing or desiring, as well as implying events in the future.

SONNET 138

When my love swears that she is made of truth,
I do believe her, though I know she lies,
That she might think me some untutored youth
Unlearned in the world's false subtleties.
Thus vainly thinking that she thinks me young,
Although she knows my days are past the best,
Simply I credit her false-speaking tongue;
On both sides thus is simple truth suppressed.
But wherefore says she not she is unjust?
And wherefore say not I that I am old?
O love's best habit is in seeming trust,
And age in love loves not t'have years told:
    Therefore I lie with her, and she with me,
    And in our faults by lies we flattered be.

Sonnet 138 is one of the more popular Dark Lady sonnets, included by three anthologies. It differs from the others in that it blames the woman less and is freer from the feeling of masochistic surrender that mars so many sonnets. The sonnet is written in a lighter tone, and is accepting of the many little and not-so-little lies that many lovers tolerate and even cultivate in their relationship. Among couples one often hears the plea, "Be less truthful, and kinder!" Or, "Must you always be truthful; can you not sometimes lie and say you love me even when you don't feel that it's true?"

In the first two lines, the Poet accepts in good grace what he found so deeply offensive in other sonnets: that his mistress is not "made of truth." He will not, in this sonnet, blame her because he is afraid that she would consider him naïve, and an "untutored youth." The Poet will accept and even "vainly think" that she regards him as young, even though she full well knows that his days are "past the best." Their relationship will be a truce, with "simple truth suppressed." Nor will he confront her lack of constancy (the word "unjust" in this context means unfaithful). In return for not saying she is unfaithful, the Poet expects her not to mention that he is old. Line 11 is a declaration of acceptance of a bitter reality: "O love's best habit is in seeming trust."

However, the lovely balance offered by the Poet will not withstand scrutiny. The two lies are not of the same order. She pretends to be faithful and the Poet pretends to be younger. Hers is a real lie, his just a pretense, but a psychoanalyst may find hidden a deeper lie, a real balance. She pretends she is faithful and he pretends not to know that this very infidelity is what attracts him to her.

This compromise may account for the sonnet's popularity. Many lovers over the generations who have accepted the fact that love is a compromise formation and that one has to live with one's own and one's partner's imperfections, have drawn comfort from this sonnet. To us, the fact that no anthology included Sonnet 137, with its savage beauty, but three anthologies included Sonnet 138, with its all too common wisdom, suggests that the wish not to be too inquisitive and even to flatter so-called "common sense" affects the selection of the sonnets. We interpret the greater popularity of a banal sonnet as a sign that poetic beauty or depth of inquiry is not the sole reason for a sonnet's popularity.

SONNET 140

Be wise as thou art cruel, do not press
My tongue-tied patience with too much disdain,
Lest sorrow lend me words, and words express
The manner of my pity-wanting pain.
If I might teach thee wit, better it were,
Though not to love, yet love to tell me so,
As testy sick men, when their deaths be near,
No news but health from their physicians know:
For if I should despair, I should grow mad,
And in my madness might speak ill of thee;
Now this ill-wresting world is grown so bad,
Mad slanderers by mad ears believed be.
    That I may not be so, nor thou belied,
    Bear thine eyes straight, though thy proud heart go wide.

Like many other sonnets, this one can be read in different ways. It can be read as the Poet asking his lady for some kind of truce—not necessarily for a resolution of their conflict, but for a respite. The image that he conveys of himself in this sonnet is not an attractive one. It is one of self-subjugation and self-pity. Whatever the differences were between the Poet's homosexual and heterosexual love, submission and masochistic tendencies appear in both choices.

In the first quatrain, the Poet advises his lady to be as wise as she is cruel, and threatens that his sorrow will lead him to attack her. Reading this, however, we feel that this supposed warning has come too late; the very attack he is trying to avoid is taking place as we read. In line 4 we find the memorable "my pity-wanting pain," a poetic expression of masochistic feeling. Unconsciously at least, being pitied may be more important to the Poet than being loved.

In the second quatrain, the Poet invites the lady to pretend to love him even if she does not. He goes on to compare himself to "testy sick men," who are short-tempered and can tolerate only good news from their physicians, suggesting again that the lady tell him only that she loves him. He accused her of being false, but now he invites her to be false. We suspect from other sonnets that unconsciously the Poet wanted a false woman, and in this sonnet he asks her directly to be false. The Poet continues to threaten her, saying he may go mad and speak ill of her, as if he had not done so already. The "ill-wresting world," is a highly condensed phrase. To wrest means to twist or turn over (as in ploughing), and to pull forth, in this case, denunciations both true and false. Burrow has noticed that this is the only place this compound word, "ill-wresting," appears. In line 12, "mad slanderers" have convinced equally mad listeners, here reduced to "mad ears." The poem ends with humiliating advice—the lady should keep her eyes "straight," meaning narrowly focused on him, and not look at other men, even though her "proud heart" desires a wide selection of admirers. Yet again, the lady is invited by the Poet to pretend that she loves him even if she cannot do so.

There is much bitterness in this sonnet. The Poet is asking for a resumption of the compromise that allowed them to "lie together" (Sonnet 138) in the double sense of the word. One anthology included this sonnet.

SONNET 141

In faith I do not love thee with mine eyes,
For they in thee a thousand errors note,
But 'tis my heart that loves what they despise,
Who in despite of view is pleased to dote.
Nor are mine ears with thy tongue's tune delighted,
Nor tender feeling to base touches prone,
Nor taste, nor smell, desire to be invited
To any sensual feast with thee alone:
But my five wits, nor my five senses can
Dissuade one foolish heart from serving thee,
Who leaves unswayed the likeness of a man,
Thy proud heart's slave and vassal wretch to be:
    Only my plague thus far I count my gain,
    That she that makes me sin, awards me pain.

There is no radical break between the previous sonnets discussed in this chapter and Sonnet 141, but when read with care there is a slight shift to a calmer self-observation.

By describing a war between the senses and the heart, Shakespeare has discovered yet another metaphor for describing intrapsychic conflict and ambivalence in loving. The five senses foster only desire, while the heart, an inner organ, is associated with a deeper feeling of love. The senses, because they are in contact with the outside world, are closer to reality. But in Shakespeare's poetry, the heart, having no contact with the outside world, represents the inwardness of the Poet. This heart dotes on the lady, disregarding the testimony of the senses, and when the heart is in love, it is stronger than all five.

The sonnet opens with "In faith," a declaration that implies the Poet feels that we might not trust him and therefore is compelled to make sure that we believe him. Today, many people are in the habit of saying, "to tell you the truth," as if someone suspected them of lying. In psychoanalysis, what one usually discovers is that the person unconsciously feels accused of lying because of the presence of an inner conflict. It is conceivable that the Poet felt he was not entirely truthful, hence, "in faith." But faith may well be the right word, because one relies on belief when there is no exter-nal evidence to support what one believes. The irrational heart is capable of denying what the eyes report as true. In this sonnet, the eyes "in thee a thousand errors note," but the heart still continues to love what the eyes, and eventually all the senses, despise. What the combined senses object to in the woman is not specified. In light of this, every reader can imagine his or her own objections. The poem thus appeals to all those who are ambiva-lent in their choice of a love object.

The sixth line is obscure: "Nor tender feeling to base touches prone." Shakespeare scholars Booth and Blackmore Evans thought this line brings in the sense of touch. They suggest that Shakespeare here alludes to what we call "petting," sexual contact short of intercourse. Such sexual touches are declared to be "base," or unbecoming to either the Poet or his lady. What is achieved by excluding all the senses is the divorce of emotional feeling from physical feeling. The heart can dote, but without the partici-pation of the senses, it cannot achieve sexual pleasure.

The traditional view that love is blind, and therefore irrational, domi-nates this sonnet. Line 9 adds the "five wits" to the five senses. The term "wits" was used to connote what psychoanalysts today call ego functions like memory, perception and imagination. Now the heart has not five but ten forces in opposition to it. Because the heart fails to listen to the combi-nation of the brain and the senses it is called foolish. Vendler noted that the word "serving" comes as a surprise in line 10 because we expect "loving." This substitution emphasizes the Poet's submissiveness. We are accustomed to the description of unloving sex as "service," but here an adversive and asexual love is reduced to "serving" the mistress. Line 11—"Who leaves unswayed the likeness of a man"—is a savage line in which the Poet attacks himself. "Unswayed" here means lacking control over himself. What the Poet seems to imply is that if the heart is so foolish as to disregard both senses and wits, what remains is no longer a human being and that he has lost the "likeness of a man." This may also be the Poet's euphemism for sexual impotence. Now he has become the "slave and vassal wretch" of her "proud heart" (but perhaps of no other body parts). The couplet is mas-ochistic. The Poet's suffering, what he calls his "plague," is his only gain. In this sonnet, again, we discover what happens when lust is banished: it is replaced by submission.

In our opinion, the most striking differences between the sonnets addressed to the Young Man and those addressed to the woman popularly known as the Dark Lady is the idealization of the young man and the inability of the Poet to idealize a woman. On this point we once more disagree with Vendler, who believes that in both genders the Poet showed "Idealization, infatuation and inevitable disillusion twice over (p. 638)." This sonnet was chosen by two anthologies.

SONNET 127

In the old age black was not counted fair,
Or if it were it bore not beauty's name:
But now is black beauty's successive heir,
And beauty slandered with a bastard shame,
For since each hand hath put on nature's power,
Fairing the foul with art's false borrowed face,
Sweet beauty hath no name no holy bower,
But is profaned, if not lives in disgrace.
Therefore my mistress' eyes are raven black,
Her eyes so suited, and they mourners seem,
At such who not born fair no beauty lack,
Slandering creation with a false esteem,
    Yet so they mourn becoming of their woe,
    That every tongue says beauty should look so.

Scholars consider Sonnet 127 to be one of the earlier sonnets because words Shakespeare later used do not appear in this sonnet. It appeared in *The Passionate Pilgrim,* printed in 1598.

When we love actively we feel that we have made the selection of the person we love. When we love passively, our experience is that we have fallen in love; when this happens we may feel victimized or bewitched by the person who evoked these feelings in us. In Sonnet 127 the Poet describes a passive form of sexual attraction. From the psychoanalytic perspective, passive love is dominated by unconscious wishes and takes place without the "permission" of the active and conscious ego. The feeling it inspires of being "bewitched" is closer to paranoia. Shakespeare understood this very well, as we learn from Othello's defense that he used no witchcraft to win Desdemona. Othello defends himself against that accusation by demonstrating that Desdemona loved him actively.

In this sonnet, the Poet mockingly complains that had he not been mislead or bewitched by the Dark Lady he would have chosen a fair beauty. The woman's mournful black eyes have caused him to perceive as beautiful features that should not entitle a woman to this claim. Such an extreme form of passive falling in love assigns all power to the other. From there, it is only one more step to the feeling that one is mistreated and misused by this all-powerful woman. Like Sonnet 20 (discussed in Chapter 1), Sonnet 127 is built around a myth created by the Poet. In both sonnets, the Poet playfully suggests that some mysterious power thwarted his purposes. In Sonnet 20 it made him fall in love with a man when he had planned to fall in love with a woman, and in Sonnet 127 he was going to fall in love with a fair woman, but a dark one usurped her place.

The first two quatrains are devoted to the development of the myth that "black beauty" usurped the place that "fair" beauty once occupied. Black beauty, according to the Poet, has no legitimate status. In line 5, "each hand put on nature's power," suggesting that cosmetic skills have usurped nature's regal power to declare what is beautiful and what is not. "Fairing the foul," making beautiful what is ugly, in Burrow's view anticipated the witches in *Macbeth:* "Fair is foul and foul is fair." The Poet suggests that once foul becomes fair the natural order of the world is overthrown as by a kind of cosmic usurpation. The Poet's sympathy is with fair beauty that as a result of the usurpation "hath no name" and "no holy bower." The O.E.D. defines the word "bower" as "a vague poetical word for an idealized abode, not realized in any actual dwelling." Thus fair beauty, a goddess or at least a queen, has lost both her good name and her home or shrine. The Poet writes that "Therefore my mistress' eyes are raven black/Her eyes so suited, and they mourners seem"—the woman's eyes seem like mourners, but are not genuine mourners. The word "therefore" may be a door to the unconscious, as if the Poet were saying because he sees her as lacking legitimacy and as a usurper of someone else's place he mistrusts the attraction that her mournful eyes have evoked in him. The woman's depressive look made her attractive to the Poet but his paranoia made him suspicious of her. Line 13—"Yet so they mourn becoming of their woe"—is not easy to interpret.

Duncan-Jones reads the word "becoming" as meaning "becoming them, making them appear beautiful." Booth noted that "the line never quite makes an assertion in any one syntax, but in general conveys the message that woe is transformed into beauty." To us the line makes sense if we read the poem as describing the Poet's inner conflict between his attraction to the woman because her eyes convey depression and his suspicion that the depressive look is deceptive.

The Poet describes a complex psychological state. He does not feel that he actively sought to fall in love with a dark, mournful-eyed beauty. That women in a state of mourning could be especially attractive to Shakespeare is likely, for we remember the way Richard III woos and wins Queen Anne, the wife of the man he murdered, while she is at the height of mourning, at her husband's funeral.

Before we succumb to the Poet's bewitching skill and accept this notion as historically valid, it may be useful to recall the biblical Song of Solomon with which Shakespeare was unquestionably familiar. In the Song of Solomon, we read:

> I am black, but comely, o ye daughters of Jerusalem, as the
> tents of Cedar, as the curtains of Solomon. Look not upon
> me, because I am black, because the sun hath looked upon
> me: my mothers' children were angry with me; they made me
> the keeper of the vineyards; but my own vineyard have I not
> kept (Song of Solomon 1.5-6).

Contrary to the Poet's assertion, there is no evidence that in "the old age," black was not "counted fair."

Today we know that the Song of Solomon, or the Song of Songs as it is called in the Hebrew bible, was originally a Hellenistic love poem that found its way into the bible and was not expurgated because it was interpreted as an allegory evoking the love between God and his chosen people. Christian theologians later interpreted the same love song as an exchange between God and his ecclesia, his church.

The Poet may be making fun of his Dark Lady, accusing her of usurpation; however, the beauty that was usurped may not have been that of another woman, as the Poet claims, but the beauty of the Young Man the

Poet praised so highly in other sonnets. This sonnet was chosen by one anthology.

SONNET 130

My mistress' eyes are nothing like the sun,
Coral is far more red than her lips red,
If snow be white, why then her breasts are dun:
If hairs be wires, black wires grow on her head:
I have seen roses damasked, red and white,
But no such roses see I in her cheeks,
And in some perfumes is there more delight,
Than in the breath that from my mistress reeks.
I love to hear her speak, yet well I know,
That music hath a far more pleasing sound:
I grant I never saw a goddess go,
My mistress when she walks treads on the ground.
    And yet by heaven I think my love as rare,
    As any she belied with false compare.

Sonnet 130 can be read as a satire on rival poets who idealize their women beyond compare, the way the Poet himself idealized the Young Man. The sonnet can also be read as the Poet's unconscious confession that he cannot idealize a woman. Homosexual men, for whom the penis of the partner is all-important, can neither desire nor idealize a woman who does not have one.

The association between black hair and black eyes and evil, central to Sonnet 127, is not repeated here. The black color of her hair in this sonnet becomes "wires," not an attractive sensual description, but devoid of the symbolism of evil. In a disparaging tone, the Poet goes on to compare the redness of her lips with coral and the whiteness of her breasts with snow, etc., in a comparative catalog of parts in which this woman is always the loser.

Burrow, in discussing this sonnet, gives an example of the kind of poems Shakespeare mocked. He quotes from Lynch's *Diella* (1592):

My mistress snow white skin does much excele
The pure soft wool Arcadian sheep do bear;
Her hair exceeds gold forced in smaller wire
In smaller threads than those Archane spun
Her eyes are crystal fountains yet dart fire (Burrow p. 640).

The couplet is of special interest. It counterbalances what the Poet said in the body of the sonnet, as if the Poet felt the need to reassure his readers that in spite of his inability to idealize his mistress, he truly loves her. Yet "I think," in line 13, can be read as an unconscious confession that the Poet is not entirely convinced of what he is saying. Vendler believes the Poet was sincere in the last two lines; we feel that both sonnet and couplet express ambivalence. We surmise that after the other poets' idealizing tendencies were mocked, the Poet experienced envy of their capacity for praise and attempted to mitigate his harsh wit in the couplet. Nothing in this sonnet strikes us as original or memorable beyond the mischievous wish to mock other poets' capacity to idealize women, and the sharp contrast between the body of the poem and the couplet. Two anthologies included this sonnet.

SONNET 131

Thou art as tyrannous, so as thou art,
As those whose beauties proudly make them cruel;
For well thou know'st to my dear doting heart
Thou art the fairest and most precious jewel.
Yet in good faith some say that thee behold,
Thy face hath not the power to make love groan;
To say they err, I dare not be so bold,
Although I swear it to my self alone.
And to be sure that is not false I swear,
A thousand groans but thinking on thy face,
One on another's neck do witness bear
Thy black is fairest in my judgment's place.
    In nothing art thou black save in thy deeds,
    And thence this slander as I think proceeds.

Like Sonnet 130, this sonnet also deals with the Poet's ambivalent feelings towards the woman. The poem opens with the accusation that the lady is "tyrannous." We are told that she is like other beautiful women whose beauty made them proud and whose pride turned into cruelty. She knows that she is the Poet's doting heart's "fairest and most precious jewel." The use of the term "doting," with its strong connotation of loving foolishly, proclaims the Poet's submissiveness. So far we are on conventional masochistic ground, but in this sonnet something unexpected happens. The second quatrain denies what the first one says. Contrary to the laws of love but in obedience to the laws of ambivalence, the Poet asks other men what they think of his lady. These others fail to admire her. The Poet did not know, but psychoanalysis has taught us, that the need of a man to have the woman he loves admired by other men shows an underlying homosexual structure which manifests itself in an insecurity that the woman chosen is not beautiful enough, or, to put it differently, the woman is valuable and valued only if other men desire her. For such men, the number of men she can attract determines the value of the woman. In these men, the heavenly alchemy of transformation which love can bring about, that makes a particular woman valuable beyond compare, has not taken place.

The Poet tells the lady that there are many who do not find her face beautiful enough to make a lover groan. Insulting her, he proclaims that he cannot disagree with her detractors in public. Only alone and to himself will he "swear" her praise; to make sure that he is not false, the Poet will swear "a thousand groans." In other words, he will pretend to idealize her. Line 11—"One on another's neck do witness bear"—has caused difficulty to interpreters. Most cite the proverb "one misfortune comes on the neck of another;" others cite the biblical "to fall on one's neck," a term of loving embrace. The language is awkward but there is a powerful implication that the Poet visualizes a different face on her neck, and the other face seems more attractive.

Like the previous sonnets, Sonnet 131 raises the question, to whom is it addressed? Vendler assumed that it was addressed to the lady herself.

Surely it is to make her behave better toward him so that the
world will forgive her and enroll her among those attractive
enough to provoke love. He appeals, therefore, to her social
self-interest to make her cease tormenting him
(Vendler p. 560).

To us the claim is not convincing; in our opinion, the poem's ultimate
audience is a circle of men who are ambivalent toward women and who
find such poems entertaining. What is unique in this sonnet is line 6: "Thy
face hath not the power to make love groan." If somewhere in the Poet's
mind she lacks this power, the poem cannot work as a love poem, even if
the statement is attributed to others.

No anthology has included this sonnet.

SONNET 137

Thou blind fool, Love, what dost thou to mine eyes
That they behold and see not what they see?
They know what beauty is, see where it lies,
Yet what the best is take the worst to be.
If eyes corrupt by over-partial looks
Be anchored in the bay where all men ride,
Why of eyes' falsehood hast thou forged hooks,
Whereto the judgment of my heart is tied?
Why should my heart think that a several plot,
Which my heart knows the wide world's common place?
Or mine eyes seeing this, say this is not,
To put fair truth upon so foul a face?
    In things right true my heart and eyes have erred,
    And to this false plague are they now transferred.

Ever in search of new metaphors to express inner conflict, the Poet
has here united eyes and heart, which he had formerly set in opposition,
against the "blind fool, Love."

In the first line, the Poet attacks Cupid for what he has done to the
Poet's eyes. He feels that his eyes no longer judge reality; they still know

how to "behold," but then deny what they have seen. It is Cupid's job to render the eyes useless, as in *A Midsummer Night's Dream:*

Helena: Love looks not with the eyes, but with the mind,
And therefore is wing'd Cupid painted blind (I.i.234-235).

The next two lines repeat the idea in different words. The eyes still know fully what beauty is and where and in what way beauty "lies," and yet the Poet accuses them of confusing the best with the worst: "Yet what the best is take the worst to be." The line literally says that the eyes see what is best and take it for the worst. What do they look at that is best? If this is a reference to the Young Man (and there is nothing else in the poem to suggest it is), then the Poet is telling us that, having fallen in love with the Dark Lady he looks upon the Young Man and no longer sees him as "best." And there is another way to read the line. If someone undergoing psychoanalysis recited the fourth line, the analyst would draw attention to the fact that the statement was inverted. Did not the Poet mean to say the opposite, that it is the crime of the eyes to have transformed the worst into the best, since he accuses himself of unrealistic idealization? The slip could then be interpreted as an unconsciously favorable view of the lady. Cases like these, where a slip corrects a paranoid attitude, are known.

The second quatrain employs two powerful and unexpected images. The eyes are said to "corrupt by over-partial looks." The word "partial" is the expected word, but "over-partial," meaning partial beyond reasonable expectation in a state of love, gives the image its striking power. These eyes that were over-partial in the fifth line become anchored "in the bay where all men ride"—a new and original metaphor to express the promiscuity of the woman, a metaphor that has become one of the best-known metaphors in the sonnets. A "bay where all men ride" refers to a vagina that gives shelter to every man. In the seventh line, the eyes that were "over-partial" become eyes of "falsehood," and they turn into "forged hooks" that tie up the judgment of the Poet. What exasperates the Poet in this sonnet is the fact that the woman's promiscuity does not, as it should, repel the Poet's desire, but instead increases it. At this point psychoanalysis can offer an explanation: men whose latent homosexuality is strong are attracted to promiscuous women because they are attractive to other men. The attraction to a promiscuous woman can be thought of as a midway station between homosexuality and heterosexuality.

In the third quatrain a new metaphor is created to differentiate fidelity from promiscuity. Promiscuity is called the "wide world's common place," while fidelity is referred to as "a several plot," meaning a private plot, enclosed and protected. Line 11 repeats that the eyes see correctly, but deny what they see, enabling the Poet to mask "so foul a face" with fair (as in beautiful) truth, and also to avoid "facing" the truth about the woman. Other parts of the body may evoke sexual attraction; but in love, the face must play the leading role. When the face is experienced as foul, one cannot speak of love. The sonnet ends on a bitter note: both eyes and heart, so often in conflict with each other, have become organs of judgment and thought only to be "transferred" to a "false plague." This is a difficult metaphor because plague loses its terror when it is designated as false, but the woman's promiscuity, in the angry language of the Poet, can be both a plague and false.

The sonnet is so harsh, the attack on the woman so savage, that even such striking expressions as "over-partial looks" and "the bay where all men ride," and the contrast between "several plot" and "common place" did not recommend it to any of the anthologizers. We feel that the capacity to put such raw feelings into a 14-line poem rich in metaphors deserves more admiration than the poem received.

SONNET 151

Love is too young to know what conscience is,
Yet who knows not conscience is born of love?
Then, gentle cheater, urge not my amiss,
Lest guilty of my faults thy sweet self prove.
For, thou betraying me, I do betray
My nobler part to my gross body's treason;
My soul doth tell my body that he may
Triumph in love; flesh stays no farther reason,
But rising at thy name doth point out thee
As his triumphant prize; proud of this pride,
He is contented thy poor drudge to be,
To stand in thy affairs, fall by thy side.
  No want of conscience hold it that I call
  Her 'love', for whose dear love I rise and fall.

We interpret Sonnet 151 differently than the traditional Shakespearean scholars do because we take the first two lines seriously.

  Love is too young to know what conscience is:
  Yet who knows not conscience is born of love?

Love being "too young" is a reference to Amor or Cupid, the god of love that the Greeks with fine intuition portrayed as a child, rather than to Venus, the mature woman who is the goddess of love. Commentators have stressed the possibility of a concealed pun, a "prick of conscience," and the Latin proverb "penis erectus non habeat conscientiam" (the erect penis has no conscience). Conscience also contains the pun "science of cunt." We have no objection to this interpretation, but we believe that the sonnet, beyond the bawdy surface, deals with more profound issues.

In our view, Sonnet 151 is unique among the sonnets because it deals with the relationship between conscience and love, inviting comparison with the better-known statement in *Hamlet:* "thus conscience doth make coward of us all and thus the native hue of resolution is sicklied o'er with the pale hue of thought (III.i.83-85)." Only a few of Shakespeare's sonnets are as complex and difficult to decipher as Sonnet 151, and yet two of the six anthologies have included it. This is all the more surprising because the sonnet contains a number of puns dealing with the penis that are reminiscent of Sonnet 20, which no anthology has included.

The opening lines of this sonnet are a brilliant meditation on the complexity of loving. The Poet startles us by immediately raising a contradiction: "Love is too young to know what conscience is," but "who knows not conscience is born of love?" The contradiction can be explained thus: love can cause people to do things their conscience would not allow, but at the same time our conscience, our regard for others, is born out of our capacity to love.

In psychoanalytic terms, we can say that love is a passion, and being a passion it can cause us to disregard social prohibitions. In that sense, "Love is too young to know what conscience is." On the other hand, love is the antidote to the destructive urges that arise when one is concerned only for the self. In that sense, "conscience is born of love." However, there is a rival interpretation, suggested by Booth, in which conscience should be read as "cunt knowledge." In this interpretation, love is too young to experience cunt knowledge (knowledge in the biblical sense, meaning sexual intercourse). The second line would then mean that everyone knows that sexual intercourse is the result of love.

In the third line, "gentle cheater" also has two interpretations. It could refer to Amor, the god of love, or to the woman. Either one could urge the Poet "amiss" and prove guilty of the "faults" that this arousal of the Poet will bring about. The Poet then turns to his mistress, asking her not to betray him lest she provoke him to yield his love (his nobler part) to his "gross body's treason," a reference to the Poet's own promiscuity.

"Betray/My nobler part to my gross body's treason" contains a complex idea that exposes the Poet's inner conflict and fear. It refers to lust, an emotion that horrified the Poet in Sonnet 129, as we discussed in the first chapter. The Poet accusingly tells the woman that her promiscuity will cause him to lose his love for her, and he fears he will be left only feeling lust. In line 8 his soul tells his body that love can triumph, but "flesh," once more a reference to the erect penis or lust, is incapable of following the dictates of reason.

From this point on the Poet is personified by his penis, and we can see that the danger to his relationship with the woman that the Poet fears has already happened. In line 9, "rising at thy name" and "doth point out" are again references to erection. The woman becomes his "triumphant prize," and "proud of this pride" he is contented to lapse into submission to the to the mistress' demands. The word "contented" in line 11 can also be read as "cunt ended," implying both that a sexual climax has been achieved and that the Poet's "end" (both his fate and his penis) are involved with the woman's genital. Then the term "drudge" would refer to the Poet's penis working to provide pleasure in intercourse: "To stand in thy affairs" with an erection, and "fall by thy side" with the subsequent loss of the erection. If this interpretation is accepted, Sonnet 151 may be read as a confession of the sexual problems the Poet experienced, becoming submissive to the woman and losing his erection.

In our reading, if not in the reading of Shakespeare's commentators, the couplet should be read as a defense and as a self-justification. The Poet who opened the sonnet with the incompatibility between love and conscience (and love and sexual intercourse) now assures us that in his love for the lady there was "no want of conscience;" yet he ends the couplet by telling us that for her "dear love I rise and fall." In other words, the Poet ends the sonnet fearing that he is in danger of losing his potency.

If our hypothesis is correct, then the very promiscuity of the woman that was so abhorrent to the Poet was the very reason why he selected her and also made it possible him to become potent with her. What he consciously abhorred, he unconsciously needed in order to counteract the homosexual wish. Thus he created what is called in psychoanalysis a compromise formation. This made an actual heterosexual relationship possible, even though the Poet's potency was always in question, as this sonnet suggests.

SONNET 147

My love is as a fever longing still,
For that which longer nurseth the disease,
Feeding on that which doth preserve the ill,
Th' uncertain sickly appetite to please:
My reason the physician to my love,
Angry that his prescriptions are not kept,
Hath left me, and I desperate now approve,
Desire is death, which physic did except.
Past cure I am, now reason is past care,
And frantic-mad with evermore unrest,
My thoughts and my discourse as mad men's are,
At random from the truth vainly expressed.
     For I have sworn thee fair, and thought thee bright,
     Who art as black as hell, as dark as night.

The idea that love is a sickness to be cured only by the presence of the beloved goes back to the poetry of ancient Egypt, between 1300 and 1100 B.C.E. (Bergmann 1987). We will cite one of these Egyptians in another chapter. What is of interest in this sonnet is that Shakespeare gave this well-known theme a radically different interpretation. Traditionally, the metaphor of love as a sickness was used to demonstrate that the mere appearance of the beloved effects a miraculous cure. Love-sickness has been transformed by the Poet into a situation where his own reason, not the beloved, is the physician, but the relationship between patient and physician is not a happy one. The patient refuses to follow the prescriptions of this supposed "physician" and the "physician" abandons the "patient." The metaphorical transformation of reason into an angry physician going off in a huff is humorous, but the implication that the Poet has therefore gone mad is not.

The first two quatrains can be read as a meditation on the state of being in love, but in the third quatrain the mood becomes more passionate and desperate. In the body of the poem the lover is not described, but in the couplet she is brought in so powerfully that we have no doubt that this sonnet belongs to group dealing with the relationship with the Dark Lady.

Love is compared to a fever of longing. However, this longing only "longer nurseth," or prolongs, the disease. Preconsciously and skillfully, the Poet connects the lover's longing back to the longing of an infant for the breast. The metaphor spills over into the third line, where the word "feeding" continues to hint at the infant at the breast. The choice of the word "nurseth" may also be a subtle clue that the poem is written to a woman. In the forth line the "uncertain sickly appetite to please," may be read as the wish to please, which also prolongs the sickness.

The second quatrain suggests a remedy to the illness. Reason is brought in as the physician who could cure this fever of longing, but the physician is angry because "his prescriptions are not kept," that is, that in the grip of desire the supposed patient disregards the voice of reason. The feverish patient feels uncared for and abandoned by reason, and therefore, now, past cure. There is a hint in line 8 that his longing turned into melancholia, for the Poet feels that "desire is death." What the Poet is telling us in this highly metaphorical language is that desire can become inimical not only to reason but also to life itself.

We know that the connection between love and madness had a special appeal for Shakespeare. Line 11 and 12 are also devoted to this idea. The Poet's thoughts and discourse (and presumably his writings) have become those of a madman, "random" and "vainly expressed." By the couplet, paranoia has won over masochism and transformed masochism into bitter hatred. Only Auden chose this sonnet for those he cited in his anthology. In our opinion, he was right to choose it because it is a sonnet of sustained power, and transforms the familiar trope of lovesickness into a disturbingly original equation of desire with disease.

SONNET 149

Canst thou O cruel, say I love thee not,
When I against my self with thee partake?
Do I not think on thee when I forgot
Am of my self, all-tyrant for thy sake?
Who hateth thee that I do call my friend,
On whom frown'st thou that I do fawn upon,
Nay if thou lour'st on me do I not spend
Revenge upon my self with present moan?
What merit do I in my self respect,
That is so proud thy service to despise,
When all my best doth worship thy defect,
Commanded by the motion of thine eyes?
    But love hate on for now I know thy mind,
    Those that can see thou lov'st, and I am blind.

The sonnet opens with the assertion that the Poet does indeed love, because he takes the woman's side against his own interest. To the Poet this is proof of love; to a more objective observer it may be taken as a sign of masochistic love. When masochism is the dominating emotion, love is measured by the amount of suffering endured. In the second quatrain, the Poet further asserts his loyalty: no one who hates her is his friend, and he does not fawn on anyone who frowns on her. What strikes us in this line is the masochistic echo of "frown" in "fawn." In line 7 the Poet sets up a link between "lour'st" and "lov'st" in line 14. The word "lour'st" means to look upon angrily or frown; when the lady frowns upon the Poet he turns the anger inward and berates himself: "Do I not spend/Revenge upon myself with present moan?" "Spend" is an Elizabethan euphemism for ejaculation, implying that the Poet masturbates to punish himself when he feels rejected by her.

The Poet shows an understanding of his masochism when he says "my best doth worship thy defect," referring to her promiscuity. What he does not know is that his homosexual wishes make a promiscuous woman attractive to him. The Poet therefore assigns the blame to the woman's cruelty. One of the significant differences between the sonnets written to the young man and those addressed to the woman is that the young man is never accused of cruelty except to himself, whereas the woman is often accused of being cruel.

The word "moan," it may be noted, is used frequently in the sonnets. There is "moan th' expense of many a vanished sight" in Sonnet 30 and "fore-bemoanéd moan" in the same sonnet, as well as "I must attend time's leisure with my moan" in Sonnet 44 and "Lest the wise world should look into your moan" in Sonnet 71.

In line 12 the Poet feels "Commanded by the motion of thine eyes." The power of his beloved lies in her eyes, as it did in the eyes of the Young Man. In the couplet the Poet encourages the woman by calling her "love" while at the same time encouraging her to continue to hate him. The Poet claims to understand her mind now, as he reaches for resolution. He closes by contrasting "those that can see," people who realistically see the Dark Lady with all her defects, with himself, who is "blind," and helpless to disobey. The translation of masochistic feelings into poetry was not easy to achieve, even for Shakespeare, yet they persist in poems addressed to both the Dark Lady and the Young Man. This sonnet was not selected by any of the anthologists.

SONNET 150

O from what power has thou this powerful might,
With insufficiency my heart to sway,
To make me give the lie to my true sight,
And swear that brightness doth not grace the day?
Whence hast thou this becoming of things ill,
That in the very refuse of thy deeds,
There is such strength and warrantise of skill,
That in my mind thy worse all best exceeds?
Who taught thee how to make me love thee more,
The more I hear and see just cause of hate?
O though I love what others do abhor,
With others thou shouldst not abhor my state.
    If thy unworthiness raised love in me,
    More worthy I to be beloved of thee.

The inner conflict between "reason"—"reality testing," psychologists call it today—and love is resumed in Sonnet 150. The general theme continues from Sonnet 149. The Poet seems, if anything, more puzzled by his love for the woman. Amazed at the power she has over him, the Poet, like many lovers, does not look for an explanation for his love in his own unconscious, but thinks the secret can be found by thinking about the woman rather than himself.

This sonnet is written in the form of an imaginary dialogue between the Poet and his mistress. Each of the quatrains opens with a question. In the first line, the Poet asks from what source his mistress derived her "powerful might" over him. Might is by definition power; why then the double "powerful might?" With the phrase "With insufficiency my heart to sway," the Poet has found a way of expressing what puzzles him about his mistress. He is drawn to her in spite of the fact that he cannot idealize her, and is mystified by the fact that her "insufficiency," encompassing all the many defects he finds in her, only enhances her attractiveness and her "might." Shakespeare used the word "insufficiency" only once more, in *Midsummer Night's Dream,* when Hermia complains, "But you must flout my insufficiency (II.ii.128)?" Strictly on analytic grounds, we might say that if the

Poet uses a rare word like "insufficiency" rather than "defect," it is because the word conveys more closely what the Poet knows unconsciously, but cannot admit consciously. Psychoanalytically speaking, we interpret "With insufficiency my heart to sway" as the Poet saying, "I am surprised that I love you even though I know you are insufficient," which in a homosexually inclined man may unconsciously mean lacking a penis. If that is unconsciously true, then the whole list of the woman's defects is an effort to keep the unconscious reason unconscious. The basic infantile idea, that a woman is a castrated man, is repressed. His inner struggle makes the Poet very unhappy, and he blames the woman. This is not yet paranoia, but it is the soil from which a paranoid attitude can emerge.

"With insufficiency my heart to sway" describes a new kind of love. The Poet may have verbalized it for the very first time in the history of love. It has traditionally been maintained that it is the excellence of a woman that evokes a man's love, but here the Poet gives us the insight that for many men the "insufficiency" of a woman is the very reason for the attraction.

In lines 3 and 4, when the woman is accused of having the power to "give the lie" to the Poet's true sight, he is forced to disregard the judgment of his eyes. She can make him swear falsely that "brightness doth not grace the day." Since blindness so often symbolizes castration, as in the case of Oedipus, the Poet's inability to use his eyes may be a veiled accusation that the woman has castrated him. Because she succeeded in evoking the Poet's love, despite being herself a castrated male in his unconscious, she is experienced as terribly powerful.

In the second quatrain, the Poet repeats his sense of bewilderment: "Whence hast thou this becoming of things ill." The Poet assigns to the lady the power to transform everything good into bad; this is elaborated in the sixth line, so that "in the very refuse of thy deeds/There is such strength." According to the Concordance, only in this sonnet does "refuse" appear as a noun. Preconsciously, the term "refuse" stands for excrement. Academic commentators come close to the psychoanalytic interpretation when the interpret "refuse" as scum, dregs or rubbish. From psychoanalysis we know that young children are capable of admiring excrement, and the Poet may have regressed to that point in his admiration of the mistress. Further abdicating his own capacity for realistic assessment, the Poet claims that in his mind "thy worse all best exceeds." In spite or perhaps even because of the fact that her actions do not meet with the Poet's approval, he feels forced to admire her strength.

In the third quatrain, we are again struck by the Poet's capacity to project his inner conflict on the woman. Despairing, he asks "Who taught thee how to make me love thee more" when in fact there is "cause for hate." The Poet expects to be rewarded for disregarding reality by loving such an undeserving woman. What is implicit, but not stated, is that destroying the woman's self-esteem, thus humbling her, will make her capable of loving him. In the couplet the Poet admits that the woman's unworthiness made him love her. He thinks he deserves her love especially because his loving is based on the woman's "insufficiency."

It is of interest that the lady's ability to make the bad look good was also characteristic of the Poet's relationship to the young man. The conflict between what reality is and what love makes the Poet believe haunted the Poet in both homo- and heterosexual relationships. Sonnet 114, addressed to a man, reads:

> Or whether shall I say mine eye saith true,
> And that your love taught it this alchemy,
> To make of monsters and things indigest
> Such cherubins as your sweet self resemble,
> Creating every bad a perfect best (lines 3-7)

No anthologist included Sonnet 150. We agree that the claim to be loved by his lady because the "refuse" of her "deeds" is attractive to the Poet alienates him from his readers, but as a poem describing the capacity of love to create a regression in a lover, this sonnet is a unique psychological document. We see it as a self-analysis that failed the Poet, because so much aggression was projected onto the woman.

SONNET 139

O call not me to justify the wrong
That thy unkindness lays upon my heart;
Wound me not with thine eye, but with thy tongue;
Use power with power, and slay me not by art.
Tell me thou lov'st elsewhere; but in my sight,
Dear heart, forbear to glance thine eye aside.
What need'st thou wound with cunning, when thy might
Is more than my o'er-pressed defense can bide?
Let me excuse thee: ah, my love well knows
Her pretty looks have been mine enemies,
And therefore from my face she turns my foes
That they elsewhere might dart their injuries.
    Yet do not so, but since I am near slain,
    Kill me outright with looks, and rid my pain.

If the sonnets were written in the sequence they were printed, the relief expressed in Sonnet 138 was of short duration. The harsher attitude toward the woman is resumed in Sonnet 139.

What is most difficult to interpret in this sonnet are not the metaphors, but the question of how seriously we are to read this poem. Is the language inflated? Was the Poet really wounded? Was he near death? Was this sonnet written half in jest? Perhaps the most difficult line is line 3, "Wound me not with thine eye, but with thy tongue." Are we to infer that the Poet does not wish his lady to look at other men in his presence, but does want to hear about her love affairs with other men? Despite what we have learned about the importance of the eye as the central organ of love for the Poet, it is not easy to empathize with his wishes in this sonnet. Still, if we keep in mind that the Poet's tragedy was that the very promiscuity he so abhorred was also what attracted him to this woman, he can regain some of our sympathy. There are those who are eager to know about the details of their partner's other love affairs, real or imaginary. Psychoanalytic experience shows that such people have the need to transform the dyadic relationship into a triadic one, where one of the three is the observer. In this case the Poet wishes be an observer, within limits: to hear about her infidelities, but not to see them.

In line 7, the Poet complains that his lady need not "wound with cunning," since her "might" is anyway so much more than he can bear. Cunning contains a pun on "cunt" or "cunny" and "powerful might" has a masculine connotation familiar from descriptions of the Young Man. It is as if the Poet wishes the lady to be masculine in her wounding.

In the third quatrain the Poet plays with the idea that the lady's promiscuity is based on her wish to spare him pain, and that she looks at other men so as not to hurt the Poet. "Dart" is a reference to Cupid, but these darts are that, if they are darts of love, will cause the Poet more pain. We are left with the question of how much mockery and criticism accompany the ambivalent love-hate feelings which are expressed in the last line: "Kill me outright with looks, and rid my pain." No anthology selected this sonnet. The masochism of the Poet is too evident to make a positive response to this sonnet easy.

SONNET 142

Love is my sin, and thy dear virtue hate,
Hate of my sin, grounded on sinful loving.
O, but with mine compare thou thine own state,
And thou shalt find it merits not reproving;
Or if it do, not from those lips of thine,
That have profaned their scarlet ornaments,
And sealed false bonds of love as oft as mine,
Robbed others' beds' revenues of their rents.
Be it lawful I love thee as thou lov'st those
Whom thine eyes woo as mine importune thee.
Root pity in thy heart, that when it grows,
Thy pity may deserve to pitied be.
    If thou dost seek to have what thou dost hide,
    By self-example mayst thou be denied.

Sonnet 142 introduces us to a moment often encountered among lovers: one of them feels guilty and attempts to diminish that guilt by claiming that the other carries the greater burden of guilt. This is not a shining moment in any relationship, and it may turn out that even Shakespeare could not transform such a moment into a significant poem.

The first line is paradoxical; the Poet's love is his sin and the lady's hate her virtue. Many commentators read this poem to mean that both the Poet and the lady are married, but while we read much about being false in vows of love, we read nothing in this text about marriage. The Poet makes it clear that he regards his love as "sinful" but he does not tell us what this sin is. It may be adultery, but based on the other poems it seems more likely that the Poet is angry with himself for being attracted to the Dark Lady.

In the first two lines, self-accusation predominates. In the next two lines, the Poet defends himself: if the woman compares the two relationships she will find nothing with which to reprimand the Poet. The implication is that the Poet is superior to the lady. Of the two, the woman deserves more condemnation and she has no right to reprove the Poet.

The second quatrain continues the quarrel. The Poet will accept no reproof from his lady's lips since they "profaned their scarlet ornaments." This scarlet has been profaned by speaking falsely and by kissing promiscuously. In ordinary language, only something sacred can be profaned, and "holy matrimony" is a sacred bond, but so are vows of love. The marriage ceremony seals the "bonds of love" but they become "false bonds" when extramarital relationships take place. If marriage is being spoken of, to have "sealed false bonds of love" is a civil crime as well as a profanation. The Poet both compliments the beauty of her lips and condemns her as even more guilty. Line 8 contains another of the Poet's real estate metaphors: "Robbed others' beds' revenues of their rent." Commentators have cited Amelia's protest in *Othello* (IV.iii.88), aimed at straying husbands who "pour our Treasures into foreign laps." We are not persuaded that these two are analogous. Amelia's complaint conveys her own sexual aliveness, calling her husband's semen her "treasure," whereas the Poet's reference to "beds' revenues" and "rent" compares sexuality with the obligation to pay a mortgage on real estate.

The third quatrain makes a transition away from crime ("Be it lawful") to other, less directly accusing metaphors. The woman woos other men with her eyes, but the Poet's own eyes "importune" her. "Importune" means to ask in an irresistible way. The word importune (derived from the

Latin "without a port") brings in the metaphor of a port as a place for ships to find safety: the eyes of the lady woo, but the eyes of the Poet, who claims greater constancy, importune her—that is, they look for a safe port.

The Poet tells his lady to "Root pity in thy heart," a traditional way for a lover to ask his lady to yield to him out of pity for his alleged sexual sufferings. Asking the woman for pity is a strange request after blaming her so severely for two earlier quatrains. The Dark Lady is no longer the one who "profaned" her "scarlet ornaments," nor is she the one who "sealed false bonds of love," but has here become the traditional chaste woman who will not take pity on her lover and have sex with him. The Poet tells her that she should do so because someday she too may find herself in love and then desire to be loved back. The couplet turns this into a clear threat: should she ever desire love from someone who, like her, withholds sexual favors, she will suffer and be denied by the example she herself has given. Shakespeare used this ploy of frightening a reluctant lover with such a possibility in *As You Like It*, when Silvius says to Phoebe:

> If ever, as that ever may be near,
> You meet in some fresh cheek the power of fancy,
> Then shall you know the wounds invisible
> That love's keen arrows make (III.v.28-31).

The sonnet was not selected in any anthology. We agree with this assessment. A sense of sin and punishment hovers over this sonnet; the Poet is harsh towards himself and towards the woman. We have met this harshness already in Sonnet 62. There, the same attitude was directed at self-love, but resulted in new self-knowledge; in this sonnet there is no growth in the Poet's understanding of himself or his relationship to the woman.

SONNET 152

In loving thee thou know'st I am forsworn,
But thou are twice forsworn to me love swearing,
In act thy bed-vow broke and new faith torn,
In vowing new hate after new love bearing:
But why of two oaths' breach do I accuse thee,
When I break twenty? I am perjured most,
For all my vows are oaths but to misuse thee:
And all my honest faith in thee is lost.
For I have sworn deep oaths of they deep kindness:
Oaths of thy love, thy truth, thy constancy,
And to enlighten thee gave eyes to blindness,
Or made them swear against the thing they see.
    For I have sworn thee fair: more perjured eye,
    To swear against the truth so foul a lie.

In discussing this sonnet we wish to remind the reader that the sonnets are not logical arguments but translations of a state of bewilderment into poetry. Sonnet 152 may proceed even less logically than other sonnets. We read this sonnet as an intrapsychic battle in which the Poet swings back and forth between accusing his partner and exonerating her by self-accusations, only to accuse her once more.

The Poet imagines confesses that he has broken faith in order to love the Dark Lady. However, his mistress is twice forsworn because she broke the "bed vow" to her husband by becoming his mistress and broke it once more when she became disloyal to him. The fourth line has caused difficulty for interpreters: "In vowing new hate after new love bearing." Duncan-Jones suggested that the woman was recently married and expressed "new hate" for her husband when she loves the Poet. To us this line contains the insight that when a new love takes place a new hate is also created towards the person previously loved, maintaining the intrapsychic balance between love and hate. This is of course not always true; many couples break up without hate. But the way the Dark Lady was seen by the Poet suggests that it was true for her as it is true for many others.

In the second quatrain the Poet takes the blame on himself; he has broken many more vows than the woman. Line 7 contains a rare insight: "all my vows are oaths but to misuse thee." Here the Poet is confessing that his vows were taken with some forethought that he will use them to hurt the woman. If previously the Poet examined the balance between love and hate in regard to his partner, he now examines the same balance within himself. He is trying to exonerate the woman by increasing self-accusation, but the effort fails. The Poet ends the second quatrain not with accusation but with a depressive note: "And all my honest faith in thee is lost."

The third quatrain again accuses. His oaths of love were based on the assumption that the lady would remain true and constant. The word "enlighten," in line 11, is the only appearance of this word in Shakespeare's work. It did not then mean what it means to us now: to correct error, or bring new information or the kinds of enlightenment the Buddha found; but more prosaically, to give light. To make the lady look better (we would say: "appear in a better light") the Poet "gave eyes to blindness," is another reference to the blindness of the god of love. That the Poet must have been blind to love this woman is a persistent self-accusation in these sonnets.

Self-accusation culminates in the couplet: "For I have sworn thee fair: more perjured eye (meaning the Poet himself, his "I", is doubly forsworn) / To swear against the truth so foul a lie." We learn that when paranoia turns into a violent self-accusation, there is no net gain of insight. Pathological self-accusations are no better than paranoid accusations of the other.

If we accept the suggestions of many scholars that Sonnets 153 and 154 were not written by Shakespeare, then this sonnet is the last of the Dark Lady sonnets. Vendler is of the opinion that in both Sonnet 151 and 152 the Poet reached "greater self knowledge," and that the Poet recognized that "he required promiscuity in the mistress in order to be attracted to her" even though he consciously detested that "she is a bay in which all men ride" (p. 643). We are unable to share her confidence. There are many insights in both sonnets, it does not seem to us that the Poet succeeded in knowing himself better after writing these last two.

In our reading of the sonnet, we are struck by how fluctuating this insight about promiscuity is. Vendler attributes to Shakespeare the kind of insight that Freud made available to us in 1912 when he recognized that promiscuity in a woman is, for some men, a precondition for loving. To us, the fluctuation takes place only between accusations against the woman and recognition that the Poet is guilty of the same offense.

Who is the audience for Sonnets 127 to 154? Surely not the woman herself. Reading them could not possibly have given her any pleasure or built up her self-esteem. Just as the audience for the love poems praising the Young Man consisted of men with some homosexual interest of their own, so also the most eager audience for the heterosexual sonnets must have been men who could not idealize a chaste woman, like the women other poets praised. The Dark Lady has one characteristic in common with the Poet himself and the Young Man; like them, she is portrayed as self-loving, and her main interest is in humiliating the Poet. She might, if she existed, have been as described; however, it is also possible that the Poet of the Sonnets projected his own self-love, faithlessness and self-loathing onto the woman.

In Elizabethan love poetry, the Poet's lament over the mistress' infidelity is a common theme. We should note that it is usually the mistress, and not the wife, who is charged with infidelity. Shakespeare (1564-1616) and John Donne (1572-1631) were contemporaries. We quote in part from Donne's "Song."

> Ride ten thousand days and nights
> Till Age snow white hairs on thee;
> Thou, when thou return'st, will tell me
> All strange wonders that befell thee,
> And swear
> No where
> Lives a woman true and fair
>
> If thou find'st one, let me know:
> Such a pilgrimage were sweet.
> Yet do not: I would not go,
> Though at next door we might meet.
> Though she were true when you met her,
> Yet she
> Will be
> False, ere I come, to two or three.

Donne's poem is written in the typical mode of the disappointed heterosexual lover, while Shakespeare's sonnets are unique in portraying a homo/heterosexual triangle.

The sonnets we assembled in this chapter are not an easy pleasure to read and they were not favored by the anthologists; but they are unique in depicting a man's attempt at being heterosexual when he felt so much more at home in loving a young man. The repetition of the theme from different angles is reminiscent of the typical repetition we encounter in psychoanalysis, in which a patient describes seemingly disparate events and feelings. Gradually themes emerge, and what appeared at first as unconnected free associations are revealed to be variations on a theme of great importance to the patient. Once these themes are understood and accepted, the patient gains considerably more control over the events of his or her life.

The self-analysis that the Poet attempted by writing the sonnets in this chapter did not tend to a successful conclusion, but as a group they give evidence of an attempt at self-knowledge that earns our interest and our respect.

CHAPTER 8:
THE TRIADIC CATASTROPHE

SONNETS 40, 41, 42, 133, 134, 144

If the Poet's aim in Sonnet 20 (Chapter 1) was to achieve a successful compromise between his asexual love for the Young Man and his acknowledgement of heterosexual desire, this chapter records the failure of this attempt.

A love triangle is not the ideal subject for the sonnet form. It would seem that such a triangulation would have been better dealt with in a dramatic play. The play could show how the situation evolved and how much the Poet himself contributed to the triangulation. A play would also give us a chance to hear the other two participants explain what happened from their point of view. The sonnet allows us only to hear the Poet's own version.

Psychoanalytic experience has shown that when there is a conflict between homosexual and heterosexual wishes, the person in conflict will start with the wish to be the sole loved one of both of the man and the woman. However, since the person is ambivalent towards both partners, he may eventually bring the two together in the hope of having them fight each other for his love. In this way, aggression is introduced into the two relationships. In real life or in fantasy, a nightmare situation can be created, or imagined, in which the two abandon the Poet to form their own relationship. The triadic sonnets deal with such an event.

As far as we know, the first to transform the feeling of ambivalence into poetry was the Roman poet Catullus.

> Lesbia loathes me night and day with her curses,
> "Catullus" always on her lips,
>> yet I know that she loves me.
> How? I equally spend myself day and night
> in assiduous execration
>> knowing too well my hopeless love.

From *Odi Et Amo* (I love and I hate):

> I hate and I love. And if you ask me how,
> I do not know: I only feel it, and I'm torn in two.

The ambivalence Catullus described was tame by comparison with the painful tangle of emotion evoked by the Poet of the Sonnets. What is strikingly lacking in this group of sonnets is any idealization of the woman, and the absence of any wish to immortalize her in his poetry the way the Poet did for the Young Man. Indeed, many critics have thought that she was nothing more than an object of sexual desire. If our interpretation of these sonnets is correct, the very opposite is true. Heterosexual desire was not strong enough; it was replaced by homosexuality and the need to suffer masochistically.

SONNET 40

Take all my loves, my love, yea, take them all;
What hast thou then more than thou hadst before?
No love, my love, that thou may'st true love call;
All mine was thine before thou hadst this more.
Then if for my love thou my love receivest,
I cannot blame thee for my love thou usest;
But yet be blamed, if thou thyself deceivest
By willful taste of what thyself refusest.
I do forgive thy robbery, gentle thief,
Although thou steal thee all my poverty;
And yet love knows it is a greater grief
To bear love's wrong than hate's known injury.
    Lascivious grace, in whom all ill well shows,
    Kill me with spites; yet we must not be foes.

Although placed early in the printed version of the sonnets, this poem deals with the Young Man's theft of the Poet's mistress, a theft the Poet is trying to understand and forgive. What is paramount in the Poet's mind, what he is trying to come to terms with, is the wrong done to him and his desire that the relationship should not be severed as a result of the theft.

In the first quatrain the Poet uses the world "love" five times. The lover is always addressed as "my love;" however, in the first line, "my loves" refers to other loves the Poet had, including the mistress. The Poet invites the lover to take them all, but in the second line he states that doing so will not bring him more love, implying that the Young Man already has all the Poet's love. In the third line the word "love" appears three times. The first time it refers to the Poet's other lovers, the second to the Young Man for whom the Poet writes the sonnet, and in the third instance it is used both to reassure the youth that the Poet had no other true love, and to warn him that if the youth takes the mistress away he will not gain a love he can call true. The lover presumably desires, and will take away, the other loves of the Poet, and the Poet is willing to let him do so because everything the Poet had was his already. The first quatrain is designed to assure the youth that he has gained nothing of real value from his transgression.

In the second quatrain the Poet makes a claim that may sound strange to heterosexual men and women, namely that the Young Man seduced the Poet's mistress for the sake of his love for the Poet. The Poet will not blame him for doing so because the young man is only "using" the Poet's love. In Sonnet 20 the Poet coined the phrase "love's use" as a metaphor for sexual intercourse. Here the idea comes back: "I cannot blame thee for my love thou usest." The first time the word "love" is used in line 6 it refers to the Poet's love; the second time it refers to the woman. We assume that the Poet knew very well that using the word "love" seven times would create a confusion that reflects the emotional confusion the Poet is feeling.

In the third quatrain, blame, only just disavowed, is reintroduced. The Poet had consoled himself with the idea that the Young Man is merely "using" his love, namely his mistress, when he is having a sexual experience with the Poet's Dark Lady, but in line 7 the Poet finds something for which the Young Man can be blamed: he deceives himself. "By willful taste" the youth "refusest" himself; we interpret the line to mean that the young man willfully refused sexual relations with the Poet and then traded their relationship for a sexual liaison with the Poet's mistress. We note that the implication of "thyself refusest" is that the Poet would have been willing to be sexually involved with the Young Man, had the Young Man been willing. Now the Young Man can be blamed because he refused the sexual relationship with the Poet in favor of a sexual relationship with the Poet's mistress, or, in our vocabulary, because he chose a solution that was a compromise formation between homo- and heterosexual relationships. The form of the sexual behavior was heterosexual, but psychologically, its meaning was homosexual. That heterosexual sex can unconsciously represent the fulfillment of a homosexual wish became understandable only after psychoanalysis made its discoveries about the special laws of logic that govern unconscious thought. One is amazed that the Poet intuitively understood this behavior of his lover. The Poet claims that the Young Man only deceived himself when he refused the homosexual relationship, and therefore "thyself deceivest" supplants "thyself refusest." In line 10, the lover is called "gentle thief" and his robbery is forgiven. All the lover managed to steal was the Poet's poverty.

Lines 11 and 12 repeat the dilemma posed by lines 1, 3 and 5: in what sense are we to understand the word "love?" For us, "love knows" is a reference to the Young Man, who knows that "love's wrong" (here, his behavior) hurts more than "hate's known injury." What the Poet is asserting is that love inflicts a deeper injury than hate.

"Lascivious grace," in line 13, are two words that it is hard to imagine anyone but Shakespeare pairing. Vendler observed that "it falls on the ear with such absolute rightness." She draws attention to the fact that it is the only "sophisticated polysyllable in a "couplet of monosyllables." Burrow interprets "lascivious grace" as lustful generosity; Duncan-Jones as "you who are graceful even when you are lustful." To us it seems significant that by pairing contradictory words the Poet succeeded in stating what he feels, namely a contradictory feeling of both blame and praise.

No anthology included this sonnet. If our interpretation is correct, this sonnet requires a greater awareness of unconscious processes than can be expected in today's culture.

SONNET 41

Those pretty wrongs that liberty commits,
When I am sometime absent from thy heart,
Thy beauty and thy years full well befits,
For still temptation follows where thou art.
Gentle thou art, and therefore to be won;
Beauteous thou art, therefore to be assailed;
And when a woman woos, what woman's son
Will sourly leave her till she have prevailed?
Ay me, but yet thou might'st my seat forbear,
And chide thy beauty and thy straying youth,
Who lead thee in their riot even there
Where thou art forced to break a twofold truth:
    Hers, by thy beauty tempting her to thee,
    Thine, by thy beauty being false to me.

We recall that in Sonnet 20 (Chapter 1) "love's use," meaning sexual experience, was available to women, but love itself was to take place only between men. Sonnet 41, like Sonnet 40, shows that this compromise created difficulty. In this sonnet the Poet is struggling to overcome his jealousy of the Young Man's heterosexuality. The jealousy is not as painful as it will become when the Poet's mistress will become the object of the young man's liberty. We assume that Sonnet 41 was written before the triadic betrayal took place.

The first line minimizes the Young Man's transgressions by fondly calling them "pretty wrongs that liberty commits." Liberty means licentiousness, as in *Measure for Measure*, when Claudio is being marched off to prison:

> *Lucio:* Why, how now, Claudio! Whence comes this restraint?
> *Claudio:* From too much liberty… (I.ii.128-129).

Here, however, the word implies that the Poet's lover had full liberty to commit these pretty wrongs, since the two are not bound to each other by moral or legal obligations. These wrongs are done when the Poet is temporarily "absent from thy heart." With this statement, the Poet admits that in the relationship the lover lacked the necessary constancy upon which any happy love relationship must be based. "When I am sometimes absent from thy heart" is an admirable and original way to express without anger the inconstancy of the other's love. In the next lines, further attempts are made to excuse this absence of constancy. The Young Man's beauty and nobility also make the transgressions understandable; temptation follows him everywhere. In line 7 the Poet uses the term "woman's son," a kind of opposite to the biblical term "son of man," used to describe Christ. The woman referred to here may be Eve, the first to succumb to temptation. Being a "woman's son" could then mean that no man can ever resist a woman who woos him, at least until she has won what she wants, and therefore he is not to blame.

As for "my seat forbear" in line 9, "forbear" means to spare or abstain from, giving one's place to someone else. Commentators frequently refer to Iago's statement in *Othello:* "I do suspect the lusty moor—had leaped into my seat." The "riot" of youth and beauty resulted in a break of a "twofold truth," which is explained in the couplet: the woman's truth with the Poet was broken when the youth's beauty tempted her, and the Young Man's truth was broken by being false to the Poet. The term "twofold truth" condenses the heterosexuality and homosexuality of the poem, and "thy beauty being false to me" suggests, even if only slightly, that the Young Man's infidelity makes his beauty less in the eye of the Poet.

No anthology included this sonnet. It is a personal communication of the Poet to his lover, and is too personal to appear significant to other readers.

SONNET 42

That thou hast her it is not all my grief,
And yet it may be said I loved her dearly,
That she hath thee is of my wailing chief,
A loss in love that touches me more nearly.
Loving offenders thus I will excuse ye:
Thou dost love her, because thou know'st I love her,
And for my sake even so doth she abuse me,
Suff'ring my friend for my sake to approve her.
If I lose thee, my loss is my love's gain,
And losing her, my friend hath found that loss,
Both find each other, and I lose both twain,
And both for my sake lay on me this cross,
    But here's the joy, my friend and I are one,
    Sweet flattery, then she loves but me alone.

Sonnet 42 is an astonishing sonnet. In it, psychological issues are articulated that had never been dealt with before, and it is a sonnet that sets Shakespeare apart from any previous writer on the subject of love. Homosexual feelings compete with heterosexual ones and triumph over them. It is the first of the sonnets to deal explicitly with the triangulation that occured when the lover and the Poet's mistress met and established their own sexual liaison, excluding the Poet. The Poet is surprisingly able to examine and transform into poetry the relative strengths of his homo- and heterosexual feelings. If the events alluded to in this sonnet never happened in reality, as indeed might be the case, the analysis of a fantasy would be just as remarkable. Although the sonnet deals with the triangle, it is addressed only to the male lover, whose loss is more important to the Poet than the loss of the woman. The Poet attempts to persuade himself that the double loss did not really happen, because it was the result of being loved by both of them. The possibility that the betrayal was motivated by aggression towards the Poet from both lovers, evoked by the Poet (possibly by their reading these sonnets), remains undiscovered or denied.

In the first three lines the Poet asks who matters more in the triangle: the man or the woman. The Poet loves the woman dearly, but that his lover has become his rival for her is "not all my grief." Rather, the fact that she possesses him is the main cause of mourning. Line 4 explains the matter: "A loss in love that touches me more nearly." In ordinary speech, we would be inclined to say, "touches me more," but the addition of "nearly" makes the love for the man more intimate, and cleverly implies that the Poet's love for the Young Man, although not, as far as we know, physical, was nearly so, and was felt in a more essential physical way. The second quatrain introduces a new thought: the Poet confesses that he loves the offenders—not a singular offender (the Young Man, whom the Poet will excuse, as he did in Sonnet 41), but both offenders—and maybe even all offenders, which may also express an insight into the Poet's masochism. "Loving offenders" is a hint that the Poet may have been aware of having contributed to the triangulation. The Poet lets us know that their union was not entirely unwelcome. To our ear, he loves them more because they are offenders toward him. This grandiose but insightful train of thought continues in line 6: "Thou dost love her, because thou know'st I love her." The youth loves the lady because he feels a kind of empathic identification with the Poet. More than just preference for the man over the woman is implied; since the two men are experienced as one it seems natural to the Poet that they will also love the same woman. The woman also loves the Young Man because of the Poet, but her attraction to the youth is caused by her wish to abuse the Poet. The same behavior receives opposite interpretations. In spite of the youth's great beauty, she does not desire him for his own sake; she is merely "suff'ring my friend."

The third quatrain begins a journey to a more soothing view. If he loses the Young Man, the Poet's loss is his mistress's gain. The triangle is evoked to protect the Poet from experiencing the loss. In line 11, the Poet faces reality, admitting to himself that since "Both find each other," he has lost both of them. But in line 12, he succumbs once more to the fantasy that they both united for his sake. This is expressed in line 12: "And both for my sake lay on me this cross." There is a kernel of truth in this belief: the two may have become united by a powerful association with the Poet, but what the Poet fails to face is that their union could also be based on mutual hostility towards him. This is blotted out by the fantasy of an identification with Christ, in the same line.

The sonnet is an extraordinary psychological document offering insight into the ways the Poet was trying to cope with what at times seemed a double betrayal. If such a betrayal never took place, then the poem unspools a projected situation in which heterosexual and homosexual love feelings are at times reconciled and at times in conflict. The Poet may have understood what is sometimes discovered in the course of psychoanalysis: a sexual relationship may be based on aggression towards a third person. A sexual relationship with the spouse's "best friend" can be based on hostility towards the spouse. In a triangle, as described in this sonnet, all three participants feel both love and hostility to the other two. The strength of either love or hate may be similar in all three or it may fluctuate widely, and thus one cannot know what the reality or the fantasy of the Poet was. He certainly experienced loneliness and jealousy of the other two in the triangle, but also identification with either or both. That such a complex set of fluctuating feelings could have been evoked and condensed into a poem of 14 lines is an astonishing achievement.

Our appreciation of the psychological complexity of this sonnet, in which it seems to us that the Poet was in touch with his own unconscious, did not impress the anthologizers, for none included it.

SONNET 133

Beshrew that heart that makes my heart to groan
For that deep wound it gives my friend and me.
Is't not enough to torture me alone,
But slave to slavery my sweet'st friend must be?
Me from myself thy cruel eye hath taken,
And my next self thou harder hast engrossed.
Of him, myself, and thee, I am forsaken:
A torment thrice threefold thus to be crossed.
Prison my heart in thy steel bosom's ward,
But then my friend's heart let my poor heart bail;
Whoe'er keeps me, let my heart be his guard;
Thou canst not then use rigour in my jail.
    And yet thou wilt, for I, being pent in thee,
    Perforce am thine, and all that is in me.

Sonnets 40, 41 and 42, although dealing with the triangle, were addressed to the male lover. With this sonnet the same subject is now addressed to the woman. The difference in tone between the way the youth was addressed and the way the mistress is addressed is one of the astounding features of the sonnets. In spite of betrayal, the man is still loved. Sonnet 40 ends with the plea "yet we must not be foes." In Sonnet 41 the Poet went out of his way to excuse the young man's behavior, and in Sonnet 42 the Poet made it clear that "thou hast her" is not nearly as painful to him as that she has the young man. We were left in no doubt that, the betrayal notwithstanding, the Poet still loves the youth. This will remain true in the three heterosexual sonnets we will discuss. However, if the Poet ever loved the woman, this is no trace of that love left in him.

This sonnet is an extraordinarily clever reworking of the themes discussed in the previous sonnets. Here the Young Man is referred to as the Poet's "next self," meaning both that they are one and that the Young Man has followed the Poet into the Dark Lady's bed. Since the Poet has never been happy to be her lover, he assumes that the Young Man is imprisoned by her, and therefore begs her to release him.

The sonnet opens dramatically with the word "beshrew," meaning fie upon, or curse upon. The word beshrew appears in Shakespeare's works 29 times, often as "beshrew me" or "beshrew my heart" or "beshrew my soul." It is an exclamation of regret but not a severe self-reproach, raising a question as to how seriously we should take that "deep wound." Is the Poet suffering or playing at suffering? Commentators have interpreted "deep wound" as a reference to Cupid's arrows, but also as a reference to the female genital. If this interpretation is accepted, then the woman, through sexual intercourse, inflicts "deep wound[s]" on the two men, and the Poet conflated sexual relations with a woman with becoming a woman. In these lines the lady is alluded to indirectly. In line 3, the Poet suggests that it should be enough for her to torture him alone and refrain from making his lover also "a slave to slavery."

In line 5, the Poet once more advances the idea that he and his lover are really one, and therefore, "me from myself thy cruel eye hath taken." The two of them were merged and their falling in love with the same woman was experienced by the Poet as a breach of their union. In the same quatrain we note with some surprise the crucial role that the eye plays, for the Poet speaks of the woman's "cruel eye" as the main offender; it was her eye that separated them. The word "engrossed" in line 6 means "to occupy wholly." She had not only occupied the heart of the Poet, but also that of his "next self," since the two of them were one. When the triangle was established, the Poet lost not only the lady and his lover, but also part of himself.

The predisposition to masochism is implied in the third quatrain, when the Poet asks the lady "to prison my heart in thy steel prison's ward." Once more the poem conveys the impression that the female genital is a prison from which only the woman can release the prisoner. To have one's heart imprisoned was for Shakespeare and other poets a rather common metaphor for love. The altruism, the pleading on behalf of his friend to free his friend from slavery to the mistress, may lack sincerity; he will be imprisoned, but "guard" (meaning keep for himself) his lover's heart. The Poet hopes that she will not use "rigour" in his "jail," but he does not believe in her kindness, because he adds in the couplet "yet thou wilt;" she will continue to be cruel, as long as he is "being pent in thee," meaning imprisoned. Only the woman seems free.

The Poet's conflation of himself with his lover means that he feels entitled to bargain for both of them. What may have been a genuine experience of oneness in Sonnets 40 and 42 is seen as a problem in this sonnet, because the lady has two prisoners instead of one. Since we praised the insight that made Sonnets 40 and 42 possible, we must now point out that the almost delusional quality of the betrayal and the double infidelity of the young man and the mistress has been transformed into blame of the woman, as if she had imprisoned the lover and is torturing both of them.

The feeling that, when the love relationship has come to an end, one has not only lost the other person but also part of oneself is familiar in desperate states of falling in love, and may well be the reason for the deep melancholia and even suicide that follows upon the loss of a lover. This desperation comes across in the poem's most rhythmically aggressive line, line 8: "A torment thrice threefold thus to be crossed. In addition, the word "crossed" here "threefold," recalls an identification with Christ that was stated in Sonnet 42. The sonnet did not find its way into any of the anthologies.

SONNET 134

So, now I have confessed that he is thine,
And I myself am mortgaged to thy will,
Myself I'll forfeit, so that other mine
Thou wilt restore to be my comfort still.
But thou wilt not, nor he will not be free,
For thou art covetous, and he is kind;
He learned but surety-like to write for me
Under that bond that him as fast doth bind.
The statute of thy beauty thou wilt take,
Thou usurer that put'st forth all to use,
And sue a friend came debtor for my sake;
So him I lose through my unkind abuse.
    Him have I lost, thou has both him and me;
    He pays the whole, and yet am I not free.

Still battling the conflict created by his triangular relationship with the Dark Lady and the Young Man, the Poet asks the woman to give the man back to him as if this were an entirely normal transaction. Her failure to give the Young Man back is a sign of her perfidity. The main difficulty in this sonnet is caused by the Poet's choice of the metaphor of a legal proceeding to express both masochistic and paranoid ideas about the woman, evoked by a real or imaginary triangulation. While the previous sonnets used the term "my next self," Sonnet 134 uses "that other me" to express both the Poet's feeling of oneness with his male lover and his conviction that the woman loves him only as a displacement of her love for the Poet, brought on by her jealousy of the Poet's love for the Young Man. In this sonnet, as in the previous one, the feeling of oneness of the two male lovers goes hand-in-hand with a submissive attitude toward the woman.

That lovers wish to undo their separate individuality and become one is a significant aspect of Western thinking on love. Its origin is in Plato's *Symposium,* as discussed in Chapter 3. Psychoanalysis has further explored this union and concluded that it goes back to a yearning of the infant to be reunited with the mother and undo the separation from her, but the Poet of the Sonnets experiences this wish for union only with the male lover and never with the woman. That this wish is directed only at the Young Man is explained by the fact that the two, in the Poet's mind, are replicas of one self and not two distinct people, while the Poet and the mistress are always "twain." It is never fully expressed, but is hinted at in both Sonnet 133 and Sonnet 134, that if the mistress has both of them, the two, enslaved by her, will find a new kind of union between them.

In the first line, the Poet uses the word "confess" as if he being accused of some imaginary misdeed. In its current context, the word "confess" means that the Poet accepts the fact that his mistress won the youth away from him. The Poet is no longer denying the relationship between lover and mistress. It is not immediately self-evident why her having conquered the beloved man should mortgage the Poet, too. What is implied is that since the two of them are really one, possessing one includes having the other. He himself is "mortgaged to thy will" (with the pun on Shakespeare's first name). The metaphor of mortgage gave the Poet a way of expressing his feelings of servility. The metaphor continues in line 3 when the Poet says, "myself I'll forfeit"—what has been mortgaged can be forfeited if the debtor fails to continue his payments. But what does it mean to "forfeit myself?" We assume that the Poet meant to convey that he has given up any freedom to make his own decisions. The Poet uses the language of law to describe the psychological process of submission to the woman's will. In exchange for this submission, he hopes the woman will restore his lover to him. In the second quatrain, this masochistic solution is at least temporarily abandoned, as the Poet realizes that neither the Dark Lady nor the Young Man will accept his offer. The Young Man does not desire the freedom from the lady that the Poet, in mock generosity, is offering him. Because she is covetous and wants to imprison both of them, she will not free the Young Man.

In lines 7 and 8, the Poet falls back on the idea that he was not betrayed by his Young Man because "He learned but surety-like to write for me;" as if his lover had signed his name on a quasi-legal document on behalf of the Poet, and wooed the lady in the Poet's name. In order to defend the lover, the Poet maintains that the Young Man acted as a kind of ambassador who was ambushed and taken hostage while he performed his mission. The lady will extract the full price that her beauty can command. Therefore, she is called a usurer. Line 11 continues the metaphor. The friend will be sued by her, even though he became indebted to her only for the sake of the Poet. The twelfth line contains a double meaning, as "my unkind abuse" refers both to the lady's ill use of the Poe and to self-blame: the Poet accuses himself of abusing his lover, presumably because he used him to woo the lady. The couplet is a summary. The Poet has lost his lover; the lover must "pay the whole," or give the lady her sexual due, and she still has both of them imprisoned.

The metaphor of a bond or mortgage may seem strained in these 14 lines, but it proved an extraordinarily fruitful one for Shakespeare when he worked it out to its full extent in *The Merchant of Venice*. Antonio has given himself over as a bond for Bassanio's borrowed money, and must pay a pound of his own flesh for the forfeiture of the bond. Antonio loves Bassanio, but must accept that Bassanio will marry Portia, a rich heiress whom he loves, and she will use her money to repay the debt. In the play, from which we get the phrase "all that glitters is not gold," the metaphors of love and a bond for money interplay through the stories of a rich daughter who must submit to her dead father's wishes, another daughter who robs her father, and the two men who must renounce their love for each other to make a happy marriage for the young man possible.

SONNET 144

Two loves I have of comfort and despair,
Which like two spirits do suggest me still,
The better angel is a man right fair:
The worser spirit a woman colored ill.
To win me soon to hell my female evil,
Tempteth my better angel from my side,
And would corrupt my saint to be a devil,
Wooing his purity with her foul pride.
And whether that my angel be turned fiend
Suspecting I may, yet not directly tell,
But being both from me, both to each friend,
I guess one angel in another's hell.
    Yet this shall I ne'er know but live in doubt,
    Till my bad angel fire my good one out.

Sonnet 144 brings the cycle of triadic sonnets to a close. The sonnet had already appeared in print in 1599 in *The Passionate Pilgrim*. In form, it resembles a medieval morality play known as a psychomachia, in which virtue and vice fight over the loyalty of the dying man; but Shakespeare adopted only the form. There is no real contest between the man as a "better angel" and the woman as the "worser spirit." The woman is victorious from the first to the last line; she is the active agent and all the Poet can do is live in doubt, leaving her to decide the future. The split between the idealized absolute good and an equally absolute evil is characteristic of paranoid thinking, whether it takes place in the realm of love, religion or politics. What characterizes paranoid thinking is the absence of ambivalence. The good and the evil are absolutely separated, with no admixture of the two. We note that the Young Man is referred to as an angel and the woman as spirit. The term "spirit" was traditionally associated with malevolent intentions towards human beings.

In the first line, the Poet admits that he has two loves and differentiates between them, conveying a great deal of information in a small space. From the first he obtains comfort and from the second, despair. The second line is equally complex in thought. The two loves, the Poet is saying, can be compared to "two spirits." The next phrase, "do suggest me still," means that the Poet is not reflecting on something past but that the two loves are speaking to him right now. It is only in the third and fourth lines that the metaphor of psychomachia is brought in. The metaphor dominates the second quatrain, but already in the fifth line the medieval competition has taken a strange turn. The evil-spirited woman has conceived a diabolical plot. Instead of competing for the Poet with his male lover, she will woo and win the lover away from the Poet. Line 7 tells us that she "would corrupt" the Poet's "saint" "to be a devil." Being herself a devil, she is not interested in him and does not love him, but, devil-like in her "foul pride," is only interested in "wooing his purity."

The sonnet has a strange ending. The certainty with which he began has left him and he succumbs to doubting. In the ninth line we learn that he does not know how successful the woman will be in converting his "angel" into a "fiend." He suspects it but cannot directly tell, since both turned away from him ("being both from me") to become allies ("both to each friend"). In the twelfth line—"I guess one angel in another's hell"—hell is interpreted as meaning the vagina. If so, it shows the Poet's fear of the female genital. Psychoanalytic experience lends some support to this idea, including references to the "fireplace" as meaning a vagina.

The last line, "Till my bad angel fire my good one out," has been difficult to interpret. It seems to us that "fire" is connected to the image of hell. An allusion to venereal disease has been suggested, but if fire is a symbol for sexual desire, what does firing out mean? There is a similar action, perhaps, in smoking a fox from its hole, but smoking out and firing out are not identical. To us, the most likely interpretation is that the Poet will wait until the evil woman has rendered the man impotent, and then "fire out" would mean that he lost his fire, and without "fire" he is no longer of any use to the woman. This last line once more emphasizes that the Poet feels that his destiny lies entirely in the hands of the woman.

So great is the Poet's skill that we accept his reaction as not only a possible one, but as a quasi-realistic one, and we, too, blame the woman for her supposed cruelty. The exploration of the love triangle comes to a climax in Sonnet 144. If we now suppose that this triangulation never happened in reality, we can see it as the Poet's attempt to confirm that his homosexual love is stronger than his heterosexual one. To substantiate his preference for homosexual love, he portrays the woman as cruel and see himself as a slave.

We have no way of knowing whether, in reality, the heterosexual sonnets were an unhappy interlude, soon overcome by the re-establishment of the love between the Poet and the Young Man or another lover, or whether the triangle that resulted from the relationship of the two men to the Dark Lady destroyed their relationship. Psychoanalytic experience has taught us that if the heterosexual drive is strong and meets with disappointment, one woman may be replaced with another. On the other hand, when the heterosexual current is weak, disappointment can reinforce self-love or bring about a homosexual choice. Real or imagined, we can conceive that this cycle of sonnets had a special appeal to a certain circle of male readers who shared the Poet's fear of women.

If we consult the anthology table, we see that among the triadic sonnets, only Sonnet 144 received two out of six votes. The other five were not selected by any anthology. The reader may find it interesting to compare this sonnet with the others, especially with Sonnet 133 and Sonnet 134. Is it that the language of Sonnet 144 is more vehement? Or is it that the comparison of the two lovers to angel and fiend proved more universal? It is clearer why, as a whole, this type of sonnet is not attractive to the contemporary reader: the Poet always exonerates the youth and always blames the woman.

CHAPTER 9:
THE POET OF THE SONNETS AND SHAKESPEARE THE PLAYWRIGHT

In the other chapters we often cited excerpts from the plays where they could throw light on the meaning or attitude of a particular sonnet. But there are many interesting comparisons between the plays and the sonnets that never came up because they contain very different attitudes. We will look at five themes we have come to know well—love, lust, homosexuality, self-love, and attitudes towards time and death—for comparison as to how these issues are treated in the plays. In general, the plays display a much wider range of attitudes, which is why we refer to the "I" in the sonnets as the Poet of the Sonnets, as if he were a character created by our best dramatist.

LOVE

In *Hamlet*, Claudius uses a highly original metaphor for the nature of love:

Time qualifies the spark and fire of it.
There lives within the very flame of love
A kind of wick or snuff that will abate it (IV.vii.114-116).

The king is speaking only about the love of Laertes for his father Polonius, who was killed by Hamlet, but the implications are wider: there is packed within the "flame of love" a mysterious kernel that will work to "abate it." In this passage, Shakespeare gave Claudius the capacity to make more profound observation than his character in general would lead us to expect. There is no comparable observation in the sonnets, but the sense that time alone will diminish or destroy love abounds.

Shakespeare the playwright gave Portia, in *Julius Caesar,* a kind of understanding of love we would not have expected from the Poet of the Sonnets.

> *Portia:* No, my Brutus;
> You have some sick offence within your mind,
> Which, by the right and virtue of my place,
> I ought to know of; and, upon my knees,
> I charm you, by my once-commended beauty,
> By all your vows of love, and that great vow
> Which did incorporate and make us one,
> That you unfold to me, your self, your half,
> Why you are heavy, and what men to-night
> Have had resort to you; for heare have been
> Some six or seven, who did hide their faces
> Even from darkness.
>
> *Brutus:* Kneel not, gentle Portia.

> *Portia*: I should not need, if you were gentle Brutus.
> Within the bonds of marriage, tell me, Brutus,
> Is it excepted I should know no secrets
> That appertain to you? Am I yourself
> But, as it were, in sort or limitation,
> To keep with you at meals, comfort your bed,
> And talk to you sometimes? Dwell I but in the suburbs
> Of your good pleasure? If it be no more,
> Portia is Brutus' harlot, not his wife (II.i.267-287).

Portia knows her rights as Brutus' wife and how to insist on those rights, and also knows the difference between wife and whore. The question "Dwell I but in the suburbs/Of your good pleasure?" is an another instance where real estate is called upon to provide a metaphor for love ("summer's lease hath all too short a date"). But what we are not prepared for by the sonnets is the picture of a husband and wife together in love, facing a difficulty together.

Shakespeare the playwright also knows how love emerges. In a wonderful passage, Othello defends himself against the accusation that he used witchcraft to win Desdemona's love:

> When I did speak of some distressful stroke
> That my youth suffer'd. My story being done,
> She gave me for my pains a world of sighs:
> She swore, in faith, ' t was strange, ' t was passing strange;
> 'T was pitiful, 't was wondrous pitiful:
> She wish'd she had not heard it, yet she wish'd
> That heaven had made her such a man; she thank'd me,
> And bade me, if I had a friend that lov'd her,
> I should but teach him how to tell my story,
> And that would woo her. Upon this hint I spake:
> She lov'd me for the dangers I had pass'd,
> And I lov'd her that she did pity them.
> This only is the witchcraft I have us'd (I.iii.157-169).

We can reconstruct the various stages in the formation of Desdemona's love for Othello. First she experienced empathy for Othello's suffering. But what had first been experienced as "pitiful" soon becomes "wondrous." It is at this point that empathy turns into love. The next emotion is ambivalence over loving, expressed in "she wished she had not heard it." But this ambivalence is immediately counteracted by identification: she wished "That heaven had made her such a man." It is only after the identification had taken place, that is, after the wish to be Othello herself has been overcome, that Desdemona finds a coy way of actively wooing Othello: "And bade me, if I had a friend that lov'd her,/I should but teach him how to tell my story." From this hint, Othello knew Desdemona loved him, and declared his love for her. In 13 lines, Shakespeare condensed the unfolding of this woman's love for a man. No woman in the sonnets seems much capable of love.

We have always admired Dr. Johnson's description of Desdemona: "The soft simplicity of Desdemona, confident of merit, and conscious of innocence, her artless perseverance in her suit, and her slowness to suspect that she can be suspected, are such proofs of Shakespeare's skills in human nature as I suppose, it is in vain to seek in any modern writer." We are in Act IV, scene III; Othello has just accused Desdemona of being an impudent strumpet.

> *Desdemona:* …Here I kneel;
> If e'er my will did trespass 'gainst his love,
> Either in discourse, or thought, or actual deed,
> Or that mine eyes, mine ears, or any sense
> Delighted them on any other form;
> Or that I do not, and ever did,
> And ever will, though he do shake me off
> To beggarly divorcement, love him dearly,
> Comfort forswear me. Unkindness may do much,
> And his unkindness may defeat my life,
> But never taint my love (IV.ii.151-161).

These words of Desdemona express the deepest imaginable declaration of love. This love is not free from submission. The horrible vindictiveness hurled at her by Othello has not evoked any aggression towards him. Her loyalty to him has not been called into question. Desdemona's love goes deeper than anything envisioned by the poet in Sonnet 116. Desdemona is not a woman whose eye is false or rolling, as is characteristic of womankind in Sonnet 20. Othello comes to think of her that way, but the play depends on our understanding that Othello has become the victim of a paranoid delusion brought on by Iago's cunning. One might say that the woman is seen to be false both in *Othello* and in the sonnets, but what is presented as sound judgment in the sonnets is acknowledged to be projection in *Othello*.

In *King Lear*, Shakespeare gave to Cordelia a speech that stands out as the example of resolution of the Oedipus complex in a young woman.

> *Cordelia:* Unhappy that I am, I cannot hear
> My heart into my mouth: I love your majesty
> According to my bond; no more nor less.

> *Lear:* How, how, Cordelia! Mend your speech a little,
> Lest you may mar your fortunes.

> *Cordelia:* Good my lord,
> You have begot me, bred me, lov'd me: I
> Return those duties back as are right fit,
> Obey you, love you, and most honour you.
> Why have my sisters husbands, if they say
> They love you all? Haply, when I shall wed,
> That lord whose hand must take my plight shall carry
> Half my love with him, half my care and duty.
> Sure I shall never marry like my sisters,
> To love my father all (I.i.93-106).

Psychoanalysis enables us to understand and appreciate these words of Cordelia in a new way. By discovering the Oedipus complex, Freud made it clear that the first love of any normal child goes to one of the two parents, hate and jealousy going to the other. Growth demands that the child learn to accept that this early love cannot be consummated (disaster follows if it is), and the hatred and jealousy for the other parent must be overcome as well. Maturity demands that this love be transferred to a new person. At the same time the father and the mother must be capable of relinquishing the now maturing child. King Lear is an example of a parent who cannot relinquish his daughters. The two older sisters pretend to agree with the father so as to obtain part of his kingdom; Cordelia refuses to do this. She speaks to the father not so much out of Oedipal love as in the language of the post-Oedipal sense of duty. In psychoanalytic terms she speaks the language of the mature superego. Through Cordelia, Shakespeare transmitted to us an understanding of the transfer of Oedipal love into a post-Oedipal relationship with a man other than the father.

Shakespeare the playwright also knows that sadism can be transformed into love. We quote Theseus from *A Midsummer Night's Dream*.

> Hippolyta, I woo'd thee with my sword,
> And won thy love doing thee injuries;
> But I will wed thee in another key,
> With pomp, with triumph, and with reveling (I.i.16-19).

We have had the opportunity to observe how masochistic the love of the Poet of the Sonnets became towards his two lovers. The masochistic theme appears in *A Midsummer Night's Dream* in Helena's love for Demetrius.

> *Helena:* The more you beat me, I will fawn on you:
> Use me but as your spaniel, spurn me, strike me,
> Neglect me, lose me; only give me leave,
> Unworthy as I am, to follow you.
> What worser place can I beg in your love,
> And yet a place of high respect with me,
> Than to be used as you use your dog?
>
> *Demetrius:* Tempt not too much the hatred of my spirit,
> For I am sick when I do look on thee.
>
> *Helena:* And I am sick when I look not on you (II.i.204-213)

Helena's love for Demetrius is so masochistic that the audience is not given a chance to develop sympathy for her. Demetrius experiences this love as a temptation to become sadistic, hence the line "Tempt not too much the hatred of my spirit." However, towards Hermia, Demetrius is himself masochistic.

Hermia: I frown upon him, yet he loves me still.
Helena: O! that your frowns would teach my smiles such skill.
Hermia: I give him curses, yet he gives me love.
Helena: O! that my prayers could such affection move.
Hermia: The more I hate, the more he follows me.
Helena: The more I love, the more he hateth me (I.i.194-199).

In *Twelfth Night*, much of the same material that is painful and serious in the sonnets is treated lightly. The clown happily accepts the very same brevity of life that evoked so much pain in the Poet of the Sonnets. Duke Orsino falls in love with Viola but can't have her because he thinks she's a boy. When he finds out she's a woman he is, of course, delighted to marry her. Could he have, would he have fallen in love with her had he known she was a woman? Meanwhile Viola woos Olivia in the Duke's name and Olivia, thinking Viola is a boy, falls in love with her. She is delighted to find that Viola has a twin who is a man.

There are many instances in the plays when men and women masquerade by changing their gender and supposedly heterosexual men and women do not recognize the disguise and fall in love along homosexual lines disguised as heterosexual. We may surmise that Shakespeare the playwright—and his audience—often got to enjoy the androgyny that the Poet of the Sonnets describes with such wonder in Sonnet 20. The customs of the Elizabethan stage did not allow women to perform on stage, so all women's roles were played by (male) actors, which must have added yet another layer of gender misrepresentation to the experience. Viola would have been played by a man playing a woman, so that when Viola is disguised as a boy the actor would be playing a woman playing a boy. When Olivia (played by a male actor of course) falls in love with this "boy" who is "really" a girl who is played by a man…well, it's no wonder Shakespeare was so fluent with such devices and made such frequent use of them.

At the beginning of *Twelfth Night*, Olivia is deaf to pleas for her love because she will not give up her mourning. Mourning, in Shakespeare, does not go with love. These have all become familiar themes to us, but in *Twelfth Night* they are worked into a dramatic structure and given comic treatment. Did the discharging of the pain in the sonnets made it possible to write *Twelfth Night*?

Clown: Journeys end in lovers meeting,
Every wise man's son doth know
. . .
What is love? 't is not hereafter;
Present mirth hath present laughter;
What's to come is still unsure:
In delay there lies no plenty;
Then come kiss me, sweet-and-twenty
Youth's a stuff will not endure (II.iii.44-45; 48-53).

The comic side of submission to love was also expressed by Shakespeare the dramatist in Act III, Scene I in *Love's Labor's Lost*. Berowne, one of the king's councilors, has this to say about love:

This signor junior, giant-dwarf, dan Cupid;
Regent of love rhymes, lord of folded arms,
The anointed sovereign of sighs and groans,
Liege of all loiterers and malcontents,
. . .
What! I love! I sue! I seek a wife!
A woman that is like a German clock,
Still a-repairing, ever out of frame,
. . .
With two pitch-balls stuck in her face for eyes;
. . .it is a plague
That Cupid will impose for my neglect
Of his almighty dreadful little might.
Well, I will love, write, sigh, pray, sue, and groan (III.i.177-201).

We note that Berowne's good-natured complaint deals with his submission to Cupid, the god of love.

We conclude that Shakespeare the playwright was not unfamiliar with the sexual and love anxieties of the Poet of the Sonnets, but the playwright had a much greater range of vision and tone. We do not know what accounts for this difference. Either Shakespeare matured after he wrote the sonnets, or regressed when he was deeply in love, or chose, when he wrote the sonnets, to create the character we have been calling the Poet of the

Sonnets, giving him limitless lyric skill but only Othello's trust in women, Hamlet's melancholia and Juliet's impatience when separated from his beloved. Unlike the writer of the sonnets, Shakespeare could understand and create women like Portia and Desdemona, who embody the full capacity of women to love their husbands. The playwright also understood the transition from Oedipal love to mature love in a woman. Perhaps the Poet of the Sonnets was not forgotten, but transformed into a comic character that the playwright outgrew.

LUST

The savage attack on lust in Sonnet 129 has little company in Shakespeare's other work.

In one of Shakespeare's earliest plays, *The Comedy of Errors,* we find this passage in which Arianna denounces lust:

> How dearly would it touch thee to the quick,
> Should'st thou but hear I were licentious,
> And that this body, consecrate to thee,
> By ruffian lust should be contaminate!
> Would'st thou not spit at me, and spurn at me,
> And hurl the name of husband in my face,
> And tear the stan'd skin off my harlot-brow,
> And from my false hand cut the wedding-ring,
> And break it with a deep-divorcing vow?
> I know thou canst; and therefore see thou do it.
> I am possess'd with an adulterate blot;
> My blood is mingled with the crime of lust (II.ii.132-143):

Arianna condemns lust as a moral failing because of its effect on the person betrayed, not because of its effect on the lustful person. If we look in the plays for passages that equal Sonnet 129 in ferocity, perhaps the closest are these lines from the "closet scene" in *Hamlet.* Hamlet is fulminating against his mother sharing her bed with Claudius, Hamlet's uncle:

…but to live/In the rank sweat of an enseamed bed,/Stew'd in corruption, honeying and making love /Over the nasty sty… (IV.iii.91-94)

Or this, from the Ghost of Hamlet's father:

So lust, though to a radiant angel link'd,
will sate itself in a celestial bed,
And prey on garbage (I.v.55-57).

In 1593 and 1594, while the London theaters were closed because of the fear of the plague, Shakespeare published the poems *Venus and Adonis* and *The Rape of Lucrece,* both dedicated to the Earl of Southampton. It is generally believed that both poems deal with lust, but the difference in their approach to sexual desire could hardly be greater.

Stephen Greenblatt, in *Will in the World* (2004), drew our attention to the differences in the dedication of the two works, written only a year apart. The first dedication is respectful and formal, while the second is intimate, personal, and full of expressions of love, raising the question of whether the sonnets to the Young Man were written between the two poems. Whatever the timing of the compositions may be, if Shakespeare expressed his love to the earl in *Venus and Adonis* disguised as Venus, might he have also expressed his guilt feelings over these desires disguised as Lucrece? Because of its link to Sonnet 129, we turn first to the later of the two poems.

THE RAPE OF LUCRECE

Under the title "The Argument," Shakespeare wrote a preface to the poem. The Roman generals at war were boasting about the chastity of their wives, but only Lucrece, the wife of Collatinus, passed the test when the generals returned to Rome, surprising the wives. The chastity of Lucrece enflamed the passion of Tarquinius, the last Roman king before the establishment of the Roman Republic. The theme of the chaste woman who arouses a special passion was of interest to Shakespeare, for he returned to this theme in *Measure for Measure.* The very idea that the Roman kingdom came to an end and was replaced by a republic because the last king was guilty of rape was of great interest to the Elizabethans.

As the poem opens, King Tarquin is born by the "trustless wings of false desire" and "bears the lightless fire which in pale embers hid." These are Shakespeare's metaphors to describe lust. Envy of the lucky husband for the possession of his beauteous mate, and the wish to destroy this happiness, are the motives for the rape.

In Sonnet 129 we followed the poet's severe condemnation of lust. The same condemnation of lust occurs in *The Rape of Lucrece* (1593-94).

> This momentary joy breeds months of pain
> This hot desire converts to cold disdain:
> Pure chastity is rifled of her store,
> and Lust, the thief, far poorer than before (690-93).
> …
> She says her subjects with foul insurrection
> Have battered down her consecrated wall
> And by their mortal fault brought in subjection
> Her immortality, and made her thrall
> To living death and pain perpetual (722-726)
> …
> She bears the load of lust he left behind,
> And he the burden of a guilty mind.
> He like a thievish dog creeps sadly thence,
> She like a wearied lamb lies panting there;
> He scowls and hates himself for his offence,
> She desperate with her nails her flesh doth tear (734-39).

Lust leaves both perpetrator and victim in an unbearable situation, burdened by guilt and self-hatred.

When we reach lines 834-840, an unexpected metaphor within the lament complicates the issue.

> If, Collantine, thine honour lay in me,
> From me by strong assault it is bereft:
> My honey lost, and I, a drone-like bee,
> Have no perfection of my summer left,
> But robbed and ransacked by injurious theft.
> > In thy weak hive a wand'ring wasp hath crept,
> > And sucked the honey which thy chaste bee kept (834-840).

Lucrece laments that the rape converted her from a honey-rich bee into a drone, that is, a masculine bee. The female genital is compared to a "weak hive" full of honey stored up by the loyal bee, but as a result of the robbery the bee became a useless drone. The metaphor, therefore, conveys the sense of gender change as a result of the rape. Rendered bereft of any further capacity to create new honey, the bee must kill herself. The rape has deprived the woman of her "honey" and she has nothing to give to her husband. Honey, the "honor" that "lay in me," has been stolen like mother's milk, reducing the husband to a nursing baby in danger of starvation.

Rape desexualizes Lucrece. This recalls an even more explicit, and willing, desexualization of Lady Macbeth as she prepares herself to become a murderess:

> *Lady Macbeth:* Come, you spirits
> That tend on mortal thoughts! unsex me here,
> And fill me from the crown to the toe top full
> Of direst cruelty; make thick my blood,
> Stop up the access and passage to remorse,
> That no compunctious visitings of nature
> Shake my fell purpose, nor keep peace between
> The effect and it! (*Macbeth,* I.vi.41-48).
>
> …

and when she is urging Macbeth to do the murder:

> I have given suck, and know
> How tender't is to love the babe that milks me:
> I would, while it was smiling in my face,
> Have pluck'd my nipple from his boneless gums,
> And dash'd the brains out, had I so sworn as you (I.vii.54-58).

VENUS AND ADONIS

Shakespeare found the story of Venus and Adonis in Chapter 10 of Ovid's *Metamorphoses.* Shakespeare changed Ovid's tale in two important ways: he made Adonis younger, not yet a man; and made him resist Venus' efforts to seduce him. The youth of Adonis lends support to our interpretation of Sonnet 104, namely that the poet, here disguised as Venus, had the tendency to fall in love with those who were not yet ripe for it.

Greek gods, more than Greek goddesses, often experienced lust for mortal women, but being all-powerful and immortal they never met refusal, with the exception of Daphne, who escaped Apollo's embraces by turning into a tree. The pain of unrequited love is virtually unknown to the gods. By the time of the Roman republic, when Ovid wrote his great poem, the Greek deities had lost much of their power, so that he could describe Venus as smitten by love:

> …Cupid it seems, was playing
> Quiver on shoulder, when he kissed his mother
> and one barb grazed her breast, she pushed him away,
> But the wound was deeper than she knew; deceived,
> charmed by Adonis' beauty…

When one is hit by Cupid's arrow one is in love, but when one is only grazed, the line of demarcation between lust and love is difficult to draw.

The dedication of *Venus and Adonis* to the earl can be read in two ways: either as a support of his resistance to marriage or, on a deeper, unconscious level, as Shakespeare putting himself into the role of Venus and declaring his desire for the young earl. In any case, Shakespeare gave Venus a magnificent vocabulary for her passion.

While *The Rape of Lucrece* was clearly a poem condemning lust and a portrayal of its consequences, *Venus and Adonis,* published a year earlier, is more difficult to categorize. The goddess of love desires Adonis. She attempts to seduce him, but does not rape or use any of her powers as a goddess could. She entreats him to stay with her:

> A thousand honey secrets shalt thou know.
>> Here come and sit, where never serpent hisses,
>> And being set, I'll smother thee with kisses (15-17).

The honey that will be stolen from Lucrece in the later poem is here freely offered in a land where "serpent never hisses." Venus is not afraid of phallic beasts or of the serpent who lured Eve into her catastrophic disobedience in the Garden of Eden.

The poet comments:

> She red, and hot, as coals of glowing fire,
> He red for shame, but frosty in desire (35-36).
>
> …
>
> Backward she pushed him, as she would be thrust,
> And governed him in strength though not in lust (41-42).
>
> …
>
> Even so she kissed his brow, his cheek, his chin,
> And where she ends, she doth anew begin (59-60).

The seductive power of Venus is expressed in a beautifully earthy metaphor:

> Within this limit is relief enough,
> Sweet bottom grass, and high delightful plain,
> Round rising hillocks, brakes obscure and rough,
> To shelter thee from tempest, and from rain:
>> Then be my deer, since I am such a park.
>> No dog shall rouse thee, though a thousand bark (235-240).

The reaction of Adonis is memorable:

> Hot, faint, and weary with her hard embracing,
> Like a wild bird being tamed with too much handling (559-560)

Though Venus' promises seem delightful, what seems to give special pleasure to the poet, and presumably to the homosexually inclined readers of the poem, is the capacity of Adonis to resist the goddess' attempt at his seduction.

After the death of Adonis, Venus' lament conveys that it was more than lust that she felt for Adonis. The Greek gods did lust after mortal men and women, but their narcissism protected them against both love and mourning for the loss of a lover. The only Greek goddess who knows love and mourning is Demeter, who mourns the loss of her daughter Persephone. But Shakespeare's Venus says:

> 'Hard-favoured tyrant, ugly, meager, lean;
> Hateful divorce of love,' thus chides she Death (931-932).
> …
> They bid thee crop a weed; thou pluck'st a flower (946).
> …
> Dost thou drink tears that thou provok'st such weeping (949)?
> …
> For he being dead, with him is beauty slain,
> And beauty dead, black chaos comes again (1019-1020).

The poem ends on a note of love between a mother and her infant:

> Lo, in this hollow cradle take thy rest:
> My throbbing heart shall rock thee day and night.
> There shall not be one minute in an hour
> Wherein I will not kiss my sweet love's flower (1185-1188).

HOMOSEXUALITY AND ITS PROJECTION

In the first chapter we came to realize that the Poet of the Sonnets waged a double struggle: first, to divorce homosexual wishes from homosexual love, and also, perhaps, to overcome sexual attraction to prepubescent boys.

An indirect reference to homosexuality appears in *Hamlet*.

> *Hamlet:* …man delights not me; no, nor woman neither, though by your smiling you seem to say so.
>
> *Ros.:* My lord, there was no such stuff in my thoughts.
>
> *Hamlet:* Why did you laugh then when I said "man delights not me (II.ii.322-325)?"

The issue is left unresolved. Did the friends suspect homosexuality or was Hamlet, in his distraught state, oversensitive?

In the famous graveyard scene, Hamlet picks up the skull of Yorick and says

> Alas! poor Yorick. I knew him, Horatio; a fellow of infinite
> jest, of most excellent fancy; he hath borne me on his back a
> thousand times; and now, how abhorred in my imagination it
> is! my gorge rises at it. Here hung those lips that I have kissed
> I know not how oft (V.i.203-210).

Shakespeare gave Hamlet a man instead of a traditional nursemaid (like the Nurse, for example, in *Romeo and Juliet*). It should be read as a hint that Hamlet and perhaps also his creator had a powerful homosexual relationship in his childhood. Freud did not pay attention to this scene because he understood *Hamlet* essentially as a drama of Oedipal inhibition, and a homosexual relationship is not recorded as a biographical fact about Shakespeare.

We have also discussed the psychoanalytic distinction between desexualized and latent homosexuality. For instance, in *Twelfth Night* (probably written in 1601-02 and published posthumously in 1623), Antonio loves Sebastian and endangers his own life for this love in an example of desexualized homosexuality. Similarly, Sir Toby and Sir Andrew have a desexualized love relationship. In contrast, the relationship between Othello and Iago is latently homosexual and leads to the destruction of their heterosexual relationships.

We would like to draw attention to Othello's absence of heterosexual passion. Shakespeare showed Othello to be first and foremost a soldier. Asexual, he is impotent. He portrays marriage as a desexualized relationship:

> Vouch with me, heaven, I therefore beg it not
> To please the palate of my appetite,
> Nor to comply with heat, the young affects
> In me defunct, and proper satisfaction,
> But to be free and bounteous to her mind;
> …
> For she is with me. No, when light-wing'd toys
> Of feather'd Cupid seel with wanton dullness
> My speculative and offic'd instruments,
> That my disports corrupt and taint my business
> (I.iii.262-266; 269-272)

Othello has no family or parents, and no personal history beyond his military achievements. He is loyal to the Serenissima but he is not a Venetian. There is little room within Othello's personality structure for heterosexual love. In such soil the paranoid, latently homosexual relationship between Iago and Othello can take root.

It has often been pointed out that Iago is a variation of the theme of the devil. Iago is a malignant character who systematically arouses Othello's suspicion of Desdemona and brings about her murder. Iago's attitude toward women resembles the attitude of the Poet of the Sonnets toward his mistress. The same suspicion is present, even if the tone is more humorous.

> *Iago:* Belles in your parlours, wild cats in your kitchens,
> Saints in your injuries, devils being offended.
> Players in your housewifery, and housewives in your beds…
> Nay, it is true, or else I am a Turk:
> You rise to play, and go to bed to work (II.110-13, 115-16)

Systematically, Iago works on fanning Othello's jealousy and extinguishing his love for Desdemona. When Iago has succeeded, we hear Othello's frightening words.

Now do I see 'tis true. Look here, Iago,
All my fond love thus do I blow to Heav'n.
'Tis gone.
Arise black vengeance from the hollow hell;
Yield up, O love, thy crown and hearted throne
To tyrannous hate (III.iii.444-449)!

This speech is one of Shakespeare's great dramatic moments, where love has been defeated by its great adversary, hate. Latent homosexuality contributed to this transformation.

To write *Othello* with the deep understanding of Iago's role in undermining Othello's trust and love for Desdemona required from Shakespeare a kind of insight into homosexuality and paranoia that we cannot attribute to the Poet of the Sonnets. Either Shakespeare did not use all his knowledge and range when he created the Poet of the Sonnets, or a profound change must have taken place for him to be able to accomplish what he did as poet and playwright. Possibly, too, a wider range of insights may have been available when he was not writing in the first person. Clearly, neither Iago nor Othello know that they are working together to kill Desdemona. The question remaining is, did their creator understand the implicit homosexuality which, in this case, is closely allied with destruction, so that the two men do not create a love bond but rather join in a bond of hatred against the woman? In the sonnets, the triangle between the Young Man, the Dark Lady and the Poet is resolved when the two join to exclude the Poet. The love the Poet of the Sonnets bestowed on the Young Man, as well as the tragic triangulation between them, is not repeated in the plays. *Othello* can be seen as the Poet's revenge, as it is the two men who get together not just to exclude the woman but to murder her.

If *Othello* were being created in Hollywood today, studio executives might suggest that Iago should be more like the Young Man and Desdemona more like the Dark Lady, who is neither beautiful nor innocent. That way the audience would not be as horrified when Desdemona is murdered. But Shakespeare, in creating *Othello*, chose to show that the suspicions against which the Poet struggles in the sonnets are baseless in reality. He wishes to show us the horrible outcome when we lose the struggle against the Iago part of us, for psychologically speaking Iago is part of Othello, just as dramatically speaking he is a completely different character. In the sonnets we saw that the Young Man who is the object of the Poet's love is often described as merged with the Poet into one person, as in Sonnet 62: 'Tis thee, myself, that for myself I praise.'

In Sonnet 62, the shock of aging turned the poet away from self-love towards love for a Young Man. In *Coriolanus*, Shakespeare the dramatist portrayed the self-destruction of a narcissistic man. Latent homosexuality appears in that play as a rivalry between Coriolanus and Aufidius, general of the Volscians, who is first Coriolanus' rival, then his friend, and finally his murderer.

The play contains two great dramatic moments. In the first, Coriolanus has the opportunity to become consul, but he has to display his wounds to win the crowd and this he refuses to or cannot do. He has only contempt for the ordinary citizens of Rome. Losing this opportunity, he goes over to the enemy, where he creates a desexualized homosexual relationship with Aufidius, their commanding general.

When Coriolanus seeks refuge in the house of Aufidius, there is a moment when the homosexuality behind their enmity becomes evident.

> *Aufidius:* Oh Marcius, Marcius!
> Each word thou hast spoke hath weeded from my heart
> A foot of ancient envy.
>
> …
>
> …noble Marcius. Let me twine
> Mine arms about that body, where against
> My grained ash an hundred times hath broke,
>
> …
>
> I lov'd the maid I married; never man
> Sigh'd a truer breath; but that I see thee here,
> Thou noble thing! More dances my rapt heart
> Than when first my wedded mistress saw
> Bestride my threshold (IV.v.107-124).

We may assume that it would not occur to a heterosexual man to compare the arrival of a former enemy with the memory of his wedding night. Shakespeare the playwright will show us how the injured homosexuality of Aufidius will cause the death of Coriolanus. As in the case of Othello, here too we must assume that Shakespeare could not have expressed Aufidius's homosexual feelings for Coriolanus the way he did had he still been under the power of the prohibition against homosexual wishes that animates Sonnet 20.

One of the important discoveries of psychoanalysis was that both latent and overt homosexuals have retained such a loyalty to their mothers that they cannot transfer their love to any other woman. In writing Coriolanus, Shakespeare showed that he understood, if not consciously, that such a loyalty to the mother ultimately leads to the destruction of Coriolanus.

Virgilia, the wife of Coriolanus, is loving and unconcerned with honors and appearances. In psychoanalytic terms, one can say that she could have acted as a "corrective emotional experience" for Coriolanus and averted his tragedy, but because he remained attached to his mother and could not transfer his love from mother to wife, he was doomed. This tragic situation is quite common. Many men and women have the good fortune to find a mate capable of healing their childhood-inflicted wounds, but their attachment to the trauma-inflicting parent is so great that they cannot use the mate to heal the wounds inflicted by the childhood trauma.[1]

In *Cymbeline* (1609-10), Posthumous, the exiled husband of Princess Imogen, meets Lachimo; the two wager a bet on whether Lachimo can seduce Imogen. The husband accepts the bet. Lachimo tries to seduce Imogen by telling her that her husband is unfaithful to her and that she should avenge herself by having a sexual relationship with him. The attempt fails, but Lachimo gains access to Imogen's chamber and brings back the bracelet that Posthumous gave his wife. The bracelet plays the same role in *Cymbeline* as the handkerchief played in *Othello,* indicating that Shakespeare, at

---

[1]The psychoanalytic studies about *Coriolanus* that we will cite all come from the 1960s and they differ significantly from the more classical studies. They no longer deal almost exclusively with the Oedipal theme; they reflect a shift in psychoanalysis itself during these decades towards a greater interest in the impact of earlier years and particularly the mother-child relationship, but they differ also in another respect: the gulf that separates the psychoanalytic interpretations from the non-psychoanalytic ones has narrowed. The vocabulary and the emphasis is still very different but not nearly as different as it was when Freud first formulated the idea that Hamlet's hesitation in killing his uncle is based on the fact that what the prince wished, the uncle did. What the psychoanalysts said about Coriolanus was not nearly as new as what Freud said about Hamlet.

least preconsciously, felt there is a close relationship between fetishism and homosexuality. Returning to Rome, Lachimo pretends to have seduced Imogen. Believing that Imogen was disloyal, Posthumous tries to have her killed. But unlike *Othello,* here all ends well. Lachimo is not as sinister a character as Iago. Nevertheless, the very fact that the two men enter into such a bet is an indication of a latent homosexual undercurrent between them, but the material is given a comic treatment instead of a deeply tragic one. History has not been kind to *Cymbeline,* which is rarely read and performed. *Othello,* by comparison, is one Shakespeare's most enduring successes.

King Lear contains a passage that shows that the playwright Shakespeare was familiar with the fear that the female genital can evoke.

> *Lear:* Down from the waist they are Centaurs,
> Though women all above:
> But to the girdle do the gods inherit,
> Beneath is all the fiend's:
> There's hell, there's darkness, there's the sulphurous pit,
> Burning, scalding, stench, consumption (IV.vi.126-131)

The last three lines go far beyond the "waste of shame" in Sonnet 129, and testify to Shakespeare's capacity to evoke a man's castration anxiety and his fear of the female genital, feelings that tend to be closer to consciousness in male homosexuals than in heterosexual men.

SELF-LOVE

In *The Rape of Lucrece* (1593-94), the beauty of a woman is praised thus: "Had Narcissus seen her as she stood, self-love had never drowned him in the flood" (265). From this passage, Shakespeare offers Narcissus the possibility of being rescued from self-love as the Poet was in Sonnet 62. Here, we also learn that Shakespeare derived the idea of self-love from Ovid's legend of Narcissus. Self-love appears frequently in Shakespeare's plays, but there it is handled with humor. The self-love that is a threat to both homo-

and heterosexual love, which we noted in the sonnets, is not repeated in the plays.

The Taming of the Shrew (1593-94) deals with self-love humorously. Petruchio and Katherine are both narcissistic characters; they cannot wed without one winning over the other. The shrew is tamed by giving up her independence.

> *Pet:* Good Lord, how bright and goodly shines the moon!
>
> *Kath.:* The moon? The sun! It is not moonlight now.
>
> *Pet.:* I say it is the moon that shines so bright.
>
> *Kath.:* I know it is the sun that shines so bright.
>
> *Pet.:* Now by my mother's son, and that's myself,
> It shall be moon, or star, or what I list,
> Or e'er I journey to your father's house.—
> …
>
> *Kath.:* Forward, I pray, since we have come so far,
> And be it moon, or sun, or what you please.
> And if you please to call it a rush-candle
> Henceforth I vow it shall be so for me.
>
> *Pet.:* I say it is the moon.
>
> *Kath.:* I know it is the moon.
>
> *Pet.:* Nay, then you lie. It is the blessed sun.
>
> *Kath.:* Then, God be blest, it is the blessed sun.
> But sun it is not, when you say it is not,
> And the moon changes even as your mind.
> What you will have it name'd, even that it is,
> And so it shall be so for Katharine (IV.v.1-22).

The battle of the sexes is resolved at the end of the play by Katherine's grateful appreciation of her husband's role. The resolution of the conflict will hardly appeal to contemporary audiences:

> *Kath.:* A woman mov'd is like a fountain troubled,
> Muddy, ill-seeming, thick, bereft of beauty,
> And while it is so, none so dry or thirsty
> Will deign to sip or touch one drop of it.
> Thy husband is thy lord, thy life, thy keeper,
> Thy head, thy sovereign; one that cares for thee,
> And for thy maintenance; commits his body
> To painful labour both by sea and land,
> To watch the night in storms, the day in cold,
> Whilst thou liest warm at home, secure and safe;
> And craves no other tribute at thy hands
> But love, fair looks, and true obedience;
> Too little payment for so great a debt (V.ii.143-55)

The woman yields, and self-love is not allowed to become an impediment to marriage.

In *Much Ado about Nothing* (1598-99) Hero describes Beatrice's self-love.

> O god of love! I know he doth deserve
> As much as may be yielded to a man;
> But Nature never fram'd a woman's heart
> Of prouder stuff than that of Beatrice;
> Disdain and scorn ride sparkling in her eyes,
> Misprising what they look on, and her wit
> Values itself so highly, that to her
> All matter else seems weak. She cannot love,
> Nor take no shape nor project of affection,
> She is so self-endeared (III.i.4-55).

In *Twelfth Night,* Olivia says: "O! you are sick of self-love, Malvolio (I.v.90)."

And Maria describes him thus:

> …the best persuaded of himself; so crammed, as he thinks,
> with excellencies, that it is his ground of faith that all that look
> on him love him (II.iii.149-51).

TIME AND DEATH

The triad of time, aging and death has revealed itself as the dominant theme of the sonnets. It is also a leading theme in the plays. Death is nearly omnipresent when the poet speaks of love. The attitude of Shakespeare the dramatist toward death is a vast subject of great interest. We offer a few of the highlights.

In the sonnets we noted that death is frequently experienced in oral terms, as a devourer. The same experience of death in oral terms is found in *Romeo and Juliet.*

> *Romeo:* thou womb of death
> Gorged with the dearest morsel of the earth
> Thus I enforce thy rotten jaws to open
> And in despite I'll cram thee with more food (V.iii.45-48).

"Devouring time," having feasted on Juliet's death, feels sated and has no desire to add Romeo, but Romeo will pry open death's "rotten jaws" and force death to accept him as additional, if unwelcome, food. Here, the mouth is the main organ for the expression of aggression.

Although physical death is usually what is meant when Shakespeare speaks to the subject of death, he described another kind of death, when remorse kills the villain metaphorically before physical death, in *Richard III* (1592-93). The ghosts of those the king killed visit him the night before he is to die; among them, the malediction of Queen Anne is the most poignant.

> *The Ghost of Lady Anne rises.*

> *Ghost [To King Richard]:* Richard, thy wife, that wretched
> Anne thy wife,
> That never slept a quiet hour with thee,
> Now fills thy sleep with perturbations:
> To-morrow in the battle think on me,
> And fall thy edgeless sword: despair, and die (V.iii.159-163)!

An interesting psychological essay could be written on Shakespeare's use of ghosts. In *Hamlet,* Shakespeare used the ghost in two different ways. When the ghost appears first, he is witnessed by a group of men but he speaks only to Hamlet. Shakespeare thus implies that the ghost is real; but when the same ghost appears again in the queen's chamber, only Hamlet sees and hears him, while the queen sees nothing. The queen believes that the ghost was, or at least may have been, Hamlet's hallucination. Audiences, actors and directors must decide for themselves whether Shakespeare meant the second appearance of the ghost to be real or a hallucination. In *Richard III,* the ghost is a form of remorse, though it is not an internalized remorse such as Christianity demands. Richard is not a repentant sinner, but projects his guilt on the outside world, on an apparition provided by Shakespeare as a primitive alternative to guilt.

A memorable exchange on the subject of death takes place in *Henry IV, Part I.* In Act V, Scene I, just before the battle of Shrewsbury, Falstaff admits being afraid to die and says to Prince Hal, "I would it were bed-time, Hal, and all well," to which the future King Henry V gives the memorable reply, "Why, thou owest God a death (lines 126-127)." Freud was deeply impressed by this statement, but being an opponent of religion transformed it into "every one owes nature a death and must expect to pay the debt (Freud 1915, p. 289)."

Falstaff's reply to Prince Hal is magnificent:

> 'Tis not due yet: I would be loath to pay him before his
> day—what need I be so forward with him that calls not on
> me? Well, 'tis no matter, honour pricks me on. Yea, but how if
> honour prick me off when I come on? how then? Can honour
> set to a leg? No. Or an arm? No. Or take away the grief of a
> wound? No. Honour hath no skill in surgery then? No. What
> is honour? A word. What is in that word honour? Air. A trim
> reckoning! Who hath it? He that died o' Wednesday. Doth
> he feel it? No. Doth he hear it? No. Is it insensible, then? Yea,
> to the dead. But will it not live with the living? No. Why?
> Detraction will not suffer it. Therefore I'll none of it. Honour
> is a mere scutcheon; and so ends my catechism (V.i.127-41).

Harold Bloom believes that Hamlet and Falstaff are among the greatest dramatic personae created by Shakespeare and that they "illuminate the sonnets more often than the sonnets give us new light upon those two giant forms" (p. 274). Bloom goes on to say "the poet's own love for the young nobleman in the sonnets was anything but grotesque or self-serving," and it does seem to be the paradigm for the Falstaff-Hal relationship (p. 295). It seems plausible to us that Falstaff was a self-image for Shakespeare, and Prince Hal the embodiment of the noble youth the poet loved. And yet, the glory of *Henry IV Part I* is its portrait of Hal as a young man growing to maturity. Any reader horrified by the efforts of the Poet of the Sonnets to hold back the development of the Young Man need look no further than this play for solace.

It was in *Hamlet* (1600-01) that Shakespeare reached the high point in his ability to express ambivalence towards both life and death.

> *Hamlet:* To be, or not to be: that is the question:
> Whether 't is nobler in the mind to suffer
> The slings and arrows of outrageous fortune,
> Or to take arms against a sea of troubles,
> And by opposing end them? To die: to sleep;
> No more; and by a sleep to say we end
> The heart-ache and the thousand natural shocks
> That flesh is heir to, 't is a consummation
> Devoutly to be wish'd. To die, to sleep;
> To sleep: perchance to dream: ay, there's the rub;
> For in that sleep of death what dreams may come
> When we have suffled off this mortal coil,
> Must give us pause (III.i.56-67).

Hamlet, and perhaps also his creator, struggled against strong suicidal wishes. These wishes are presented in abstract philosophical terms. They are not the reflections of a Christian believer, but neither are they the reflections of a convinced atheist. It is this vacillating position between two world views that endows this soliloquy with its unique power.

Gertrude tells Hamlet, "Thou knowest is common; All that lives must die/Passing through nature to eternity (I.ii.72-73)."

In the sonnets as well as in the dramatic works, Shakespeare anthropomorphizes both time and death, portraying them as persons. In *Troilus and Cressida* (1601-02), Ulysses says:

> Time hath, my lord, a wallet at his back,
> Wherein he puts alms for oblivion;
> A great-siz'd monster of ingratitudes:
> Those scraps are good deeds past; which are devour'd
> As fast as they are made
>
> …
>
> Love, friendship, charity, are subjects all
> To envious and calumniating time (III.iii.145-49, 173-74)

In *Measure for Measure* (1604) a "naked" fear of death is expressed by Claudio, who has been condemned to die, and who gives us a vivid description of his imagined "life" after death.

> *Claudio:* Ay, but to die, and go we know not where;
> To lie in cold obstruction, and to rot;
> This sensible warm motion to become
> A kneaded clod; and the delighted spirit
> To bathe in fiery floods, or to reside
> In thrilling region of thick-ribbed ice;
> To be imprison'd in the viewless winds
> And blown with restless violence round about
> The pendent world: or to be worse than worst
> Of those that lawless and incertain thought
> Imagine howling,——'tis too horrible!
> The weariest and most loathed worldly life
> That age, ache, penury and imprisonment
> Can lay on nature, is a paradise
> To what we fear of death (III.i.117-31).

In the same play, the attitude of Barnardine is the very opposite of that of Claudio, offering comic relief to the otherwise gruesome scene.

Pompey: Master Barnardine! You must rise and be hanged, Master Barnardine.

Abhorson: What hoa, Barnardine!

Bar.: [within.] A pox o' your throats! Who makes that noise there? What are you?

Pom.: Your friends, sir, the hangman. You must be so good, sir, to rise and be put to death.

Bar.: [within.] Away, you rogue, away; I am sleepy.

Abhor.: Tell him he must awake, and that quickly too.

Pom.: Pray, Master Barnardine, awake till you are executed, and sleep afterwards (IV.iii.22-35).

Also in *Measure for Measure,* the other side of the argument is presented by the Duke:

> Be absolute for death; either death or life
> Shall thereby be the sweeter. Reason thus with life:
> If I do lose thee, I do lose a thing
> That none but fools would keep: a breath thou art,
> Servile to all the skyey influences,
> That do this habitation, where thou keep'st,
> Hourly afflict. Merely, thou art death's fool;
> For him thou labour'st by thy flight to shun,
> And yet runn'st toward him still (III.i.5-13).

The Duke and Isabella represent Shakespeare's mature attitude towards death, but to reach this attitude, Shakespeare implies, we have to lose our love for life. It is a stunning idea that we are death's fools and work for him as long as we are in flight, trying to shun death. In the same speech quoted earlier the Duke says:

> What's yet in this
> That bears the name of life? Yet in this life
> Lie hid more thousand deaths; yet death we fear,
> That makes these odds all even (III.i.38-41).

Macbeth has a beautiful speech evoking death as an end to suffering.

> We have scotch'd the snake, not kill'd it:
> She'll close and be herself, whilst our poor malice
> Remains in danger of her former tooth.
> But let the frame of things disjoint, both the worlds suffer,
> Ere we will eat our meal in fear, and sleep
> In the affliction of these terrible dreams
> That shake us nightly. Better be with the dead,
> Whom we, to gain our peace, have sent to peace,
> Than on the torture of the mind to lie
> In restless ecstacy. Duncan is in his grave;
> After life's fitful fever he sleeps well;
> Treason has done his worst: nor steel, nor poison,
> Malice domestic, foreign levy, nothing
> Can touch him further (III.ii.13-26)!

It is worth noting that Gilbert Murray remarked, "I have heard good critics say that the most musical verse in English poetry is, 'After life's fitful fever he sleeps well' (Cairns 1940, p. 640)." Also noteworthy is Shakespeare's description of the effect of a troubled mind on the body in the state of anxious insomnia as "on the torture of the mind to lie in restless ecstasy."

In *Cymbeline* (1609-10) we encounter a very different attitude towards death, as a place where no new narcissistic injuries can be inflicted. In the play the brothers Guiderius and Arviragus have just discovered Imogen, whom they believe to be dead. She is disguised as a man. They lament her death.

Gui.: Fear no more the heat o' the sun,
Nor the furious winter's rages;
Thou thy worldly task hast done,
Home art gone, and ta'en thy wages:
Golden lads and girls all must,
As chimney-sweepers, come to dust.

Arv.: Fear no more the frown o' the great,
Thou art past the tyrant's stroke;
Care no more to clothe and eat;
To thee the reed is as the oak:
The scepter, learning, physic, must
All follow this, and come to dust.

Gui.: Fear no more the lightning-flash,

Arv.: Nor the all-dreaded thunder-stone;

Gui.: Fear not slander, censure rash;

Arv.: Thou hast finish'd joy and moan;

Both.: All lovers young, all lovers must
Consign to thee, and come to dust.

Gui.: No exorciser harm thee!

Arv.: Nor no witchcraft charm thee!

Gui.: Ghost unlaid forbear thee!

Arv.: Nothing ill come near thee!

Both: Quiet consummation have;
And renowned be thy grave (IV.ii.258-81)!

This lamentation, frequently quoted, is regarded by many as the best part of the play. The scene is comic, because the audience knows that Imogen is a woman and that she is alive. Shakespeare is treating an idea with humor that at other times disturbed him greatly: death is the ultimate sanctuary, offering comfort from injuries inflicted upon our self-love. In

Sonnet 66, we encountered a list of the ills of the world framed by the Poet's desire: "Tir'd with all these, from these would I be gone."

We have left for the end the suicide of Cleopatra in *Antony and Cleopatra* (1606). Cleopatra's suicide is Shakespeare's most original contribution to the literature that transforms death into an act of love.

> *Re-enter Iras with a robe, crown, etc.*
>
> *Cleo.:* Give me my robe, put on my crown; I have
> Immortal longings in me; now no more
> The juice of Egypt's grape shall moist this lip.
> Yare, yare, good Iras; quick. Methinks I hear
> Antony call; I see him rouse himself
> To praise my noble act; I hear him mock the luck of Caesar,
> which the gods give men
> To excuse their after wrath: husband, I come:
> Now to that name my courage prove my title!
> I am fire and air; my other elements
> I give to baser life (V.ii.282-92).

We recall how well the Poet of the Sonnets used the four elements to deal with his separation from his lover. In the same way, Cleopatra, at the moment of ecstatic suicide, identifies herself with the two nobler elements, fire and air, and leaves the baser elements behind her.

We come now to the scene of the suicide. That Cleopatra committed suicide by a snakebite is recorded in history, but Shakespeare transformed this suicide into an astonishing love and death scene between mother and child.

To the asp, which she applies to her breast.

Cleo.: With thy sharp teeth this knot intrinsicate
Of life at once untie; poor venomous fool,
Be angry, and dispatch. O! could'st thou speak,
That I might hear thee call great Caesar ass
Unpolicied.

Char.: O eastern star!

Cleo.: Peace, peace!
Dost thou not see my baby at my breast,
That sucks the nurse asleep (V.ii.307-15)?

To the readers that are willing to "learn to read what silent love hath writ," Shakespeare, as the writer of the sonnets, revealed a great deal that was often painful and more difficult than most interpreters have been willing to face. It seems that Shakespeare wrote the poems as a way of coping with what could not be repressed or ignored. The sonnets were written to be shared with a small group of men who could be expected to understand them. The great miracle is that in our time the number of readers willing to face some of these difficult problems has so markedly increased. Many of the plays in this chapter deal with the same problems, but Shakespeare the playwright presents the material with a much greater sense of emotional mastery.

Philosophers and theologians are under obligation to give us a coherent view of the meaning of both love and death. Shakespeare the dramatist is not under such an obligation; he can, through different characters, present a view of life that is contradictory. Many readers have asked Shakespeare for a coherent philosophy of life and death, but Shakespeare refuses to take heed. However, he gives us something that may well be more precious: the record of a brilliantly creative man's lifetime struggle with various attitudes towards life, love, and death.

In no play did Shakespeare deal with the complexity of loving, or with the battle between homosexual and heterosexual love, and between love for the other and self-love, as he dealt with them in the sonnets. Nowhere else did he so free himself from the constraints of narrative, and leave us, instead of a story, the record of the feelings that the story evoked as it un-folded.

APPENDIX: PSYCHOANALYSIS AND SHAKESPEARE

There is a long history of psychoanalytic interest in Shakespeare. Many a psychoanalyst has felt at home with this author whose work combines a great deal of honesty about difficult human emotions with enviably beautiful writing. This appendix is offered to those readers who wish to know more about this chapter in the history of critical studies of Shakespeare, though this book is probably as different from other psychoanalytic studies of Shakespeare as it is from other books about the sonnets.

FREUD AND SHAKESPEARE

Shakespeare's spirit was present at the very moment when psychoanalysis was born. Many psychoanalysts consider Freud's discovery of the Oedipus complex the birthday of the new discipline and that date is known from a letter that Freud wrote to his friend Wilhelm Fliess. It was on October 15, 1897 that Freud wrote:

> Being totally honest with oneself is a good exercise. A single idea of general validity dawned upon me. I have found, in my own case too, [the phenomenon of] being in love with my mother and jealous of my father, and I now consider it a universal event in early childhood (Masson p. 272).

Freud continues, later in the letter:

> If this is so, we can understand the gripping power of *Oedipus Rex*… Everyone in the audience was once a budding Oedipus in fantasy and each recoils in horror from the dream fulfillment here transplanted into reality… Fleetingly the thought passed through my head that the same thing might be at the bottom of *Hamlet* as well. I am not thinking of Shakespeare's conscious intention… How does Hamlet the hysteric justify his words, "Thus conscience does make cowards of us all?" How does he explain his irresolution in avenging his father by the murder of his uncle—the same man who sends his courtiers to their death without a scruple and who is positively precipitate in murdering Laertes (Masson p. 272-73)?

Freud discovered his own Oedipus complex as a result of self-analysis, including questioning his mother, but there can be no doubt that Sophocles and Shakespeare did their share in making this discovery possible; they were midwives in attendance at the hour when the centrality of the Oedipus complex dawned on Freud. This fact may have endeared Shakespeare to future psychoanalysts. It is conceivable that had Sophocles and Shakespeare not come to his aid, the discovery of the Oedipus complex may have been significantly delayed or may never have taken place at all.

The need to contrast *Oedipus Rex* with *Hamlet* occupied Freud for 30 years, for in 1928, in the essay "Dostoevsky and Parricide," he returned to it. (S.E. 21 p. 188). In the Greek drama the hero himself commits the crime, but as Freud observed, "poetic treatment is not possible without softening and disguise. The naked admission of an intention to commit parricide, as we arrive at it in [psycho-]analysis, seems intolerable without analytic preparation." The Greek drama solved the dilemma by substituting destiny, a force beyond the control of Oedipus, for the unconscious intent of the hero. The parricide was committed unintentionally and uninfluenced by the mother. The father, however, is symbolically present in the sphinx that has to be overcome before the mother becomes sexually available to the son. Oedipus acknowledges the unconscious wish in the way he accepts the punishment and blinds himself upon learning that he has killed his father and married his mother. In *Hamlet* the uncle carries out the murder of Hamlet's father. It may represent sibling rivalry for the queen but not parricide. The Oedipus complex, however, shows itself in Hamlet by his inability to carry out the command of his father's ghost who demands that he murder his uncle. There are many reasons, of course, why one might not wish to murder one's uncle on the say-so of a ghost, and it could be argued that the outcome of *Hamlet,* in which the entire court is killed, makes a very good case against Hamlet following the ghost's wishes. But Hamlet is nor portrayed by Shakespeare as a man of peace. He is remorseless about killing the father of the woman he once loved and casual about ordering the deaths of two friends from school. But what has made Hamlet interesting to every generation of actor and theater-goer since he was first penned is his deep conflict over whether or not to kill Claudius his uncle. It is in this wracking conflict that Freud discerned the Oedipus Complex, arguing that Claudius, by murdering Hamlet's father and marrying Hamlet's mother had done what Hamlet himself had wished, unconsciously, to do himself. This rage at Claudius combined with unconscious identification is what paralyzes Hamlet's will to act and fills him depression and self-loathing.

Although *Oedipus Rex* and *Hamlet* came to Freud's mind at the same moment, the two plays are very different in the ways they throw light on the Oedipus complex. In the play by Sophocles, Freud's contribution was the realization that what in Greek mythology was the fate of one man was in fact a universal wish. In *Hamlet* the task was to use the Oedipus complex to explain features of Hamlet's character, mainly his inability to carry out the task assigned to him by the ghost and kill his uncle.

It took a number of years for Freud to develop the initial insight of the Oedipus complex into a coherent theory of cure based on this insight, but in 1916 he wrote:

While he is still a small child, a son will already begin to
develop a special affection for his mother, whom he regards
as belonging to him; he begins to feel his father as a rival who
disputes his sole possession. And in the same way a little girl
looks on her mother as a person who interferes with her af-
fectionate relation to her father and who occupies a position
which she herself could very well fill.

…

The Oedipus complex can, moreover, be developed to a
greater or less strength, it can even be reversed; but it is a
regular and very important factor in a child's mental life, and
there is more danger of our underestimating rather than over-
estimating its influence and that of the developments which
proceed from it. Incidentally, children often react in their
Oedipus attitude to a stimulus coming from their parents,
who are frequently led in their preferences by difference of sex,
so that the father will choose his daughter and the mother her
son as a favourite, or, in case of a cooling-off in the marriage,
as a substitute for a love-object that has lost its value (*Introduc-
tory Lectures* p. 207).

In classical psychoanalysis the resolution of the lingering Oedipus
complex became the main aim of the psychoanalytic treatment. As Freud
put it in the same *Introductory Lectures*:

These tasks are set to everyone; and it is remarkable how
seldom they are dealt with in an ideal manner—that is, in one
which is correct both psychologically and socially. By neurot-
ics, however, no solution at all is arrived at: the son remains all
his life bowed beneath his father's authority and he is unable
to transfer his libido to an outside sexual object. With the rela-
tionship changed round, the same fate can await the daughter.
In this sense the Oedipus complex may justly be regarded as
the nucleus of the neuroses (*Introductory Lectures* p. 337).

Other uses of Shakespeare are also of interest. In 1913 Freud pub-
lished an essay under the title "The Theme of the Three Caskets." Ernest

Jones, Freud's biographer, called the essay one of the three most "charming" essays Freud ever wrote (Jones 1955 p. 341). The essay is based on an insight Freud derived from the suitor's choice between three caskets in *The Merchant of Venice* and King Lear's choice between his three daughters. In Freud's interpretation Cordelia, "the silent one," stands for death since in dreams dumbness is a common representation of death. The essay is an illustration of the creativity released in Freud by his recognition of how the unconscious works in dreams. Freud first noticed that caskets symbolize women and therefore it is not Portia who chooses between three suitors but man who has the choice between three women. However, even that choice is illusory because death is not a choice but a necessity. As Freud put it:

> Choice stands in the place of necessity, of destiny. In this way man overcomes death, which he has recognized intellectually. No greater triumph of wish-fulfillment is conceivable. A choice is made where in reality there is obedience to a compulsion; and what is chosen is not a figure of terror, but the fairest and most desirable of women (p. 299).
>
> …
>
> But Lear is not only an old man: he is a dying man. In this way the extraordinary premises of the division of his inheritance loses all its strangeness. But the doomed man is not willing to renounce the love of women; he insists on hearing how much he is loved. Let us now recall the moving final scene, one of the culminating points of tragedy in modern drama. Lear carried Cordelia's dead body on to the stage. Cordelia is Death. If we reverse the situation it becomes intelligible and familiar to us. She is the Death-goddess who, like the Valkyrie in German mythology, carries away the dead hero from the battlefield (p. 301).
>
> …

> The three inevitable relations that man has with a woman—
> the woman who bears him, the woman who is his mate and
> the woman who destroys him;…the three forms taken by the
> figure of the mother in the course of a man's life—the mother
> herself, the beloved who is chosen after her patterns, and lastly
> mother earth who receives him once more. But it is in vain
> that the old man yearns for the love of woman as he had it
> first from his mother; the third of the fates alone, the silent
> goddess of death, will take him into her arms (p. 301).

From these remarks of Freud, we can extract a basic feature of a psychoanalytic interpretation, that deciphering an unconscious idea may include representation by its opposite, thus choice in the manifest content may stand for necessity in the latent content and Cordelia being dead represents Death. Since the rules of Aristotelian logic do not apply to the unconscious, it often seems that psychoanalytic deductions have no limit, but this is not the way Freud conceived of the unconscious; it has different rules from conscious thinking but it too has a logic of its own. It only means that there are rules of interpretation of the unconscious way of thinking that transcend Aristotelian logic.

At this point an interesting difference between Shakespeare and Freud emerges. To Shakespeare, in the sonnets as well as in the plays, death is personified as the poet's competitor for the love of the Young Man. To Freud death is the third mother figure. In the theme of the three caskets, Freud, in our view, attempted to "libidinize," that is, transform death into a mother figure. Freud could experience death as a third mother figure; to Shakespeare the writer of the sonnets, death was a permanent enemy.

RICHARD III

In 1916, while World War I was raging, Freud found time to write an important essay based not on clinical but on literary evidence, titled "Some Character-Types Met with in Psycho-Analytic Work (S.E. 14)." No other work of Freud's reflects Shakespeare's influence on Freud's thinking as does this essay. The first section of the essay is titled "The Exceptions" and its prime example was Shakespeare's *Richard III*. Freud's originality in this case was his ability to generalize and create a psychologically valid type based on one of Shakespeare's characters. Freud discusses a type of patient who cannot submit to necessity or the reality principal and cannot renounce or at least postpone some satisfaction for the sake of a better future. These people claim that they have suffered enough, renounced enough and that they should be excused from further postponement or curtailment of their satisfaction. Some degree of claiming such a status of exception is frequently encountered, but Richard III exhibits it on a vaster scale. In the case of *Richard III* Freud did not assume that the motive of the exception was either unknown or repressed by the protagonist. Freud quotes Richard III's famous soliloquy (delivered before he becomes king):

> But I, that am not shaped for sportive tricks,
> Nor made to court an amorous looking-glass;
> I that am rudely stamp'd, and want love's majesty
> To strut before a wanton ambling nymph:
> I, that am curtail'd of this fair proportion,
> Cheated of feature by dissembling Nature,
> Deform'd, unfinish'd, sent before my time
> Into this breathing world, scarce half made up,
> And that so lamely and unfashionable,
> That dogs bark at me as I halt by them;
> …
>
> And therefore, since I cannot prove a lover,
> To entertain these fair well-spoken days,
> I am determined to prove a villain,
> And hate the idle pleasures of these days (I.i.14-23; 28-31).

Because he is deformed and unfinished, Richard feels exempt from all moral laws and therefore can kill his brother and woo and win his widow, Queen Anne, as she is burying her slain husband. In *Richard III,* as in *Hamlet,* the Oedipal wish and the Oedipal crime is carried out by the brother (Richard kills his brother, the king, and marries his widow).

The recognition of the category of "the exception" proved productive. In psychoanalytic work, in addition to self-aware exceptions like Richard III, people who survive accidents or serious illnesses, or who are very beautiful or unusually gifted, have a tendency to feel that they are exceptions. Many activities such as reckless driving, non-payment of income taxes and taking unnecessary chances can turn out to be based on unconscious feelings of being an exception.

Ultimately what distinguishes the exception is the belief that being an exception, he or she need not pay heed to the incest taboo. Freud used Richard III to illustrate his concept of the exception, but King Richard is more than just such an example, as the following lines illustrate.

> What do I fear? Myself? There's none else by;
> Richard loves Richard, that is, I am I.
> …
> Alack, I love myself. Wherefore? For any good
> That I myself have done unto myself?
> O no, alas, I rather hate myself
> For hateful deeds committed by myself (V.iii.183-84; 188-91).

Belatedly, to be sure, King Richard ultimately has to pay attention to his superego and, accused by conscience, his former self-love turns into self-hate.

In the same essay, while discussing another type frequently encountered in psychoanalysis—"those who are wrecked by success," that is, people who succumb to depression or anxiety precisely when they encounter good fortune beyond their expectations—Freud cited Lady Macbeth as an example. Lady Macbeth, unlike her husband, showed no signs of inner conflict and no hesitation in prodding her husband to murder King Duncan. She was ready to sacrifice her womanliness for her murderous intentions, as we already quoted in Chapter 9.

Shakespeare was, however, either preconsciously or even consciously aware of the fact that regicide is unconsciously parricide; this is preconsciously experienced by Lady Macbeth, who says:

> …Had he not resembled
> My father as he slept, I had done it (II.ii.13-14).

Shakespeare's understanding of the unconscious in this scene is truly amazing. Being a woman, the unconscious equation of King Duncan = my father deterred Lady Macbeth from killing the king herself. At the very same moment she also recognized that killing the father is the same as killing the nursing baby. Psychoanalytically speaking, a normal functioning superego would have warned Lady Macbeth against Duncan's murder because she would experience feelings of guilt. By contrast a pathological superego lets her commit the murder (or rather, urge her husband to commit it) and punishes her after the fact. It is only after the murder succeeded that she develops the idea that "all the perfumes of Arabia will not sweeten this little hand (V.i.55)." All Lady Macbeth's symptoms appear as a result of guilt after the murder. It is of interest to know that Freud admitted that he could not explain what the motives could have been, which in so short a space of time could turn the hesitating ambitious man into an unbridled tyrant, and his steel-hearted instigator wife into a sick woman gnawed by remorse (Ibid p. 332-333).

To us it seems likely that after Duncan's murder the couple underwent a mutual identification. Macbeth acquired the determination his wife had, and Lady Macbeth the pangs of remorse that he had. Whether such an exchange in identities actually happens in real life is not what matters if we keep in mind that a character on stage must convey psychic reality but need not be a real person.

Freud goes on to quote Ludwig Jekel's article on *Macbeth* that appeared in 1917, in which Jekel's noted that Shakespeare often splits a persona into two characters. If so, Macbeth and his wife are one person, but splitting them makes a great drama possible.

In the examples cited—Shakespeare's *Hamlet,* the three caskets of *The Merchant of Venice, Richard III* and Lady Macbeth—Freud raided Shakespeare in search of his own need to expand his knowledge of human types. To our knowledge no other psychoanalyst was capable of using Shakespeare in such a creative way. However, other psychoanalysts did succeed in understanding plays by Shakespeare in a way not open to those academicians unfamiliar with psychoanalytic thinking. Most psychoanalysts after Freud used Shakespeare's plays primarily to confirm already known psychoanalytic findings. This approach to Shakespeare determined much of the psychoanalytic literature on Shakespeare. The hope of emulating

Freud's creativity spurred on the interest in Shakespeare, but the results were at best clinical observations on various plays. These should not be disparaged, but they are a very different approach to Shakespeare than the founder of psychoanalysis was capable of taking.

Freud learned a great deal from Shakespeare, and understood him in a way Shakespeare was never seen before. We hope that in this book we have demonstrated that examining Shakespeare's sonnets from a psychoanalytic point of view is a rich experience.

Shakespeare, in *Macbeth,* came close to discovering psychoanalysis as a therapeutic method, but decided in favor of self-analysis.

> *Macbeth:* Canst thou not minister to a mind diseased;
> Pluck from the memory of a rooted sorrow;
> Raze out the written troubles of the brain;
> And with some sweet oblivious antidote
> Cleanse the stuff'd bosom of that perilous stuff
> Which weighs upon the heart?
>
> *Doctor:* Therein the patient
> Must minister to himself (*Macbeth,* V.iii.40-47).

Macbeth's words remain a magnificent formulation of what all those who suffer psychologically would like their physician to achieve.

The player king in *Hamlet* says:

> Our wills and fates do so contrary run
> That our devices still are overthrown,
> Our thoughts are ours, their ends none of our own (III.ii.221-223)

By differentiating between will and fate, Shakespeare acknowledges the power of unconscious wishes, which may run contrary to conscious wishes. These unconscious wishes can overthrow our conscious devices. We own up to our thoughts but where our thoughts ultimately lead us, expressed as "their ends," is not consciously available to us. The statement could be read as man's helplessness in the face of the power of fate, but it makes more sense to read it as a poetic acknowledgement of the power of the unconscious. An arbitrary Fate is not dramatically interesting, but when fate emerges from a character's motives, even when those motives are hidden from the character himself the drama satisfies us. This satisfaction is available to us even if there is something mysterious about the logic of the events we have witnessed.

When, in 1923, in *The Ego and the Id,* Freud suggested that we look upon personality as consisting of three mental structures—superego, ego and id—he opened a new way of looking at guilt. Freud saw the superego as a moral punitive agency that had access not only to our conscious desires and wishes but also to those that survived, repressed, in the unconscious. Our guilt feelings therefore include not only our actions and our conscious forbidden wishes but also our unconscious ones. To solve this problem, psychoanalysis had to introduce a triad: what is objectively real, what is psychically real to the patient without being objectively true, and what is regarded as fantasy.

Some wishes as well as fears are psychically real to us without being objectively true. When this happens we refuse to accept what our sense of reality tells us is true. We also have the capacity to fantasize, to pretend that something is real when we fully know it is not. The player king in *Hamlet* is aware of these complexities.

In *Measure for Measure* Angelo promises to spare Isabella's brother's life if she will yield to him sexually. Isabella refuses with the insight that to do so would be a kind of incest, but at the end of the play she pleads for Angelo's pardon with the memorable words:

> For Angelo,
> His act did not o'ertake his bad intent,
> And must be buried as an intent
> That perish'd by the way. Thoughts are no subjects,
> Intents but merely thoughts (V.i.455-459).

Traditional religious thinking tends to blur the distinction between intent and action, as exemplified by Jesus' teaching that

> Whosoever looketh on a woman to lust after her hath com-
> mitted adultery in his heart (Matt. 5:28),

Isabella and psychoanalysis take a different view, attempting to reduce unconscious guilt.

It was the differentiation between "intent" and "subject" which enables Shakespeare to turn the gruesome story of *Measure for Measure* into a comedy. The question of what is real and what is not was of great interest to Shakespeare, and we have often seen the Poet of the Sonnets worrying that his eye is being deceived. To the extent that the audience can identify with Angelo, the burden of their own conscience will be eased at least temporarily and this in turn may be the unconscious power of this play.

In the same play, the Duke asks Escalus, "I pray you sir, of what disposition was the Duke?" and received the psychoanalytic answer: "One that, above all others strifes, contended especially to know oneself (III.ii.245-246)." Much of psychoanalysis is condensed in this sentence. Though the commandment to "know thyself" was inscribed by the ancient Greeks upon the temple of the oracle at Delphi, It is psychoanalysis that understood that strife, in psychoanalytic language intrapsychic conflict, leads one to the need to know oneself and another kind of strife, in which the patient learns to glimpse the unconscious and accept what is there is required to succeed.

The Merchant of Venice opens with a declaration of Antonio that he is sad but does not know why he is sad, clearly implying the presence of an unconscious force, unbeknown to his consciousness.

> In sooth, I know not why I am so sad:
> It wearies me; you say it wearies you;
> But how I caught it, found it, or came by it,
> What stuff 'tis made of, whereof it is born,
> I am to learn;
> And such a want-wit sadness makes of me,
> That I have much ado to know myself (I.i.1-7).

The unconscious as a force is implied by Lafeu in *All's Well That Ends Well*.

Hence it is that we make trifles of terrors, ensconcing ourselves into seeming knowledge, when we should submit ourselves to an unknown fear (II.iii.3-6).

In his book *The Psychopathology of Everyday Life* (SE 6 p. 96), Freud cited a slip of Portia in *The Merchant of Venice* that betrayed her love for Bassanio, which shows that Shakespeare knew that slips of the tongue divulge unconscious wishes. Portia says: "One half of me is yours, the other half yours (III.ii.16)."

Shakespeare's capacity to communicate with his audience using symbols is often astonishing. Desdemona's loss of the handkerchief plays a crucial role in Othello's suspicion.

> *Othello:* That handkerchief
> Did an Egyptian to my mother give.
> She was a charmer, and could almost read
> The thoughts of people; she told her, while she kept it
> 'Twould make her amiable and subdue my father
> Entirely to her love; but if she lost it
> Or made a gift of it, my father's eye
> Should hold her loathed, and his spirits should hunt
> After new fancies. She, dying, gave it me,
> And bid me, when my fate would have me wived,
> To give it her. I did so; and take heed on't;
> Make it a darling like your precious eye;
> To loose't or give't away were such a perdition
> And nothing else could match (*Othello*, III.iii.55-68).

That the Egyptian gave the handkerchief to Othello's mother is understandable; it assured her dominion over Othello's father's fancies. But why did the mother bequeath it to her son? This is the only reference in the play to Othello's mother, the only reference to his childhood. The handkerchief links wife and mother. As long as this link prevails, Othello will love Desdemona as he loved his mother. Once the handkerchief is lost the bridge linking the two women is broken and the homosexuality held in check becomes translated into paranoia.

Shakespeare gave the villain Iago the capacity to understand and use the frail connection between Othello's mother and Desdemona to bring about Desdemona's murder.

One of the basic discoveries of psychoanalysis is the recognition of the power of early memories and the wish to return to childhood that characterizes many people. Shakespeare understood this and created some striking examples.

When Lear gives away his kingdom to his daughters he is told by the fool, "Thou makest thy daughters thy mothers," revealing Lear's unconscious wish to become a child once more in his old age (revealed, as we already said, in the metaphor "crawl toward death").

Shakespeare's sensitivity to the relationship between guilt and insomnia was expressed in many places, but found a superb expression in *Henry IV, Part II.*

> How many thousand of my poorest subjects
> Are at this hour asleep! O Sleep! O gentle Sleep!
> Nature's soft nurse, how have I frightened thee,
> That thou no more wilt weigh my eyelids down
> And steep my senses in forgetfulness (III.i.4-8)?

Psychoanalysts working with patients suffering from insomnia have noted that people who are angry or feel deserted cannot fall asleep. One can sleep well when one is in harmony with a good internal object, either in the present or in the past. Shakespeare made the king experience sleep as "Nature's soft nurse," an implicit memory of a childhood nurse who puts the child to sleep. The king, suffering from insomnia, longs to find contact with this nurse but feels deserted by her. He blames himself for having done something that frightened the mother or nurse to stay away. In the next two lines a popular image is evoked, that sleep has the capacity to weigh down the eyelids. Finally in the last line we are told that the "soft nurse" is the one who can "steep" the king's senses in forgetfulness, but she has been frightened away. All this has been condensed into five lines.

> Canst thou, O partial Sleep! give thy repose
> To the wet sea-boy of an hour so rude,
> And in the calmest and most stillest night,
> With all appliances and means to boot,
> Deny it to a king? Then happy low, lie down!
> Uneasy lies the head that wears a crown (*Henry IV, Part II,* III.i.26-30).

Jealousy towards all those who can sleep speaks in these lines; sleep is called "partial sleep" because it bestows or withholds its balm arbitrarily. To those in the audience who have no difficulty in sleeping, Shakespeare offers the comforting thought that they are more fortunate than a king.

Insomnia plays a significant role in both *Macbeth* and *Hamlet*.

> Sleep that knits up the ravell'd sleave of care,
> The death of each day's life, sore labour's bath,
> Balm of hurt minds, great nature's second course,
> Chief nourisher in life's feast (*Macbeth,* II.ii.34-37)

> O God, I could be bounded in a nutshell,
> And count myself a king of infinite space,
> Were it not that I have bad dreams (*Hamlet,* II.ii.254-256).

Both *Macbeth* and *Hamlet* pay homage to sleep. Sleep as a woman is implicit in *Macbeth* as it was for King Henry; she is the "chief nourisher in life's feast," to the psychoanalytic ear a striking reference to mother's breast.

Shakespeare may also have surmised the connection between dreaming and the unconscious.

> …it shall be called Bottom's Dream, for it hath
> no bottom (*A Midsummer Night's Dream,* IV.i.221).

Shakespeare showed understanding of what psychoanalysis now designates Oedipal rivalry, the rivalry between father and son. In *Henry IV, Part II,* King Henry IV admonishes his son, who puts his father's crown on his head while the king is sleeping.

> *King:* Thy wish was father, Harry, to that thought (IV.v.93).

That wishes are fathers of thoughts assigns priority to wishes over thoughts is a cornerstone of Freud's theory of dream formation. In *The Interpretation of Dreams* (SE 5 p. 484), Freud commented on this scene: "Shakespeare's Prince Hal could not even at his father's sickbed resist the temptation of trying on the crown." Freud then goes on to quote from Shakespeare's *Julius Caesar:* "As he was ambitious, I slew him."

The most impressive example of Shakespeare's familiarity with the unconscious is in the close affinity between love, poetry and madness.

Lovers and madmen have such seething brains,
Such shaping fantasies, that apprehend
More than cool reason ever comprehends.
The lunatic, the lover, and the poet,
Are of imagination all compact:
One sees more devils than vast hell can hold,
That is the madman; the lover, all as frantic,
Sees Helen's beauty in a brow of Egypt:
The poet's eye, in a fine frenzy rolling,
Doth glance from heaven to earth, from earth to heaven;
And, as imagination bodies forth
The forms of things unknown, the poet's pen
Turns them to shapes, and gives to airy nothing
A local habitation and a name (*A Midsummer Night's Dream*, V.i.2).

"Cool reason" is Shakespeare's equivalent to what Freud will call the secondary process, and "imagination all compact" is what Freud will call primary process thinking.

Shakespeare brings together under one conceptual roof the madman, the lover and the poet, for they all have in common "seething brains." The word seething literally means "to come to a boil," and metaphorically as "to become excited." Only the poet can transform this madness and give local habitation to "eerie nothings." In 15 lines, Shakespeare gives insight into the nature of madness, the nature of love, and the nature of poetic activity. The third line, "More than cool reason can comprehend," is Shakespeare's way of acknowledging the power of the unconscious.

The reader has seen that Freud made creative use of many of Shakespeare's ideas. Critics of Freud have deplored the fact that the psychoanalytic interpretation of a work of Shakespeare is reductive in nature. The charge contains a kernel of truth: when Freud suggested that Hamlet's hesitation can only be understood as due to the fact that he is paralyzed by his own Oedipal wishes and therefore cannot kill the guilty uncle, the richness of *Hamlet* suffers reduction. For some time to come, the interpretation that Hamlet hesitates because he too has Oedipal wishes could not easily co-exist with other ideas about Hamlet, but this insight into Hamlet is now beginning to take its place among other insights that together enrich our understanding and appreciation of the play.

It is of interest that the French heretic psychoanalyst Jacques Lacan did much to give back to *Hamlet* the richness and mystery that Freud's approach of necessity downplayed. For Lacan, Hamlet is a man "who has lost the way of his desire… [He is] confronted on one hand with an eminent, idealized, exalted object—his father—and on the other with the degraded, despicable object Claudius, the criminal and adulterous brother, Hamlet does not choose" ("Desire and the Interpretation of Desire in *Hamlet*" p. 12). Greek tragedy knows madness but Hamlet is the first to feign madness. Lacan invites us to notice that Hamlet, after the encounter with the ghost, no longer treats Ophelia like a woman; she becomes, in his eyes, only a child-bearer. Only after her death, when she can no longer be the object of his desire, does Hamlet proclaim his love for Ophelia jumping into her grave scene. We would note that dead Ophelia combines two of the three women Freud discerned in the Three Caskets, and that as a suicide she also has done the act which Hamlet thought of for himself in the "To Be or Not To Be" soliloquy.

PSYCHOANALYTIC STUDIES OF SHAKESPEARE AFTER FREUD

The psychoanalytic literature on Shakespeare's plays is voluminous. In 1966 Norman Holland published a book titled *Psychoanalysis and Shakespeare* and already at that time it was a major task to discuss this literature in a book of 400 pages. In 1970 Faber published another book of 550 pages titled *The Design Within: Psychoanalytic Approaches to Shakespeare*. What follows, therefore is not an exhaustive survey of the field but a look at some of the uses that psychoanalysts after Freud have made of Shakespeare's plays.

Psychoanalytic interpretations have in common that they assume that the action or at least the decisive part of the action makes no sense, unless we assume that some unconscious wish determines a character's irrational action and that this wish must be unconscious not only to the character in the play but also to the author. The result, because the unconscious of the audience also glimpses the character's hidden reasons, is a play that is more lifelike than a play in which everything is clear. Once a psychoanalytically oriented critic has surmised the unconscious motive, the play becomes understandable in a new perspective. As to whether the reader will find the psychoanalytic interpretation convincing depends on two very different factors: the skill of the interpreter in convincing the reader that this interpretation is convincing, and the general readiness of the reader to accept the assumptions upon which the psychoanalytic enterprise rests. The question of whether this unconscious understanding enhances or diminishes the pleasure of reading the play is important and not easily answered. A benevolent attitude towards psychoanalysis is helpful for such interpretations to be experienced as enhancing the comprehension of the play, but sometimes a really satisfying interpretation that adds to the enjoyment of the play may make a reader more sympathetic to the psychoanalytic view of human motivations. What further has to be kept in mind is that Shakespeare was a poet and a writer of plays; his aim was to captivate our interest and to hold our attention riveted to what he wrote, not to offer moral lessons or psychotherapeutic cure.

There are, in our opinion, two main reasons for the psychoanalytic interest in Shakespeare's plays. The first is rooted in psychoanalysts' interest in the early history of their field: a solution to the puzzle of Hamlet's inability to act occurred to Freud at the very moment when he discovered the Oedipus complex. The second, as we have already seen, is Shakespeare's interest in unconscious motivation and his adept use if unconscious themes in his dramatic work. Even outside of professional psychoanalysis, Stephen Greenblatt, in his recently published *Will in the World,* recognized the astonishing role Shakespeare assigned to unconscious forces; Shakespeare's plays imply that the choices people make in love are inexplicable and irrational (p. 324). Greenblatt emphasized that whenever Shakespeare adapted a pre-existing plot he tore away the coherent and superficial structure given to the story by his predecessors and by eliminating the obvious reasons he uncovered the deeper, that is unconscious, motives of the characters.

In 1929 the English psychoanalyst Ella Freeman Sharpe, writing under the influence of Melanie Klein's ideas, wrote a paper titled "The Impatience of Hamlet." Unlike Freud, she did not attempt to explain Hamlet's indecision but rather interpreted the play as evidence of pre-Oedipal fixations and the play as a tragedy of impatience. She also believed that the same impatience is at the core of *Romeo and Juliet, Othello* and *King Lear.* She saw all the characters as "introjections thrown out from his [Shakespeare's] mind (p. 200)." The ghost represents the ideal father image and Claudius the embodiment of the wicked father (p. 206). The wicked father became incorporated in the ego and the ghost was incorporated in the superego. Ophelia is Hamlet's feminine counterpart; the madness of both is the urgency towards self-destruction. Freud's emphasis on the Oedipal interpretation of *Hamlet* and Sharpe's emphasis on the oral and pre-Oedipal features of the play mirror the classical and post-classical developments within psychoanalysis.

In 1949 Moloney and Rockelein wrote a paper titled "A New Interpretation of *Hamlet*" in which they drew attention to a number of scenes where "under no circumstances did Hamlet want the responsibility of becoming an adult, of besting the father and winning the Queen (p. 94)." "His mother's remarriage quickly supplied a substitute father, enabling Hamlet to resume the role of child (p. 95)."

If the scholarly assumption that *Hamlet* was written in 1600-01 and *Macbeth* in 1606 is correct, then a trend of thought left unfinished in *Hamlet* may well have been resumed in *Macbeth,* where the married couple conspire together to kill the guest king, a representative of the father image. In *Oedipus Rex* and in *Hamlet* the Oedipal wish and the Oedipal crime have taken place, but in Hamlet the crime was carried out not by the child but by the child's uncle; the child is asked to avenge the crime and he cannot fulfill that task.

Moloney and Rockelein also pointed out that Hamlet's relationship with Ophelia deteriorates after the encounter with the ghost and how gradually his relationship with his mother becomes hostile. These are valid and interesting additions to Freud's insight, but in no way comparable in magnitude to Freud's original observation. Reviewing this paper suggests to us some further observations: the task of avenging the father becomes a duty for Hamlet, bringing the full force of the superego to bear. Increasingly horrified by the implications of the Oedipus complex, Hamlet retreats from heterosexuality, telling Ophelia "Get thee to a nunnery." Deferring the murder of his uncle, Hamlet is resolved (consciously, at least, to prevent his uncle from going to heaven) to kill him only in certain conditions.

> When he is drunk asleep, or in his rage,
> Or in the incestuous pleasure of his bed,
> At gaming, swearing, or about some act
> That has no relish of salvation in 't (III.iii.89-92).

As the play goes on Hamlet's heterosexuality deteriorates. Both mother and Ophelia should abstain from sexual intercourse.

Reflecting on this scene, we were struck by the ambiguity that surrounds Gertrude's role in the murder. The ghost tells Hamlet:

> Taunt not thy mind, nor let thy soul contrive
> against thy mother aught: leave her to heaven.

This is not, it seems to us, an exoneration of the role of the mother, but neither is she an accomplice to the crime.

Both Freud and Ernst Jones' further elaboration on this theme have shown the connection between a repressed wish and an inhibition of the action. The conflict that cannot be solved manifests itself in a depression.

At a further distance of 100 years from the time of Freud's initial writings on the play we can express our admiration for Shakespeare's capacity to find, as Sophocles did, a way in which the Oedipal wish is carried out displaced enough to be intriguing yet acceptable to the audience.

So what does the psychoanalytic, Oedipal reading of the play really add? Hamlet is old enough to be king and might have expected to come home to rule when his father died. Instead he finds his uncle on the throne. The psychoanalytic interpretation draws attention to the fact that he is being forced to watch an Oedipal spectacle: his uncle doing what he himself unconsciously would have wished to do. In the first court scene Hamlet has asked his uncle for permission to return to school and Claudius refuses his request. The text is silent on whether or not Hamlet made that request before or after seeing the ghost and receiving the command to kill Claudius, but it is certain that his denial of Hamlet's wish to leave leads to his death. The text is also silent on whether he came home to find the relationship between Claudius and Gertrude already consummated or whether he had to witness Claudius usurping his place—consciously—on the throne and unconsciously with his mother. The psychoanalytic focus makes us realize, too, that killing Claudius will be killing another father figure. The fact is that the first time Hamlet tries to kill Claudius he kills Polonius by mistake, and Polonius is the only actual father in the play.

In 1971, under the title *Discourse on Hamlet and Hamlet*, Kurt Eissler published a book of 656 pages that substantially affected the psychoanalytic approach to Shakespeare's plays. As the title indicates, the first Hamlet refers to the prince of Denmark, the second *Hamlet* to Shakespeare's play. Until Eissler psychoanalysts were satisfied in throwing light on one or another aspect of the hero or the play. Now Eissler undertook the examination of both the hero and the play. The double task required the analysis of many other characters beyond Hamlet himself. Thus about Gertrude, Eissler pointed out that nothing can be said about her character with any degree of certainty (p. 266). Fortinbras takes over where Hamlet has left off. Unlike Hamlet, Fortinbras has been spared the effects of an Oedipal conflict, which under extreme conditions can be devastating (p. 129).

In Eissler's view the soliloquies can be understood as the landmarks of an extensive process of reorganizing the defensive approaches, bringing out proper relationships with a changed internal milieu (p. 136). In the play within the play, Hamlet lets a nephew commit the murder (p. 134). This indicates to Eissler, as it did to Freud, Hamlet's unconscious belief that he was his father's murderer. Freud saw Hamlet as incapable of acting because he is burdened by Oedipal guilt; Eissler is interested in the developments that take place within the person as the play unfolds.

Oremland, in a recently published book titled *Death and the Fear of Finiteness in "Hamlet"* (2005), grapples, as Eissler did, with both Hamlet the character and *Hamlet* the play. Oremland argues: "…the point is not whether Hamlet is psychotic, as is usually argued, but how does his psychosis make the play into a masterpiece (p. 114)." To Oremland "…Hamlet makes visible the excruciatingly terrifying fear of nonexistence (p. 114)" in his conversation with Rosencrantz and Guildenstern.

Hamlet: ...I have of late, but wherefore
I know not, lost all my mirth, forgone all custom
of exercises; and indeed it goes so heavily with my
disposition that this goodly frame the earth seem to
me a sterile promontory, this most excellent canopy
the air, look you, this brave o'erhanging firmament
this majestical roof fretted with golden fire, why, it
appeareth nothing to me but a foul and pestilent congregation
of vapours (II.ii.295-303).

We hear the echo of the magnificent description of depression in Sonnet 29: "with what I most enjoy contented least." To Oremland, what Hamlet is voicing is a profound sense of meaninglessness (p. 62). In Oremland's view, Hamlet, during the play, develops from despair into psychosis and finally into reintegration. To Oremland, Hamlet evolves into "typus Christi," making *Hamlet* at a basic level into a passion play.

In 1988 Blechner offered another interpretation of *King Lear*. *King Leir,* the source upon which Shakespeare drew, had a sensible plot. None of the daughters are married but the two older ones have accepted their suitors while Cordelia had not. The king wants to force Cordelia to choose a suitor out of her love for her father. The story ends happily when Cordelia's husband, the king of France, reconquers England and restores Leir. Shakespeare's play ends tragically with the dead Cordelia in her father's arms. In Blechner's interpretation the king becomes infuriated when he hears that Cordelia does not plan to give all her love to him. In the last scene the incestuous wishes are symbolically granted but both father and daughter pay with their lives for the gratification of the forbidden wish.

Greenblatt has pointed out that the Cordelia motif had a discernible biographical basis; Shakespeare had a strong attachment to his daughter Susanna. In *The Tempest* Prospero relinquishes his hold on Miranda, abdicating as well all his magical powers. In addition to *King Lear,* three of Shakespeare's plays—*Pericles, The Winter's Tale* and *The Tempest*—are centered on the father-daughter relationship. In these three plays the incest motif is resolved as the father renounces his claim to the daughter. Seen as self-psychotherapy, these works offer a healthier solution but as works of art none compares in depth to *King Lear.*

In discussing *Hamlet*, and *Lear* analysts traversed the same territory already discussed by Freud. We turn now to psychoanalytic interpretations of the plays not discussed by Freud.

OTHELLO

In his essay "*Othello:* the Tragedy of Iago" (1950), Martin Wangh developed the basic idea that Iago loves Othello and is jealous of Desdemona and therefore hates her. The idea that a homosexual desire that undergoes repression can become transformed into paranoid suspicion had been developed by Freud in 1922 in a paper titled "Some Neurotic Mechanisms in Jealousy, Paranoia and Homosexuality." In that essay Freud cites examples of men who become jealous of their wives' imagined disloyalty because they themselves are unconsciously sexually attracted to the men with whom they fear their wives are having extramarital relations. Besides *Othello*, Shakespeare's *The Winter's Tale* is a story of such a jealousy. Iago is jealous of Othello's heterosexual relationship.

What kind of evidence does Wangh supply to support his assertion?

1. During the first night after the wedding, when Othello and Desdemona have retired, Iago creates an uproar to disturb their first nuptial togetherness.

2. He does the same when they arrive at Cyprus.

When we are dealing with an unconscious emotion in a work of literature we are confronted with the question of whether the homosexuality of Iago was unconscious to him, and also unconscious to Shakespeare when he created Iago? Wangh cites the following scene.

> *Iago* …I lay with Cassio lately
> And, being troubled with a raging tooth,
> I could not sleep.
> …
> In sleep I heard him say, 'Sweet Desdemona,
> Let us be wary, let us hide our loves!'
> And then, sir, would he gripe and wring my hand,
> Cry, 'O, sweet creature!' and then kiss me hard,
> As if he pluck'd up kisses by the roots
> That grew upon my lips; then laid his leg
> Over my thigh, and sigh'd, and kiss'd; and then
> Cried, 'Cursed fate, that gave thee to the Moor!'
> (III.iii.413-415, 419-426)

This is a homosexual scene only thinly disguised by an imagined heterosexual dream. However, since the scene never took place and was fabricated to fan Othello's jealousy, the homosexuality of Iago remains implicit, and we do not know whether Shakespeare consciously wanted to convey the impression of homosexuality or did so preconsciously without facing the implicit homosexuality of his character. We know from the sonnets, however, that at least asexual homosexual love was not abhorrent to Shakespeare.

Wangh notes:

> The dream begins with an imagined toothache which prevented Iago from sleeping. A tooth is one of the commoner universal symbols of the penis in dreams. "A raging tooth" would then indicate sexual excitement. Iago's saying that he was "troubled" with a raging tooth has two meanings: first—resistance to his homosexual excitement; second, the wish for and the fear of castration. "Kisses plucked up by the roots" can be similarly understood as a phrase heavy with castration symbolism, and the whole fantasy is replete with oral erotism. We can conclude that it is in part a fantasy of fellatio. "He laid his leg over my thigh is self-explanatory (Faber p. 163-164)."

Wangh's paper was based on Freud's assumption that there is an intimate connection between paranoia and latent homosexuality, transforming love into its opposite, hate. This is confirmed in Iago's speech:

> ...I hate the Moor,
> And it is thought abroad that 'twixt my sheets
> He hath done my office: I know not if't be true,
> But I, for mere suspicion in that kind,
> Will do as if for surety (I.iii.392-96).

Iago is describing here what he will do to Othello, in whom he turns the suspicion he creates into a motive for the worst kind of action. A neurotic can be suspicious on the basis of no or only minor evidence but it requires a disturbance beyond ordinary neurosis to confuse suspicion with fact. Iago, when he makes the above statement, is not yet psychotic; Shakespeare may have endowed Iago with the insight to know that he is gliding into madness, but he took care to make us, his audience, aware of the possibility of Iago's madness.

It is interesting to see how psychoanalysis changed the understanding of Iago. In the pre-psychoanalytic literature, Iago's behavior is that of a villain, and villainy as a psychological category requires no further elucidation. This is how Hazlitt (1817), writing before Freud, explained the character of Iago:

> The character of Iago is one of the supererogations of
> Shakespear's genius. Some persons, more nice than wise, have
> thought this whole character unnatural, because his villainy
> is *without a sufficient motive*. Shakespear, who was as good a
> philosopher as he was a poet, thought otherwise. He knew
> that the love of power, which is another name for the love of
> mischief, is natural to man (p. 54).

Iago in fact belongs to a class of characters, common to Shakespear and at the same time peculiar to him; whose heads are as acute and active as their hearts are hard and callous. Iago is...of diseased intellectual activity, with an almost perfect indifference to moral good or evil...he is quite or nearly as indifferent to his own fate as to that of others; he runs all risks for a trifling and doubtful advantage; and is himself the dupe and victim of his ruling passion—an insatiable craving after action of the most difficult and dangerous kind (p. 55).

The comparison between Hazlitt's pre-Freud interpretation of Iago's character with Wangh's post-Freud interpretation can serve us as a good illustration of the difference psychoanalysis made in the understanding of one of Shakespeare's characters. Wangh elucidates the territory referred to by Hazlitt's phrase "without sufficient motive," although there is nothing in Wangh that makes Hazlitt obsolete. Homosexual jealousy does not, in and of itself, explain villainy, as the lives of many good people who are homosexuals testifies. What Wangh offers us is some insight into why we accept Iago's actions as convincing, why we do not experience the play as hopelessly, pointlessly melodramatic.

It is interesting to compare Wangh's psychoanalytic interpretation with a contemporary non-psychoanalytic one. Harold Bloom (1998) agrees with Wangh concerning Iago's supremacy in the play: he speaks eight soliloquies, Othello only three. He sees Othello as "a great soul hopelessly outclassed in intellect and drive by Iago (p. 438)." Bloom cites the differences between Shakespeare and Cinthio's Ensign, from where Shakespeare took the plot as: "Cinthio's Ensign Iago falls passionately in love with Desdemona, but wins no favor with her, since she loves the moor (p. 436)." The ensign assumes that Desdemona is in love with another captain and plots to remove the rival together with Desdemona. The difference between the psychoanalytic and general point of view is that the non-psychoanalytic Iago remains within the heterosexual domain and the psychoanalytic Iago demands a repressed homosexual component as the crucial explanation for his character.

FALSTAFF AND PRINCE HAL

In 1933 the psychoanalyst Franz Alexander published "A Note on Falstaff." The essay opens with a question, what is the specific appeal of this mass of fat, the cowardly, boasting and loquacious knight, this drunkard and gourmand? The play *Henry IV* is so successful because the childish, ir-

responsible hedonism of Falstaff is contrasted to the self-sacrificing mascu-
line heroism of Hotspur. In Alexander's view, Shakespeare succeeded in this
play to make us look alternately at two aspects of life that are in permanent
conflict with each other, our social self, which admires the heroism of Hot-
spur, and the other part of our personality, identified with the personality
of Falstaff. Implicit in this view is a psychoanalytic theory of pleasure in art.
We derive pleasure from seeing our own not-verbalized conflicts projected
on the stage in sharp contrast and if we respond positively to Falstaff we
thereby also respond positively to our own hedonistic wishes.

Alexander comments:

> King Henry IV, lying in his last death struggle, the crown
> beside him on a pillow, falls asleep as Prince Henry enters.
> Henry puts on the crown and declaims:
>
> Why doth the crown lie there upon his pillow,
> Being so troublesome a bedfellow?
> O polished perturbation! golden care!
> That keep'st the ports of slumber open wide
> To many a watchful night—sleep with it now!
> Yet not so sound and half so deeply sweet
> As he whose brow with homely biggin bound
> Snores out the watch of night! (IV.v. 21-28)
>
> The King, awaking and learning that his heir has taken the
> crown, accuses his son of being greedy for power and not be-
> ing able to wait for his death, but the Prince explains:
> Coming to look on you, thinking you dead,—
> And dead almost, my liege, to think you were,—
> I spake unto the crown as having sense,
> And thus upbraided it: The care on thee depending
> Hath fed upon the body of my father;
> Therefore thou, best of gold, art worst of gold (IV.v.156-161).

We may indeed believe that the Prince is telling the truth. We saw the
other side of his personality, in his reckless enjoyment of life with Falstaff.
He changed chiefly from a sense of duty and he cannot but consider his
rank and position as an undesirable burden. He became a hero and he will

become a great king under the pressure of his social self, but his deepest urges are not gratified by this change. The monologue with the crown in his hands demonstrates this with the utmost clarity. Falstaff is the representative of the nonsocial portions of his personality (p. 505).

The self-coronation act, in Alexander's view, is no longer a simple Oedipal act, but a real sacrifice. The inheritance of the father's position has become a duty. The prince is sincere when he calls the crown "an evil gold." We cannot resist pointing out that Alexander has here overlooked Prince Hal's statement:

> "I'll so offend to make offense a skill,
> Redeeming time when men think least I will."
> (*Henry IV Part I,* 1.2.204-5)

Which implies that Prince Hal regards hedonistic behavior as proper to his youth and responsible behavior as something he plans all along to adopt after everyone (meaning his father) has given up on him.

Alexander sees the banishment of Falstaff to ten miles from the king's body to eliminate the king's temptation to regress to childish hedonism. This banishment, according to Alexander, is the psychoanalytic equivalent of repression. Falstaff's self-satisfaction is more infantile than the forgiving attitude towards oneself that Freud considers the essence of humor, but we love him because Falstaff stands for what we all had to repress in ourselves.

In 1948 Ernst Kris' published an essay entitled "Prince Hal's Conflict." In Kris' interpretation, Prince Hal (the future King Henry V), has two father figures, his own father King Henry IV, who could not serve as a model of a father figure because he himself committed regicide on Richard II, and symbolic parricide because Richard II had favored Prince Hal. The other father figure to Prince Hal is Falstaff, whom the prince disowned when he became king.

The father, Henry IV, in a parallel position, has two sons: his true eldest son, Hal, and the son he wishes for, Harry Percy, or Hotspur.

> *Henry IV:* Yea, there thou mak'st me sad, and mak'st me sin
> In envy that my Lord Northumberland
> Should be the father to so blest a son;
> A son who is the theme of honour's tongue;
> Amongst a grove the very straightest plant;
> Whilst I, by looking on the praise of him,
> See riot and dishonour stain the brow
> Of my young Harry. O! that it could be prov'd
> That some night-tripping fairy had exchang'd
> In cradle-clothes our children where they lay,
> And called mine Percy, his Plantagenet
> Then would I have his Harry, and he mine (*I Henry IV*, I.i.78-90)

In Kris' interpretation Percy is Hal's double. Both father and son are burdened by the father's guilt over regicide.

> *Henry IV:* How I came by the crown, O God forgive!
> And grant it may with thee in true peace live
> (*2 Henry IV,* IV.v.219-220).

In *Henry V* the night before the battle of Agincourt the king (the former Prince Hal) prays to avert divine retaliation for his father's regicide.

> *Henry V:* My father made in compassing the crown.
> I Richard's body have interred new,
> And on it have bestow'd more contrite tears
> Than from it issued forced drops of blood.
> Five hundred poor I have in yearly pay,
> Who twice a day their wither'd hands hold up
> Toward heaven, to pardon blood; and I have built
> Two chantries, where the sad and solemn priests
> Sing still for Richard's soul. More will I do;
> Though all that I can do is nothing worth,
> Since that my penitence comes after all,
> Imploring pardon (*Henry V,* IV.i.311-322).

The same logic that was followed by Freud in *Hamlet,* Kris ascribes to Henry V. Prince Hal tries to dissociate himself from the crime his father had committed; he avoids contamination with regicide because the impulse to regicide (which for the prince is identical with patricide, alive in his unconscious). When the King's life is threatened he saves the King and kills the adversary, who is his alter ego. In shunning the court for the tavern he expresses his hostility to his father and escapes the temptation to parricide. He can permit himself to share Falstaff's vices because he does not condone the King's crime; but hostility to the father is only temporarily repressed (p. 399). When Prince Hal becomes King Henry V, he turns against Falstaff, the debased father substitute, with the full hatred that the original Oedipal conflict has awakened in him.

Kris further points out that only one part of the Oedipal conflict is presented in this play, the hostility to the father. The other component, the love for the mother, remaining repressed, went into the formation of the superego, which further explains the harsh treatment of the hedonistic Falstaff. If we compare Alexander's view with that of Kris, we will note that Kris is the more orthodox Freudian, focusing on the Oedipal conflict in the future. Henry V. Alexander, on the other hand, follows more in the steps of Freud in *Beyond the Pleasure Principle,* highlighting the difficulty in overcoming the domination of the pleasure principle.

It is of interest to compare Kris' study with the study by Harold Bloom (1998, chapter 5, *Henry V*). For Bloom the major player is not the prince but Falstaff. In Bloom's view Hal's ambivalence "has resolved itself into a murderous negativity (1998, p. 272)." He noted the wordplay fall/staff and shake/spear. The relationship of Falstaff to Prince Hal bears a similarity to Shakespeare's attitude to the noble youth celebrated in the sonnets. The rejection of Falstaff by King Henry V echoes Shakespeare's rejection by the young nobleman of the sonnets. In Bloom's opinion both Hamlet and Falstaff illuminate the sonnets rather than the other way around. It is Falstaff "who speaks what is still the best and most vital prose in the English language (p. 275)."

Bloom may not agree with us but it seems to us that he too was influenced by Freud. If he is right then Shakespeare transformed his rejection by a young aristocrat into the creation of a magnificent and universally loved old man, a kind of subtle revenge that only a genius could have thought of, a more interesting idea than Kris' standard psychoanalytic application.

CORIOLANUS

Because we have four psychoanalytic studies of *Coriolanus* to draw upon—by Charles Hofling (1957), Rufus Putney (1962), D.B. Barron (1962) and Robert Stoller (1966)—and many non- psychoanalytic studies of this play, *Coriolanus* lends itself to a comparison between the psychoanalytic and the general approach.

We cite Harold Bloom as an example of a non-psychoanalytic approach to *Coriolanus*. Bloom called Coriolanus "a one-man army, the greatest killing machine in all Shakespeare," a dramatic personage of "most limited consciousness…his own enemy" and a man "in chains…an infant Mars (1998 p. 577-578)." Shakespeare has portrayed a number of unsympathetic characters, including Richard III, Iago and Shylock; through his genius he found ways of making these types understandable in their own terms (581). "The poetry of Coriolanus is properly harsh, even strident, since so much of the play is a tirade." About Volumnia, Coriolanus' mother, Bloom says she "must be the most unpleasant woman in all Shakespeare, not excluding Goneril and Regan… like everyone else in the play, [she] has only an outward self (p. 584)."

Bloom quotes William Hazlitt:

> Wrong dressed out in pride, pomp, and circumstance, has
> more attraction than abstract right. Coriolanus complains of
> the fickleness of the people: yet, the instant he cannot gratify
> his pride and obstinacy at their expense, he turns his arms
> against his country (Bloom 1998 p. 577).

Since Shakespeare took plot from the famous Roman writer Plutarch, a quote from Plutarch may be illuminating:

> For this Marcius' natural wit and great heart did marvelously
> stir up his courage to do and attempt noble acts. But on the
> other side, for lack of education, he was so choleric that he
> would yield to no living creature; which made him churlish,
> uncivil, and altogether unfit for any man's conversation…but
> Marcius began from his childhood to give himself to handle
> weapons, and daily did exercise himself therein (quoted by
> Losey p. 803).

By comparison with Plutarch, Shakespeare greatly magnified the role of the mother, and by so doing transformed a story of patriotism and treason into a story of a mother-son relationship and how the tie of the son to his mother results in a latent homosexual tie to the enemy general and treason to his city. Volumnia makes the following interesting distinction between herself and her son:

> Thy valiantness was mine, thou suck'dst it from me
> But owe thy pride thyself (III.ii.129-130).

This is how Menenius describes the fury of Coriolanus, magnificently expressed by Shakespeare:

> What his breast forges, that his tongue must vent;
> And, being angry, does forget that ever
> He heard the name of death (III.i.258-260).

In these three lines Shakespeare put together two character traits not usually combined. The first is the inability to feel something without immediately expressing it, and the second is an absence of the usual fear of death.

From a psychoanalytic point of view *Coriolanus* is of special interest because it is the only play in which the mother-son relationship is central and the play contains many more childhood memories than was customary in Shakespeare's plays. In general, Shakespeare avoided dealing with the mother-son relationship; besides Coriolanus only Hamlet has, psychologically speaking, a mother, and their relationship is also a complicated one. It is not unfair to say that Shakespeare, as a dramatist, is a motherless child and we have seen that the mother image in the sonnets, when not entirely absent, also does not fare well.

Holfling's interpretation of the character of Coriolanus was written under the influence of Wilhelm Reich's character analysis. Reich resigned, although some believe he was asked to resign, from the Psychoanalytic International in 1934, but before that he was an influential leader of psychoanalysis and his famous book *Character Analysis* appeared in 1933 (English translation 1949).

Hofling interpreted the character of Coriolanus as a phallic-narcissistic character, as described by Reich. Self-confident, often arrogant, haughty, aggressive, outspoken, resentful of subordination, courageous and dominated by irrational forces. Coriolanus was traumatized by his mother, Volumnia, an unfeminine, non-maternal woman who molded her son to gratify her own masculine or, more likely, pseudo-masculine wishes. She withheld any praise and affection from any achievement except aggressive and exhibitionistic ones. By contrast to the mother, the wife, Virgilia, is the very opposite and under favorable conditions could have acted as a "corrective emotional experience" to the traumatized Coriolanus, but she is no match for the mother.

All psychoanalytic writers on *Coriolanus* have paid special attention to a dialogue between Volumnia, the mother, and Virgilia, the wife of Coriolanus.

> *Volumnia:* I pray you, daughter, sing; or express yourself in a
> more comfortable sort. If my son were my husband, I should
> freelier rejoice in that absence wherein he won honour than in
> the embracements of his bed where he would show most love.
> When yet he was but tender-bodied, and the only son of my
> womb, when youth with comeliness plucked all gaze his way,
> when for a day of king's entreaties a mother should not sell
> him an hour from her beholding, I, considering how honour
> would become such a person, that it was no better than pic-
> ture-like to hang by the wall, if renown made it not stir, was
> pleased to let him seek danger where he was like to find fame.
> To a cruel war I sent him; from whence he returned, his brows
> bound with oak. I tell thee, daughter, I sprang not more in joy

at first hearing he was a man-child than now in first seeing he
had proved himself a man.

Virgilia: But had he died in the business, madam, how then?

Volumnia: Then his good report should have been my son;
I therein would have found issue. Hear me profess sincerely:
had I a dozen sons, each in my love alike, and none less dear
than thine and my good Marcius, I had rather had eleven die
nobly for their country than one voluptuously surfeit out of
action (I.iii.1-28).

The dialogue is a magnificent exchange between two fundamentally
different women, one narcissistic and using the man for her own self-ag-
grandizement, the other loving the man. Virgilia, one could argue, was
potentially Coriolanus' cure from Volumnia as a mother, but Shakespeare
showed how much more powerful the mother is in shaping the son's char-
acter than the wife.

We are struck by "then his good report would have been my son."
Volumnia is willing to sacrifice her son so that she would be able to enjoy
his "good report." In Volumnia, Shakespeare created a character of great
complexity. More than just masculine wishes and treating her son as a
phallus are involved; all these wishes have amalgamated in the service of a
harsh, unloving mother.

In keeping with the phallic narcissistic nature of his character, Corio-
lanus cannot tolerate being in the passive position. He cannot ask for the
support of the Roman citizens and displays his war wounds in order to
be elected. Coriolanus is not a politician and quickly loses his temper and
becomes the victim of the tribune.

Sicinius: I do demand,
If you submit you to the people's voices,
Allow their officers, and are content
To suffer lawful censure for such faults
As shall be proved upon you?

Coriolanus: I am content (III.iii.43-47).

Menenius speaks on Coriolanus' behalf, but the situation soon deteriorates.

> *Sicinius:* We charge you, that you have contriv'd to take
> From Rome all season'd office, and to wind
> Yourself into a power tyrannical;
> For which you are a traitor to the people.

> *Coriolanus:* How! traitor!

> *Menenius:* Nay, temperately; your promise.

> *Coriolanus:* The fires I' the lowest hell fold-in the people!
> Call me their traitor! Thou injurious tribune!
> Within thine eyes sat twenty thousand deaths,
> In thy hands clutched as many millions, in
> Thy lying tongue both numbers, I would say
> "Thou liest" unto thee with a voice as free
> As I pray the gods.

> *Sicinius:* Mark you this, people?

> *Plebeians:* To the rock! To th' rock with him (III.iii.64-75)!

The accusation that Coriolanus was seeking "a power tyrannical" translated into the unconscious means that he wished to possess his mother and this Oedipal accusation Coriolanus cannot tolerate. The decision to sack Rome is in the unconscious of Coriolanus to attack his mother and this he cannot do.

Hofling assumed that the relationship between Coriolanus and his mother reflected Shakespeare's own attitude and the play, together with Mary Shakespeare's death, made it possible for Shakespeare to return to Stratford.

Hofling notes that Coriolanus reacts with the greatest violence when he is called traitor and boy.

Putney (1962) uses a somewhat different vocabulary but the basic ideas are the same:

That Coriolanus can face death at her command is not sur-
prising; that he has been doing since his youth. Faced with the
choice of destroying his mother or losing his own life, he can
only, though reluctantly, choose death. Coriolanus's inexorable
maternal superego decrees that he sacrifice himself (p. 372).

Barron (1962) argued that the chilliness of Volumnia created the ag-
gression in her son.

Stoller (1966) draws attention to the absent father in Coriolanus. Vo-
lumnia uses her son both as a boy and as a man; he was hers to com-
mand. There is, she says, "no man in the world more bound to's mother
(V.vii.159)."

Coriolanus' inability to sack Rome results in his death at the hands of
Aufidius.

> *Aufidius:* Read it not, noble lords:
> But tell the traitor in the highest degree
> He hath abus'd your powers.
>
> *Coriolanus:* Traitor! How now!
>
> *Aufidius:* Ay, traitor, Marcius.
>
> *Coriolanus:* Marcius!
>
> *Aufidius:* Ay, Marcius, Caius Marcius. Dost thou think
> I'll grace thee with that robbery, thy stol'n name
> Coriolanus in Corioli?
> You lords and heads o' the state, perfidiously
> He has betray'd your business, and given up,
> For certain drops of salt, your city Rome,
> I say 'your city,' to his wife and mother;
> Breaking his oath and resolution like
> A twist of rotten silk, never admitting
> Counsel o' the way, but at his nurse's tears
> He whin'd and roar'd away your victory,
> That pages blush'd at him, and men of heart,
> Look'd wondering each at other.

> *Coriolanus:* Hear'st thou, Mars?
>
> *Aufidius:* Name not the god, thou boy of tears.
>
> *Coriolanus:* Ha!
>
> *Aufidius:* No more.
>
> *Coriolanus:* Measureless liar, thou hast made my heart
> Too great for what contains it. Boy! O slave (V.v.84-104)!

Stoller comments on the discussion between wife and mother:

> For such a mother, a son is the literal embodiment of her
> phallus which from infancy she had wished to attain by one
> means or another. Subjected to such relentless pressures, her
> son may either surrender and become virtually emasculated,
> or he may be able partially to salvage his virility by acting
> out his mother's fantasy as her surrogate until his repressed
> (feminine) identification with her—and his guilt about his
> repressed hatred of her— ead him to contrive his destruction
> (p. 332).

Stoller cannot demonstrate all of these ideas to be present in the text of the play itself and it is characteristic of many psychoanalytic interpretations that they are not demonstrable but rather inferences that the analyst transports from clinical experience to the Shakespearean text. It is this technique that evoked in many readers skepticism about psychoanalytic interpretations.

KING LEAR

In the British Psychoanalytic Society, under the influence of Melanie Klein, Shakespearean studies took a different direction. Bolder, more intuitive and more radical interpretations were favored. Ella Freeman Sharpe, a teacher of English before she became a psychoanalyst, was the leading

Shakespearean interpreter. Her article "From *King Lear* to *The Tempest*" was published in 1946.

The fool in the play tells King Lear "Thou hast made thy daughters thy mothers." This insight by Shakespeare is elaborated by Sharpe: "The three daughters of Lear represent three different 'aspects' of one mother, 'aspects' that accord with the anger felt against her or the longing for her experienced by the child (p. 223)." Lear has to prove that his mother does not love him (p. 224). Sharpe declares that "mother-Goneril's pregnancy is the cause of child Lear's 'storm' in the play" (p. 225). Lear's mother had two additional pregnancies; one occurred when his sphincter control was not stabilized and the second occurred when the child was accustomed to walk about independently. The child Lear had a long reign of sovereignty in an adoring household, which carried out the child's bidding (p. 226). That Lear stayed with each daughter for one month Sharpe connects with mother's menstruation. The three sons-in-law represent three aspects of the father. The dominant motif in King Lear is banishment, becoming an outcast. The whole play is seen as a traumatic reliving of early childhood experiences before speech was available to the child. Where Kris saw an articulation of the Oedipal conflict, Sharpe goes to earlier traumatic experiences based on a mother's repeated pregnancies in early childhood.

When Sharpe speaks of the infant Lear, she knows full well that Lear never was a child and is Shakespeare's creation. She shows from the little that is known of the playwright's biography that it is, as far as we can tell, compatible with what she attributes to the rage of Lear the child.

It is of interest to compare Sharpe's analytic approach with interpretations of Shakespeare scholars who are not psychoanalytically oriented. Stephen Greenblatt called the last chapter of his book "The Triumph of the Everyday." He sees Shakespeare as brooding over the perils of retirement in 1604 when he wrote *King Lear;* Shakespeare had just turned 40. Greenblatt can find "no easy, obvious link between what Shakespeare wrote—here a tremendous explosion of rage, madness and grief—and the known circumstances of his own life (p. 356)." Greenblatt mentions a widely discussed lawsuit in 1603 where the two elder daughters of a doddering gentleman attempted to get their father declared insane and obtain his estate while the youngest daughter, named Cordell, protested (p. 357). Greenblatt has no answer to the question of what motivated the playwright to embark upon this play, though we know from the sonnets that Shakespeare considered 40 to be a time of old age.

MEASURE FOR MEASURE

Hans Sachs was a member of Freud's inner circle, the so-called secret committee, and one of the recipients of Freud's rings. [See chapter six of Ernst Jones' biography of Freud, volume two, 1955.] Together with Otto Rank, he edited the journal *Imago,* the psychoanalytic journal that was devoted to expanding the scope of psychoanalysis beyond clinical boundaries. Sachs is therefore particularly well qualified to speak in the name of classical psychoanalysis.

In 1942 a study by Sachs appeared, titled "The Measure in *Measure for Measure.*" Shakespeare wrote *Measure for Measure* during the period of his great tragedies, *King Lear* and *Othello.* Sachs calls it "a comedy without gaiety" in which the possibility of tragedy is barely averted.

Shakespeare prepared the happy ending from the start by keeping the Duke in disguise present and informed of Angelo's villainous intentions, instead of bringing him in at the end as a sort of *deus ex machina.* This constitutes a great mitigation of the painful tension: the audience knows all the time that the powers of darkness will not prevail, and it brightens the sequence of gloomy events with the reassurance that they are only "much ado about nothing" (p. 70-71).

As to how Shakespeare avoided making *Measure for Measure* a tragedy, Sachs wrote:

Shakespeare eliminated all the dreadfulness of the crimes by having none of them committed actually, but he retained, he even deepened, their appalling effect as far as Angelo's mind is concerned (p. 89).

The psychological center of gravity of *Measure for Measure* is the gradual deterioration of Angelo's resolve.

> *Angelo:* What dost thou, or what art thou, Angelo?
> Do thou desire her foully or those things
> That make her good?
> Never could the strumpet,
> With all her double vigour, art and nature
> Once stir my temper; but this virtuous maid
> Subdues me quite.——Ever till now
> When men were fond, I smiled and wondered how
> (II.ii.173-175, 181-187)

Sachs comments:

> As this first monologue shows, Angelo's abstinence was found-
> ed on his indifference to ordinary sensuality and to "fond-
> ness," that is…love in the form of tenderness. Isabella was his
> first serious temptation because she aroused something in him
> to which no other woman had appealed before, a desire that
> had been slumbering—or rather waiting for its time (p. 75).

At this point Sachs, in our opinion, did not go far enough. In our view Isabella tempted Angelo precisely because she aroused not only his sexual desire but also his aggression "to destroy the sanctuary." This appears in an adjacent part of the same speech.

> …Can it be
> That modesty may more betray our sense
> Than woman's lightness? Having waste ground enough,
> Shall we desire to raze the sanctuary,
> And pitch our evils there (II.ii.168-172)?

In our interpretation Shakespeare endowed Angelo with the capacity to surmise that his sexual attraction for Isabella is based more on the wish to destroy than on love. We recognize Angelo's attraction from the hetero-sexual sonnets; once again a man is attracted to a woman but he holds no good opinion of this attraction calling his desire (and all men's desires) "our evils." The Dark Lady of the sonnets is unfaithful and promiscuous. Isa-bella is the oposite, a pure woman more like Desdemona and it is this very purity that arouses Angelo, a different tragedy from the Poet of the Sonnets who was aroused by the Dark Lady's promiscuity. Sachs comments on this passage:

> Thus stimulated and exposed to the storm of desire, his cruelty loses every aspect of sublimation and falls back, regressively, to its original source, revealing its primeval, sensual form (1942 p. 78).

Isabella's own need for a strict Superego is beautifully illustrated in her conversation with the nun Francesca.

> *Isabella:* And have you nuns no further privileges?
>
> *Francesca:* Are not these large enough?
>
> *Isabella:* Yes, truly: I speak not as desiring more,
> But rather wishing a more strict restraint (IV.i.1-4).

Commenting on the marriage of the Duke and Isabella, Sachs says:

> The Duke and Isabella are, therefore, well matched in every respect: they are both good and virtuous and not much in love with life (p. 96).

Sachs concludes the essay:

> Shakespeare's pessimism not only speaks through the mouths of his hero and heroine, it pervades the whole play and imparts to it the pungent and bitter taste that aroused the displeasure of the critics. In showing up all sorts of depravity, he tears away the last shred of pretense from them and mocks their repulsive nakedness with exultant despair. It is all so ugly and distressing, but just for this reason he does not want to delude himself about the truth. Life is not good—then let us find out how bad it can be! Lust and cruelty, one is as horrible as the other, as long as one takes man seriously. Don't take him seriously and the horrible thing becomes a comedy—the bitterest comedy ever written (p. 96-97).

One can, in our opinion, see *Measure for Measure,* like *Hamlet,* as one of Shakespeare's plays that anticipates Freud's death instinct.

Duke: Reason thus with life:
If I do lose thee, I do lose a thing
That none but fools would keep

…

Merely, thou art death's fool;
For him thou labour'st by thy flight to shun,
And yet runn'st toward him still.

…

For thou dost fear the soft and tender fork
Of a poor worm. Thy best of rest is sleep,
And that thou oft provok'st; yet grossly fear'st (III.i.6-8, 11-13, 16-18).

THE TEMPEST

The Tempest, Shakespeare's last play, presents unusual difficulties to commentators, whether they try to understand the play from a general or psychoanalytic point of view. Bloom argues that the play is virtually plotless and that the characters lack inwardness. Prospero's magic is not a persuasive substitute for the waning inwardness of this play. Psychoanalytic commentators have also found it difficult to make exciting observations.

The best known part of this play is Prospero's abdication speech.

You do look, my son, in a mov'd sort,
As if you were dismay'd: be cheerful, sir.
Our revels now are ended. These our actors,
As I foretold you, were all spirits and
Are melted into air, into thin air;
And, like the baseless fabric of this vision,
The cloud-capp'd towers, the gorgeous palaces,
The solemn temples, the great globe itself,
Yeah, all which it inherit, shall dissolve
And, like this insubstantial pageant faded,
Leave not a rack behind. We are such stuff
As dreams are made on, and our little life

> Is rounded with a sleep. Sir, I am vex'd;
> Bear with my weakness; my old brain is troubled:
> Be not disturb'd with my infirmity,
> If you be pleas'd, retire into my cell
> And there repose: a turn or two I'll walk
> To still my beating mind (IV.i.146-163).

> …graves at my command
> Have waked their sleepers, oped, and let them forth
> By my so potent art. But this rough magic
> I here abjure (V.i.48-51).

Since the speech appears close to the end of Shakespeare's last play many have read it as Shakespeare's farewell to writing plays. In Bloom's opinion it presents Shakespeare as a nihilist, a kind of benign Iago. When the curtain falls we are left wondering whether a magician can ever abjure his magic and return from his enchanted island to civilian life in Milan.

In Sachs's paper titled "The Tempest" (1919, English translation 1923) the psychoanalytic part of the essay begins with the statement that if Prospero is Shakespeare himself, then Prospero's breaking the magic wand means that the poet is saying farewell to his poetry. This is not a difficult symbolic interpretation and many non-psychoanalytic commentators have effortlessly reached the same conclusion.

As Caliban says:

> …the isle is full of noises,
> Sounds and sweet air, that give delight and hurt not (III.ii.144-145).

Ariel, who quickens the island with his music, who both entangles the senses and sets them free again, is the embodiment of Shakespeare's art. Setting Ariel free is parting with the poetic muse.

Of special interest to any psychoanalytically interested person is Prospero's attempt to overcome Miranda's childhood amnesia.

Prospero: …Canst thou remember
A time before we came unto this cell?
I do not think thou canst, for then thou wast not
Out three years old.

Miranda: Certainly, sir, I can.

Prospero: By what? by any other house or person?
Of anything the image tell me that
Hath kept with thy remembrance.

Miranda: 'Tis far off;
And rather like a dream than an assurance
That my remembrance warrants. Had I not
Four or five women that once tended me?

Prospero: Thou hadst, and more, Miranda.
But how is it
That this lives in thy mind? What seest thou else
In the dark backward and abysm of time?
If thou remember'st aught ere thou cam'st here
How thou cam'st here, thou may'st.

Miranda: But that I do not (I.ii.38-52).

Such interest in childhood memories before Freud is one more example of the close affinity between Shakespeare and Freud. Miranda's statement that her memory lacks assurance and is rather like a dream is familiar to psychoanalysts, often mirrored when analysands begin to recall their childhood memories.

K.R. Eissler devoted the last chapter of his book *Discourse on* Hamlet *and Hamlet* (1971) to *The Tempest,* in an essay titled "*The Tempest* and the Christian Dogma." His evaluation is similar to that of Bloom:

The Tempest is devoid at times of that overwhelming rush of
dynamic psychological development that makes Shakespeare's
great plays precisely what they are. We may call *The Tempest*
a truly static play, in which there is almost no psychological
development (p. 560).

As to the reasons for the decline in Shakespeare's creative capacity, Eissler assumes:

> I can also imagine that a man who has gone through the
> nightmares of Hamlet, Othello, Lear and Macbeth has in-
> curred psychic injuries… In going through the thousands of
> deaths, the crimes, the shattering outbreaks of passion that he
> put on the stage, Shakespeare may himself have been trauma-
> tized (p. 557-558).

The idea that a creative artist can wound himself with his creations is original to Eissler. When psychoanalysts first became interested in the creative process, Otto Rank, in 1907, published *The Artist,* in which he described the artist as the opposite of the neurotic, the man who heals himself through his creativity. Later, when artists became psychoanalytic patients, this view had to be modified. Great creativity turned out to be compatible with neuroses and even paranoia in private life. Nevertheless the psychoanalytic concept of sublimation implies that creativity is in some way beneficial, a more or less successful effort to resolve psychic conflict. Ella Freeman Sharpe, in a 1929 essay "The Impatience of Hamlet," ex-pressed the typical psychoanalytic point of view:

> The poet is not Hamlet. Hamlet is what he might have been if
> he had not written the play *Hamlet.* The characters are all in-
> trojections thrown out again from his mind… He had ejected
> all of them symbolically and remains a sane man, through a
> sublimation that satisfies the demands of the super-ego and
> the impulses of the id (p. 205).

This traditional and optimistic view of what creativity means to the artist was disputed by Eissler. Eissler's belief that Shakespeare experienced nightmares when writing his great plays questions this assumption and suggests that the creative process at its height, because it demands identifi-cation with the created characters, can lead to exhaustion and thus become a traumatic experience for the artist.

In general, psychoanalysts use the word trauma to describe a disrup-tive event that befalls a person from without, like death of a sibling, but in Eissler's use of the term artists can traumatize themselves by the work they choose to do. In Eissler's view *The Tempest* is Shakespeare's attempt to deny the tragic lives that he had created (p. 558). Eissler further assumes that all great creative efforts leave in their creators a sense of guilt.

This survey of the psychoanalytic literature demonstrates three different ways of using Shakespeare's plays. The first and most creative was employed only by Freud himself; it used Shakespeare's plays as a stimulus to make original discoveries like the Oedipus complex and the category that Freud called the exception. The second method was to explore what was unconscious to the character but not to the playwright; Wangh's Iago and Kris' Prince Hal are examples of such endeavors. The third way employs a more intuitive approach to guess at the infantile and the unconscious of Shakespeare himself, hiding behind a dramatic personality. This approach is exemplified by Ella Sharpe's analysis of King Lear. Only two psychoanalytic authors, Eissler and Oremland, went beyond the analysis of a character in a play to analyze the play itself. To compare these two books is to realize that there is a considerable agreement among psychoanalysts about a character. One can speak of a psychoanalytic understanding of a Hamlet, or a Coriolanus or a Prince Hal, but to judge from the two examples cited psychoanalysis is not a school of literary criticism that can contribute a coherent approach to the understanding of a play by Shakespeare.

To illuminate the sonnets from a psychoanalytic point of view is a very different task, since the sonnets lack a cohesive plot. The technique we resorted to was borrowed from the clinical field. We read the sonnets until a coherent image of the Poet of the Sonnets emerged. However convincing this exercise may have been it have us the pleasurable sense of getting to know the character and getting to know the poems, which are easier to grasp once one has mastered their major themes and the skillful way in which the Poet has interwoven them.

LIST OF SONNETS DISCUSSED IN THIS BOOK

INDEX OF SONNET FIRST LINES

A

D

Dante
61–62. *See also* Beatrice

Dark Lady
5–6, 51, 249–250, 250, 250–251,
251–252, 255–256, 260, 261–262,
262–263, 267–268, 273, 275, 281–282,
282, 283–285, 284–285, 285, 290–291,
296–298, 299–300, 300, 303, 322–323,
378–379, 379

David and the Ignudi
7. *See also* Sistine Chapel

death
2, 7, 10, 13, 51, 53–54, 54, 56–58,
57–58, 58, 59, 60–62, 61–62, 62, 63–64,
65, 66, 68, 70, 72, 77–78, 80, 84–85,
86–87, 87, 88, 91–92, 92, 95, 96, 97–98,
98, 99–101, 100–101, 101, 102–103,
105–106, 106, 107, 108, 109, 109–110,
110, 115, 116–118, 117–118, 121–122,
122, 126–127, 135, 137–139, 138–139,
139, 152, 172, 182, 183, 183–184, 185,
186–187, 187, 187–188, 190, 192,
193–194, 194, 197, 198, 201, 203–204,
207, 208, 208–209, 209, 213–214, 225,
226, 233–234, 246, 272, 273, 279–280,
305, 315, 318–319, 323–325, 328,
329, 330, 331, 332, 333, 334–335, 335,
336–337, 340, 343, 343–344, 344, 352,
353, 355, 358–359, 365, 370, 370–371,
373, 374, 379, 380, 383–384

Death and the Fear of Finiteness in Hamlet
359. *See also* Oremland

"Death be not proud"
108. *See also* Donne, John

defensive
359

Delphi
35, 350

Demetrius
310. *See also A Midsummer Night's Dream;*
Bottom; Helena; Hermia; Oberon; The-
seus; Titania

denial
8, 30–32, 213–214, 358–359

Desdemona
261–262, 307, 307–308, 308, 308–309,
313, 321, 322–323, 351, 351–352, 361,
362, 364, 378–379. *See also Othello;* Iago

desexualization
32, 316

desexualized homosexuality
32, 320. *See also* homosexuality

desire
2, 8, 11–12, 32, 44, 48, 49–50, 50,
50–51, 51, 126–127, 129, 153, 167–168,
182, 185, 186, 196, 203, 204, 225, 226,
228–229, 235, 236, 240, 241, 258,
258–259, 263, 265, 267–268, 273, 282,
287, 288, 289–291, 294–295, 300,
302–303, 314, 315, 317, 318, 328, 335,
355, 361, 378, 378–379, 379

"Diana"
135. *See also* Constable, Henry

Diella
263

Diotima
184, 185, 186–187. *See also* Plato; *Sympo-
sium;* Aristophanes; Socrates

G

I

Iago
292–293, 309, 320, 321, 322, 322–323, 325, 351–352, 361, 362, 363, 363–364, 364, 369, 381, 384. *See also Othello;* Desdemona

id
349, 383

idealization
8, 111–112, 249–250, 260, 267–268, 288

Iliad
134. *See also* Homer; Helen of Troy

Imago
377. *See also* Rank, Otto; Sachs, Hans

Imogen
324–325, 325, 333, 334–335. *See also Cymbeline;* Guiderius and Arviragus; Posthumous; Lachimo

impotence
125–127, 126–127, 128, 259. *See also* impotent

impotent
125–127, 126–127, 128, 259. *See also* impotence

infidelity
72, 74, 144, 145–146, 146, 147–148, 150, 155, 173–174, 174, 256, 285, 293, 298

inner conflict
7–8, 9, 10, 114, 150–151, 151, 164–165, 165, 251, 258–259, 262, 266–267, 270–271, 276–278, 278, 346

insight
1–2, 15, 32, 38–39, 43, 113–114, 114, 150, 161, 174, 178–179, 187, 203–204, 206–207, 277–278, 283–285, 284–285, 294–295, 295, 298, 322–323, 341, 343, 349, 354–355, 357–358, 363, 364, 376

insomnia
10, 216–217, 222–223, 333, 352

intercourse
29–32, 129, 187, 190, 197–198, 201, 259, 270–271, 271, 290–291, 297–298, 358

internalization
216–217, 217, 219, 220–221, 223, 229, 230, 231, 232

intrapsychic
8, 10

Introductory Lectures
342. *See also* Freud

irony
32, 228–229

Isabella
332, 349, 349–350, 378, 378–379, 379. *See also Measure for Measure;* Angelo; Claudio; Duke; Escalus; Francesca; Lucio

J

Jakobson, Roman
46–47, 47, 48

James I
69, 69–70

jealous
112–114, 150, 240, 241, 252, 253, 340, 361. *See also* jealousy

metaphor
11–12, 12, 12–13, 13, 14, 14–15, 15, 16,
27–28, 40–41, 41–43, 42–43, 46–47,
57–58, 59–62, 60–62, 64, 68, 73–74,
75–76, 78–79, 79, 80–81, 86–87, 88,
90–92, 91–92, 94, 94–95, 97–98,
102–103, 106, 109–110, 115, 123–124,
126–127, 131–132, 132, 133–134,
134, 137, 145–146, 146, 147–148, 150,
150–151, 152, 153, 157, 158, 163, 164–
165, 171, 172, 173–174, 176, 183, 187,
191–192, 192, 195–196, 196, 197–198,
198, 200, 200–201, 201, 204, 207, 208–
209, 211, 216–217, 218–219, 219, 226,
226–227, 227–229, 228–229, 229, 234,
235, 237–238, 238, 239, 240–241, 241,
252, 253–254, 258–259, 267–268, 268,
272–273, 273, 282, 290–291, 297–298,
299–300, 300, 300–301, 302–303, 305,
307, 315, 316, 318, 352

metaphors
7, 11–12, 12–13, 13, 15, 16, 43,
113–114, 119–122, 144–146, 146,
149–150, 150, 150–151, 158–159, 188,
193–194, 196, 201, 203–204, 216–217,
238, 239, 242, 246, 266–267, 267–268,
268, 279–280, 281–282, 300–301, 315.
See also metaphor

Michelangelo
6–7, 7, 218–219

Middle Ages
6–7, 36–38, 44, 79, 107, 140–141,
197–198

Middleton Murray, J.
4

Millay, Edna St. Vincent
103. *See also* St. Vincent Millay, Edna

mimeses
114–115

Miranda
360, 381, 382. *See also The Tempest;*
Prospero

Moloney and Rockelein
357–358. *See also* "A New Interpretation
of Hamlet"

Moncrief, Scott
117–118

mother-child love
254

mother-son relationship
370, 370–371

mourning
77–78, 88, 99–101, 100–101, 101,
101–103, 116–118, 117–118, 118,
118–119, 119, 206–207, 233–234, 262,
294–295, 311, 319

Mourning and Melancholia. See also Freud

Much Ado About Nothing
28. *See also* Beatrice; Benedick; Don
Pedro; Hero

Murray, Gilbert
333

Murray, J. Middleton
4. *See also* Middleton, Murray J.

mythology
25–26, 26–28, 341, 343–344

N

narcissism
28, 34, 35, 37–38, 38, 38–39, 39, 50,
54, 61–62, 113–114, 130, 147–148,
148, 156–157, 158–159, 159, 164–165,
167–168, 168, 175–176, 179, 182, 183,
186–187, 190, 191–192, 192, 193–194,
198, 203–204, 206, 208–209, 240–241,
319, 323, 326, 333, 371, 372. *See
also* narcissistic

narcissist. *See also* narcissism and narcissistic

narcissistic
28, 34, 37–38, 38, 38–39, 39, 66, 68,
69–70, 82, 105–106, 106, 130, 147–148,
148, 167–168, 168, 175–176, 179,
191–192, 192, 206, 240–241, 323, 326,
333, 371, 372. *See also* narcissism

Narcissus
14, 33–34, 35, 36, 37–38, 183, 191–192,
203–204, 325–326

nature
3, 10, 13, 14, 26, 27–28, 28, 31–32, 32,
33–34, 34–35, 38, 40–41, 41, 43, 46–47,
51, 59, 59–62, 60–62, 62, 63–64, 66, 74,
78–79, 81, 83, 84–85, 85, 88, 90, 90–92,
91–92, 92, 101–103, 102–103, 104,
105–106, 106, 111–112, 114, 118–119,
136, 136–137, 137, 141, 144–146,
145–146, 146, 147–148, 149–150, 150,
151, 152, 156, 156–157, 161, 172, 175,
183, 184, 190, 193, 193–194, 205, 206,
218–219, 232, 244–246, 260, 261–262,
305, 308, 316, 329, 330–331, 331, 353,
354–355, 372, 378

Nazis
94

Nemesis
35

neurotic
12, 160–161, 363, 383

New Testaments
75–76

O

Oberon
28, 105–106. *See also A Midsummer
Night's Dream;* Bottom; Demetrius; Helena; Hermia; Theseus; Titania

Odysseus
242. *See also* Homer; Penelope

Oedipus
173–174, 277–278, 309, 309–310,
339–340, 340, 340–341, 341, 342,
356–358, 357–358, 384

Oedipus complex
309, 309–310, 339–340, 340–341, 341,
342, 356–358, 357–358, 384

Oedipus Rex
340, 340–341, 341, 357–358

Old Testament
75–76, 205

Olivia
311, 327. *See also Twelfth Night;* Duke
Orsino; Malvolio; Maria; Sir Andrew; Sir
Toby

Y

Alexander, F. (1933) "A Note on Falstaff." In *The Scope of Psychoanalysis 1921-1961: Selected Papers of Franz Alexander*, 1961. New York: Basic Books Inc. pp. 501-510.

Auden, W.H. *Lectures on Shakespeare*. Ed. A. Kirsch. Princeton, New Jersey: Princeton University Press.

Auden, W. H. and Pearson, N. H., eds. (1950). *Poets of the English Language II: Marlowe to Marvell*. New York: The Viking Press.

Bak, R. C. (1946). "Masochism in Paranoia." *The Psychoanalytic Quarterly*, 15.

Barron, D.B. (1962). "*Coriolanus*: portrait of the artist as infant." *American Imago*, 19: 171-193.

Barthes, R. (1978). *Lovers Discourse*. New York: Hill & Wang.

Bate, J. (2000). "Shakespeare's Ovid." *Ovid's Metamorphosis*, The Arthur Golding Translation. Philadelphia: Paul Dry Books.

Bender, R.M. and Squier, C.L. (1967). *The Sonnet*. New York: Washington Square Press.

Bergmann, M.S. (1987). *The Anatomy of Loving*. New York: Columbia University Press.

Bion, W.R. (1977). *Seven Servants*. New York: Jason Aronson.

Blackmore Evans, G. B., ed. (1996) *The Sonnets*. Cambridge University Press.

Blechner, M.J. (1988). King Lear: King Leir and incest wishes. *American Imago*, 45: 309-325.

Bloom, H. (1994). *The Western Canon: The Books and School of the Ages*. New York: Harcourt Brace & Company.

(1998). *Shakespeare: The Invention of the Human*. New York: Riverhead Books.

(2004). *The Best Poems of the English Language: From Chaucer Through Frost*. New York: HarperCollins Publishers.

Booth, S. (1977) *Shakespeare's Sonnets*. New Haven: Yale University Press.

Bradley, A.C. (1904). *Shakespearean Tragedy: Lectures on Hamlet, Othello, King Lear, Macbeth*. New York: St. Martin's Press.

Burrow, Colin, ed. (2002). *The Oxford Shakespeare Complete Sonnets and Poems*. Oxford: Oxford University Press.

Byatt, A.S. (1990) *Possession*. New York: Vintage International.

Cairns, H., ed. (1948) *The Limits of Art*. Bollingen Series XII. Pantheon Books. Dover, K.J. (1978) *Greek Homosexuality*. Cambridge, Mass.: Harvard University Press.

Duncan-Jones, K., ed. (1997). *Shakespeare's Sonnets*. Arden Shakespeare series, Thomson Pub. Co.

Eissler, K.R. (1971). *Discourse on Hamlet and* Hamlet: *a Psychoanalytic Inquiry*. New York: International Universities Press.

Eliot, T. S. (1957) "The Three Voices of Poetry." *On Poetry and Poets*. New York: Farrar, Straus and Cudahy.

Ellenberger, H. F. (1970) *The Discovery of the Unconscious*. London: The Penguin Press.

Faber, M.D., ed. (1970). *The Design Within: Psychoanalytic Approaches to Shakespeare*. New York: Science House.

Fenton, J. (2000). Auden at Home. *The New York Review of Books*.

Ferenczi, S. (1933) "Confusion of Tongue between Adults and the Child." In *Final Contributions to Problems and Methods of Psychoanalysis*. London: Hogarth Press, 1955.

Fineman, J. (1986). *Shakespeare's Perjured Eye*. Berkeley: University of California Press.

Fowler, H.W. (1926). *A Dictionary of Modern English Usage*. London: Oxford University Press.

Freud, S. (1910). The antithetical meaning of primal words. *The Standard Edition of The Complete Psychological Works of Sigmund Freud, Volume 11*. London: The Hogarth Press.

(1912). On the universal tendency to debasement in the sphere of love (contributions to the psychology of love II). *The Standard Edition, Volume 11*. London: The Hogarth Press.

(1913). The Theme of the Three Caskets. *The Standard Edition, Volume 12*. London: The Hogarth Press.

(1914). "On Narcissism: An Introduction." *The Standard Edition, Volume 14*. London: The Hogarth Press.

(1915). "Instincts and Vicissitudes." *The Standard Edition, Volume 14*. London: The Hogarth Press.

(1915). "Thoughts for the Times on War and Death." *The Standard Edition, Volume 14*. London: The Hogarth Press.

(1915). "On Transience." *The Standard Edition, Volume 14*. London: The Hogarth Press.

(1916-17). "Introductory Lectures on Psycho-Analysis." *The Standard Edition, Volume 15-16*. London: The Hogarth Press.

(1916). "Some Character-Types Met with in Psycho-Analytic Work." *The Standard Edition, Volume 14*. London: The Hogarth Press.

(1917). "Mourning and Melancholia." *The Standard Edition, Volume 14*. London: The Hogarth Press.

(1922). "Some Neurotic Mechanisms in Jealousy, Paranoia and Homosexuality." *The Standard Edition, Volume 18*. London: The Hogarth Press.

(1923). "The Ego and the Id." *The Standard Edition, Volume 19*. London: The Hogarth Press.

BIBLIOGRAPHY

(1937). "Constructions in Analysis." *The Standard Edition, Volume 23*. London: The Hogarth Press.

Frye, Northrop. (1986). *Northrop Frye on Shakespeare*. New Haven, Conn.: Yale University Press.

Furness, H.F. (1966). *Twelfe Night, or, What You Will* (A New Variorium Edition). New York: American Scholar Publications, Inc.

Gibbons, R. (1979). *The Poet's Work*. Boston: Houghton Mifflin.

Graves, R. (1955). *Greek Myths*, two volumes. New York: Penguin Books.

Green, A. (1975). The analyst, symbolization and the absence in the analytic setting (on changes in analytic practice and analytic experience). *International Journal of Psycho-Analysis* 56: 1-22. Also in: *On Private Madness*. Madison, Ct: International University Press.

Green, A. (2001). *Life Narcissism Death Narcissism*. New York: Free Association Books.

Greenblatt, S. (2004). *Will in the World: How Shakespeare Became Shakespeare*. New York: W.W. Norton & Company.

Hecht, A. (1996). Introduction to *The Sonnets* (Evans, G.B., ed). Cambridge University Press.

Hazlitt, W. (1817). *Characters of Shakespeare's Plays*. London.

Hofling, C.K. (1957). An Interpretation of Shakespeare's *Coriolanus*. American Imago. 14: 407-437. Reprinted in *The Design Within: Psychoanalytic Approaches to Shakespeare*. M.D. Faber, ed. 1970. New York: Science House. 289-305.

Holland, N.N. (1964). *Psychoanalysis and Shakespeare*. New York: McGraw-Hill.

Honan, P. (1998). *Shakespeare: a Life*. Oxford, England: Oxford University Press.

Humphries, R., trans. (1955). *Ovid's Metamorphoses*. Bloomington, Indiana: Indiana University Press.

Jakobson, R. and Jones, L.G. (1971). Shakespeare's Verbal Art in "th'Expence of Spirit" from "Concealed Structures." In *Romantic Poets, Critics, and Other Madman* C. Rosen, 1998, Cambridge: Harvard University Press.

Jebb, R.C., trans. Sophocles' Oedipus the King. In *The Complete Greek Drama, Volume One*. Whitney J. Oates and Eugene O'Neill, Jr., eds. 1938. New York: Random House. 369-417.

Jekels, L. (1943). The Riddle of Shakespeare's *Macbeth*. In *The Design Within: Psychoanalytic Approaches to Shakespeare*. M.D. Faber, ed. 1970. New York: Science House. 233-249.

Jones, E. (1955). *The Life and Work of Sigmund Freud, Volume II: 1901-1919, Years of Maturity*. New York: Basic Books, Inc.

Jones, E., ed. (1991). *The New Oxford Book of Sixteenth Century Verse*. Oxford: Oxford University Press.

Kerrigan, J., ed. (1986). *The Sonnets and A Lover's Complaint*. New York: Penguin Books.

Kohut, H. (1971). *The Analysis of the Self.* New York: International University Press.

Kohut, H. (1972). "Thoughts on Narcissism and Narcisstic Rage." *The Psychoanalytic Study of the Child* 27: 360-400.

Kris, E. (1948). "Prince Hal's Conflict." *Psychoanalytic Quarterly.* 17: 487-506. Reprinted in *The Design Within: Psychoanalytic Approaches to Shakespeare.* M.D. Faber, ed. 1970. New York: Science House. 389-407.

Kubie, L.S. (1974). "The Drive to Become Both Sexes." *Psychoanalytic Quarterly,* 43: 349-426.

Lacan, J. (1959). "Desire and the Interpretation of Desire in *Hamlet.*" *Literature and Psychoanalysis* (1982), ed. Shoshana Felman. Baltimore: The John Hopkins University Press. 11-52.

Langer, S. K. (1942). *Philosophy in a New Key.* Cambridge: Harvard University Press.

1953). *Feeling and Form: A Theory of Art.* New York: Charles Scribner's Sons.

Lewin, B. (1948). "The Nature of Reality, the Meaning of Nothing." *Psychoanalytic Quarterly* 17: 524-526.

Losey, F.D. (1926) Introduction to *Coriolanus.* In *Shakespeare: the Complete Dramatic and Poetic Works of William Shakespeare.* Philadelphia: The John C. Winston Company.

Mahony, P. (1979). "Shakespeare's sonnet 20 and its symbolic nuclear principle." *American Imago* 36: 69-79.

Masson, J.M., trans. and ed. (1985). *The Complete Letters of Sigmund Freud to Wilhelm Fliess, 1887-1904.* Cambridge, Mass.: The Belknap Press of Harvard University Press.

Moloney, J.M. and L. Rockelien. (1949). A New Interpretation of *Hamlet. International Journal of Psychoanalysis.* 30: 92-107.

Nims, J.F., ed. (2000). *Ovid's Metamorphoses.* The Arthur Golding Translation. Philadelphia: Paul Dry Books.

Oremland, J. (2005). *Death and the Fear of Finiteness in* Hamlet. San Francisco: Lake Street Editions.

Painter, G. D. (1959). *Proust: The Early Years.* Boston: Little, Brown, and Company.

(1965). *Proust: The Later Years.* Boston: Little, Brown, and Company.

Panofsky, E. (1960). *Renaissance and Renaissances in Western Art.* Stockholm: Almquist and Wiksell.

Petersson, R.T. (1970). *The Art of Ecstasy: Saint Teresa, Bernini and Crashaw*. London: Routledge & Kegan Paul.

Putney, R. (1962). Coriolanus and His Mother. *Psychoanalytic Quarterly*. 31: 364-381.

Rank, O. (1907). *Art and Artist*. English trans., 1932. New York: Knopf.

Reich, W. (1949). *Character Analysis*. Oregon Institute Press.

Rosen, C. (1998) *Romantic Poets, Critics, and Other Madmen*. Cambridge: Harvard University Press.

Sachs, H. (1923). The Tempest. *International Journal of Psychoanalysis*. 4: 43-88.

Sachs, H. (1942). The Measure in *"Measure for Measure."* In *The Creative Unconscious: Studies in the Psychoanalysis of Art*. Cambridge, Massachusetts: Sci-Art Publishers. 63-99.

Sharpe, E.F. (1940) Psycho-Physical Problems Revealed in Language. In *An Examination of Metaphor in Collected Papers on Psycho-Analysis*. (1950) London: the Hogarth Press, Ltd.

Sharpe, E. (1946). "From *King Lear* to *The Tempest*." In *Collected Papers on Psycho-Analysis*. (1950). London: The Hogarth Press, Ltd. 214-241.

Sharpe, E. (1929). "The Impatience of Hamlet." In *Collected Papers on Psycho-Analysis*. (1950). London: The Hogarth Press, Ltd. 203-213.

Smith, B. R. (1991). *Homosexual Desire in Shakespeare's England*. Chicago: The University of Chicago Press.

Spitz, R.A. (1965). *The First Year of Life*. New York: International University Press.

Spivak, M. (1973). *The Harvard Concordance to Shakespeare*. Cambridge, Mass.: Harvard University Press.

Spurgeon, C. F. E. *Shakespeare's Imagery and What It Tells Us*. Boston: Beacon Hill Press.

Steiner, G. (1996). A Reading Against Shakespeare (1986). 108-128. In *No Passion Spent*. New Haven: Yale University Press.

Stoller, R. J. (1966). Shakespearean Tragedy: Coriolanus. *Psychoanalytic Quarterly*. 35: 263-274. Reprinted in *The Design Within: Psychoanalytic Approaches to Shakespeare*. Faber, M.D., ed., 1970. New York: Science House. 329-339.

Thomas, D (1951) Poetic Manifesto. In *The Poet's Work: 29 Masters of 20th Century Poetry on the Origins and Practice of Their Art*. Gibbons, R., ed. (1979). Boston: Houghton Mifflin Company.

Untermeyer, L., ed. (1942). *A Treasury of Great Poems: English and American*. New York: Simon and Schuster.

Vendler, H. (1997). *The Art of Shakespeare's Sonnets*. Cambridge: Harvard University Press.

Wangh, M. (1950) Othello: the tragedy of
Iago. *Psychoanalytic Quarterly.* 19: 202-12.
Reprinted in *The Design Within: Psycho-
analytic Approaches to Shakespeare.* Faber,
M.D., ed. (1970). New York: Science
House. 157-168.

Whyte, L. L. (1960) *The Unconscious
Before Freud.* New York: Basic Books.

Wilson, Dover

Wilson, J.W. (1966) *The Sonnets.* Cam-
bridge University Press.

Wollheim, R. (1987). *Painting as an Art.*
Princeton, N.J.: Princeton University
Press. Bollingen Series 35.